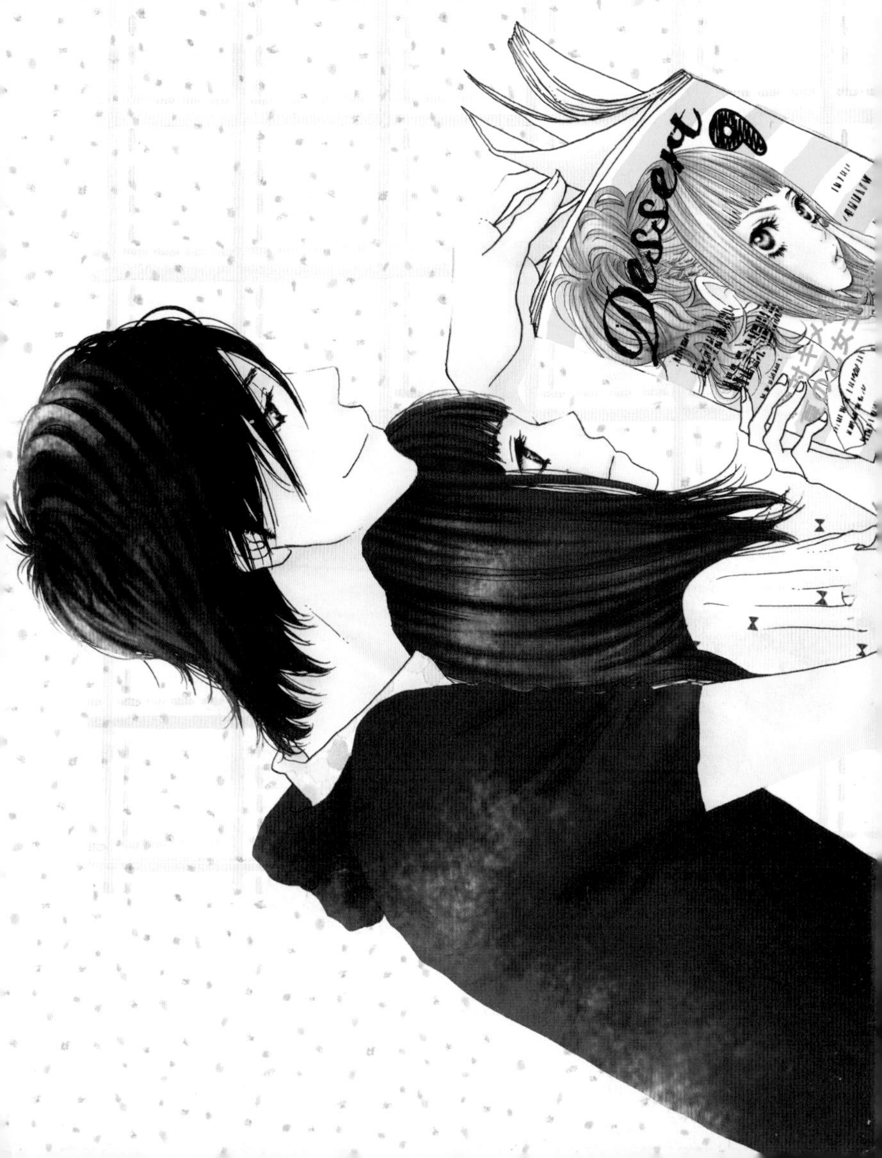
Dessert

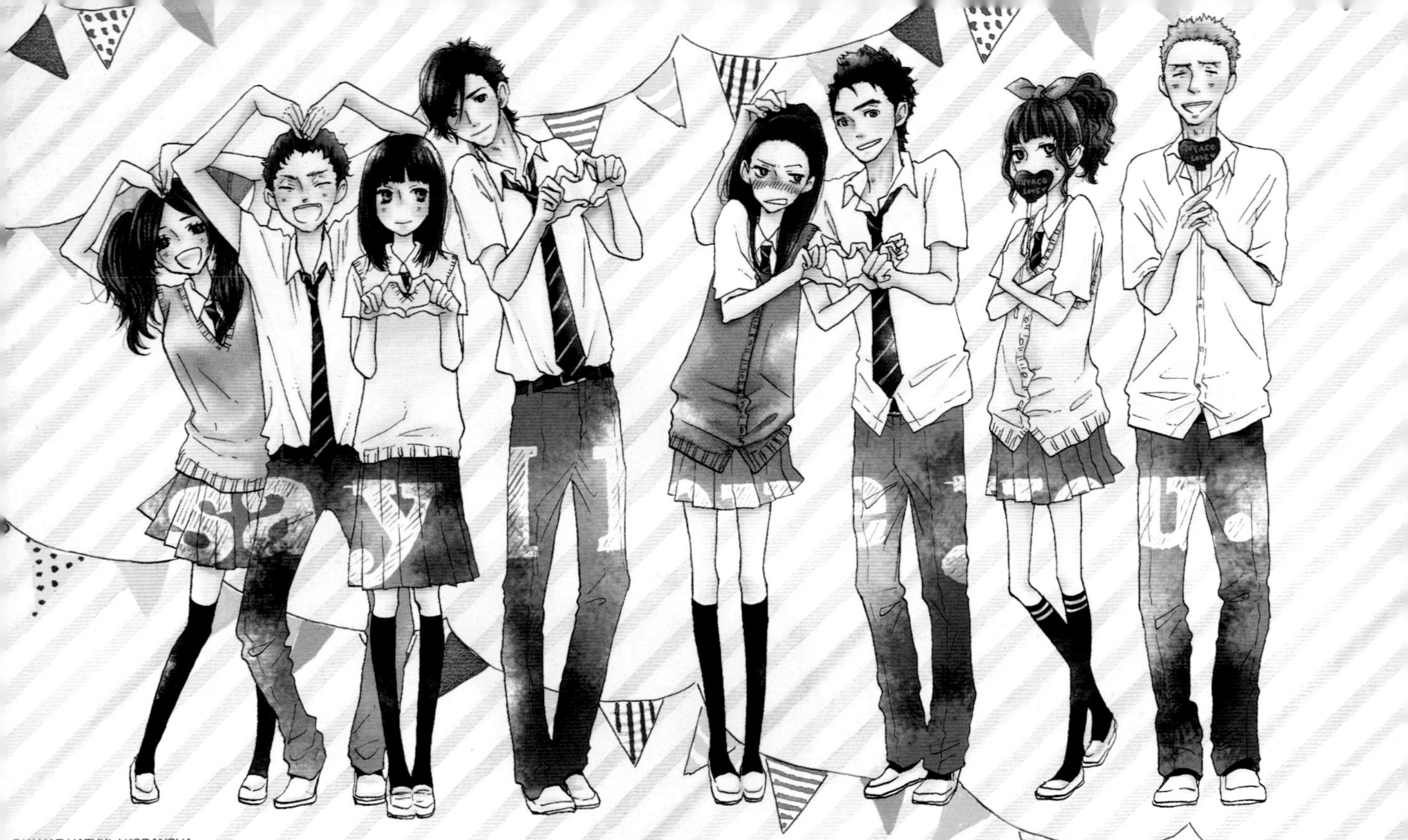

Say I Love You.

by
Kanae
Hazuki

13

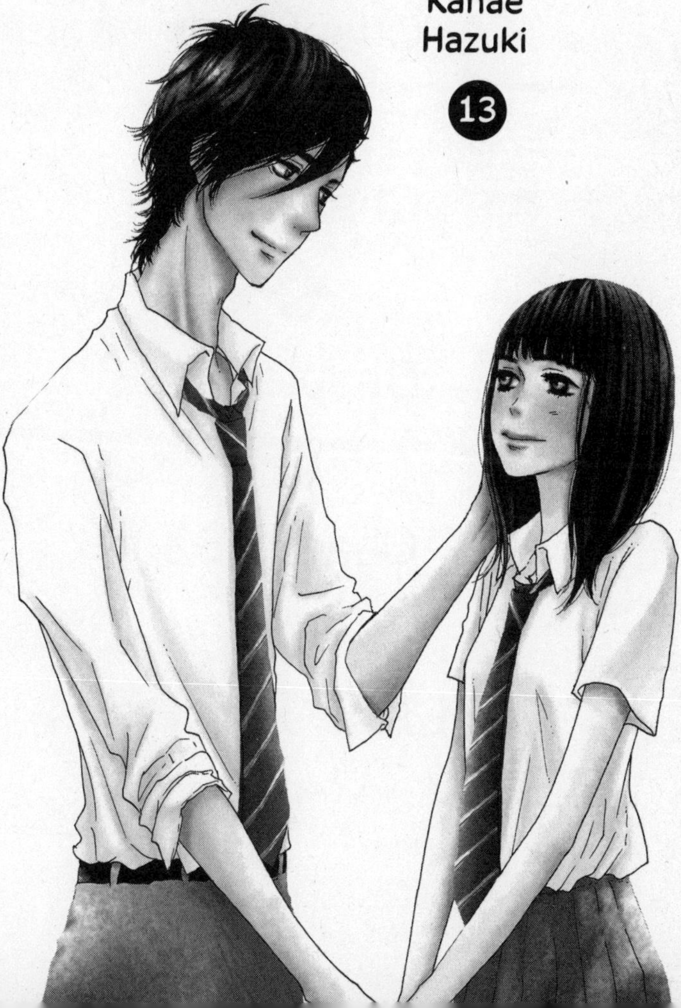

Kanae Hazuki
presents

Say I Love You.

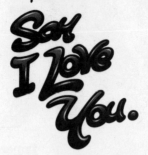

CHARACTER

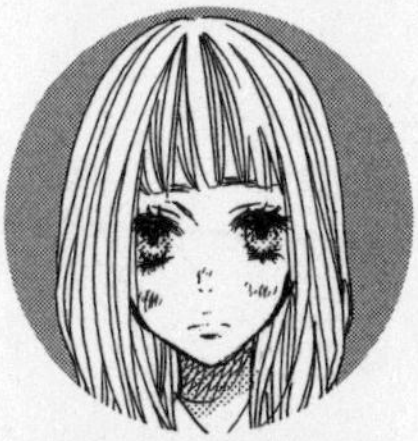

Mei Tachibana

A girl who hasn't had a single friend, let alone a boyfriend, in sixteen years, and has lived her life trusting no one. She finds herself attracted to Yamato, who, for some reason, just won't leave her alone, and they start dating.

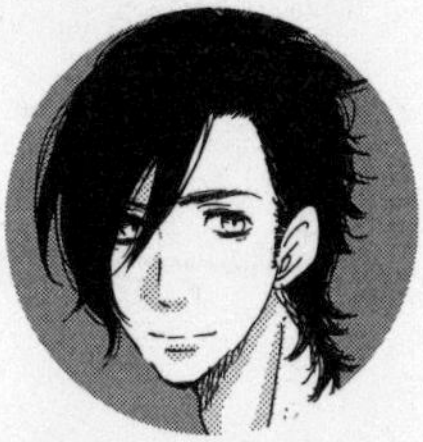

Yamato Kurosawa

The most popular boy at Mei's school. He has the love of many girls, yet for some reason, he is obsessed with Mei, the brooding weirdo girl from another class. ♡

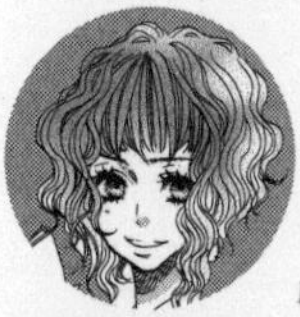

Megumi

An amateur model who had her sights set on Yamato. She transferred to his school and got him a modeling job, and the two gradually grew closer. In the end, Yamato rejected her, but now she has moved on and is going forward with a positive outlook.

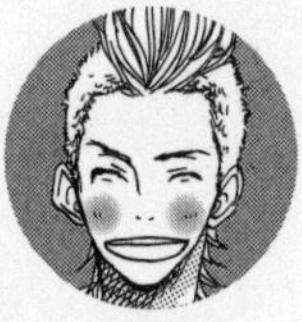

Kai

Yamato's classmate from middle school who had been the victim of bullying. For his own reasons, he started high school a year late. He likes Mei and told her so, but...?

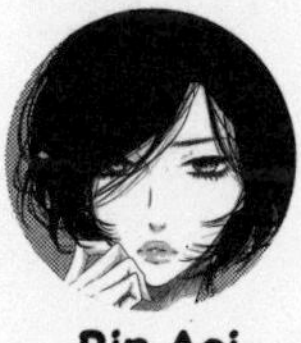

Rin Aoi

A new student at Mei's school, who is currently modeling under the name RIN. Kai caught her with one hand when she tripped on the stairs, and she fell in love at first sight?!

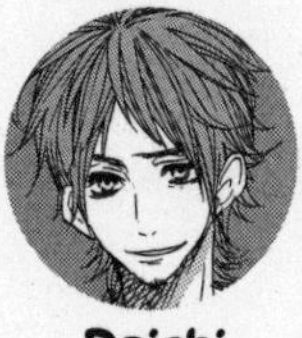

Daichi

Yamato's brother and a hairstylist. He helped Mei out for the fireworks show and the beauty contest. He had a hard time forgetting his previous girlfriend, but currently, he is ♡♡.

STORY

Mei Tachibana spent sixteen years without a single friend or boyfriend, but now it's been two years since she started dating Yamato Kurosawa, the most popular boy in her school. Mei and her friends have entered their final year of high school, and each of them is starting to worry about where they will go next. Yamato begins to work towards becoming a photographer, and Mei, through her volunteer experience at a preschool, develops an interest in childcare. Megumi determines to go to Paris to advance her modeling career. Meanwhile, a new student at their school, the model Rin, goes on her first date with Kai, and out of nowhere, she confesses her love and kisses him...?!

Say "I love you".

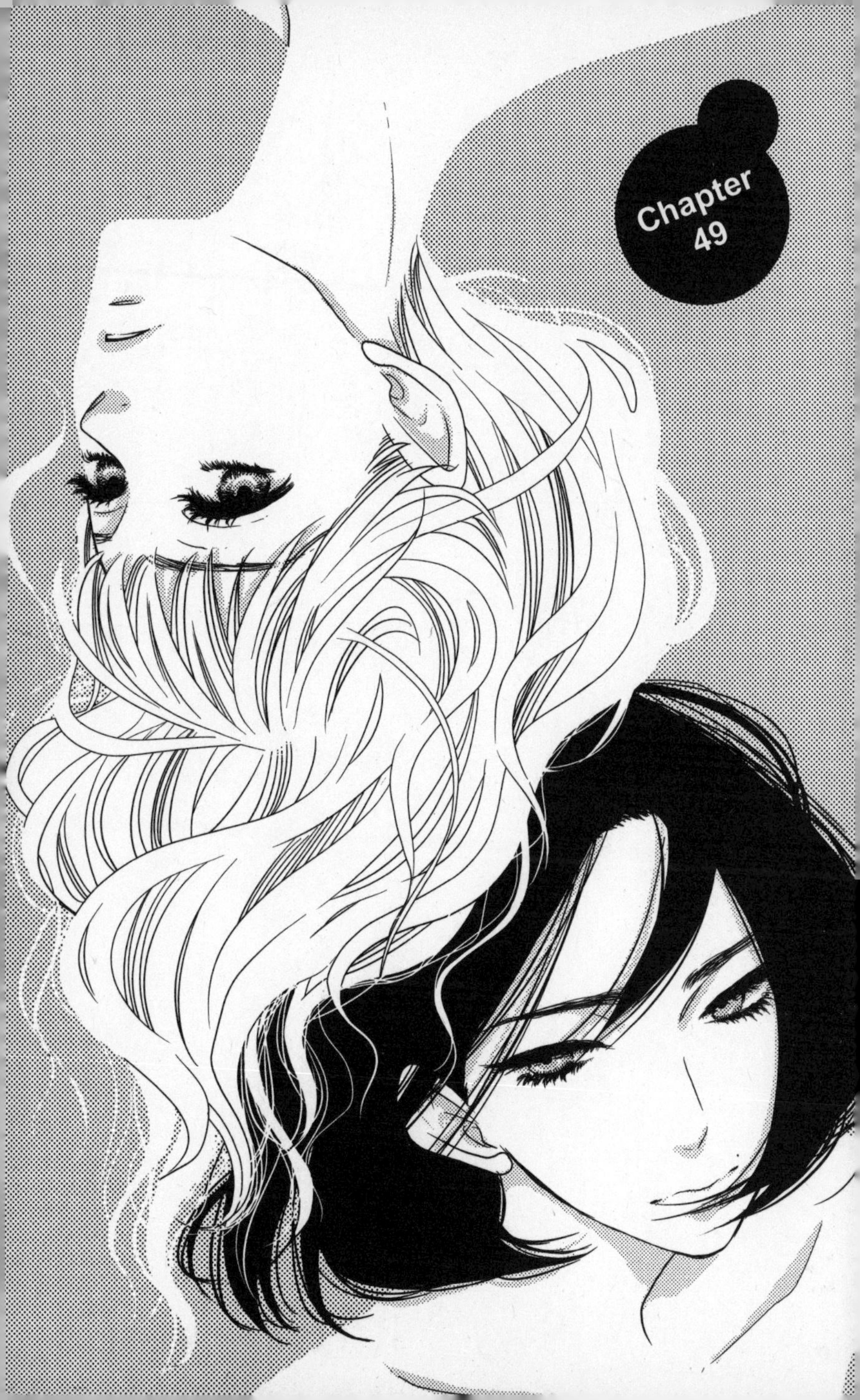
Chapter
49

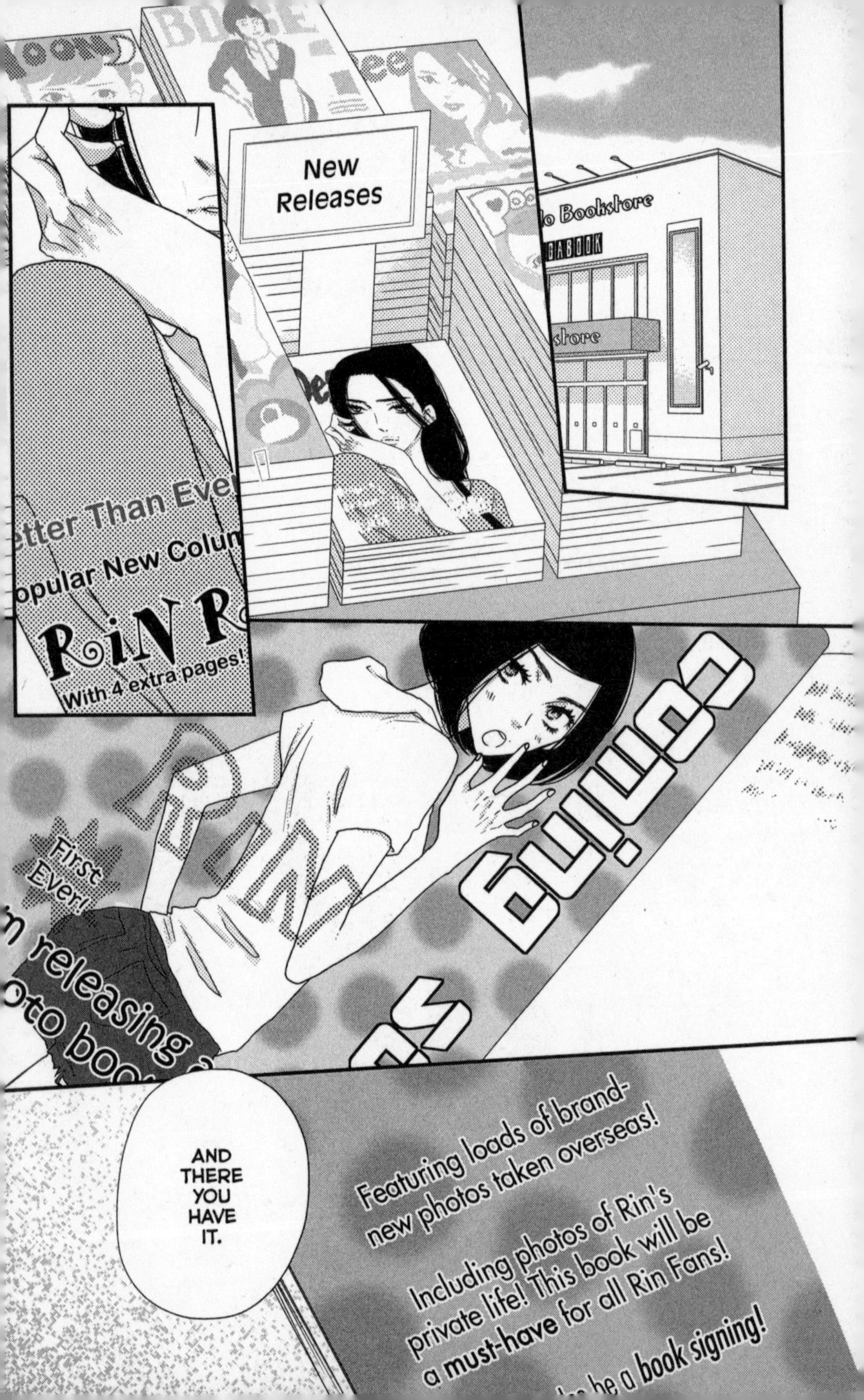

o Bookstore
store
New Releases
etter Than Eve
opular New Colum
RiN R
With 4 extra pages!
First Ever!
releasing
oto boo
AND THERE YOU HAVE IT.
Featuring loads of brand-new photos taken overseas!
Including photos of Rin's private life! This book will be a must-have for all Rin Fans!
be a book signing!

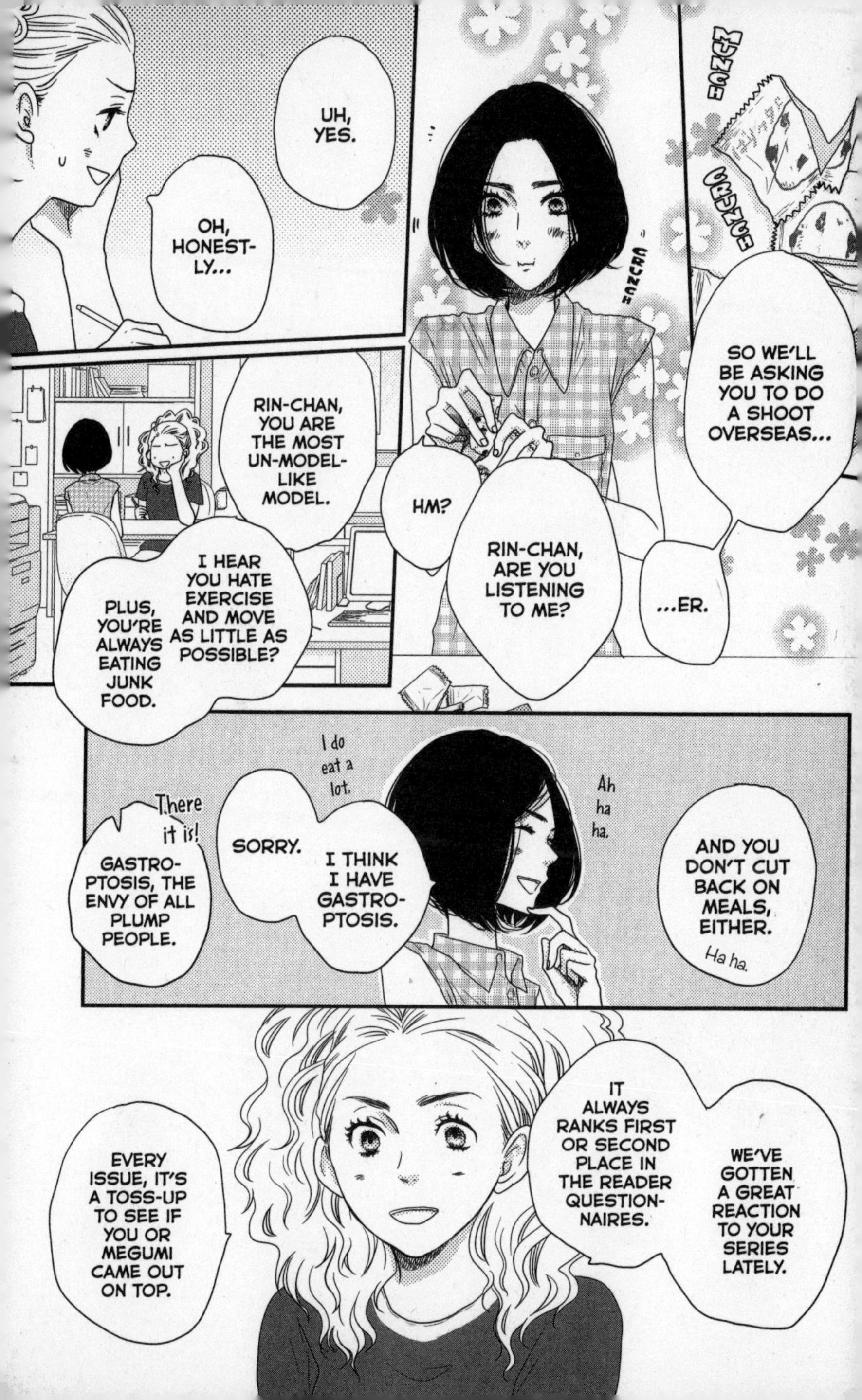
MUNCH
CRUNCH
SO WE'LL BE ASKING YOU TO DO A SHOOT OVERSEAS...
CRUNCH
...ER.
RIN-CHAN, ARE YOU LISTENING TO ME?
HM?
UH, YES.
OH, HONESTLY...
RIN-CHAN, YOU ARE THE MOST UN-MODEL-LIKE MODEL.
I HEAR YOU HATE EXERCISE AND MOVE AS LITTLE AS POSSIBLE?
PLUS, YOU'RE ALWAYS EATING JUNK FOOD.
AND YOU DON'T CUT BACK ON MEALS, EITHER.
Ha ha.
Ah ha ha.
I do eat a lot.
I THINK I HAVE GASTROPTOSIS.
SORRY.
There it is!
GASTROPTOSIS, THE ENVY OF ALL PLUMP PEOPLE.
WE'VE GOTTEN A GREAT REACTION TO YOUR SERIES LATELY.
IT ALWAYS RANKS FIRST OR SECOND PLACE IN THE READER QUESTIONNAIRES.
EVERY ISSUE, IT'S A TOSS-UP TO SEE IF YOU OR MEGUMI CAME OUT ON TOP.

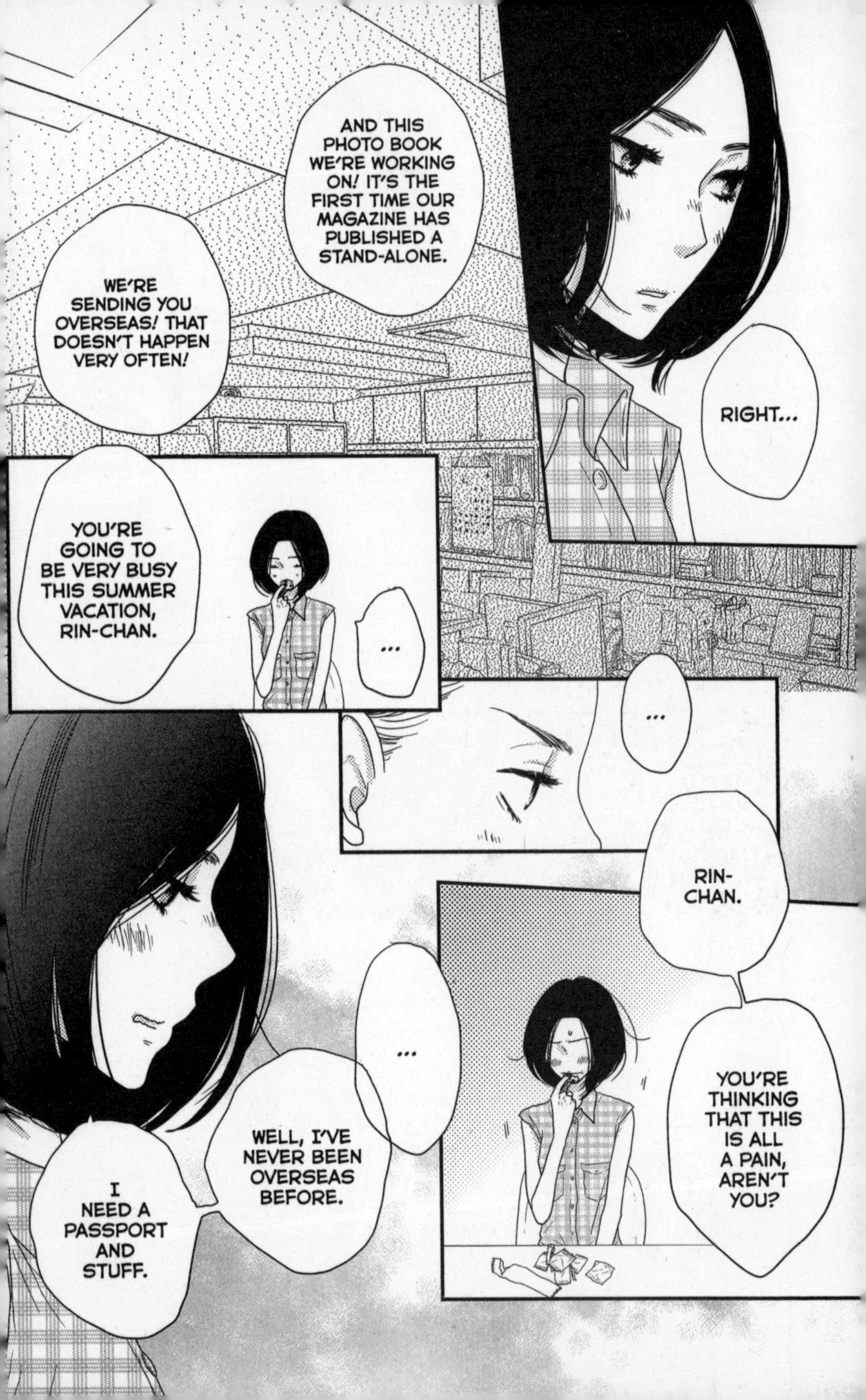
AND THIS PHOTO BOOK WE'RE WORKING ON! IT'S THE FIRST TIME OUR MAGAZINE HAS PUBLISHED A STAND-ALONE.
WE'RE SENDING YOU OVERSEAS! THAT DOESN'T HAPPEN VERY OFTEN!
RIGHT...
YOU'RE GOING TO BE VERY BUSY THIS SUMMER VACATION, RIN-CHAN.
...
...
RIN-CHAN.
YOU'RE THINKING THAT THIS IS ALL A PAIN, AREN'T YOU?
...
WELL, I'VE NEVER BEEN OVERSEAS BEFORE.
I NEED A PASSPORT AND STUFF.

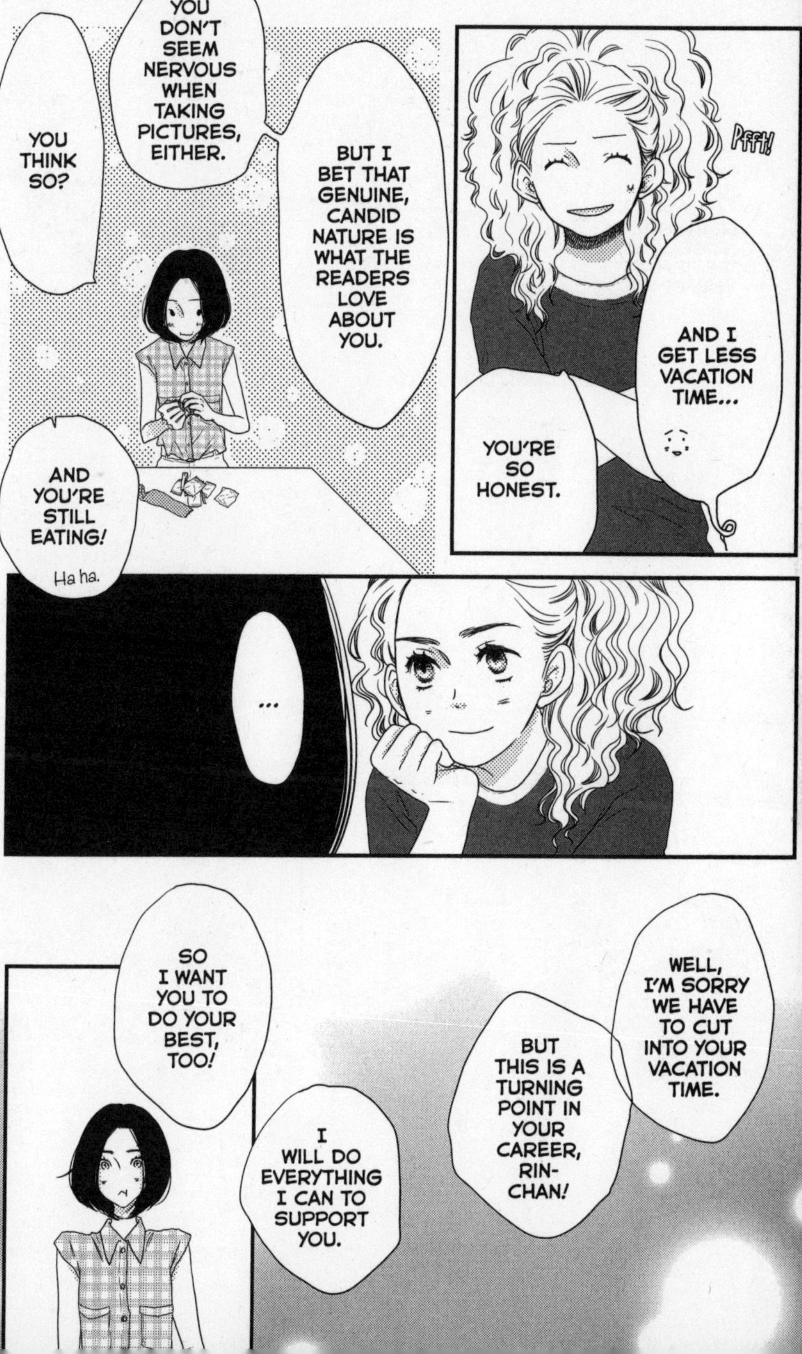
Pfft!
AND I GET LESS VACATION TIME...
YOU'RE SO HONEST.
YOU DON'T SEEM NERVOUS WHEN TAKING PICTURES, EITHER.
YOU THINK SO?
BUT I BET THAT GENUINE, CANDID NATURE IS WHAT THE READERS LOVE ABOUT YOU.
AND YOU'RE STILL EATING!
Ha ha.
...
WELL, I'M SORRY WE HAVE TO CUT INTO YOUR VACATION TIME.
BUT THIS IS A TURNING POINT IN YOUR CAREER, RIN-CHAN!
I WILL DO EVERYTHING I CAN TO SUPPORT YOU.
SO I WANT YOU TO DO YOUR BEST, TOO!

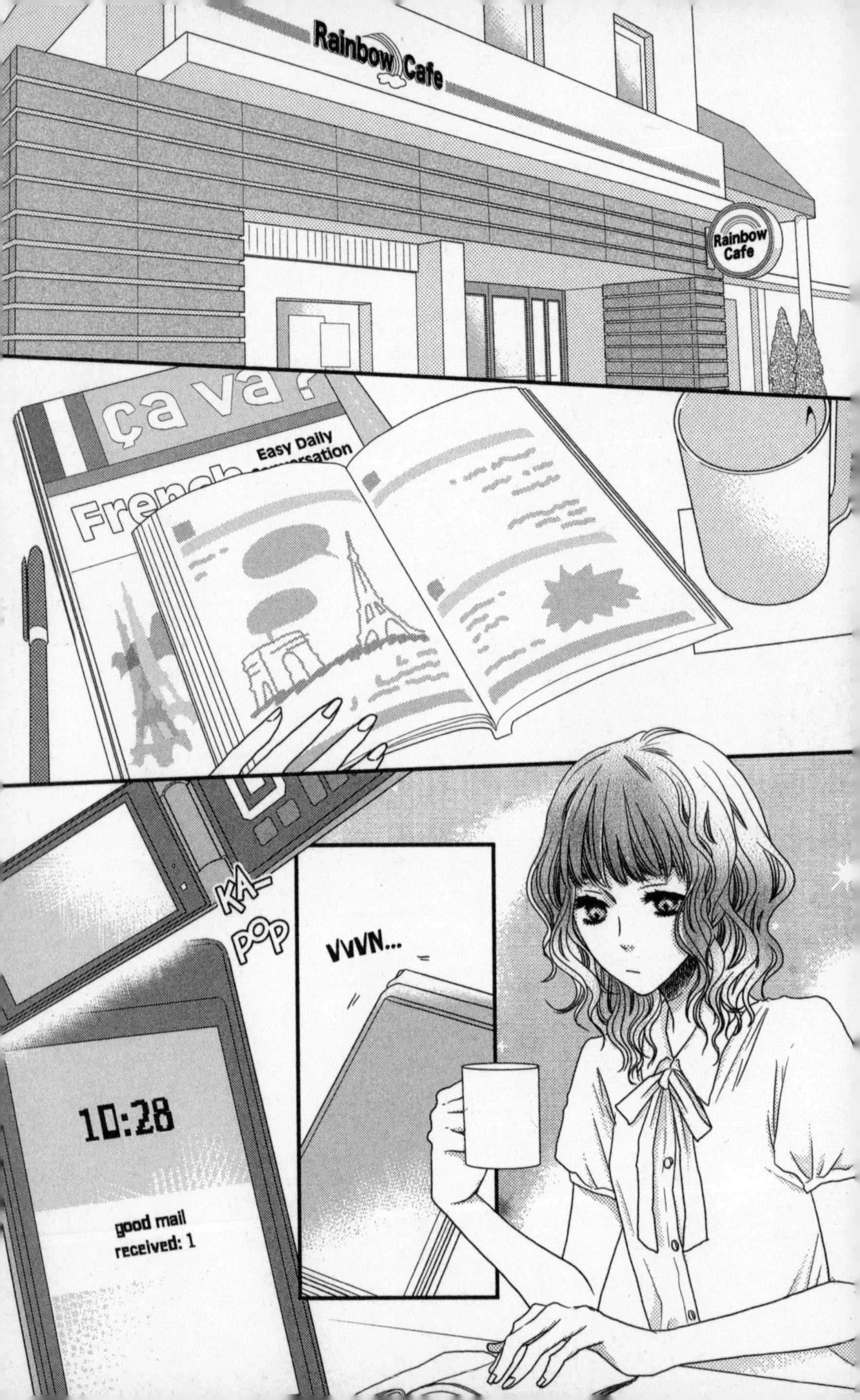
Rainbow Cafe
Rainbow Cafe
ça va ?
Easy Daily
VVVN...
KA-POP
10:28
good mail
received: 1

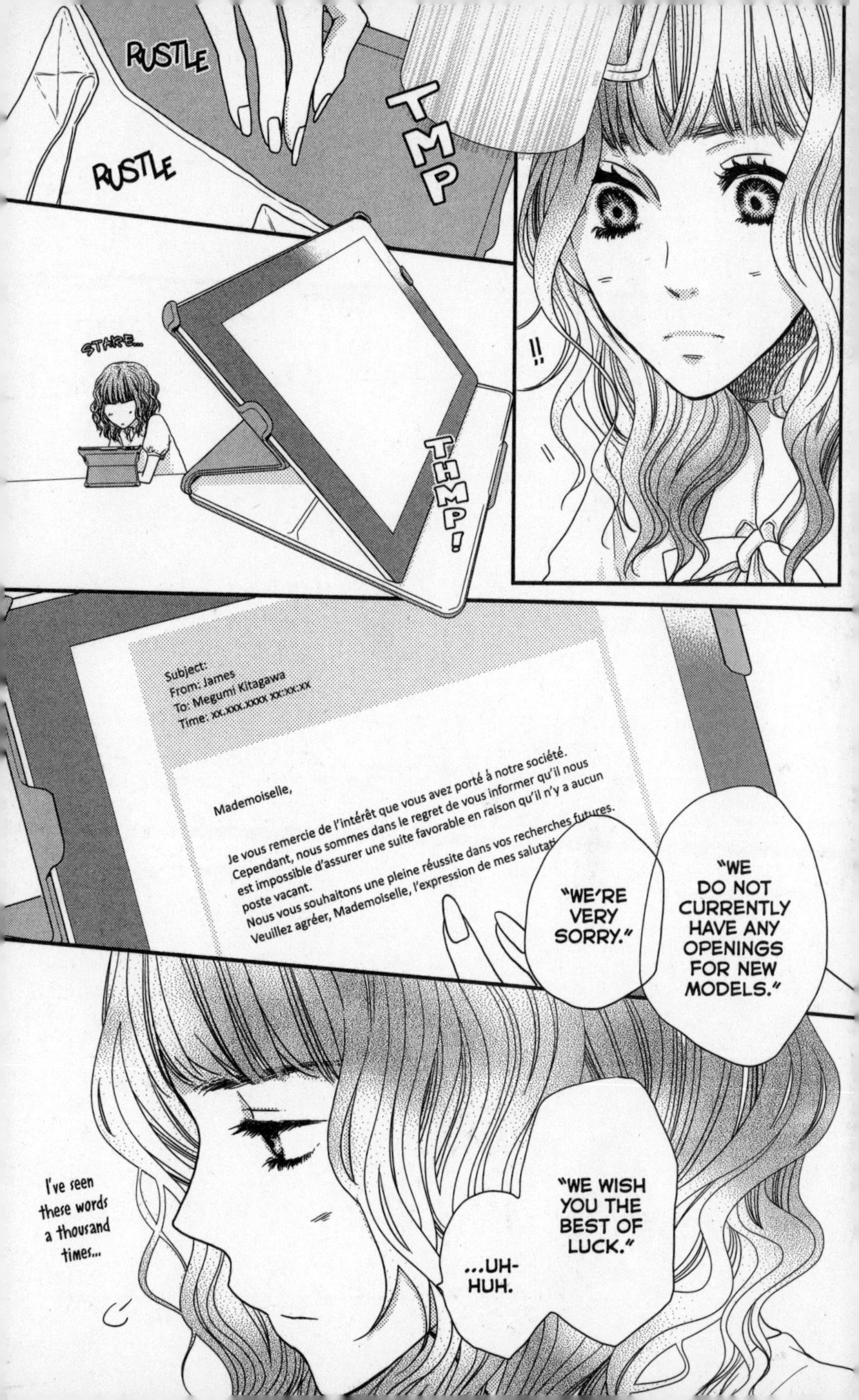
RUSTLE
TMP
RUSTLE
!!
STARE...
THMP!
Subject:
From: James
To: Megumi Kitagawa
Time: xx.xxx.xxxx xx:xx:xx
Mademoiselle,
Je vous remercie de l'intérêt que vous avez porté à notre société. Cependant, nous sommes dans le regret de vous informer qu'il nous est impossible d'assurer une suite favorable en raison qu'il n'y a aucun poste vacant.
Nous vous souhaitons une pleine réussite dans vos recherches futures.
Veuillez agréer, Mademoiselle, l'expression de mes salutati
"WE DO NOT CURRENTLY HAVE ANY OPENINGS FOR NEW MODELS."
"WE'RE VERY SORRY."
"WE WISH YOU THE BEST OF LUCK."
...UH-HUH.
I've seen these words a thousand times...

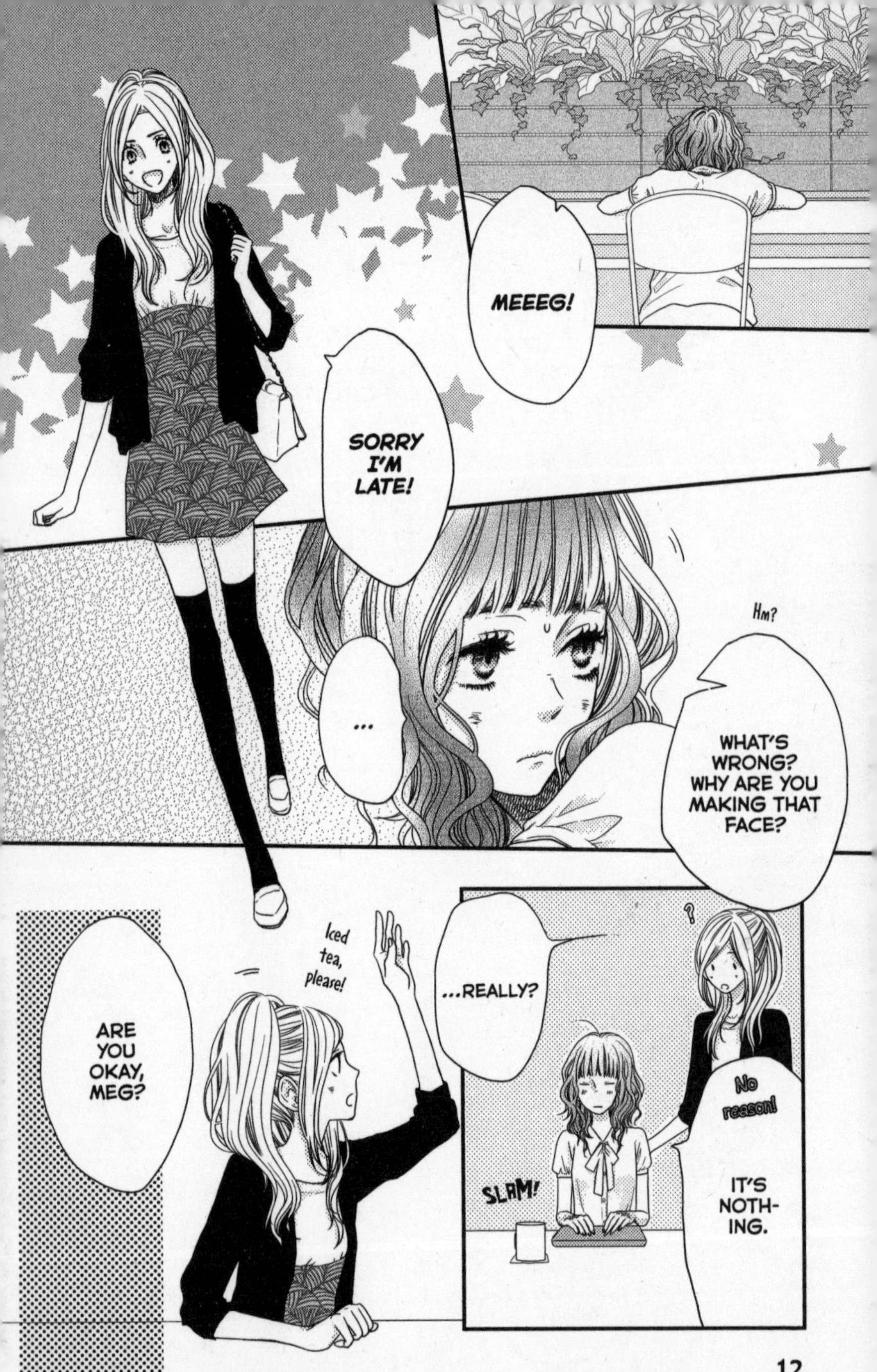
MEEEG!
SORRY I'M LATE!
...
Hm?
WHAT'S WRONG? WHY ARE YOU MAKING THAT FACE?
?
No reason!
IT'S NOTHING.
...REALLY?
SLAM!
Iced tea, please!
ARE YOU OKAY, MEG?

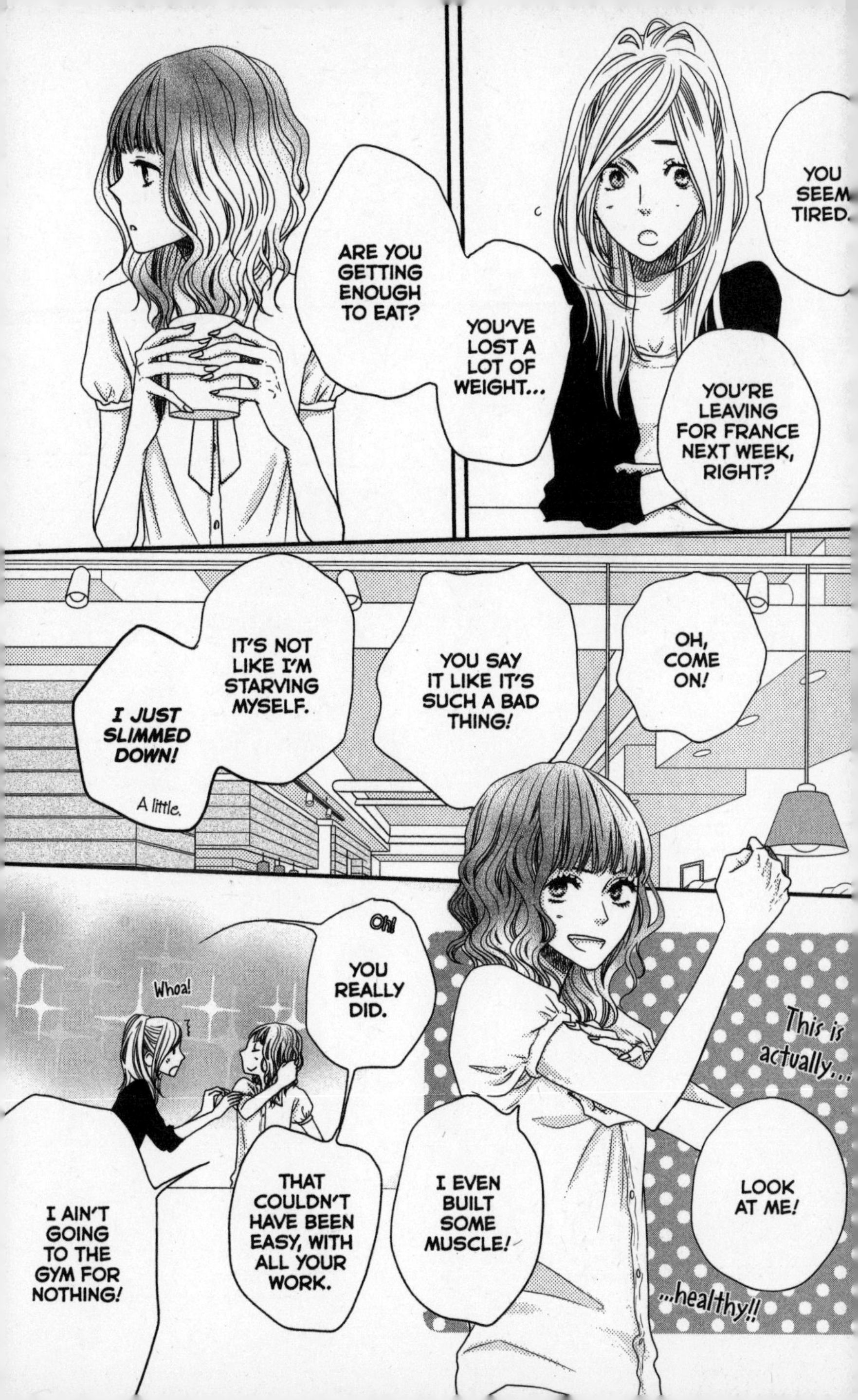
YOU SEEM TIRED.
YOU'RE LEAVING FOR FRANCE NEXT WEEK, RIGHT?
YOU'VE LOST A LOT OF WEIGHT...
ARE YOU GETTING ENOUGH TO EAT?
OH, COME ON!
YOU SAY IT LIKE IT'S SUCH A BAD THING!
IT'S NOT LIKE I'M STARVING MYSELF.
I JUST SLIMMED DOWN!
A little.
This is actually...
LOOK AT ME!
I EVEN BUILT SOME MUSCLE!
...healthy!!
Oh!
YOU REALLY DID.
Whoa!
THAT COULDN'T HAVE BEEN EASY, WITH ALL YOUR WORK.
I AIN'T GOING TO THE GYM FOR NOTHING!

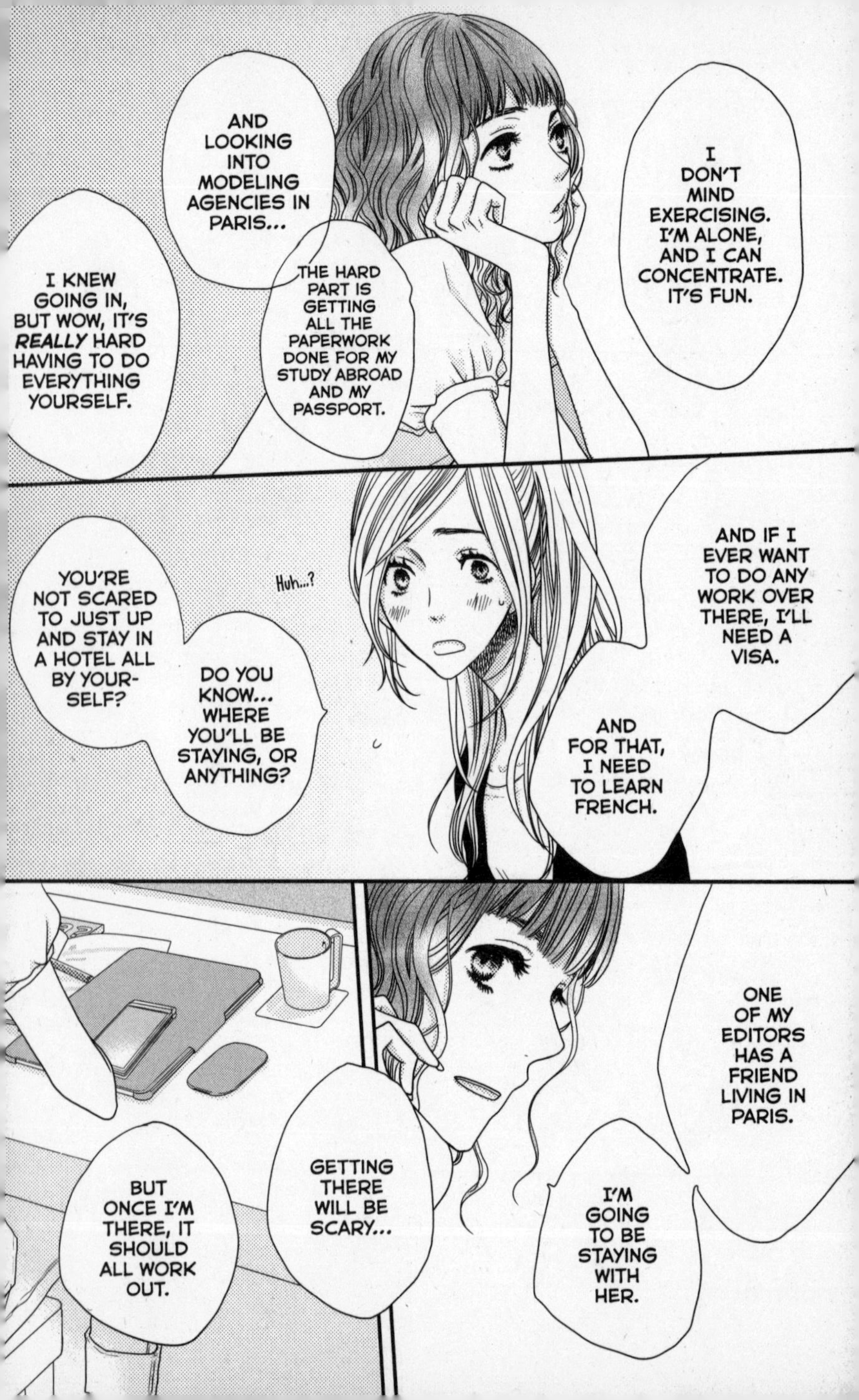

I DON'T MIND EXERCISING. I'M ALONE, AND I CAN CONCENTRATE. IT'S FUN.
THE HARD PART IS GETTING ALL THE PAPERWORK DONE FOR MY STUDY ABROAD AND MY PASSPORT.
AND LOOKING INTO MODELING AGENCIES IN PARIS...
I KNEW GOING IN, BUT WOW, IT'S *REALLY* HARD HAVING TO DO EVERYTHING YOURSELF.
AND IF I EVER WANT TO DO ANY WORK OVER THERE, I'LL NEED A VISA.
AND FOR THAT, I NEED TO LEARN FRENCH.
Huh...?
DO YOU KNOW... WHERE YOU'LL BE STAYING, OR ANYTHING?
YOU'RE NOT SCARED TO JUST UP AND STAY IN A HOTEL ALL BY YOURSELF?
ONE OF MY EDITORS HAS A FRIEND LIVING IN PARIS.
I'M GOING TO BE STAYING WITH HER.
GETTING THERE WILL BE SCARY...
BUT ONCE I'M THERE, IT SHOULD ALL WORK OUT.

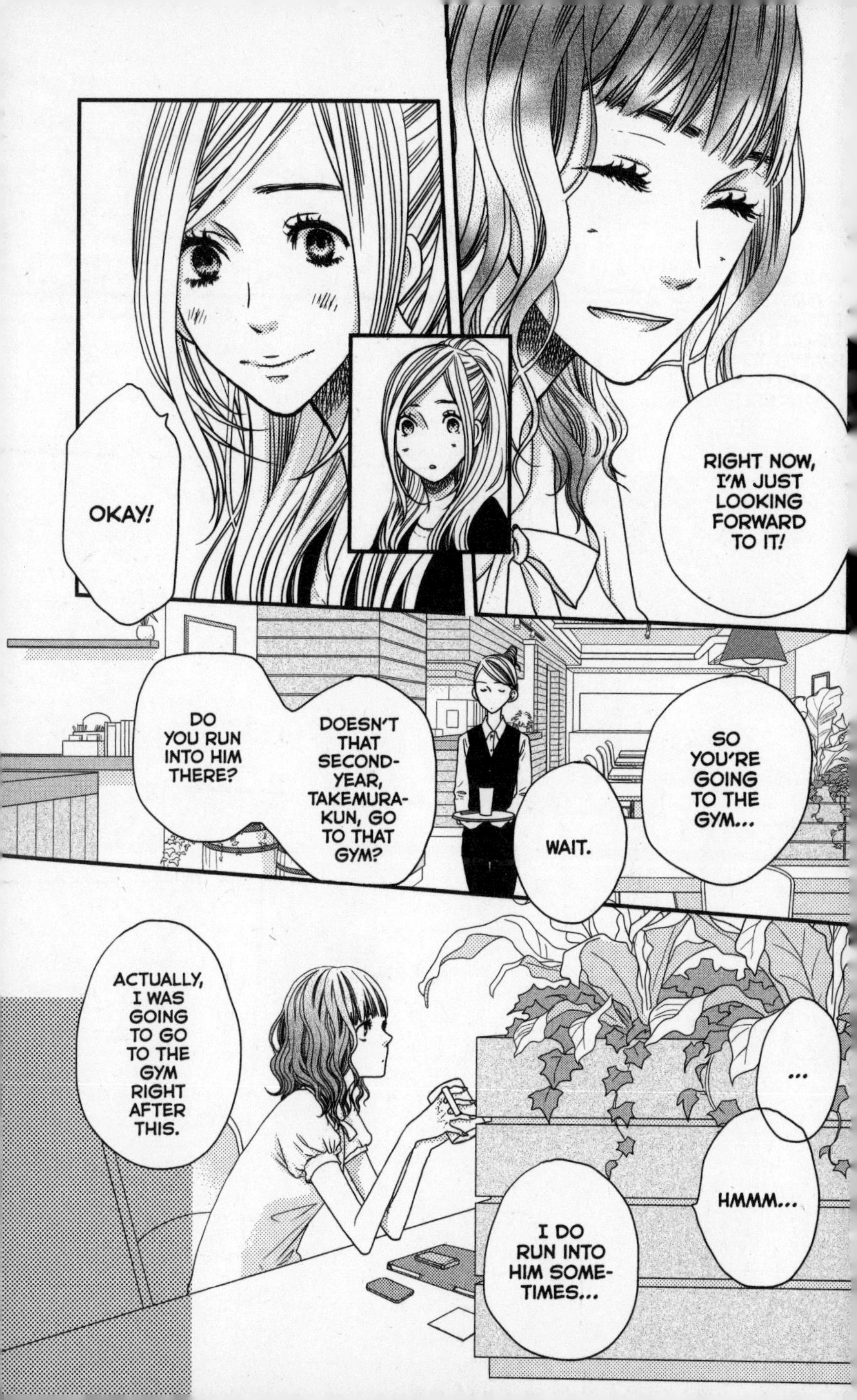
RIGHT NOW, I'M JUST LOOKING FORWARD TO IT!
OKAY!
SO YOU'RE GOING TO THE GYM...
WAIT.
DOESN'T THAT SECOND-YEAR, TAKEMURA-KUN, GO TO THAT GYM?
DO YOU RUN INTO HIM THERE?
...
HMMM...
I DO RUN INTO HIM SOME-TIMES...
ACTUALLY, I WAS GOING TO GO TO THE GYM RIGHT AFTER THIS.

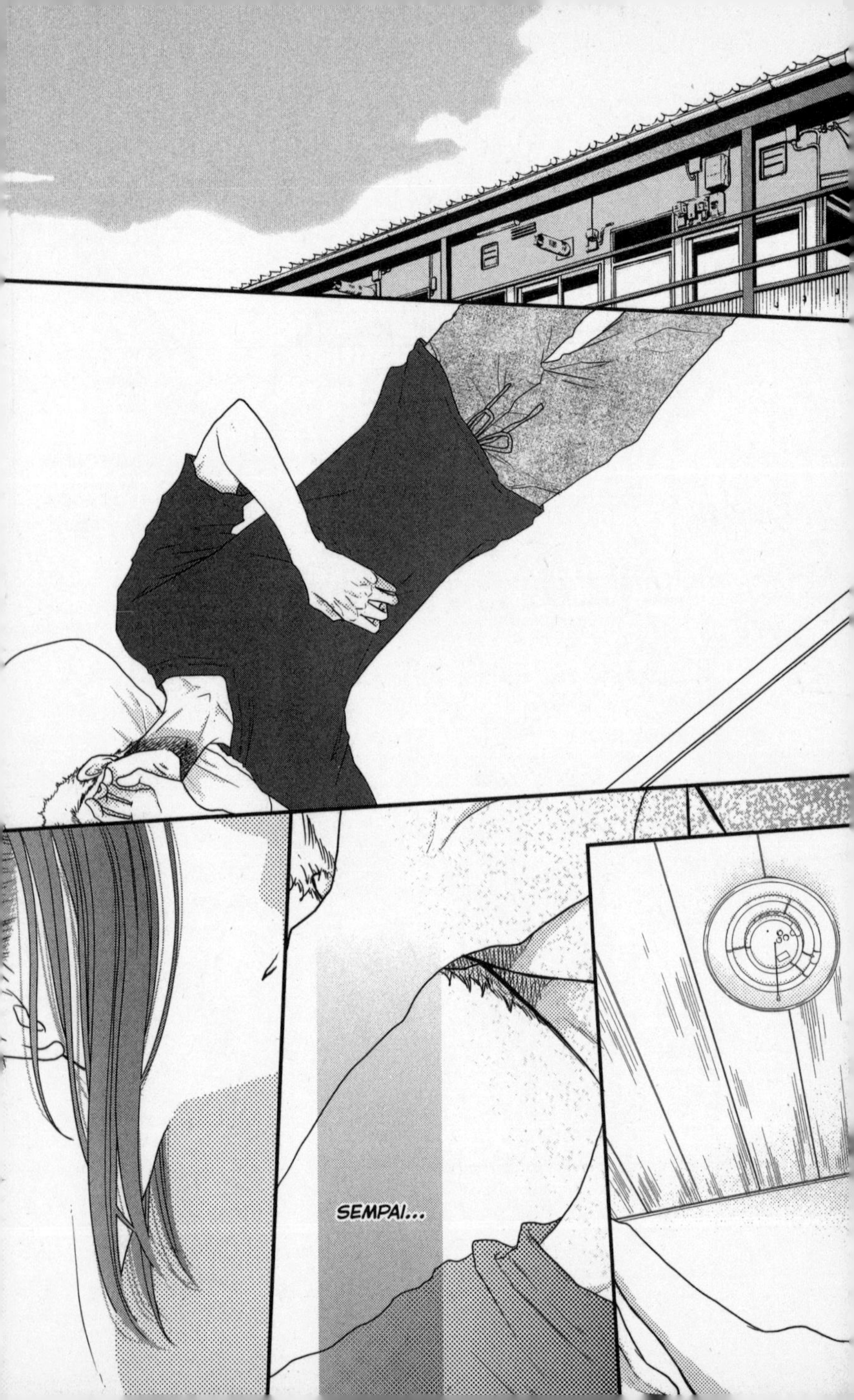
SEMPAI...

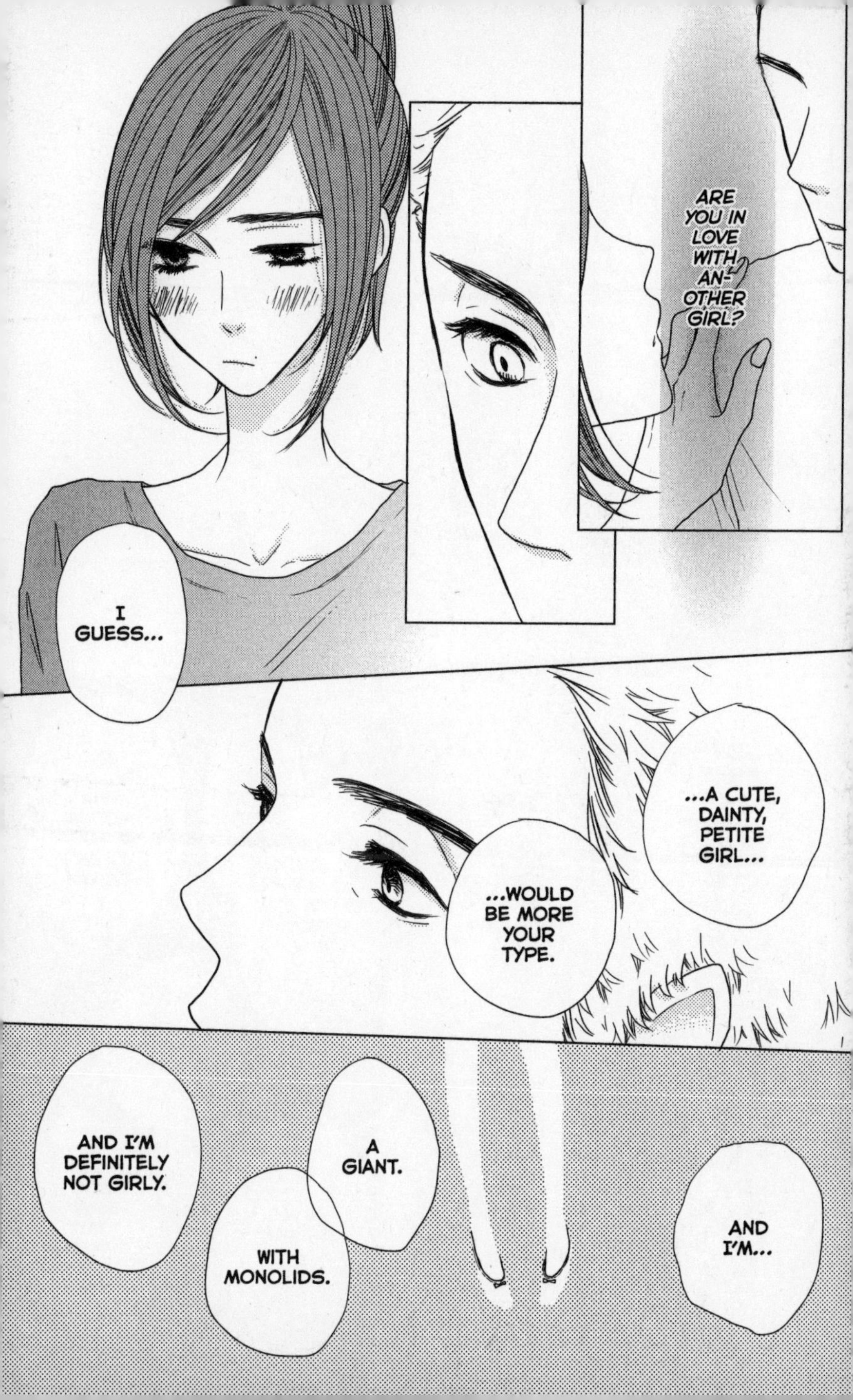
ARE YOU IN LOVE WITH AN-OTHER GIRL?
I GUESS...
...A CUTE, DAINTY, PETITE GIRL...
...WOULD BE MORE YOUR TYPE.
AND I'M...
A GIANT.
WITH MONOLIDS.
AND I'M DEFINITELY NOT GIRLY.

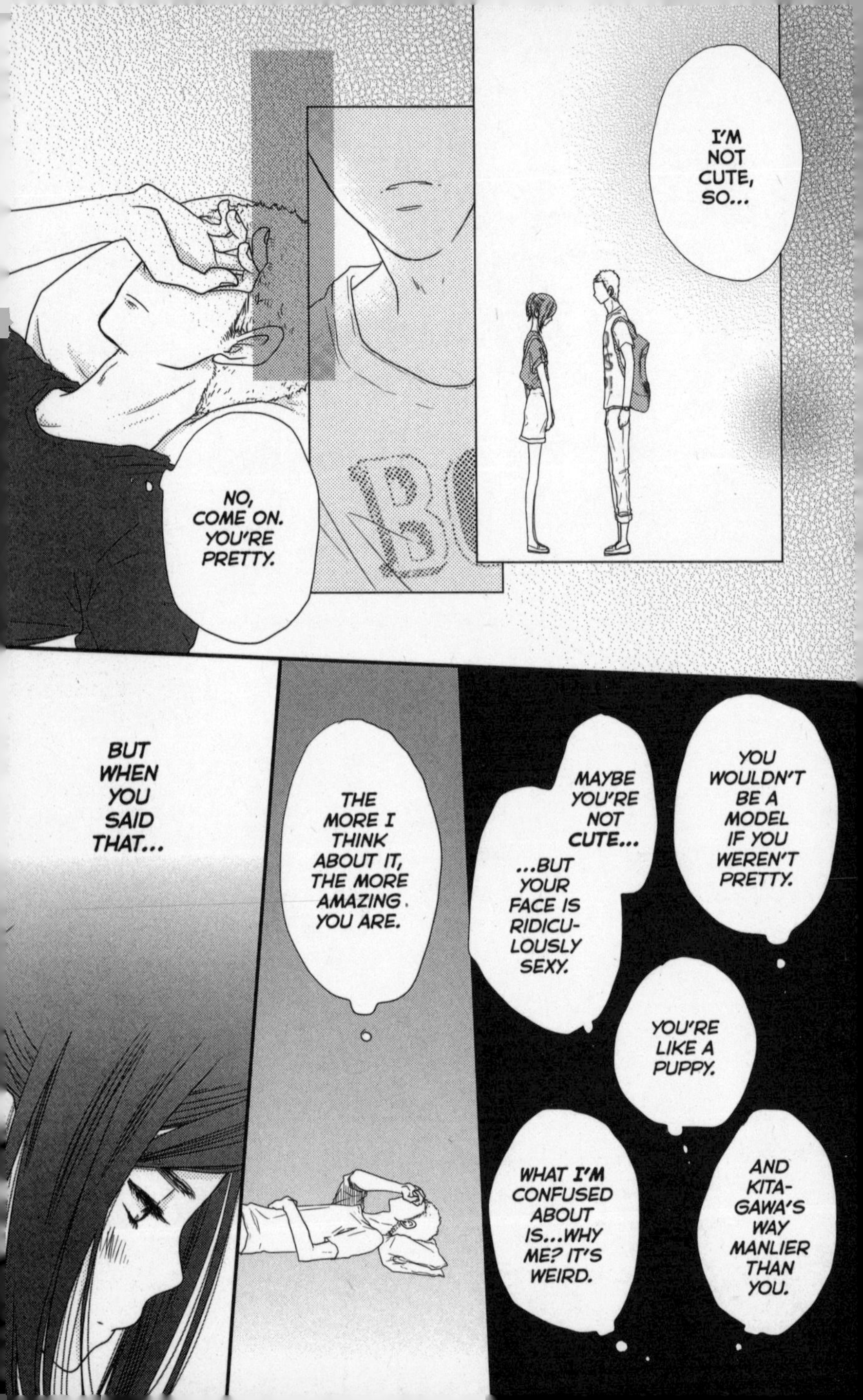

I'M NOT CUTE, SO...
NO, COME ON. YOU'RE PRETTY.
YOU WOULDN'T BE A MODEL IF YOU WEREN'T PRETTY.
MAYBE YOU'RE NOT CUTE... ...BUT YOUR FACE IS RIDICU-LOUSLY SEXY.
YOU'RE LIKE A PUPPY.
AND KITA-GAWA'S WAY MANLIER THAN YOU.
WHAT I'M CONFUSED ABOUT IS...WHY ME? IT'S WEIRD.
THE MORE I THINK ABOUT IT, THE MORE AMAZING YOU ARE.
BUT WHEN YOU SAID THAT...

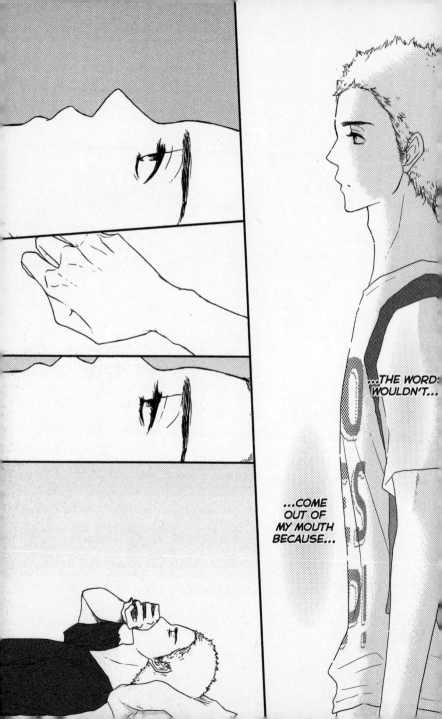

...THE WORDS WOULDN'T...

...COME OUT OF MY MOUTH BECAUSE...

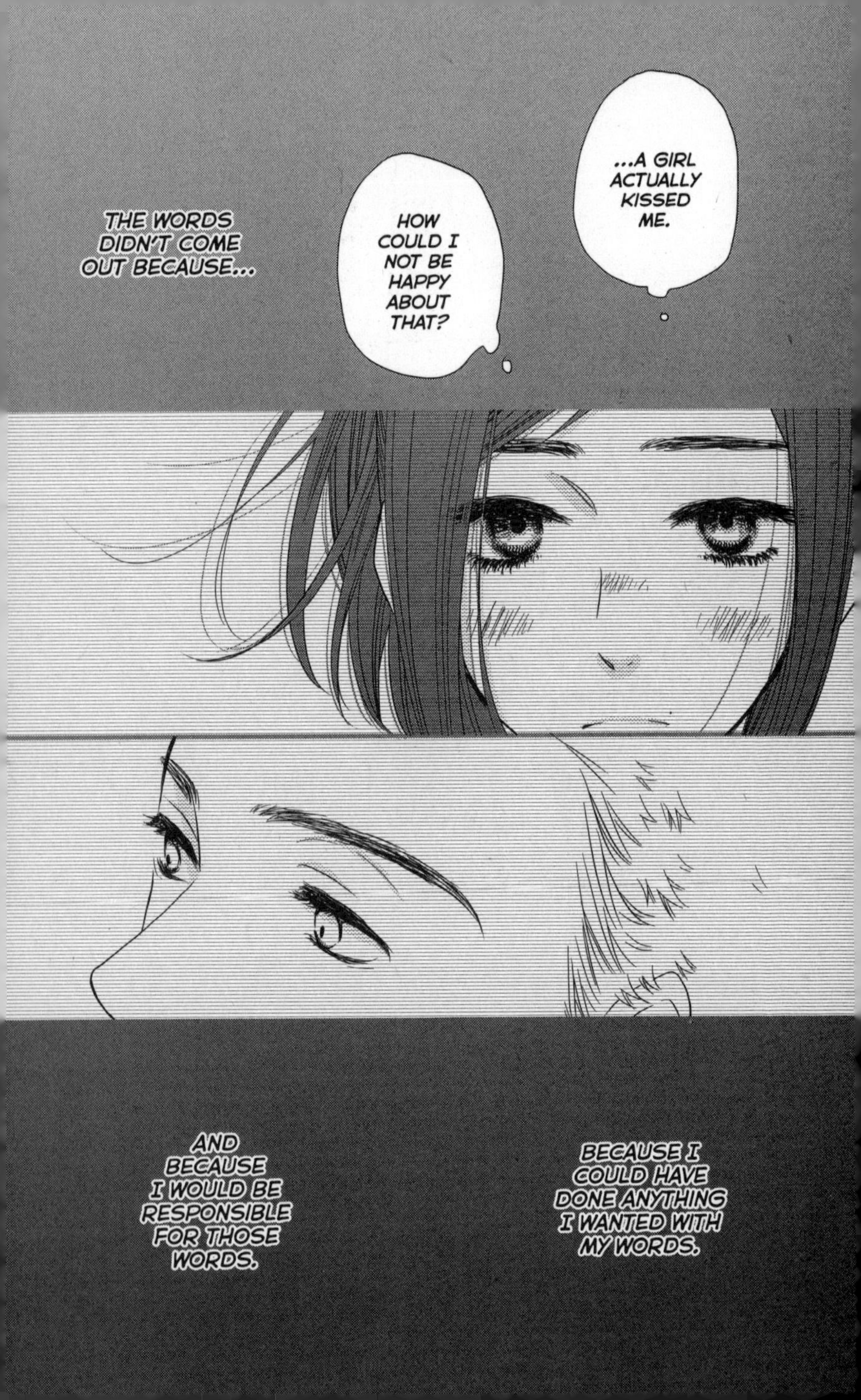
...A GIRL ACTUALLY KISSED ME.
HOW COULD I NOT BE HAPPY ABOUT THAT?
THE WORDS DIDN'T COME OUT BECAUSE...
BECAUSE I COULD HAVE DONE ANYTHING I WANTED WITH MY WORDS.
AND BECAUSE I WOULD BE RESPONSIBLE FOR THOSE WORDS.

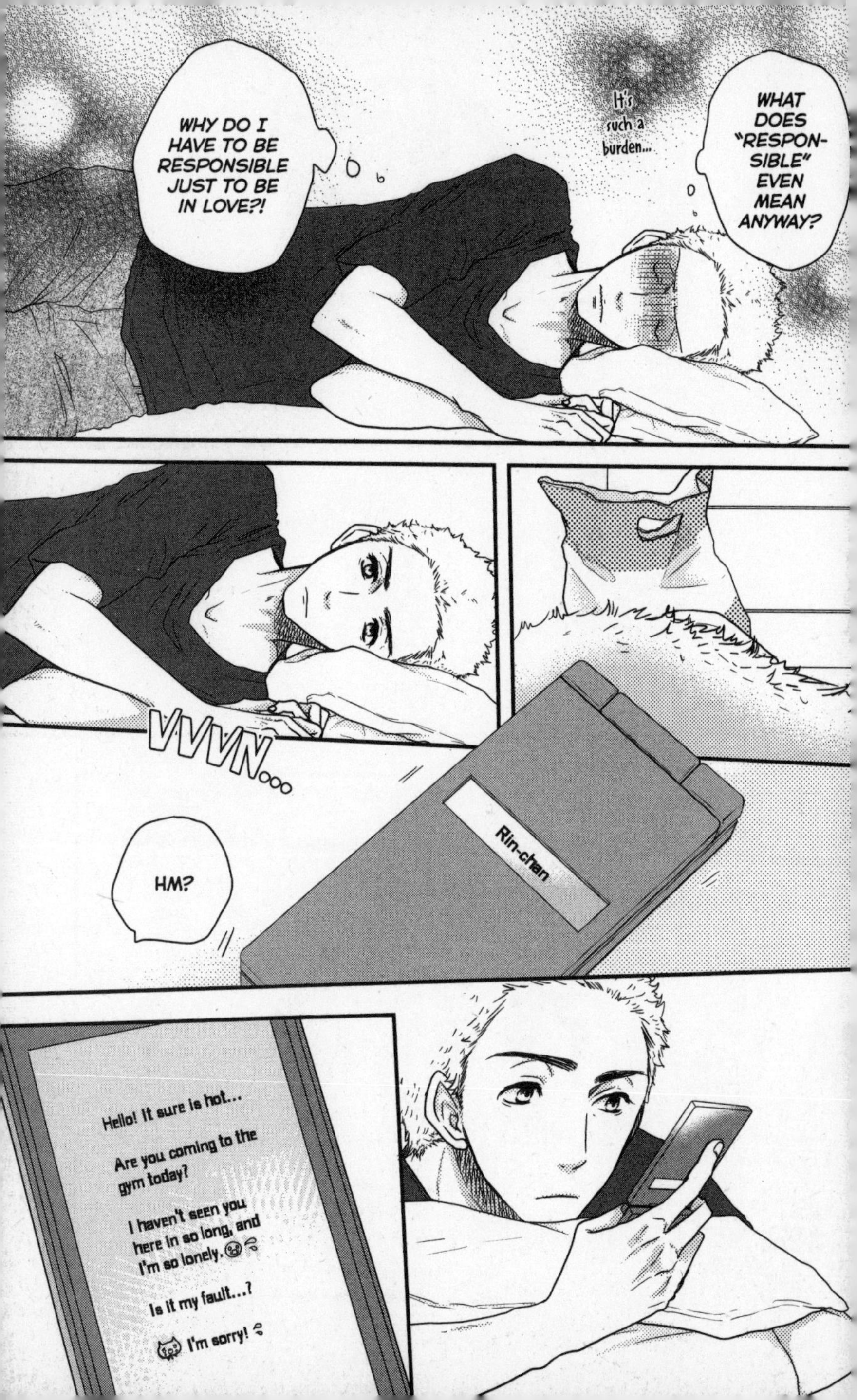
WHAT DOES "RESPONSIBLE" EVEN MEAN ANYWAY?
It's such a burden...
WHY DO I HAVE TO BE RESPONSIBLE JUST TO BE IN LOVE?!
VVVN...
Rin-chan
HM?
Hello! It sure is hot...
Are you coming to the gym today?
I haven't seen you here in so long, and I'm so lonely.
Is it my fault...?
I'm sorry!

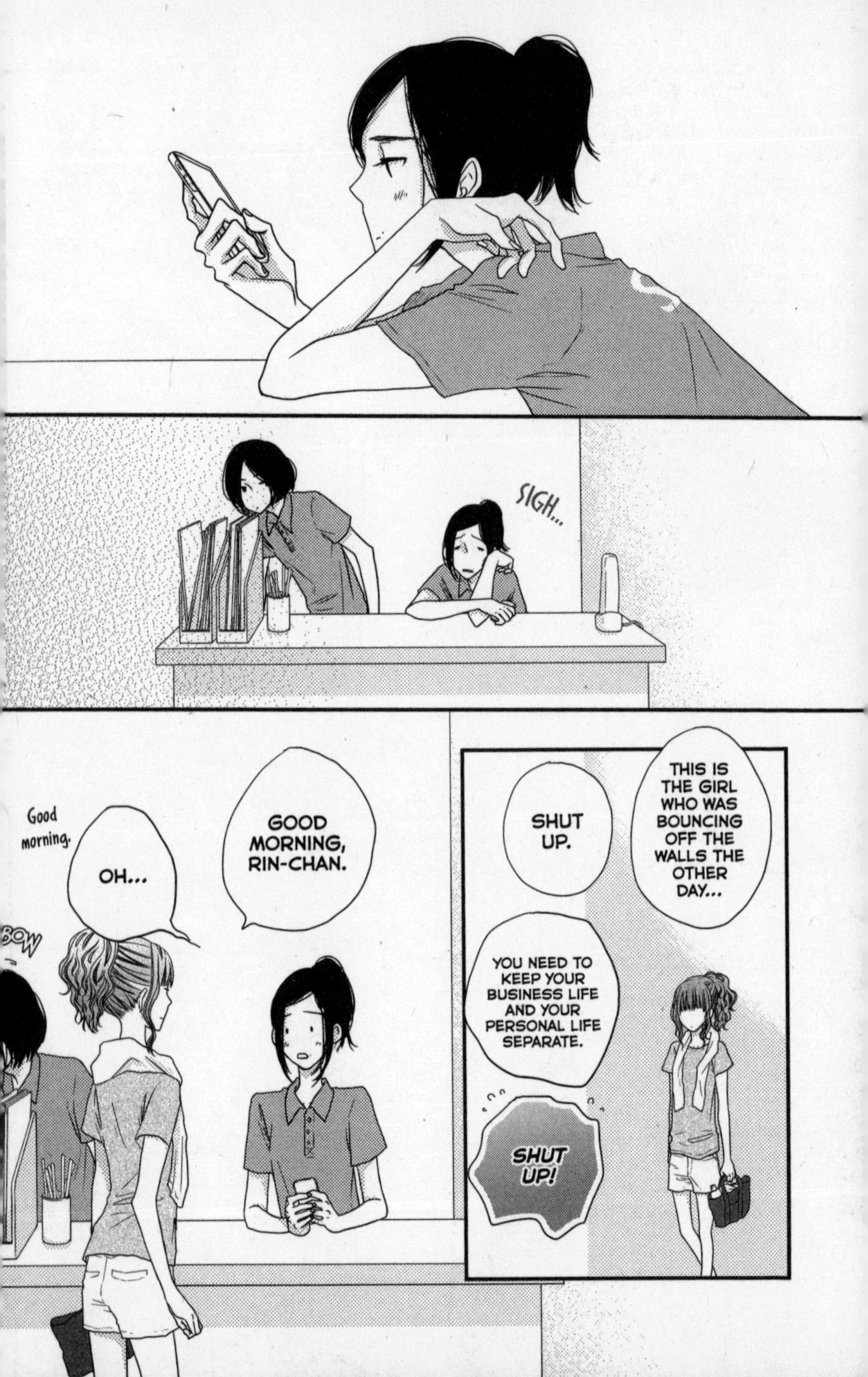
SIGH...
THIS IS THE GIRL WHO WAS BOUNCING OFF THE WALLS THE OTHER DAY...
SHUT UP.
YOU NEED TO KEEP YOUR BUSINESS LIFE AND YOUR PERSONAL LIFE SEPARATE.
SHUT UP!
GOOD MORNING, RIN-CHAN.
OH...
Good morning.
BOW

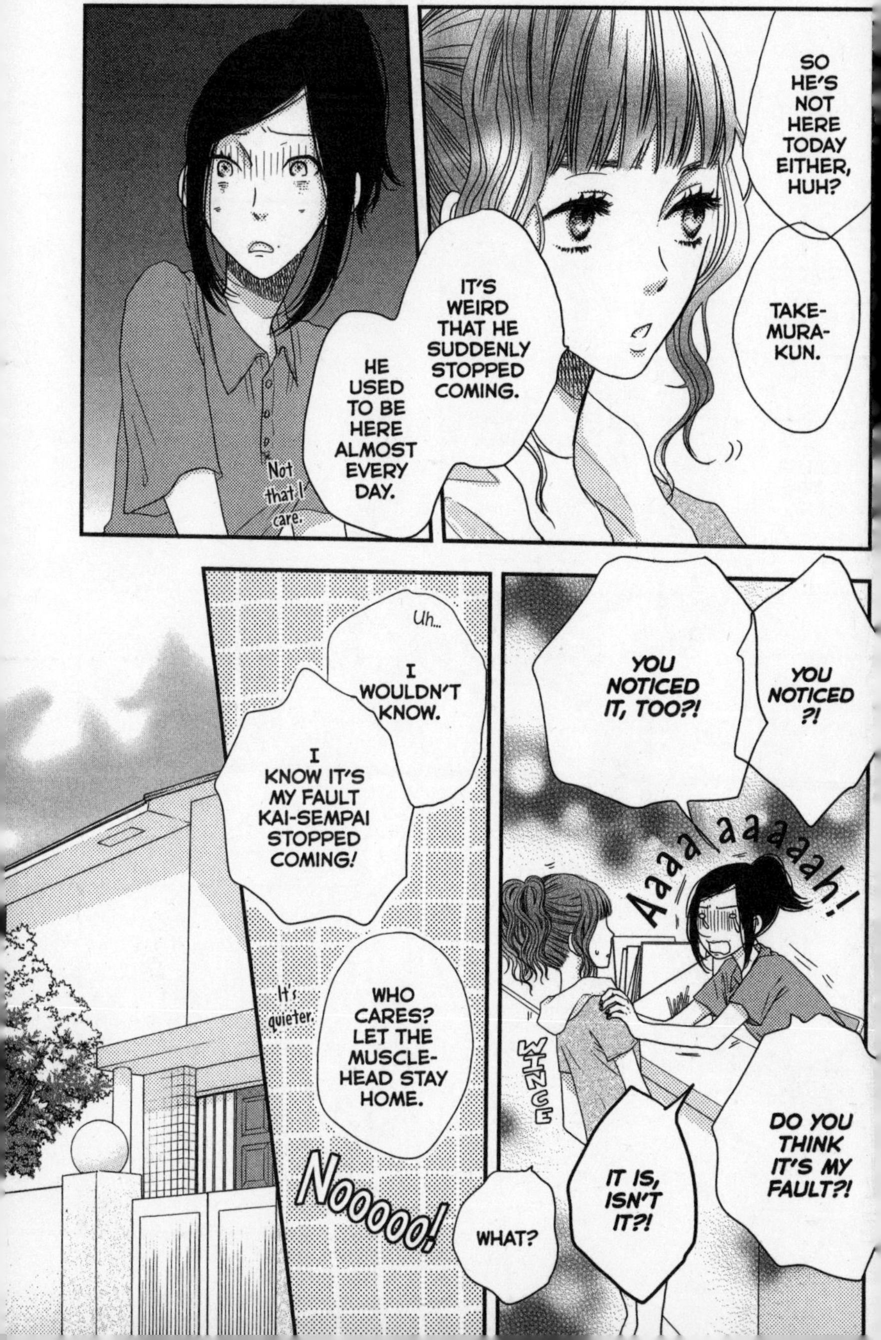
SO HE'S NOT HERE TODAY EITHER, HUH?
TAKE-MURA-KUN.
IT'S WEIRD THAT HE SUDDENLY STOPPED COMING.
HE USED TO BE HERE ALMOST EVERY DAY.
Not that I care.
YOU NOTICED ?!
YOU NOTICED IT, TOO?!
Aaaa aaaaaah!
WINCE
DO YOU THINK IT'S MY FAULT?!
IT IS, ISN'T IT?!
WHAT?
Uh...
I WOULDN'T KNOW.
I KNOW IT'S MY FAULT KAI-SEMPAI STOPPED COMING!
WHO CARES? LET THE MUSCLE-HEAD STAY HOME.
It's quieter.
Noooooo!

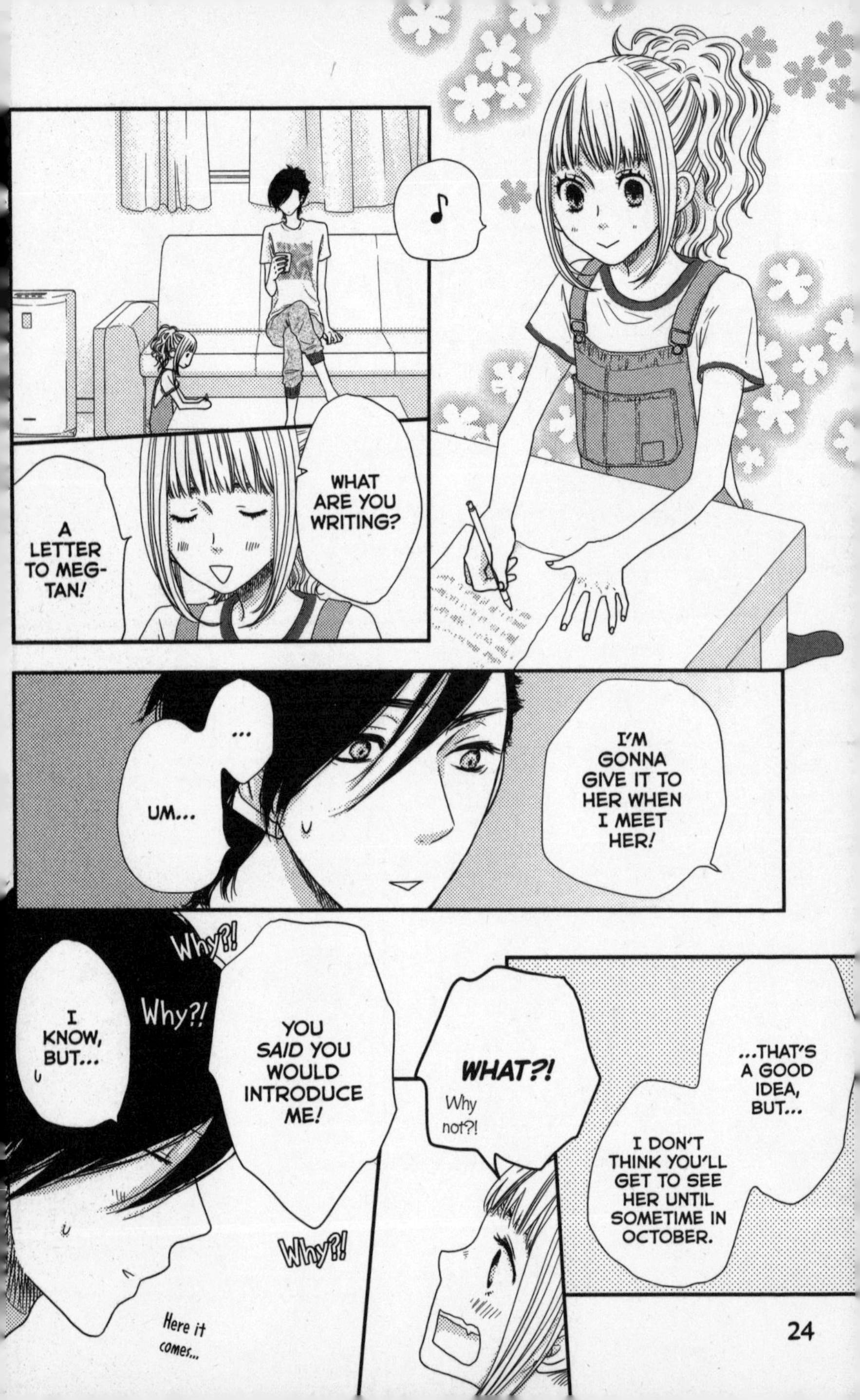

♪
WHAT ARE YOU WRITING?
A LETTER TO MEG-TAN!
I'M GONNA GIVE IT TO HER WHEN I MEET HER!
...
UM...
...THAT'S A GOOD IDEA, BUT...
I DON'T THINK YOU'LL GET TO SEE HER UNTIL SOMETIME IN OCTOBER.
WHAT?!
Why not?!
YOU SAID YOU WOULD INTRODUCE ME!
Why?!
Why?!
Why?!
I KNOW, BUT...
Here it comes...

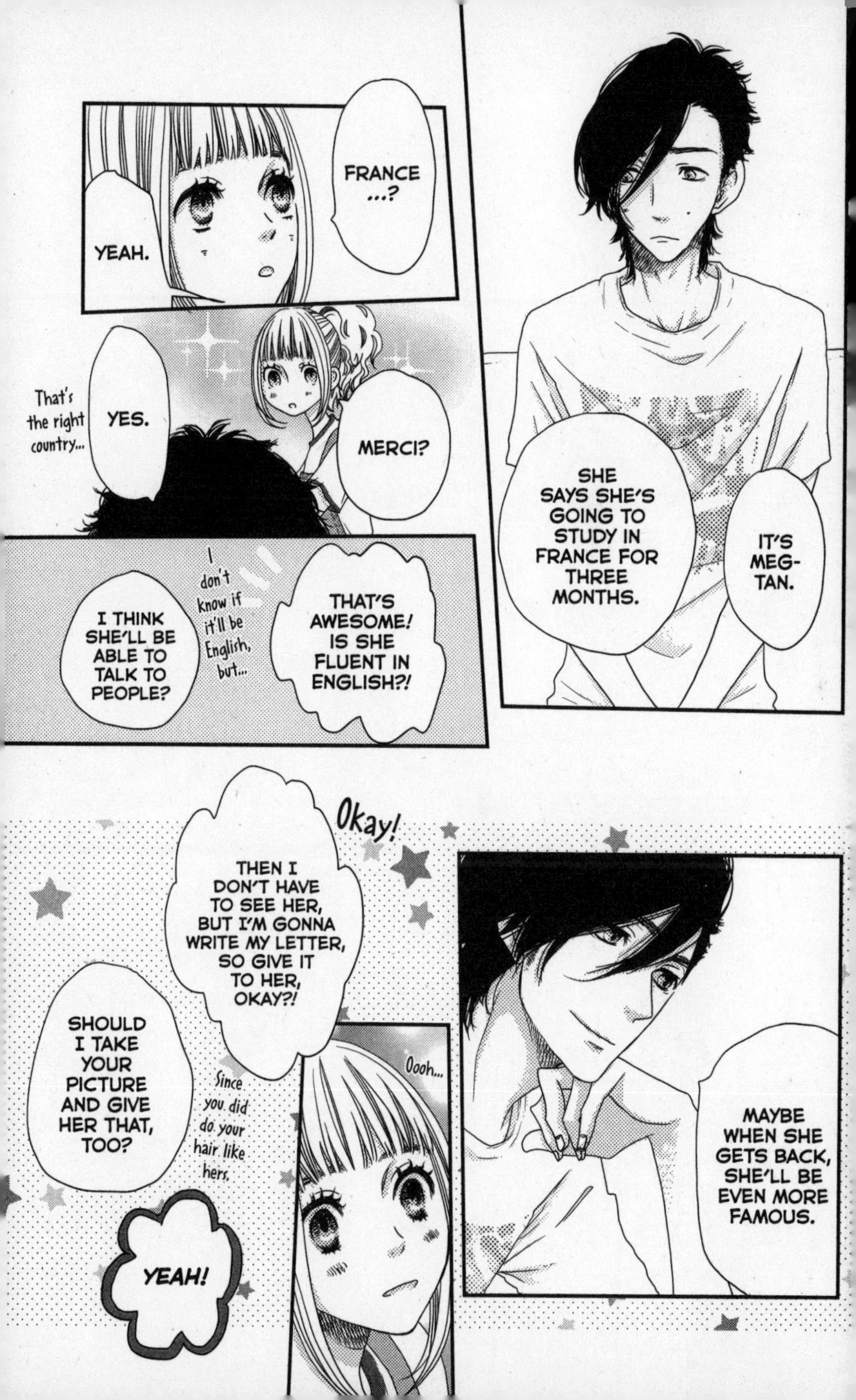
IT'S MEG-TAN.
SHE SAYS SHE'S GOING TO STUDY IN FRANCE FOR THREE MONTHS.
FRANCE ...?
YEAH.
MERCI?
YES.
That's the right country...
THAT'S AWESOME! IS SHE FLUENT IN ENGLISH?!
I don't know if it'll be English, but...
I THINK SHE'LL BE ABLE TO TALK TO PEOPLE?
MAYBE WHEN SHE GETS BACK, SHE'LL BE EVEN MORE FAMOUS.
Okay!
THEN I DON'T HAVE TO SEE HER, BUT I'M GONNA WRITE MY LETTER, SO GIVE IT TO HER, OKAY?!
Oooh...
Since you did do your hair like hers.
SHOULD I TAKE YOUR PICTURE AND GIVE HER THAT, TOO?
YEAH!

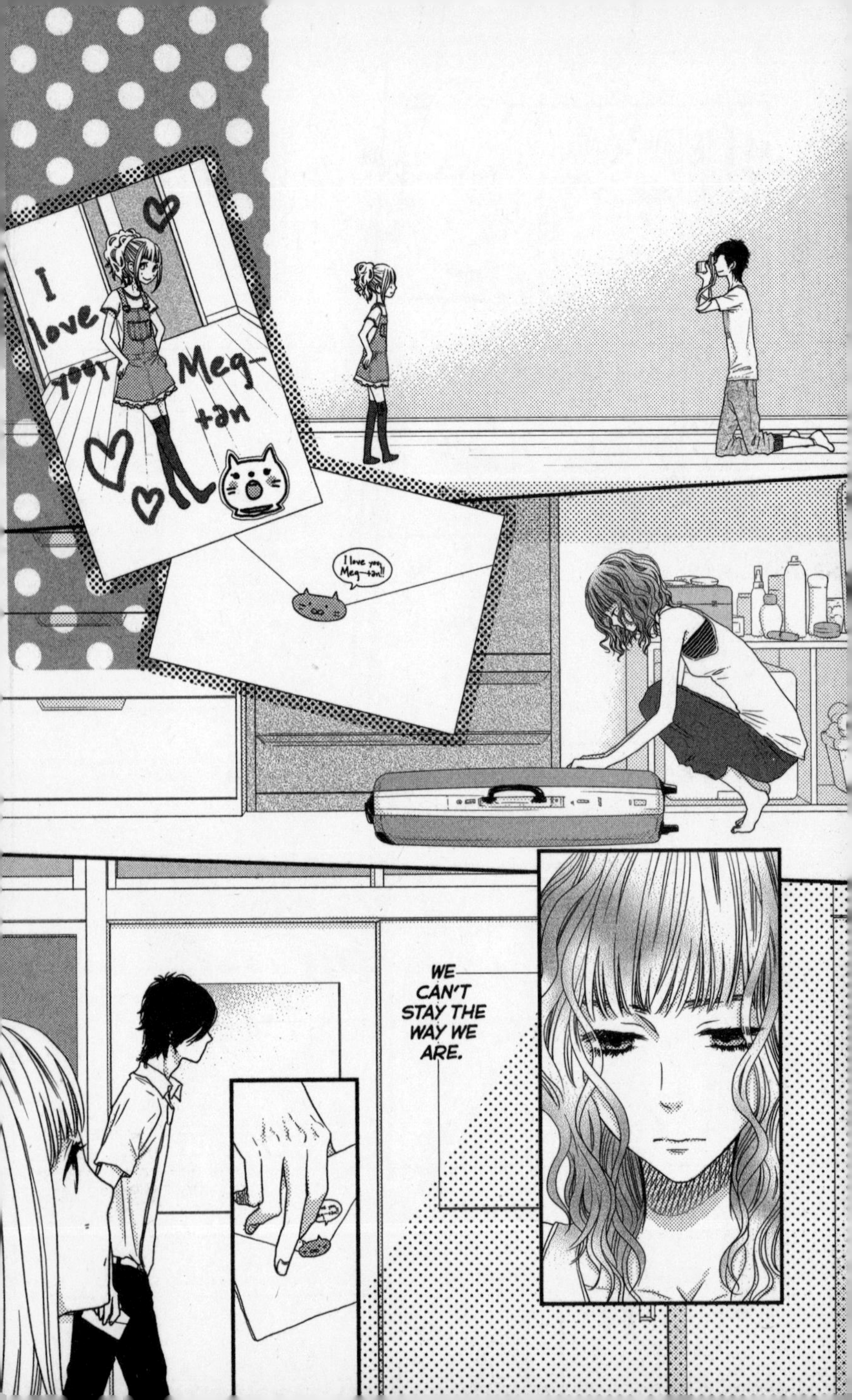
I love you, Meg-tan
I love you, Meg-tan!!
WE CAN'T STAY THE WAY WE ARE.

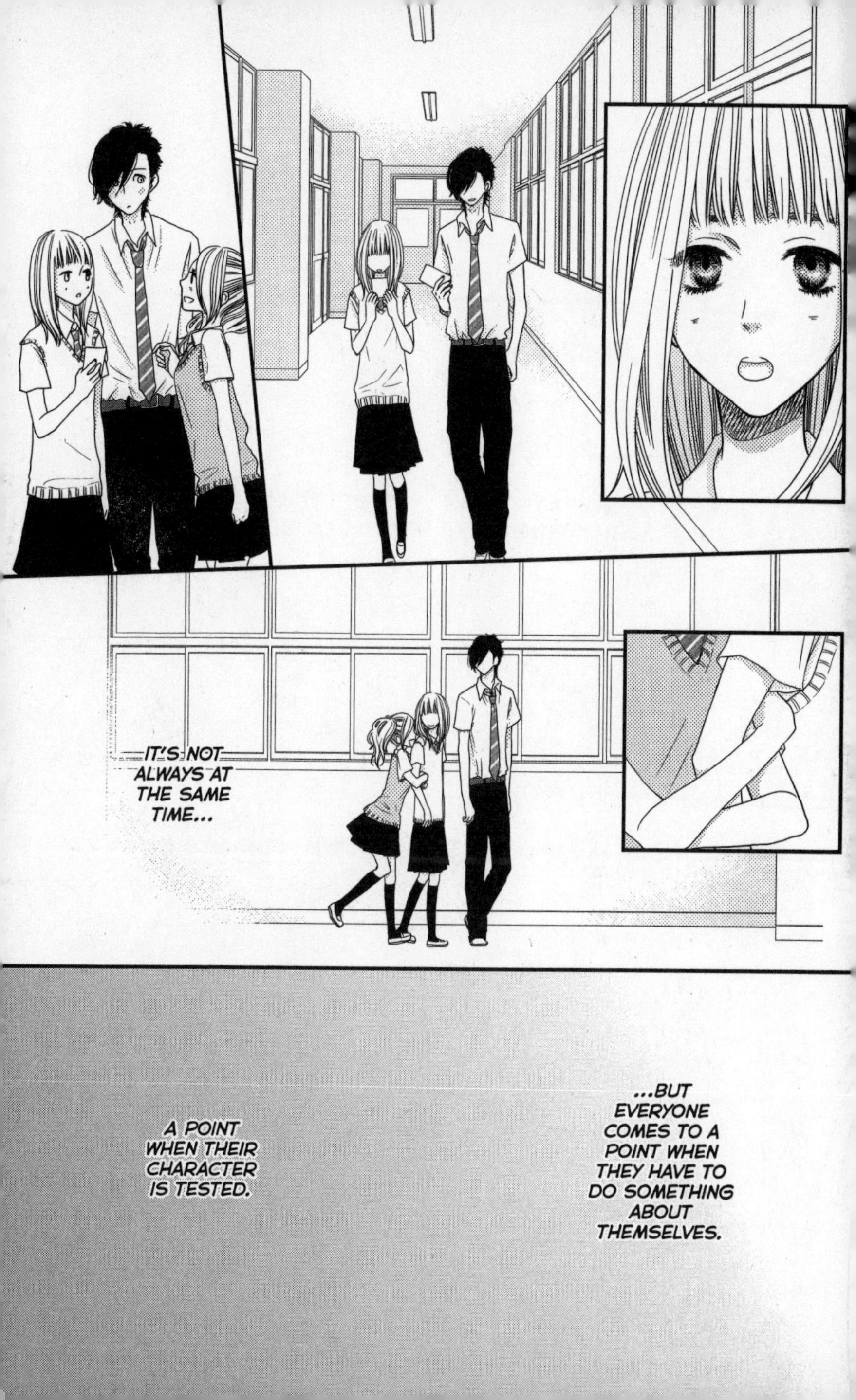
IT'S NOT ALWAYS AT THE SAME TIME...
...BUT EVERYONE COMES TO A POINT WHEN THEY HAVE TO DO SOMETHING ABOUT THEMSELVES.
A POINT WHEN THEIR CHARACTER IS TESTED.

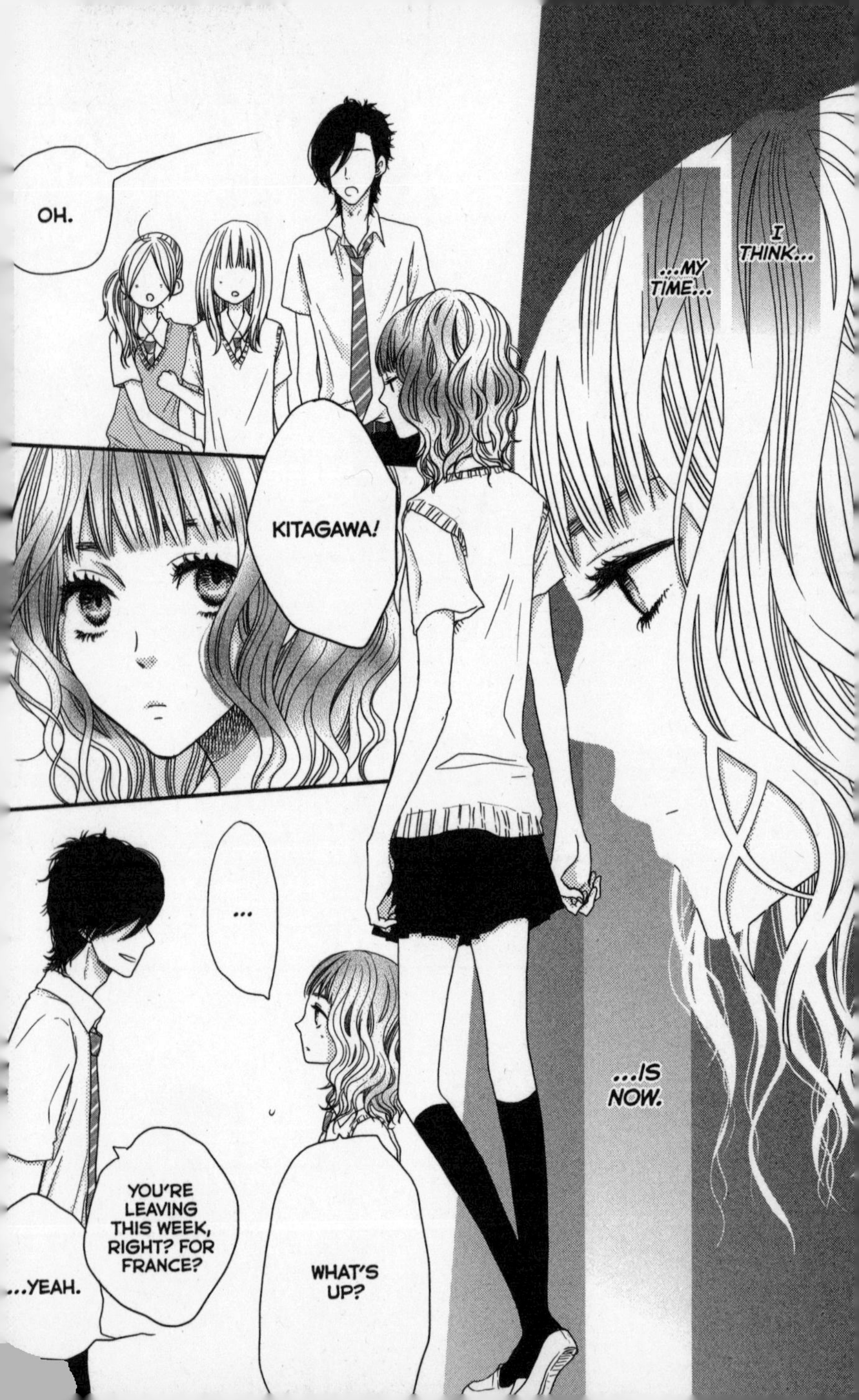
I THINK...
...MY TIME...
...IS NOW.
OH.
KITAGAWA!
...
WHAT'S UP?
YOU'RE LEAVING THIS WEEK, RIGHT? FOR FRANCE?
...YEAH.

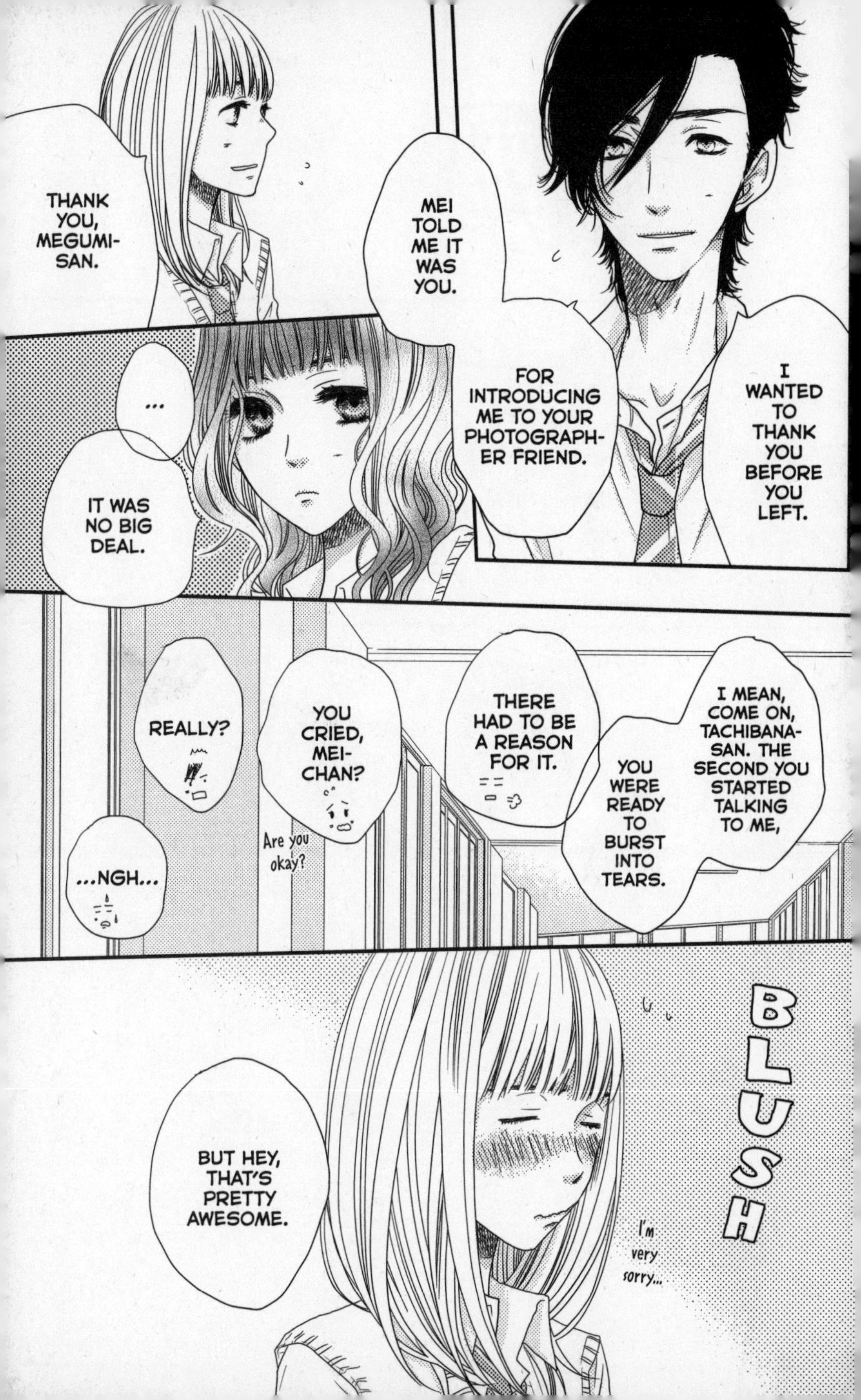
MEI TOLD ME IT WAS YOU.
I WANTED TO THANK YOU BEFORE YOU LEFT.
FOR INTRODUCING ME TO YOUR PHOTOGRAPHER FRIEND.
THANK YOU, MEGUMI-SAN.
...
IT WAS NO BIG DEAL.
I MEAN, COME ON, TACHIBANA-SAN. THE SECOND YOU STARTED TALKING TO ME,
YOU WERE READY TO BURST INTO TEARS.
THERE HAD TO BE A REASON FOR IT.
YOU CRIED, MEI-CHAN?
Are you okay?
REALLY?
...NGH...
BLUSH
I'm very sorry...
BUT HEY, THAT'S PRETTY AWESOME.

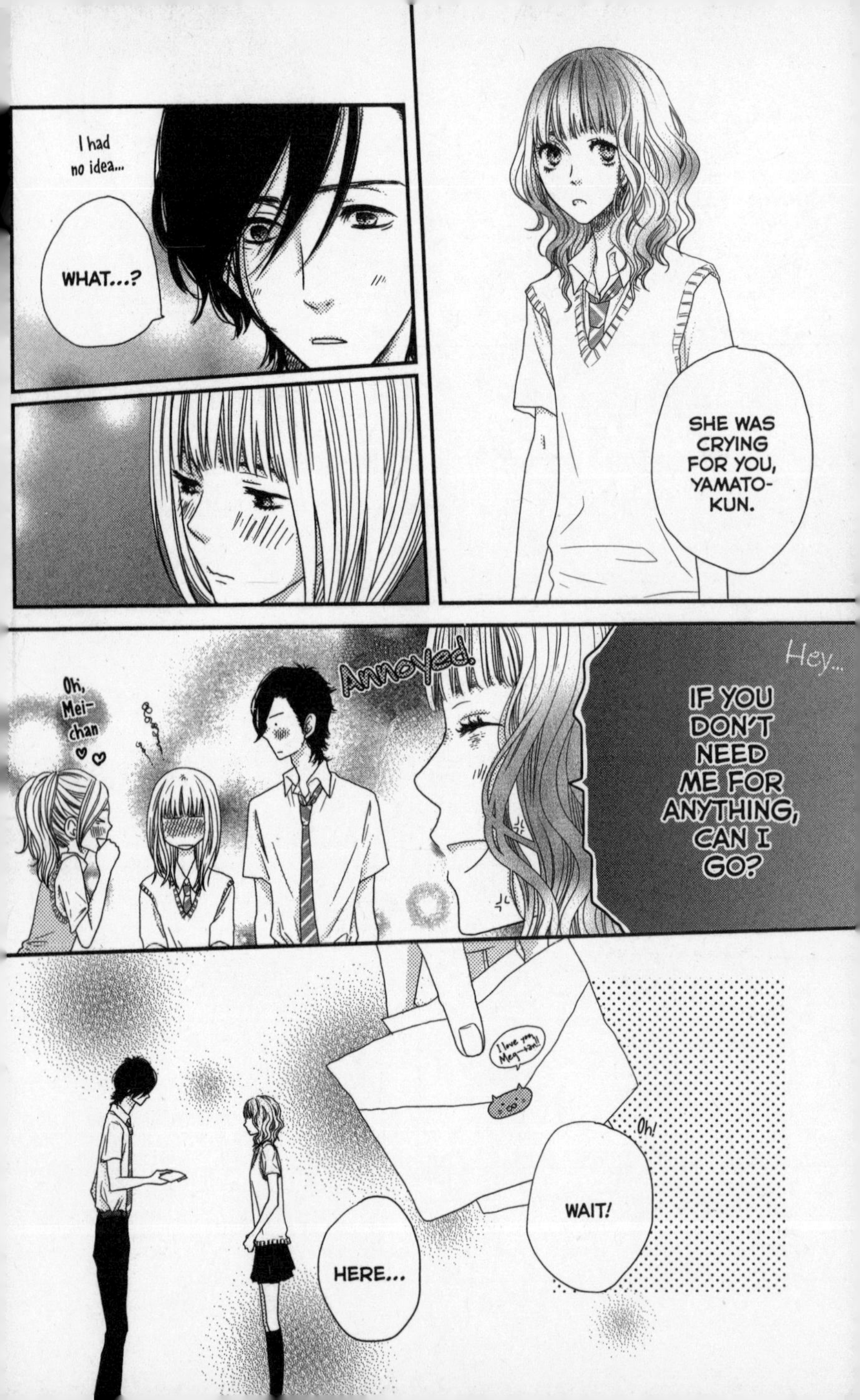
SHE WAS CRYING FOR YOU, YAMATO-KUN.
I had no idea...
WHAT...?
Hey...
IF YOU DON'T NEED ME FOR ANYTHING, CAN I GO?
Annoyed
Oh, Mei-chan
I love you, Meg-tan!!
Oh!
WAIT!
HERE...

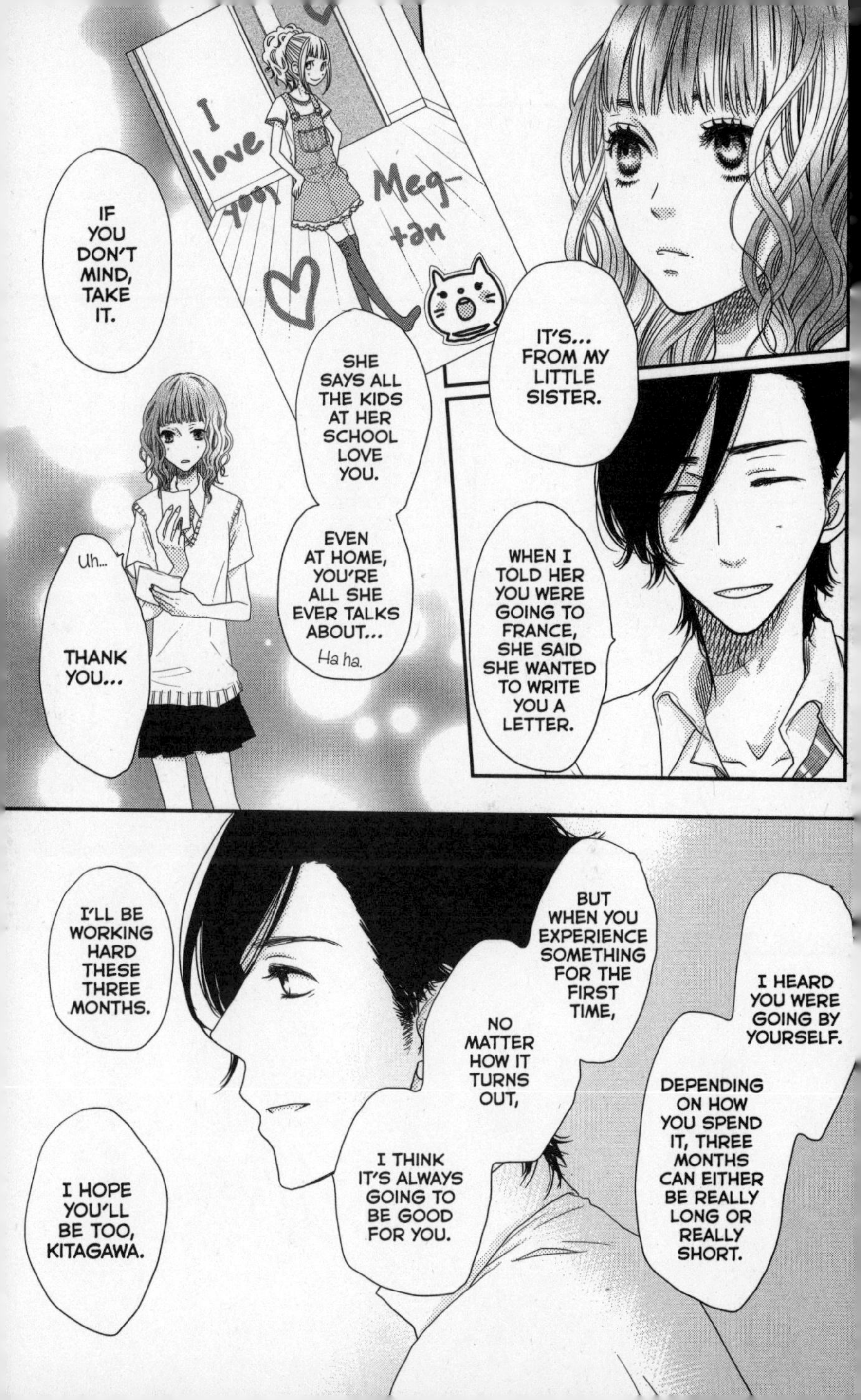
IT'S... FROM MY LITTLE SISTER.
WHEN I TOLD HER YOU WERE GOING TO FRANCE, SHE SAID SHE WANTED TO WRITE YOU A LETTER.
I love you
Meg-tan
SHE SAYS ALL THE KIDS AT HER SCHOOL LOVE YOU.
EVEN AT HOME, YOU'RE ALL SHE EVER TALKS ABOUT...
Ha ha.
IF YOU DON'T MIND, TAKE IT.
Uh...
THANK YOU...
I HEARD YOU WERE GOING BY YOURSELF.
DEPENDING ON HOW YOU SPEND IT, THREE MONTHS CAN EITHER BE REALLY LONG OR REALLY SHORT.
BUT WHEN YOU EXPERIENCE SOMETHING FOR THE FIRST TIME,
NO MATTER HOW IT TURNS OUT,
I THINK IT'S ALWAYS GOING TO BE GOOD FOR YOU.
I'LL BE WORKING HARD THESE THREE MONTHS.
I HOPE YOU'LL BE TOO, KITAGAWA.

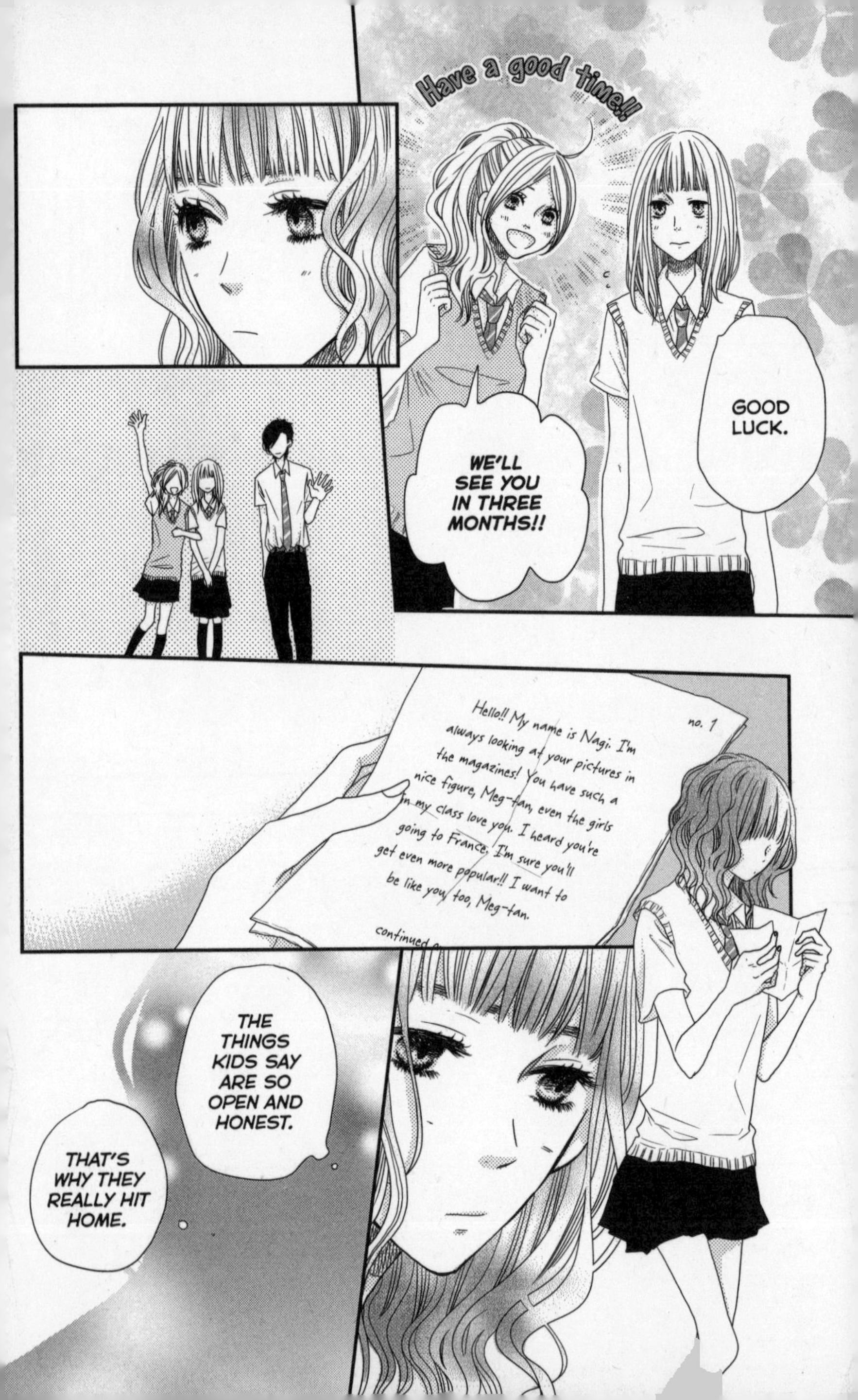
Have a good time!!
GOOD LUCK.
WE'LL SEE YOU IN THREE MONTHS!!
no. 1
Hello!! My name is Nagi. I'm always looking at your pictures in the magazines! You have such a nice figure, Meg-tan, even the girls in my class love you. I heard you're going to France. I'm sure you'll get even more popular!! I want to be like you, too, Meg-tan.
continued
THE THINGS KIDS SAY ARE SO OPEN AND HONEST.
THAT'S WHY THEY REALLY HIT HOME.

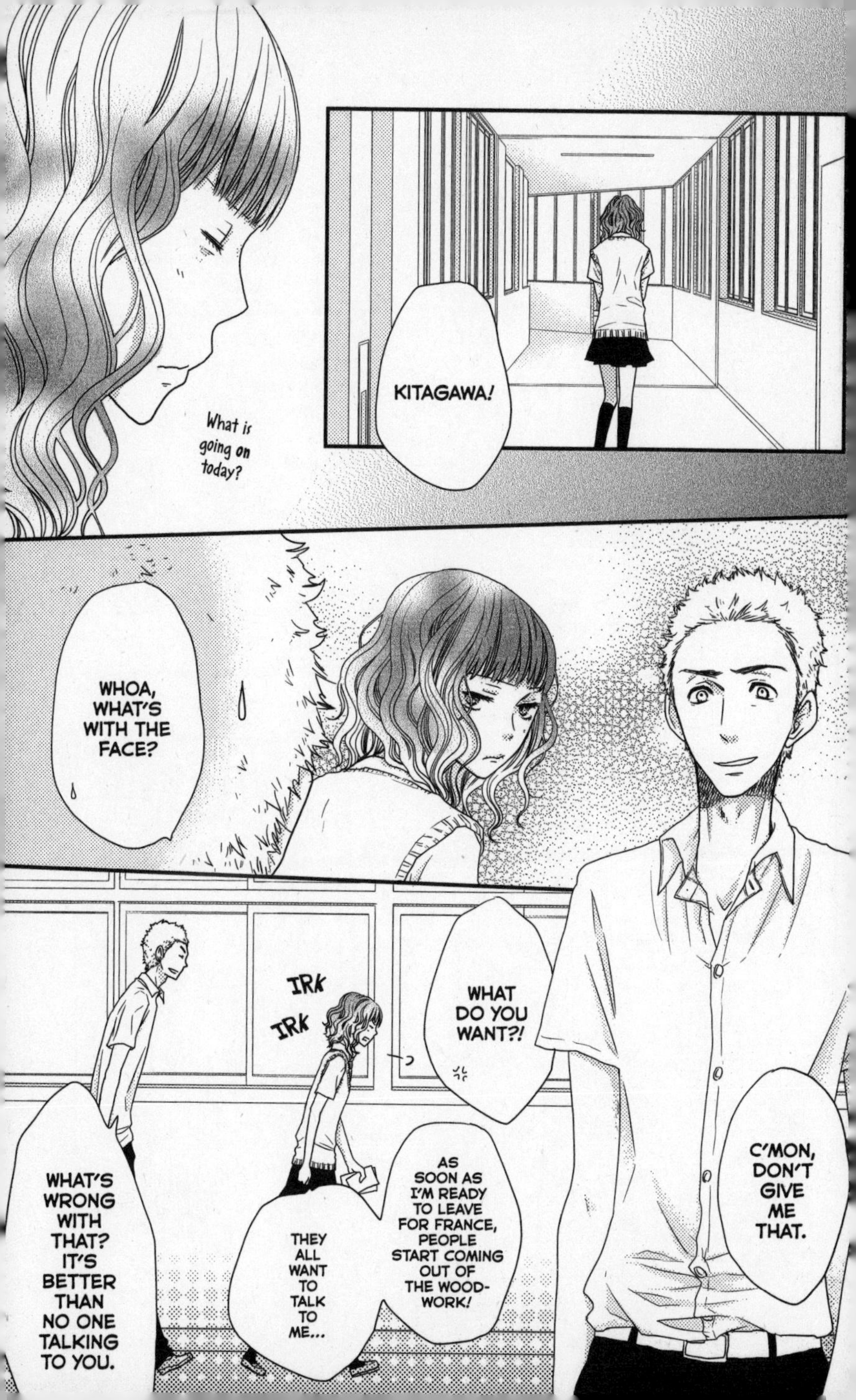
KITAGAWA!
What is going on today?
WHOA, WHAT'S WITH THE FACE?
WHAT DO YOU WANT?!
C'MON, DON'T GIVE ME THAT.
IRK
IRK
AS SOON AS I'M READY TO LEAVE FOR FRANCE, PEOPLE START COMING OUT OF THE WOOD-WORK!
THEY ALL WANT TO TALK TO ME...
WHAT'S WRONG WITH THAT? IT'S BETTER THAN NO ONE TALKING TO YOU.

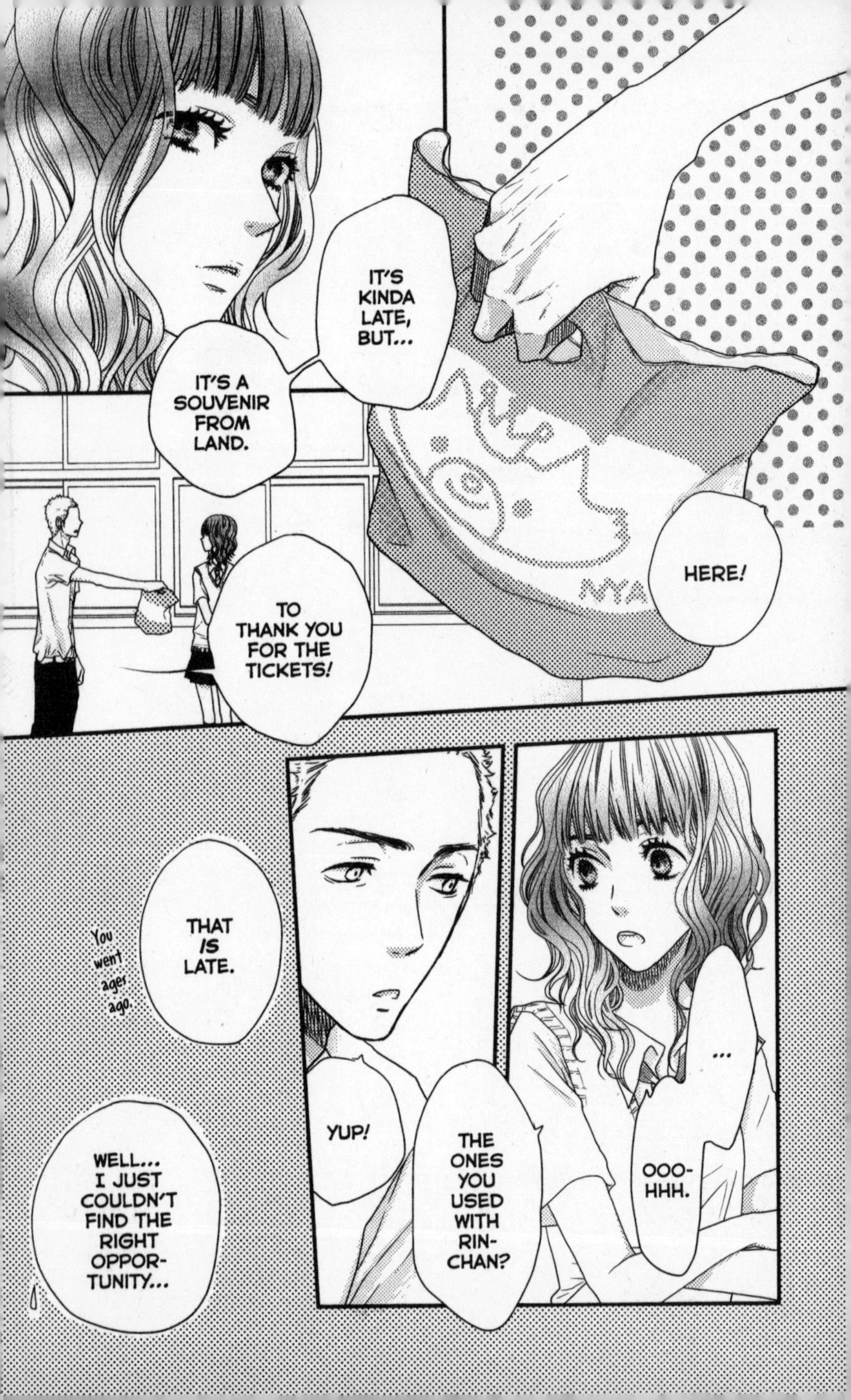
HERE!
IT'S KINDA LATE, BUT...
NYA
IT'S A SOUVENIR FROM LAND.
TO THANK YOU FOR THE TICKETS!
...
OOO-HHH.
THE ONES YOU USED WITH RIN-CHAN?
YUP!
THAT *IS* LATE.
You went ages ago.
WELL... I JUST COULDN'T FIND THE RIGHT OPPOR-TUNITY...

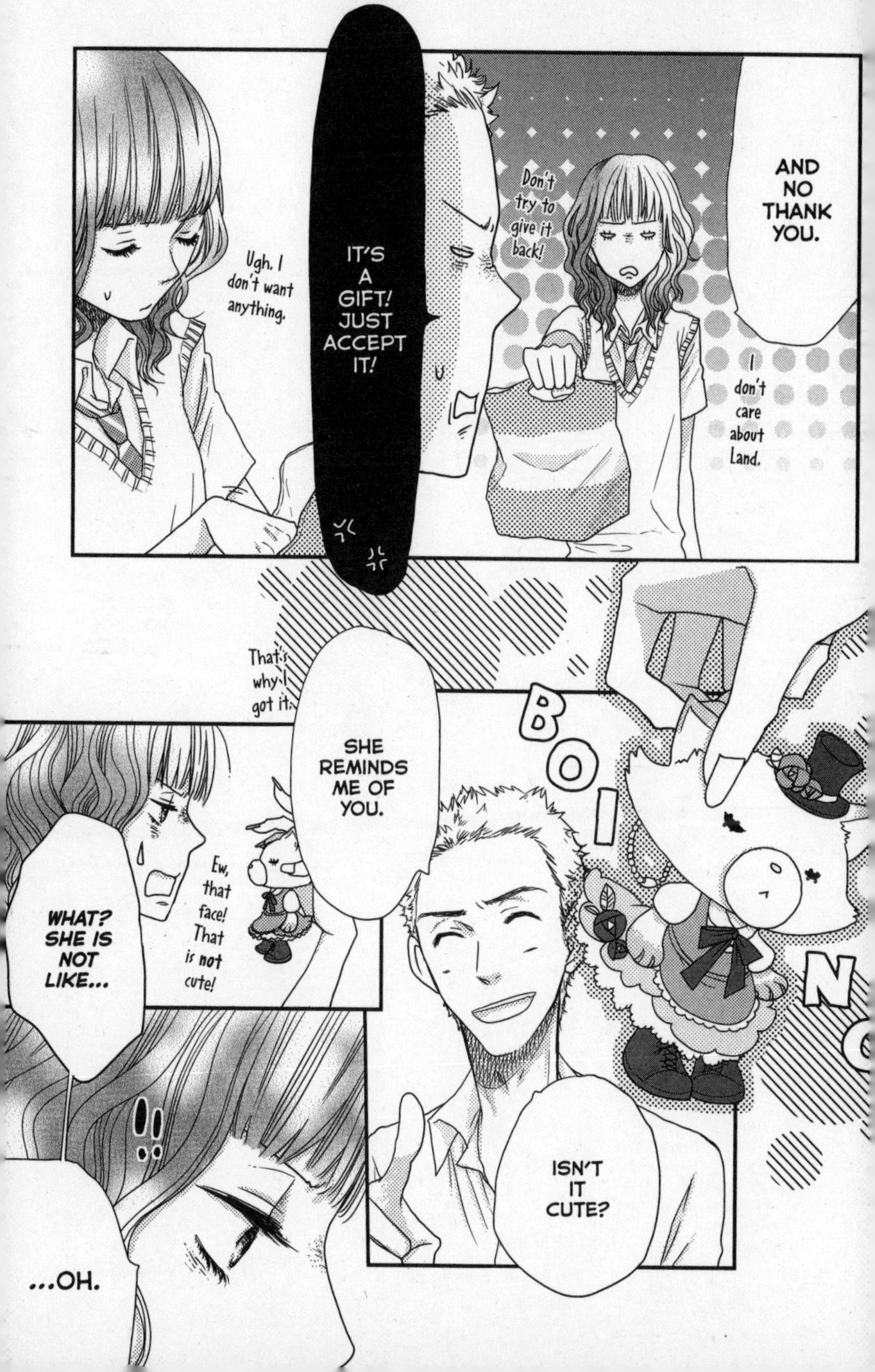
AND NO THANK YOU.
I don't care about Land.
Don't try to give it back!
IT'S A GIFT! JUST ACCEPT IT!
Ugh. I don't want anything.
BOING
SHE REMINDS ME OF YOU.
That's why I got it.
ISN'T IT CUTE?
Ew, that face! That is not cute!
WHAT? SHE IS NOT LIKE...
!!
...OH.

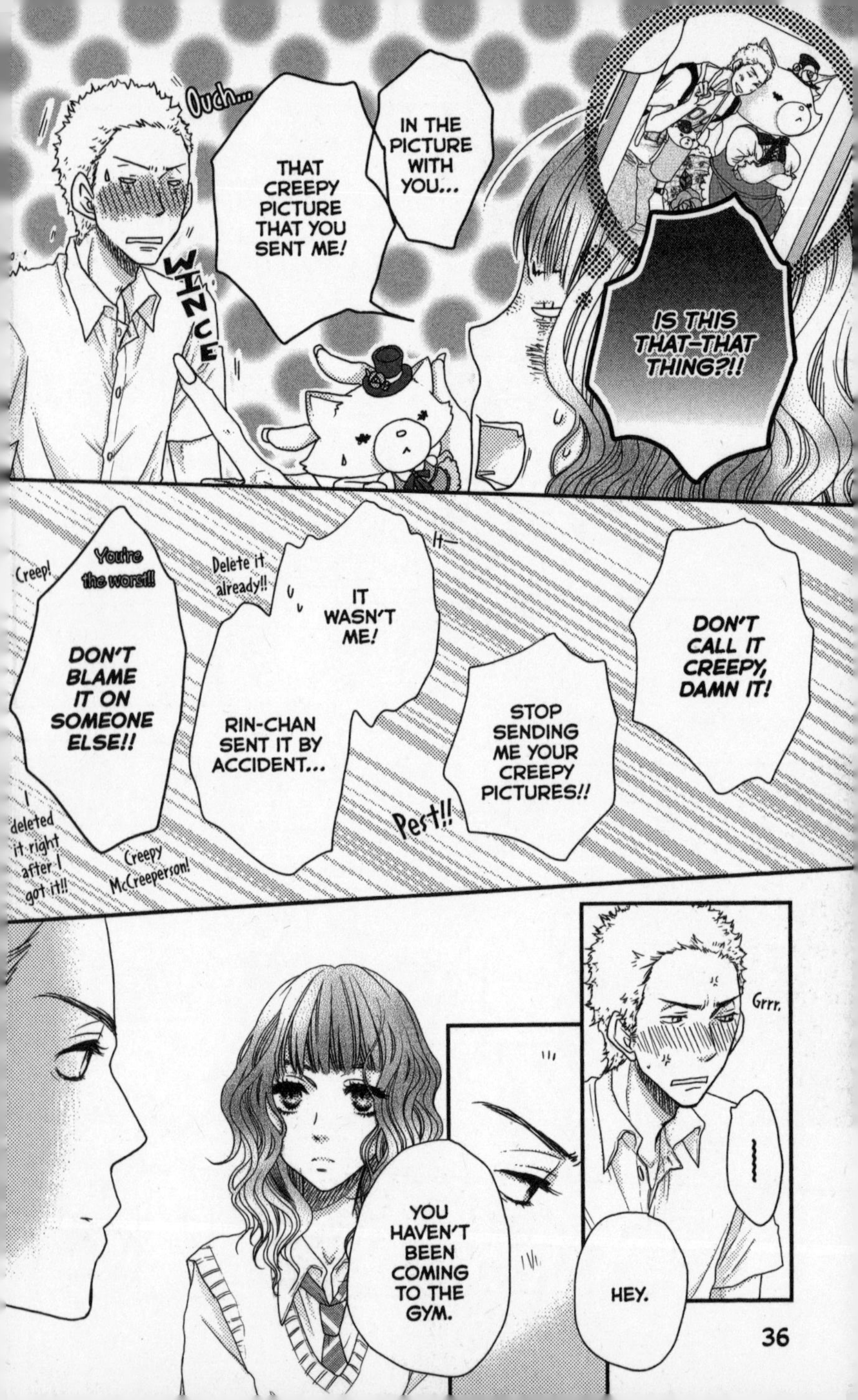
IS THIS THAT-THAT THING?!!
IN THE PICTURE WITH YOU...
THAT CREEPY PICTURE THAT YOU SENT ME!
Ouch...
WINCE
DON'T CALL IT CREEPY, DAMN IT!
STOP SENDING ME YOUR CREEPY PICTURES!!
Pest!!
It—
IT WASN'T ME!
RIN-CHAN SENT IT BY ACCIDENT...
Delete it already!!
You're the worst!!
Creep!
DON'T BLAME IT ON SOMEONE ELSE!!
I deleted it right after I got it!!
Creepy McCreeperson!
Grrr.
HEY.
YOU HAVEN'T BEEN COMING TO THE GYM.

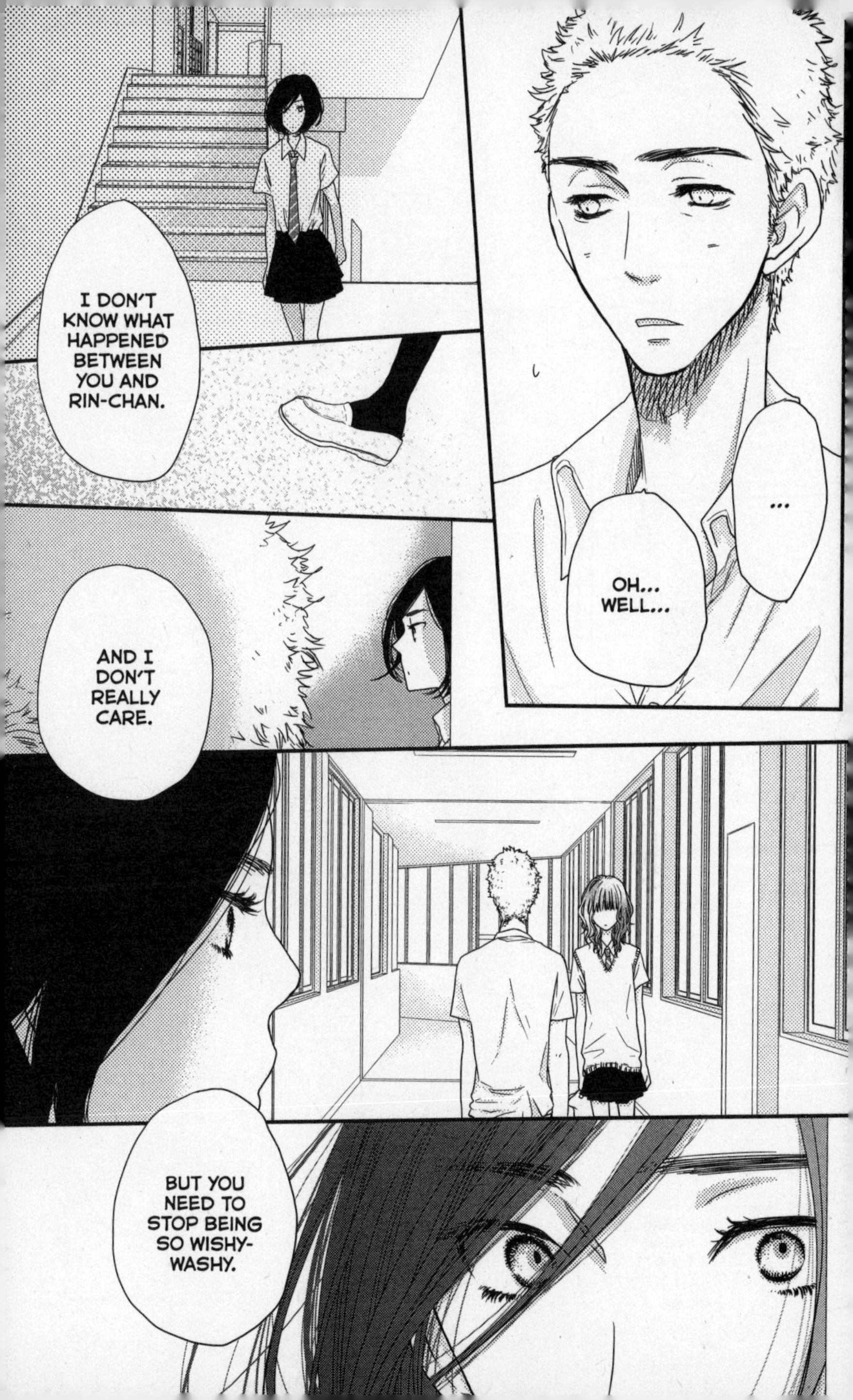
...
OH... WELL...
I DON'T KNOW WHAT HAPPENED BETWEEN YOU AND RIN-CHAN.
AND I DON'T REALLY CARE.
BUT YOU NEED TO STOP BEING SO WISHY-WASHY.

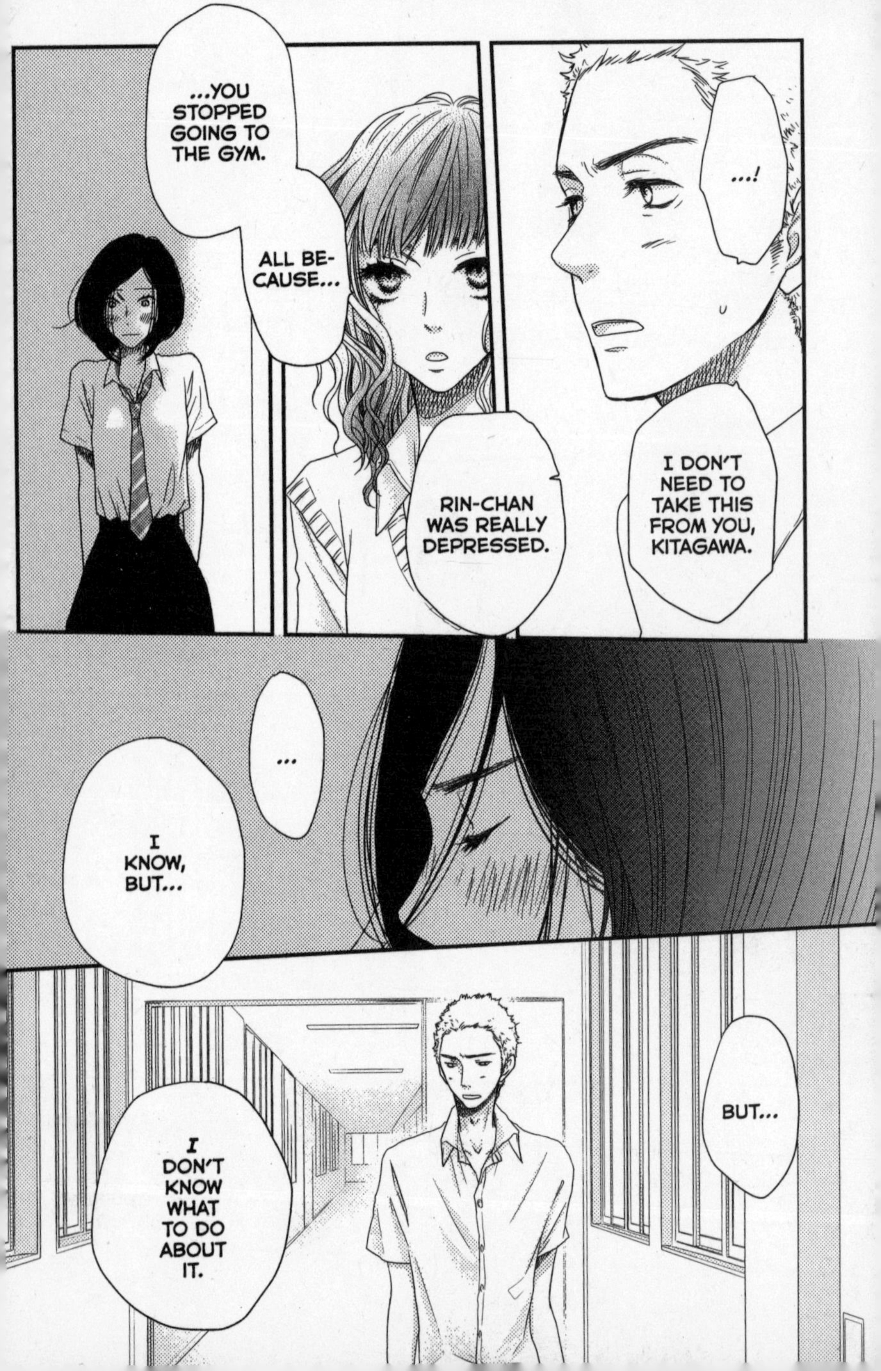
...!
I DON'T NEED TO TAKE THIS FROM YOU, KITAGAWA.
RIN-CHAN WAS REALLY DEPRESSED.
ALL BE-CAUSE...
...YOU STOPPED GOING TO THE GYM.
...
I KNOW, BUT...
BUT...
I DON'T KNOW WHAT TO DO ABOUT IT.

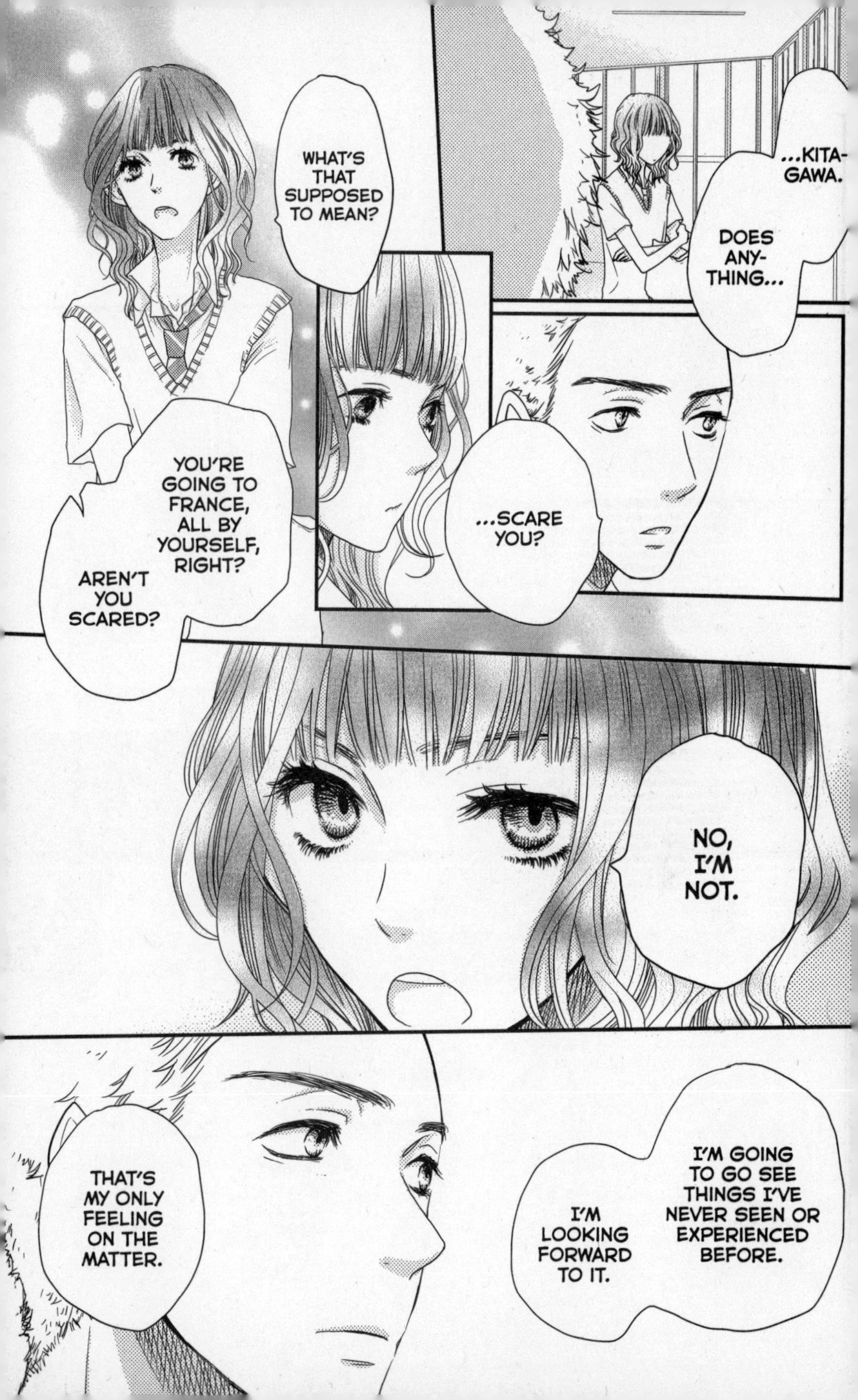
...KITA-GAWA.
DOES ANY-THING...
...SCARE YOU?
WHAT'S THAT SUPPOSED TO MEAN?
YOU'RE GOING TO FRANCE, ALL BY YOURSELF, RIGHT?
AREN'T YOU SCARED?
NO, I'M NOT.
I'M GOING TO GO SEE THINGS I'VE NEVER SEEN OR EXPERIENCED BEFORE.
I'M LOOKING FORWARD TO IT.
THAT'S MY ONLY FEELING ON THE MATTER.

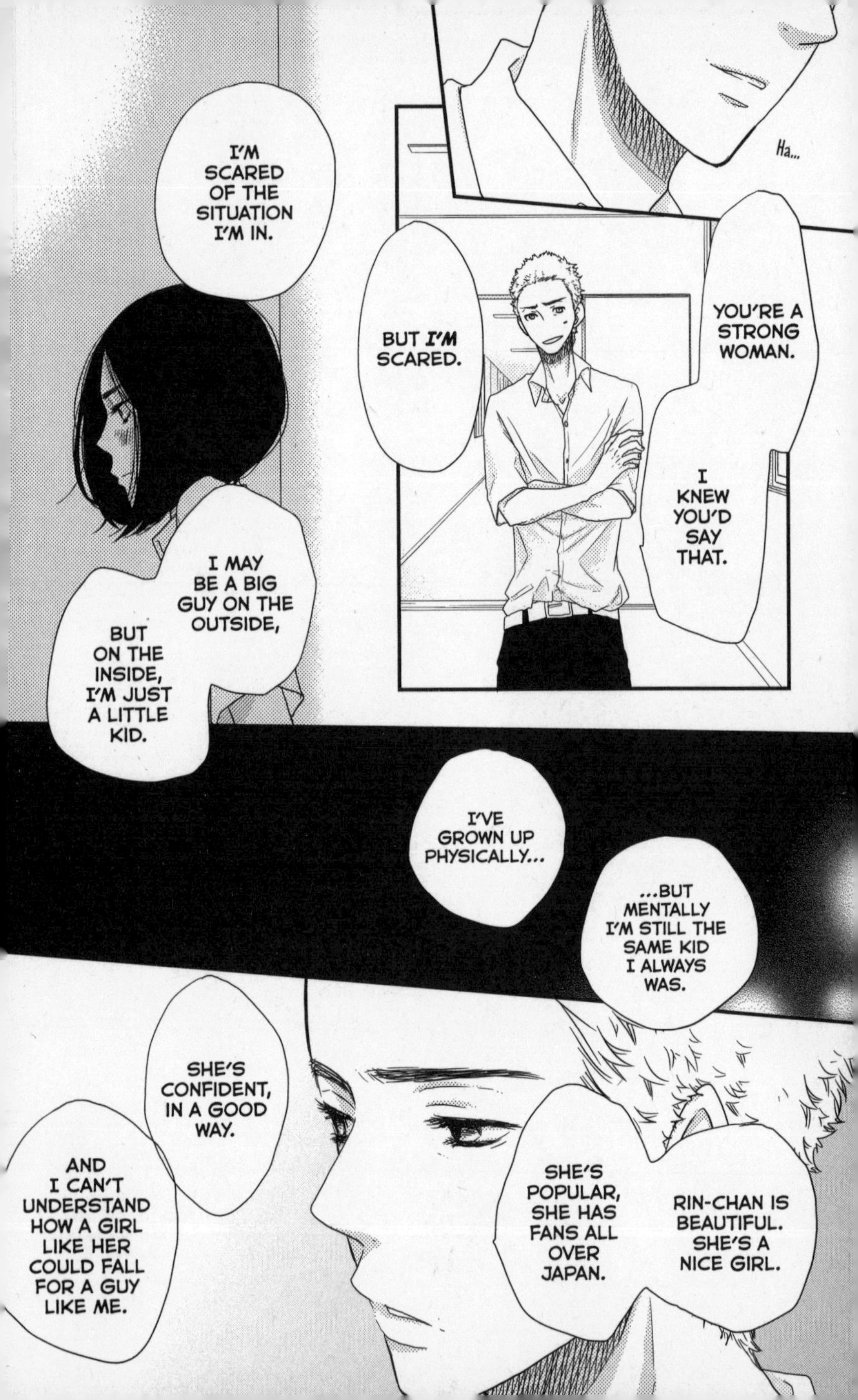
Ha...
YOU'RE A STRONG WOMAN.
I KNEW YOU'D SAY THAT.
BUT *I'M* SCARED.
I'M SCARED OF THE SITUATION I'M IN.
I MAY BE A BIG GUY ON THE OUTSIDE,
BUT ON THE INSIDE, I'M JUST A LITTLE KID.
I'VE GROWN UP PHYSICALLY...
...BUT MENTALLY I'M STILL THE SAME KID I ALWAYS WAS.
RIN-CHAN IS BEAUTIFUL. SHE'S A NICE GIRL.
SHE'S POPULAR, SHE HAS FANS ALL OVER JAPAN.
SHE'S CONFIDENT, IN A GOOD WAY.
AND I CAN'T UNDERSTAND HOW A GIRL LIKE HER COULD FALL FOR A GUY LIKE ME.

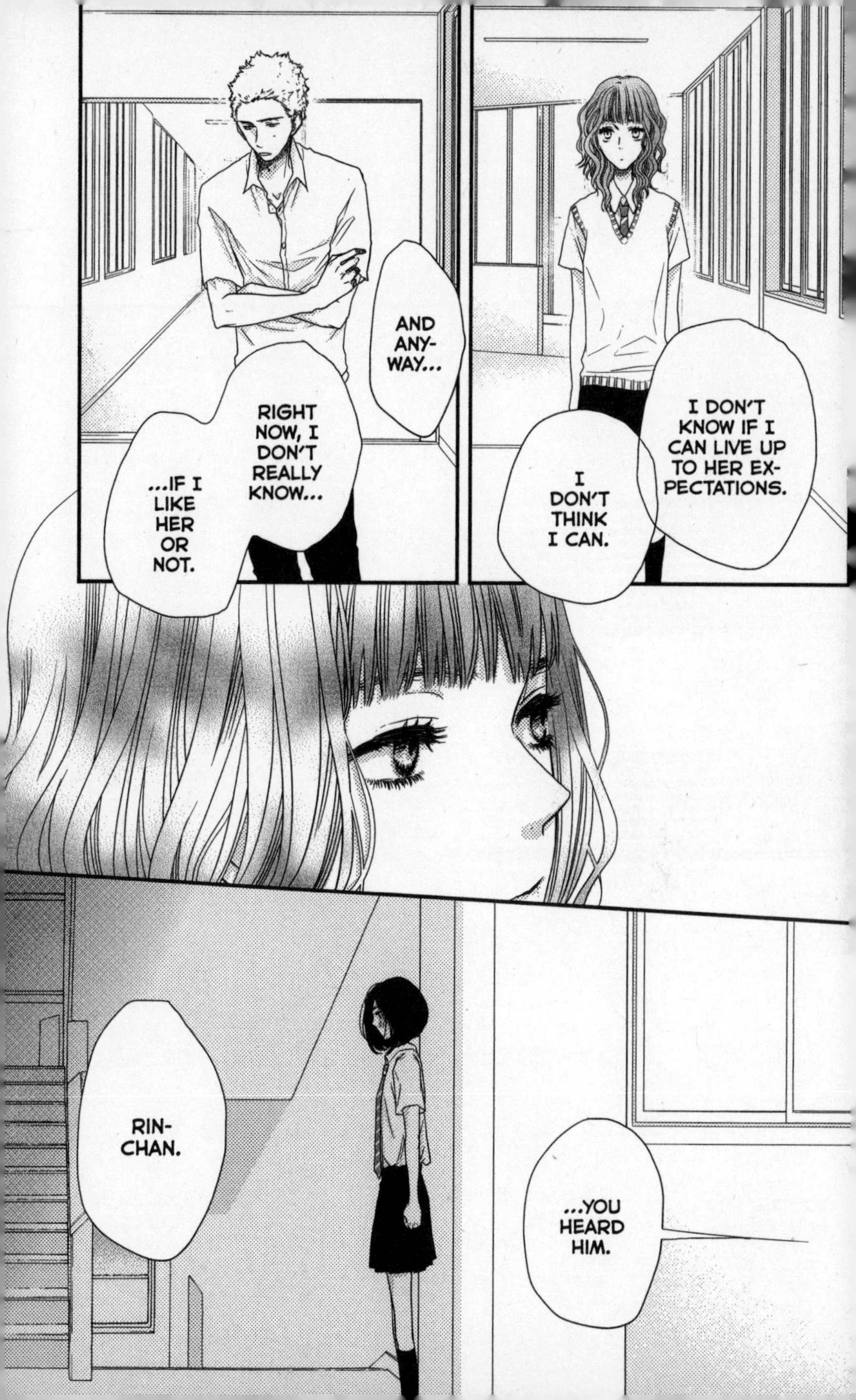
I DON'T KNOW IF I CAN LIVE UP TO HER EX-PECTATIONS.
I DON'T THINK I CAN.
AND ANY-WAY...
RIGHT NOW, I DON'T REALLY KNOW...
...IF I LIKE HER OR NOT.
RIN-CHAN.
...YOU HEARD HIM.

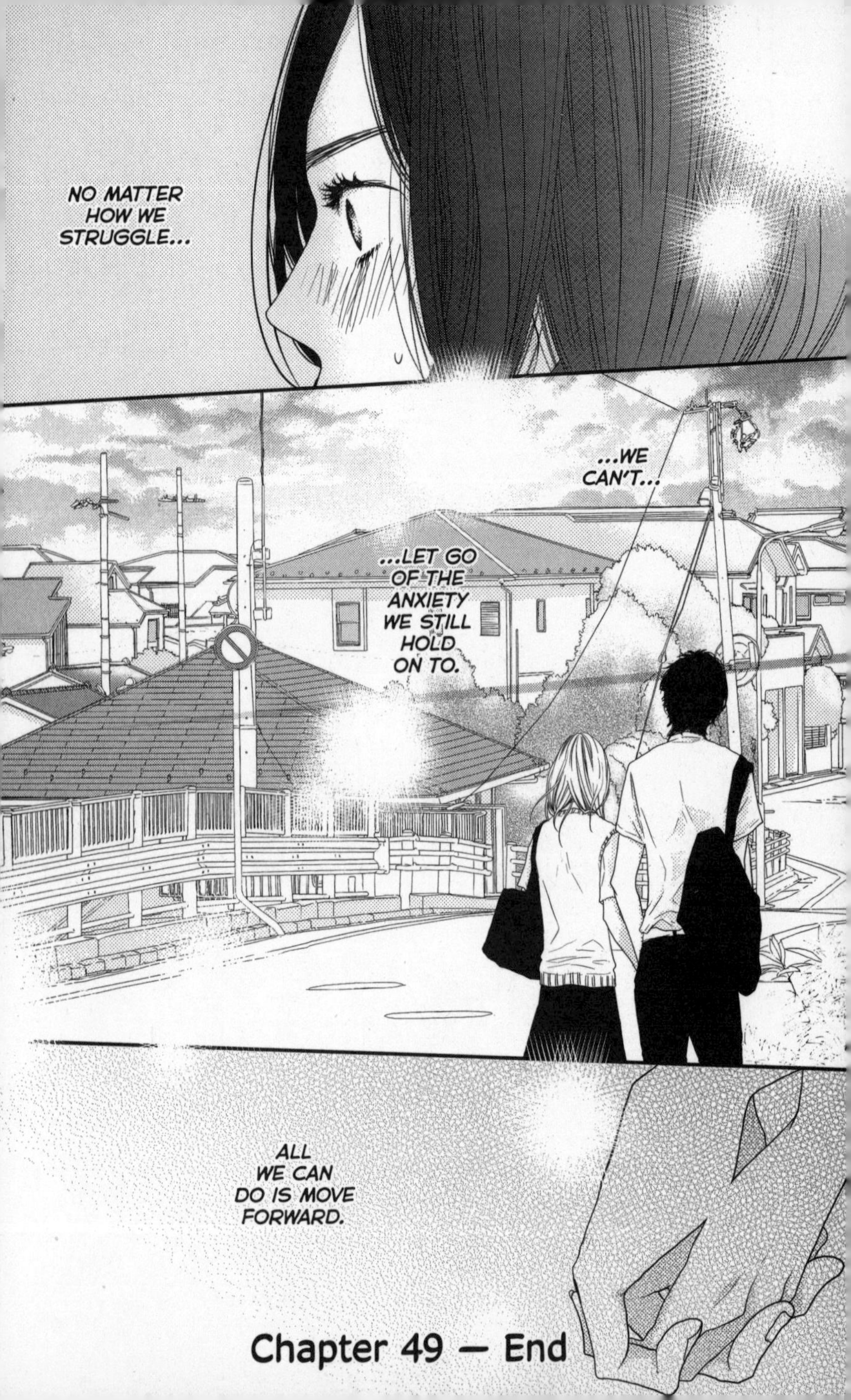
NO MATTER HOW WE STRUGGLE...
...WE CAN'T...
...LET GO OF THE ANXIETY WE STILL HOLD ON TO.
ALL WE CAN DO IS MOVE FORWARD.

Chapter 49 — End

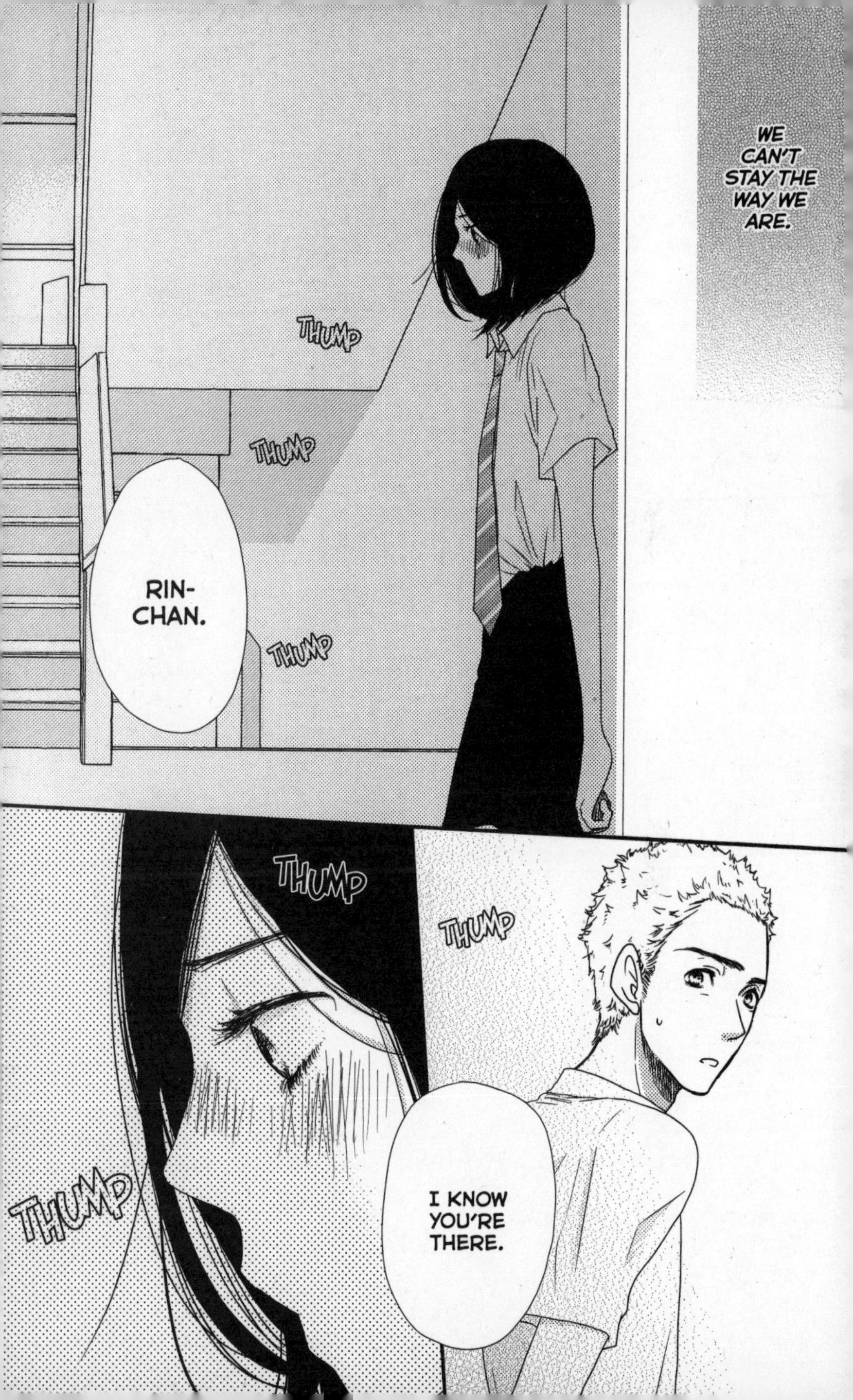
WE CAN'T STAY THE WAY WE ARE.
THUMP
THUMP
RIN-CHAN.
THUMP
THUMP
I KNOW YOU'RE THERE.
THUMP
THUMP

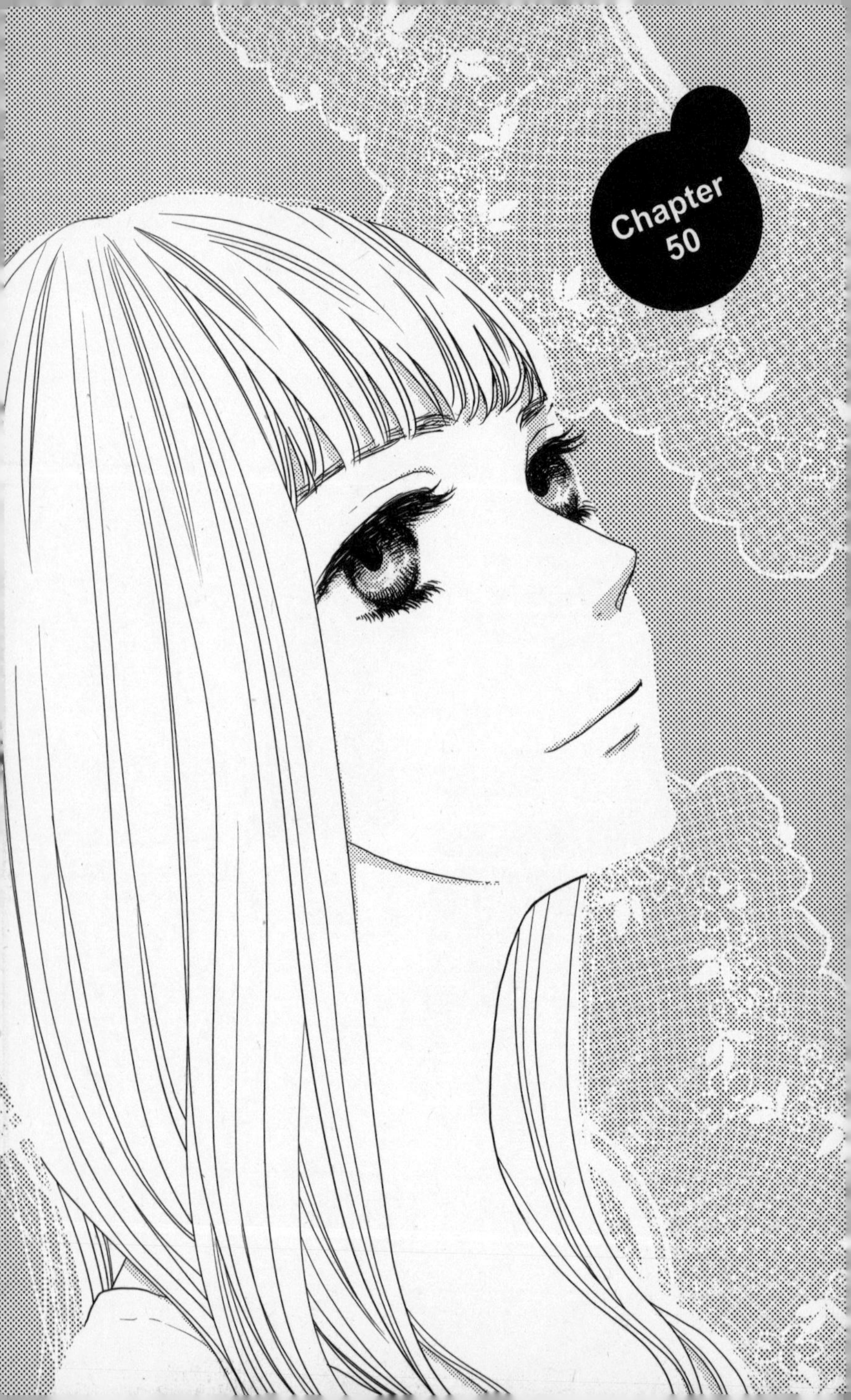
Chapter
50

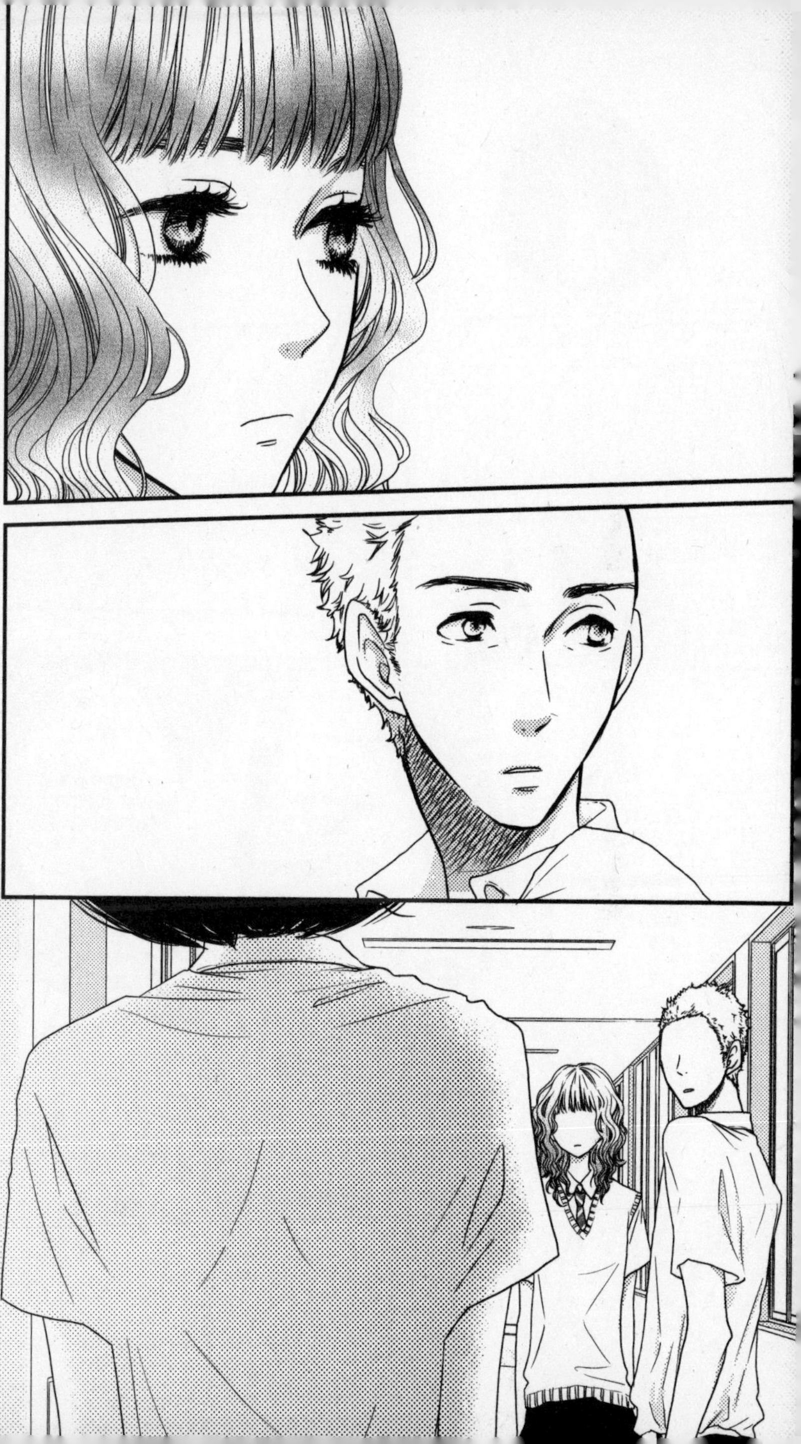

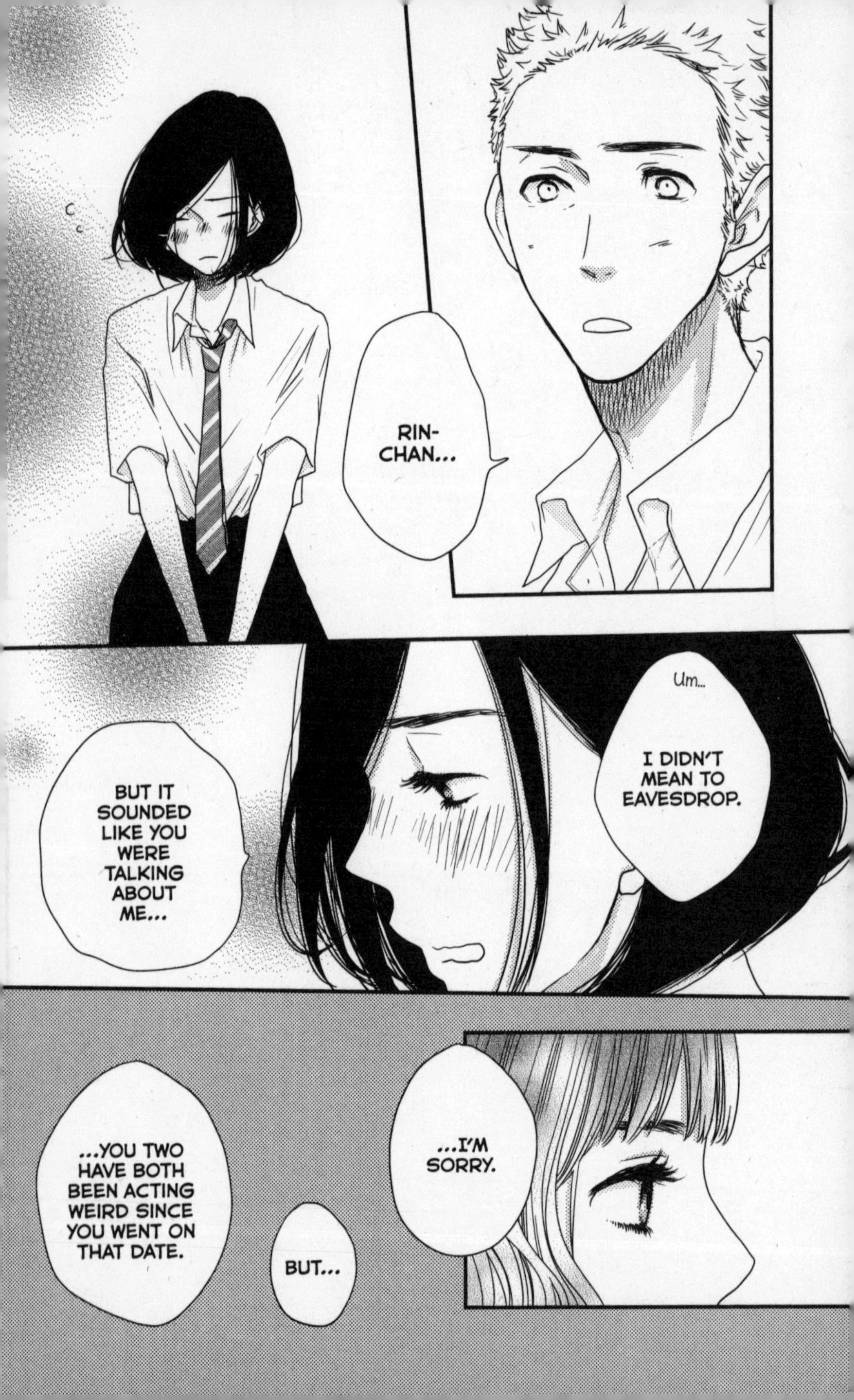
RIN-CHAN...
Um... I DIDN'T MEAN TO EAVESDROP.
BUT IT SOUNDED LIKE YOU WERE TALKING ABOUT ME...
...I'M SORRY.
BUT...
...YOU TWO HAVE BOTH BEEN ACTING WEIRD SINCE YOU WENT ON THAT DATE.

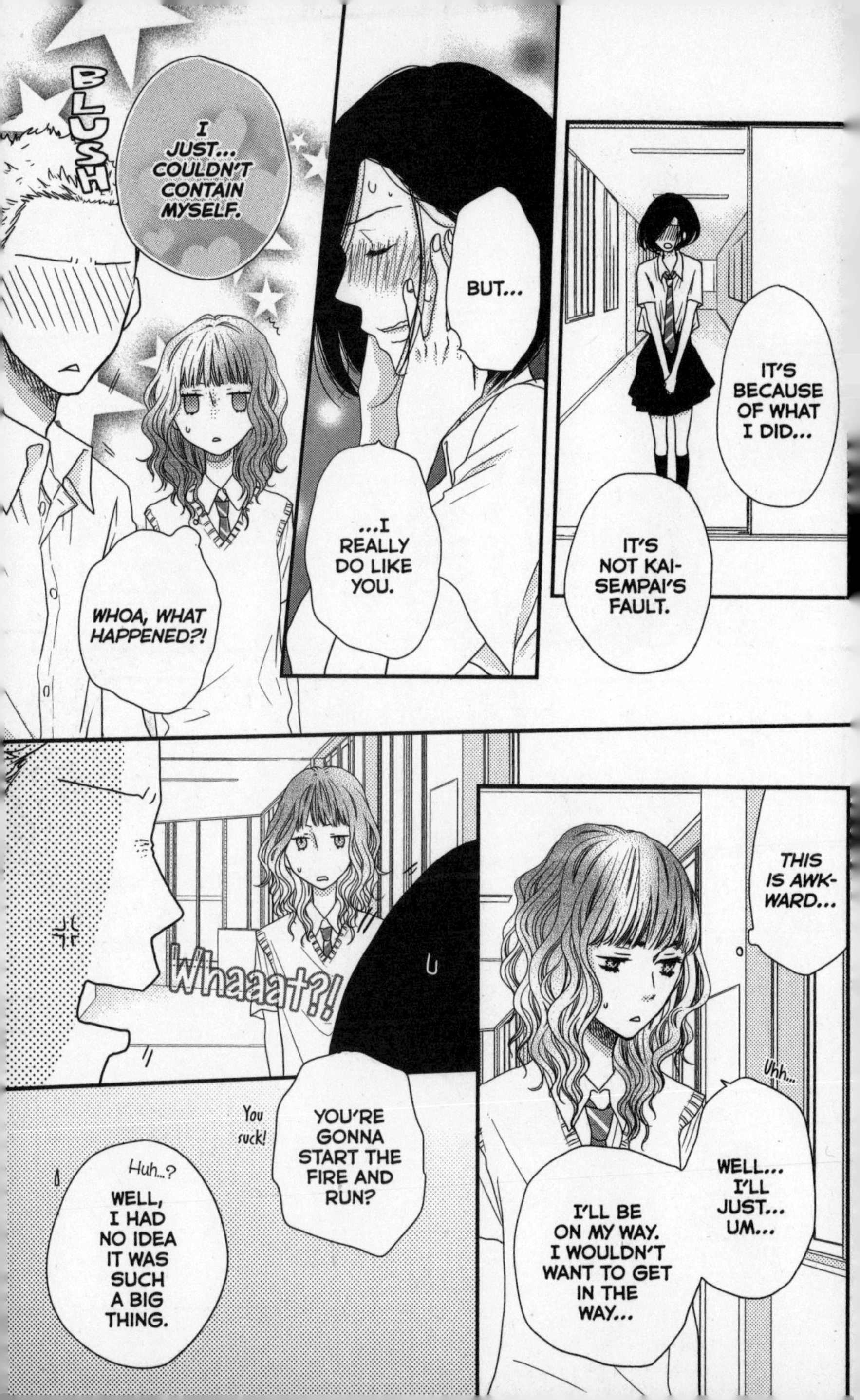
IT'S BECAUSE OF WHAT I DID...
IT'S NOT KAI-SEMPAI'S FAULT.
BUT...
...I REALLY DO LIKE YOU.
BLUSH
I JUST... COULDN'T CONTAIN MYSELF.
WHOA, WHAT HAPPENED?!
THIS IS AWKWARD...
Uhh...
WELL... I'LL JUST... UM...
I'LL BE ON MY WAY. I WOULDN'T WANT TO GET IN THE WAY...
Whaaat?!
YOU'RE GONNA START THE FIRE AND RUN?
You suck!
Huh...?
WELL, I HAD NO IDEA IT WAS SUCH A BIG THING.

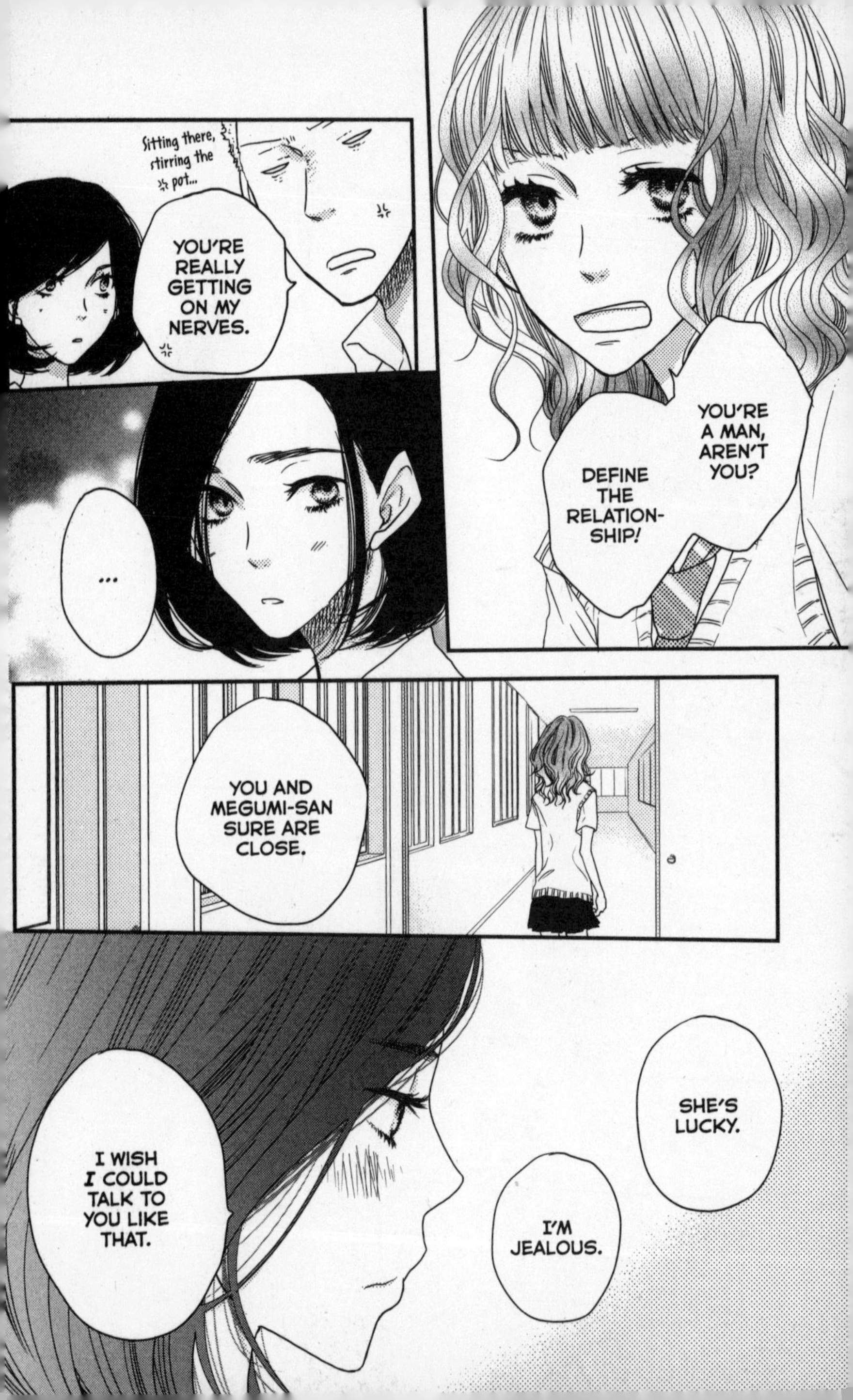
YOU'RE A MAN, AREN'T YOU?
DEFINE THE RELATIONSHIP!
Sitting there, stirring the pot...
YOU'RE REALLY GETTING ON MY NERVES.
...
YOU AND MEGUMI-SAN SURE ARE CLOSE.
SHE'S LUCKY.
I'M JEALOUS.
I WISH *I* COULD TALK TO YOU LIKE THAT.

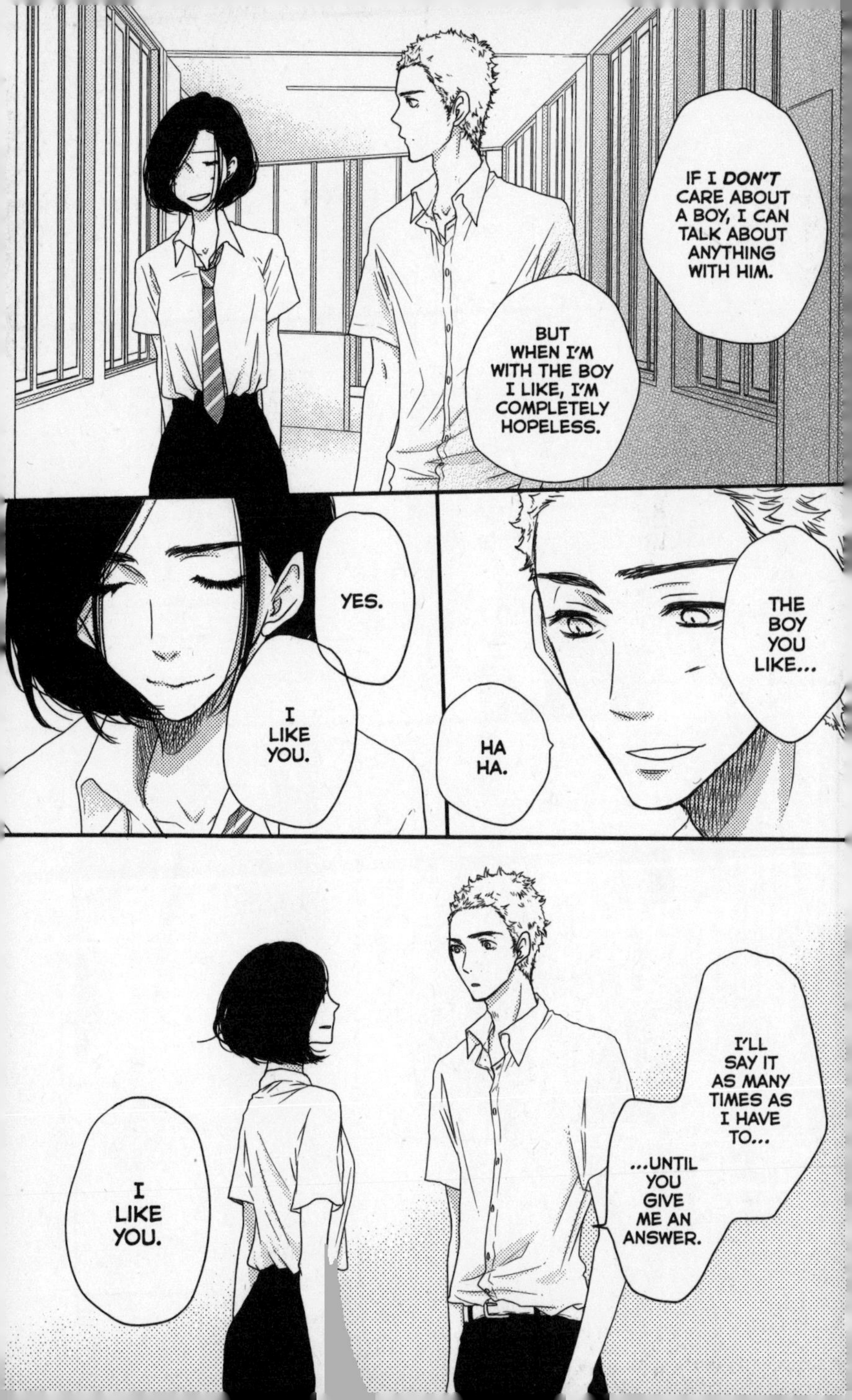
IF I *DON'T* CARE ABOUT A BOY, I CAN TALK ABOUT ANYTHING WITH HIM.
BUT WHEN I'M WITH THE BOY I LIKE, I'M COMPLETELY HOPELESS.
THE BOY YOU LIKE...
HA HA.
YES.
I LIKE YOU.
I'LL SAY IT AS MANY TIMES AS I HAVE TO...
...UNTIL YOU GIVE ME AN ANSWER.
I LIKE YOU.

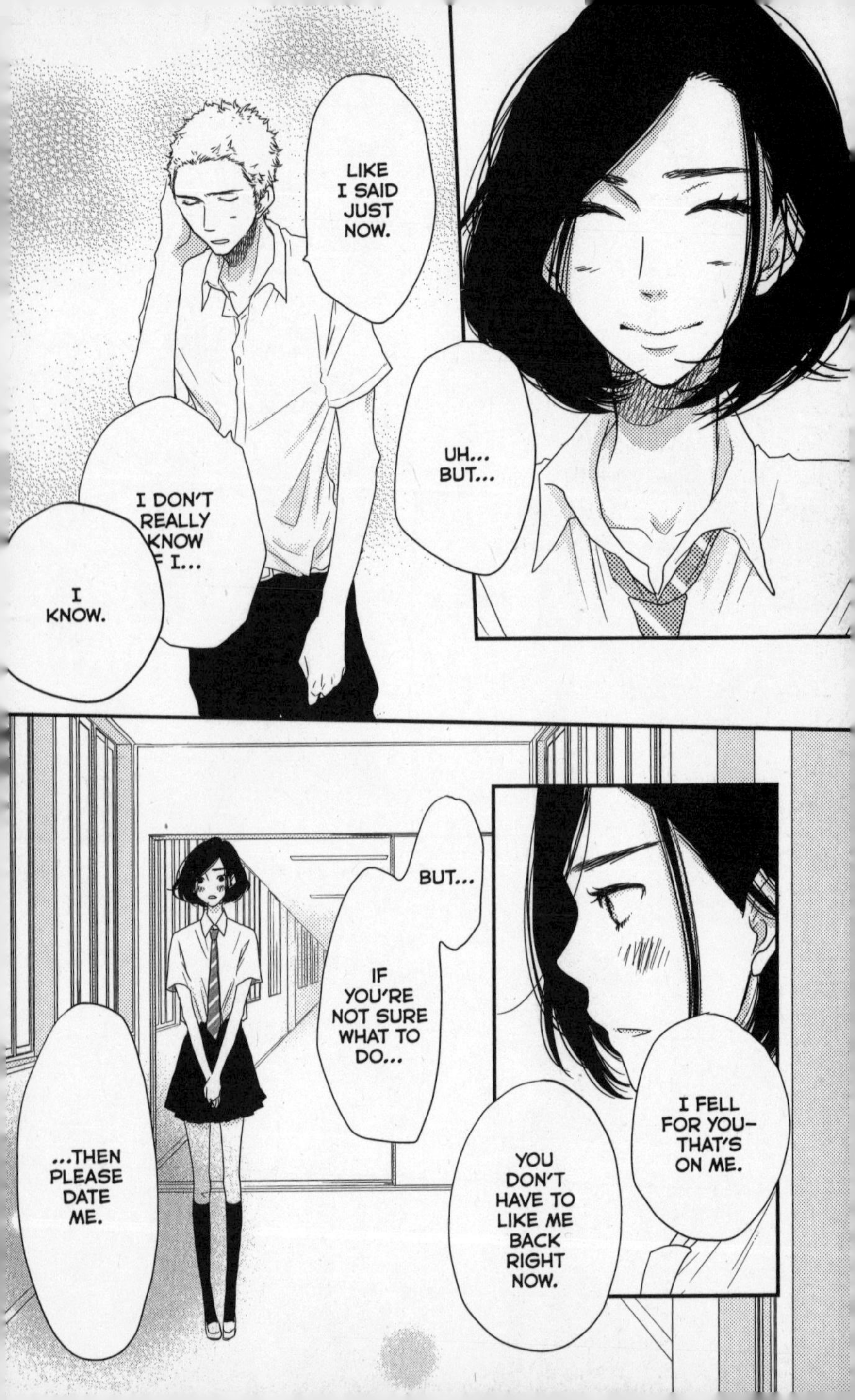
UH... BUT...
LIKE I SAID JUST NOW.
I DON'T REALLY KNOW F I...
I KNOW.
I FELL FOR YOU— THAT'S ON ME.
YOU DON'T HAVE TO LIKE ME BACK RIGHT NOW.
BUT...
IF YOU'RE NOT SURE WHAT TO DO...
...THEN PLEASE DATE ME.

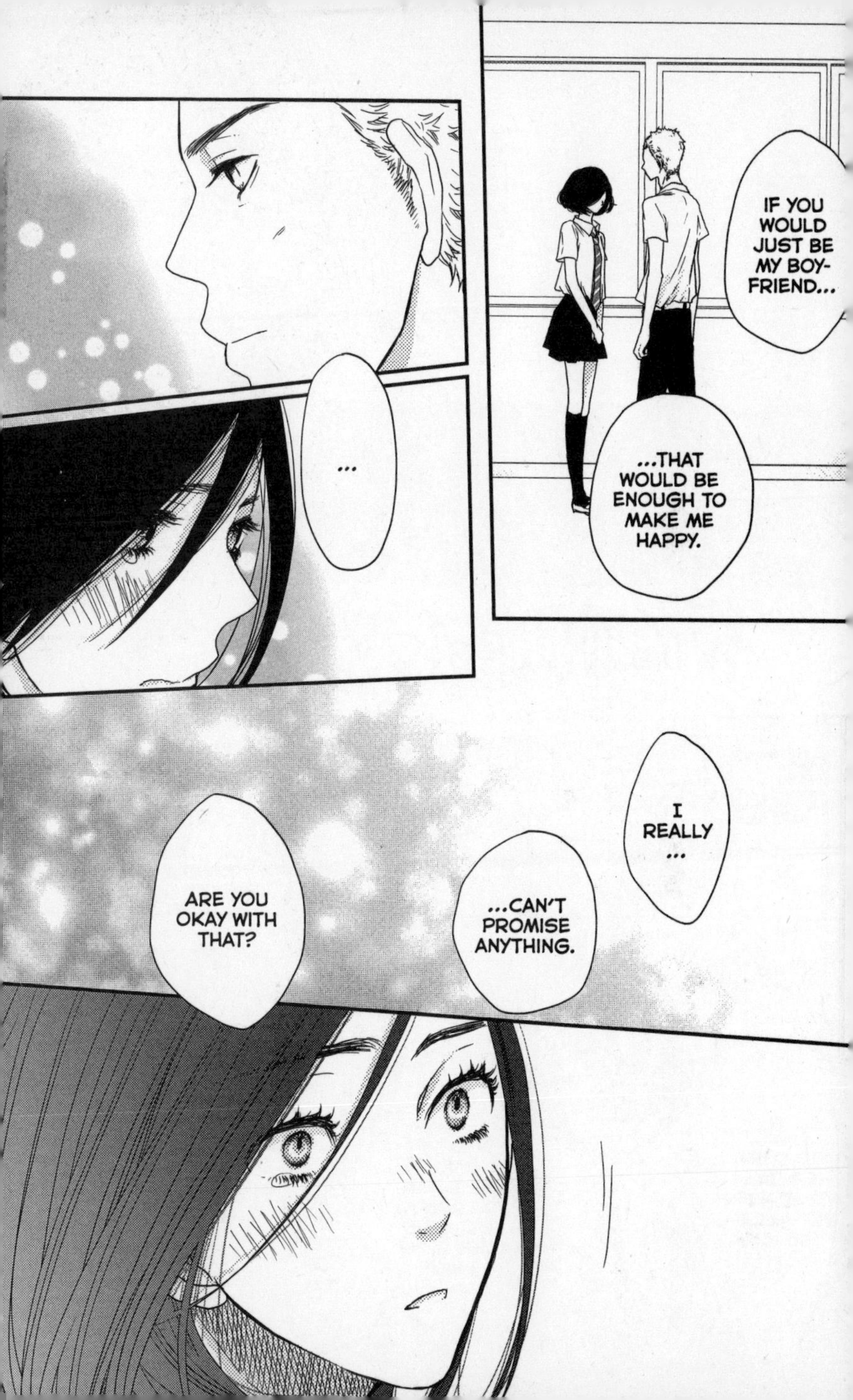
IF YOU WOULD JUST BE MY BOY-FRIEND...
...THAT WOULD BE ENOUGH TO MAKE ME HAPPY.
...
I REALLY ...
...CAN'T PROMISE ANYTHING.
ARE YOU OKAY WITH THAT?

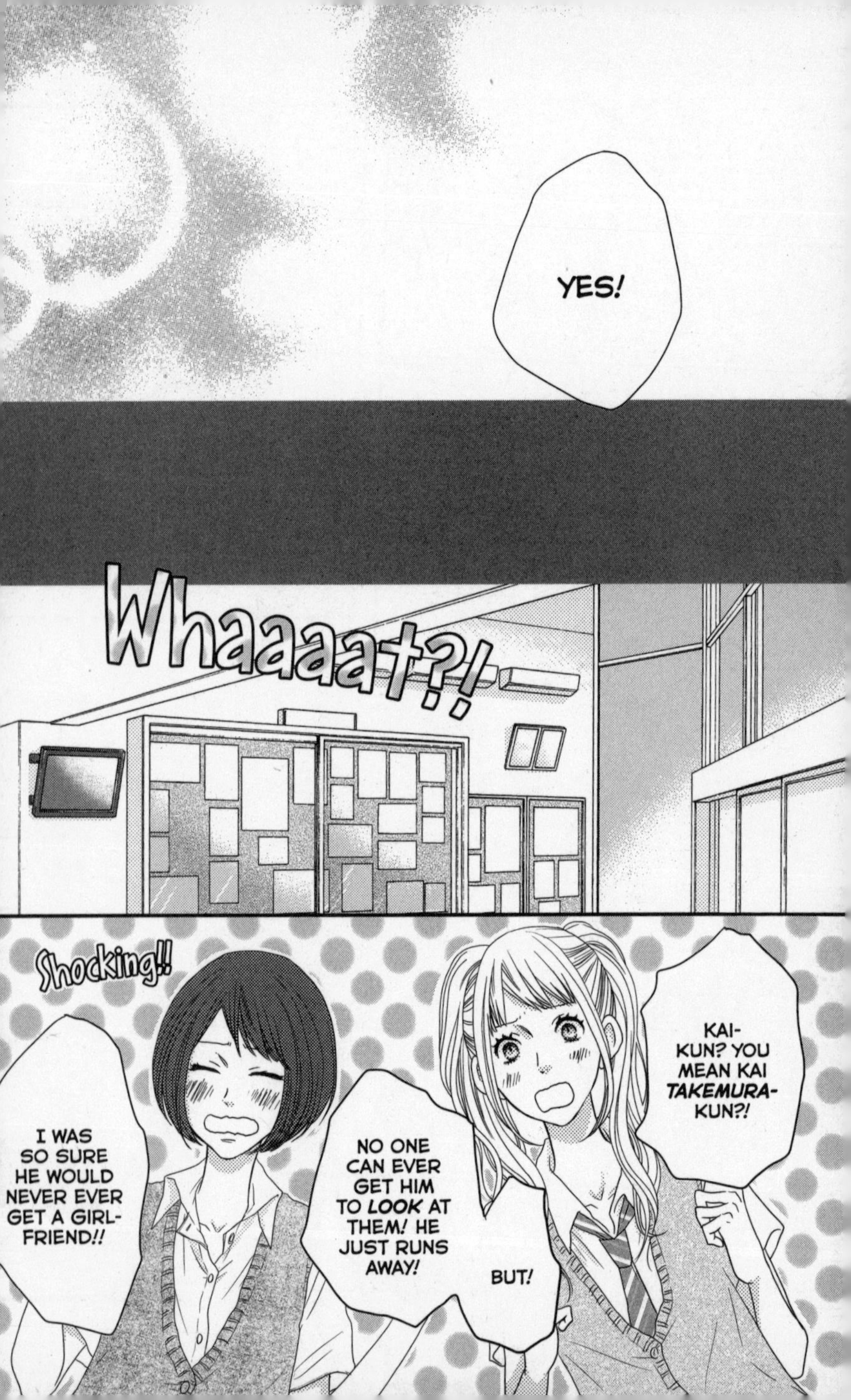
YES!
Whaaaaat?!
KAI-KUN? YOU MEAN KAI *TAKEMURA*-KUN?!
BUT!
NO ONE CAN EVER GET HIM TO *LOOK* AT THEM! HE JUST RUNS AWAY!
Shocking!!
I WAS SO SURE HE WOULD NEVER EVER GET A GIRLFRIEND!!

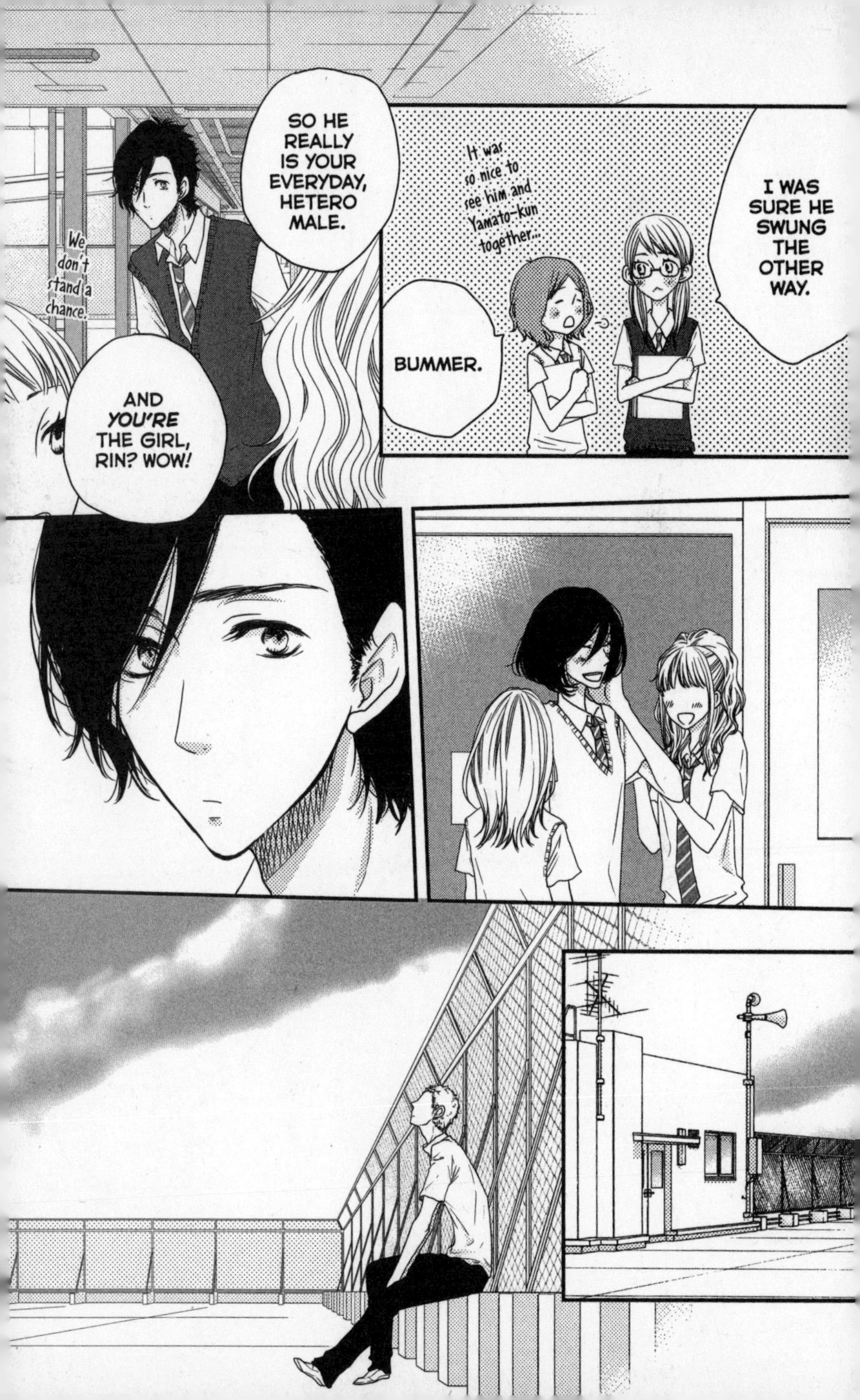
I WAS SURE HE SWUNG THE OTHER WAY.
It was so nice to see him and Yamato-kun together...
BUMMER.
SO HE REALLY IS YOUR EVERYDAY, HETERO MALE.
We don't stand a chance.
AND YOU'RE THE GIRL, RIN? WOW!

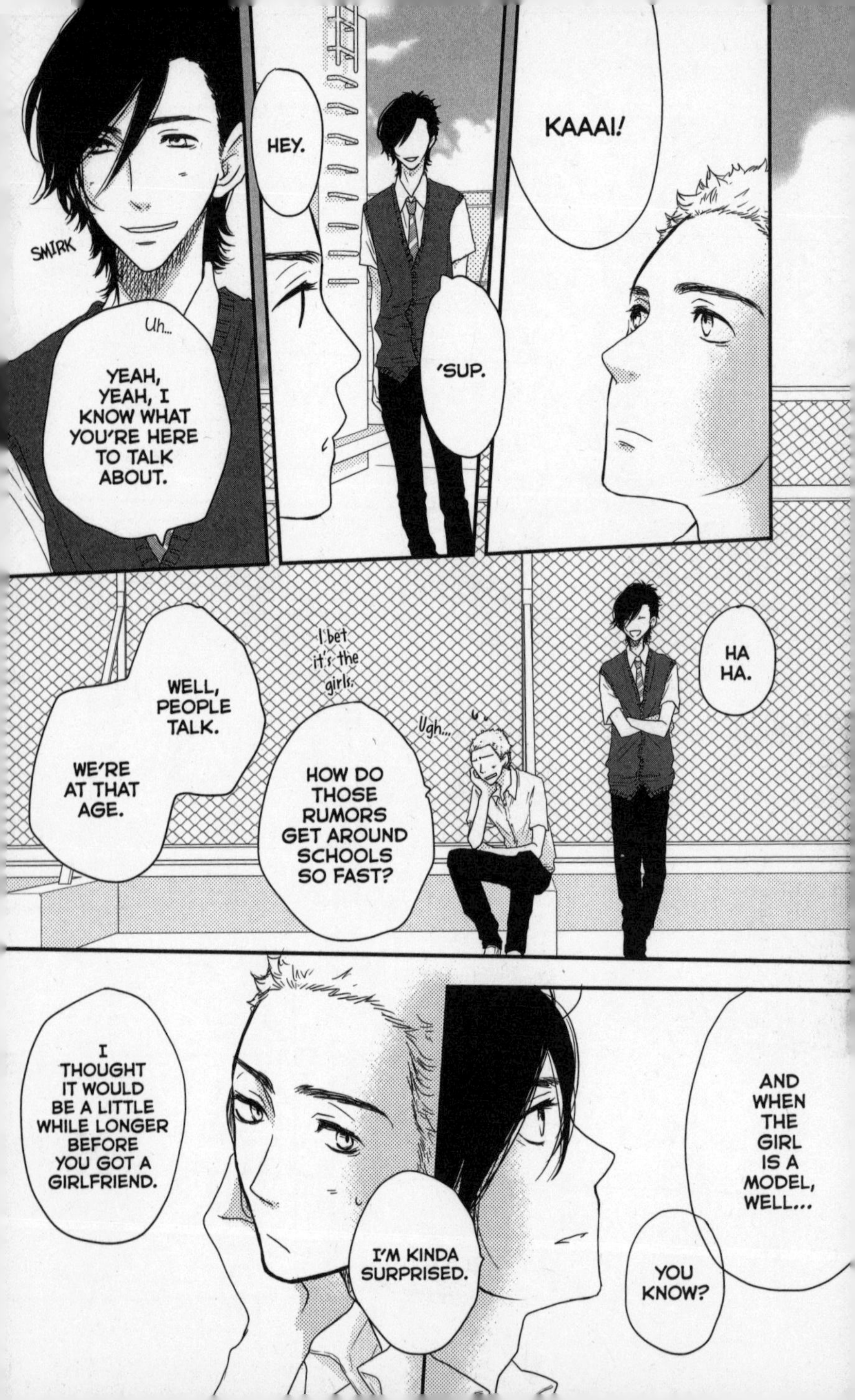

KAAAI!
HEY.
'SUP.
SMIRK
Uh...
YEAH, YEAH, I KNOW WHAT YOU'RE HERE TO TALK ABOUT.
HA HA.
Ugh...
I bet it's the girls.
HOW DO THOSE RUMORS GET AROUND SCHOOLS SO FAST?
WELL, PEOPLE TALK.
WE'RE AT THAT AGE.
AND WHEN THE GIRL IS A MODEL, WELL...
YOU KNOW?
I'M KINDA SURPRISED.
I THOUGHT IT WOULD BE A LITTLE WHILE LONGER BEFORE YOU GOT A GIRLFRIEND.

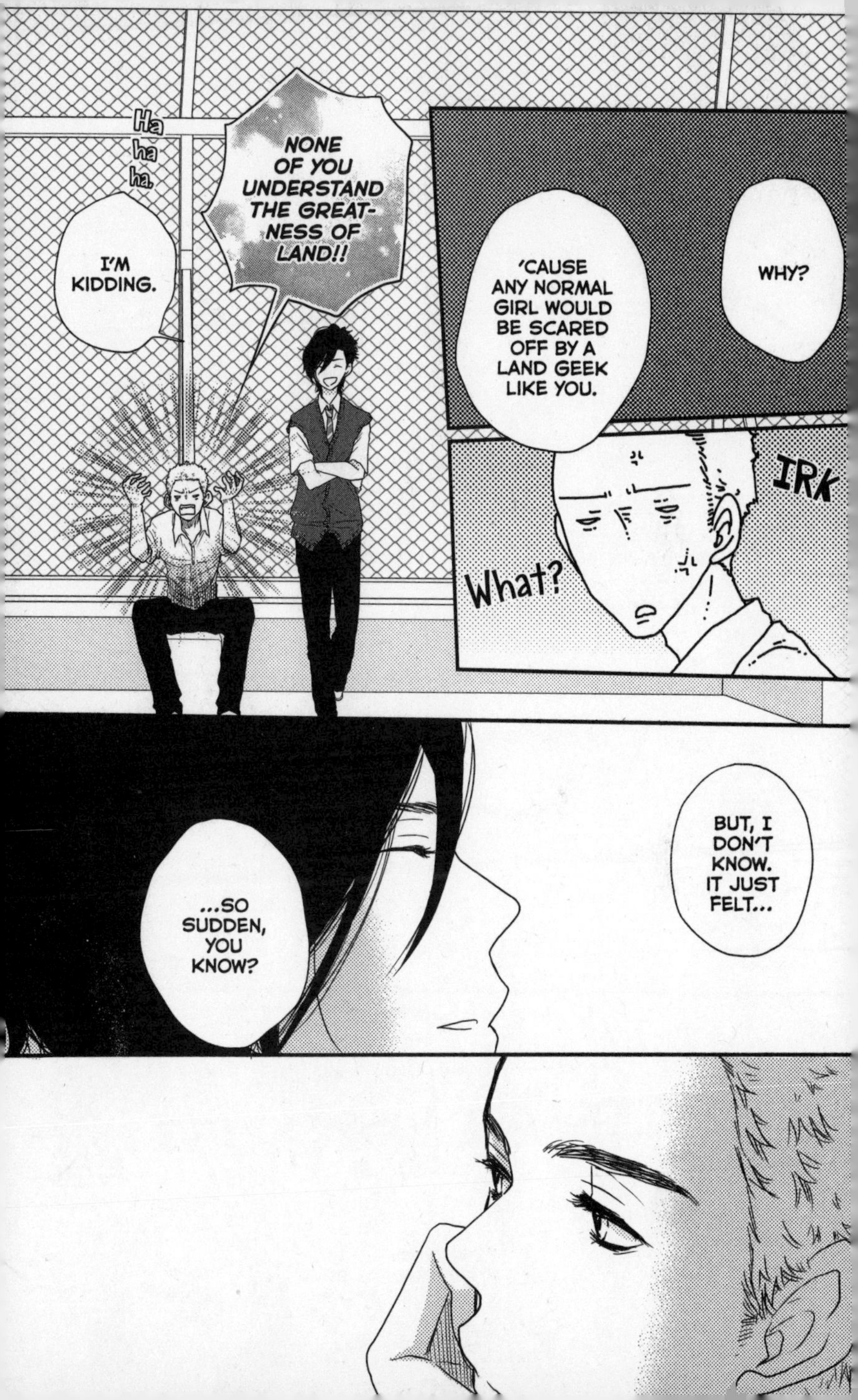
WHY?
'CAUSE ANY NORMAL GIRL WOULD BE SCARED OFF BY A LAND GEEK LIKE YOU.
IRK
What?
NONE OF YOU UNDERSTAND THE GREAT-NESS OF LAND!!
Ha ha ha.
I'M KIDDING.
BUT, I DON'T KNOW. IT JUST FELT...
...SO SUDDEN, YOU KNOW?

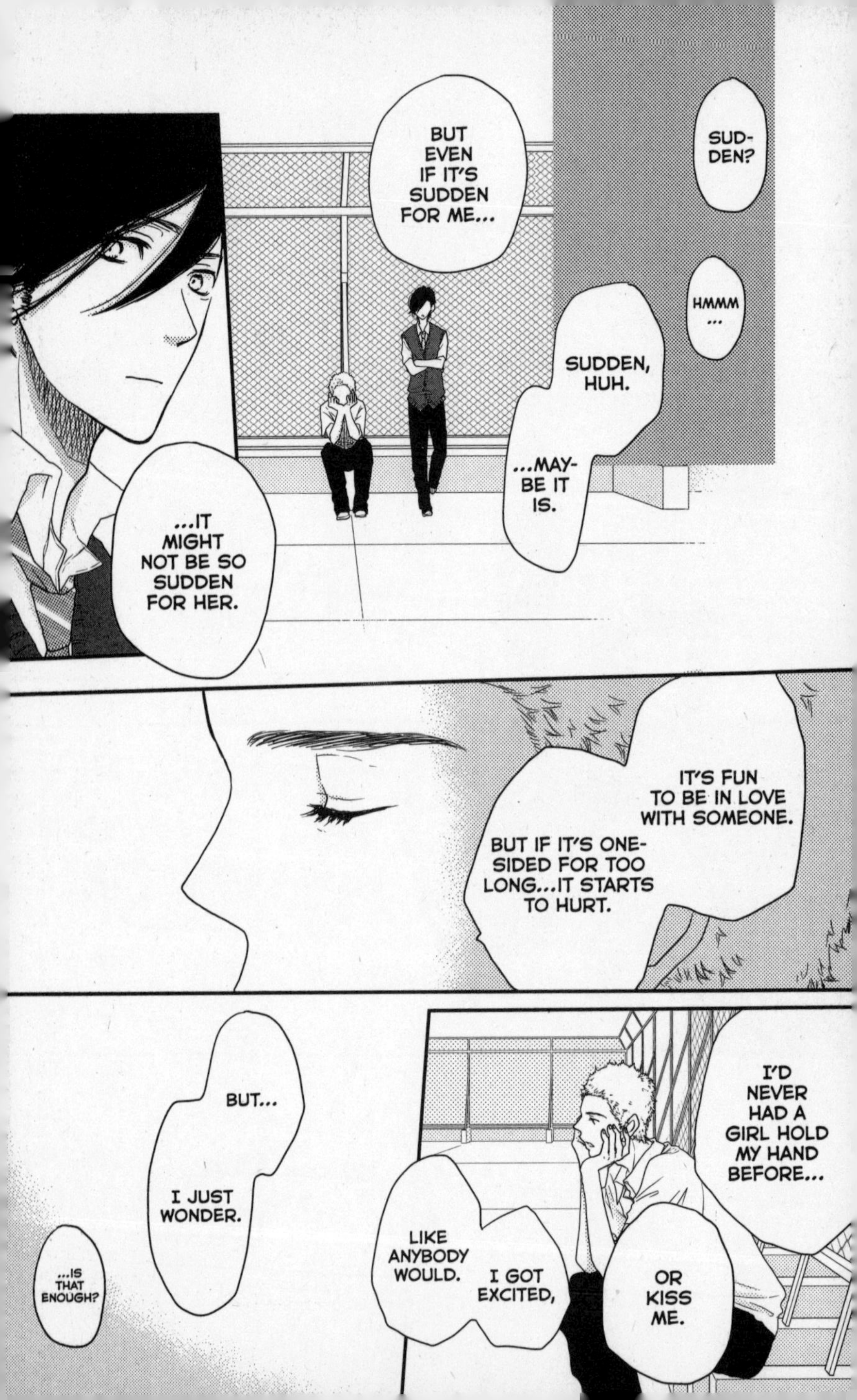
SUD-DEN?
HMMM...
BUT EVEN IF IT'S SUDDEN FOR ME...
SUDDEN, HUH.
...MAY-BE IT IS.
...IT MIGHT NOT BE SO SUDDEN FOR HER.
IT'S FUN TO BE IN LOVE WITH SOMEONE.
BUT IF IT'S ONE-SIDED FOR TOO LONG...IT STARTS TO HURT.
I'D NEVER HAD A GIRL HOLD MY HAND BEFORE...
OR KISS ME.
I GOT EXCITED,
LIKE ANYBODY WOULD.
BUT...
I JUST WONDER.
...IS THAT ENOUGH?

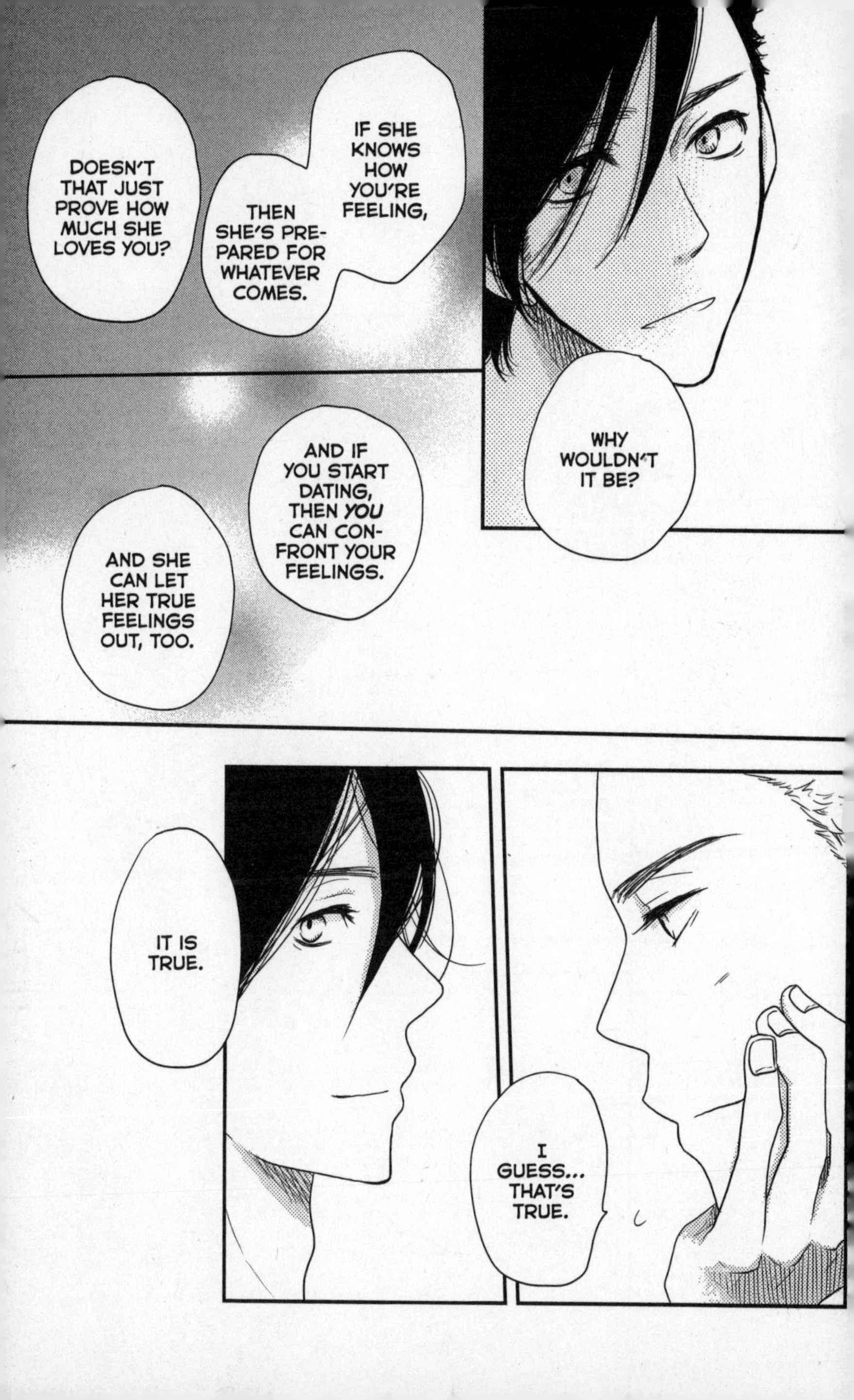

WHY WOULDN'T IT BE?
IF SHE KNOWS HOW YOU'RE FEELING,
THEN SHE'S PRE-PARED FOR WHATEVER COMES.
DOESN'T THAT JUST PROVE HOW MUCH SHE LOVES YOU?
AND IF YOU START DATING, THEN *YOU* CAN CON-FRONT YOUR FEELINGS.
AND SHE CAN LET HER TRUE FEELINGS OUT, TOO.
I GUESS... THAT'S TRUE.
IT IS TRUE.

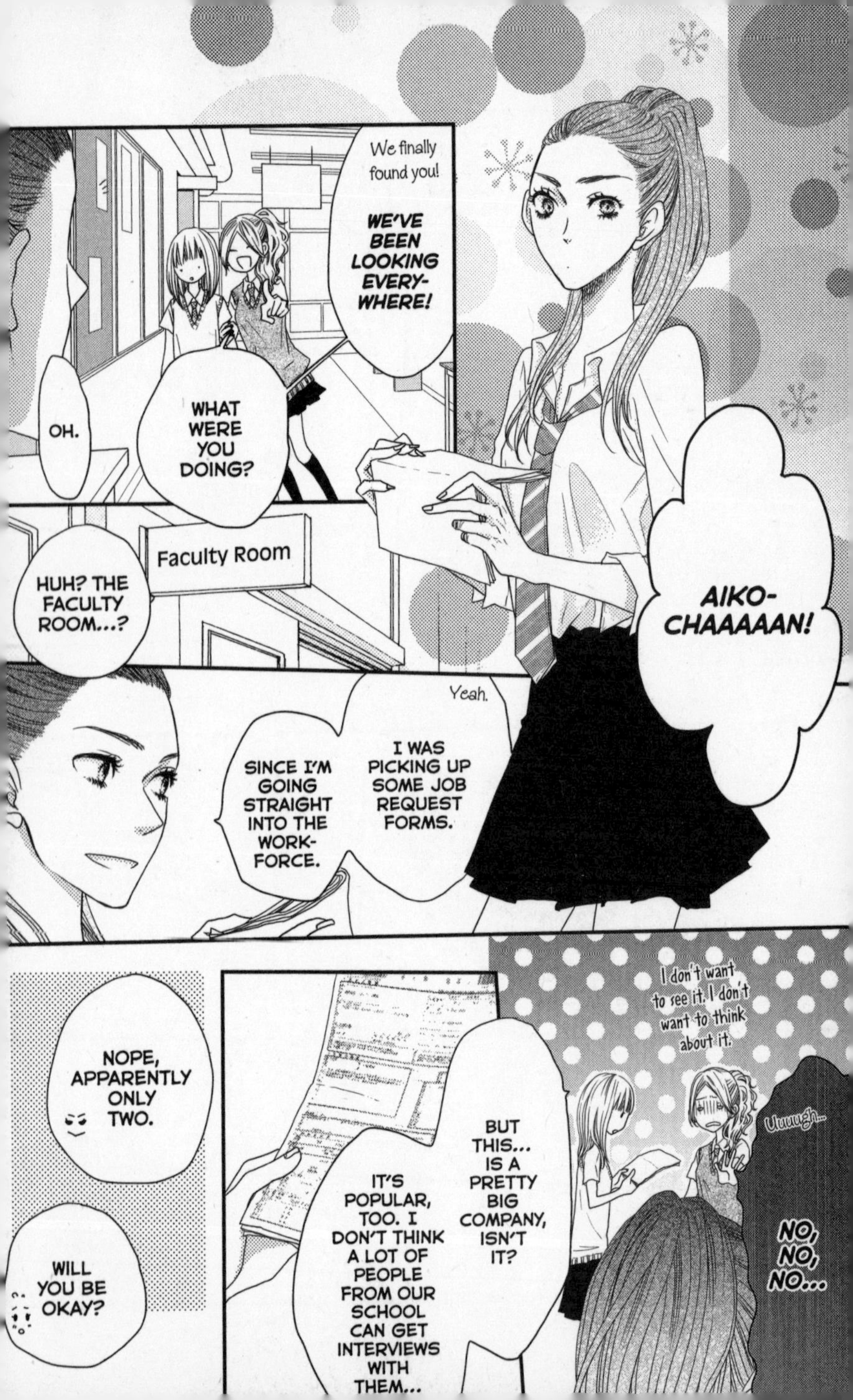
AIKO-CHAAAAAN!
We finally found you!
WE'VE BEEN LOOKING EVERY-WHERE!
WHAT WERE YOU DOING?
OH.
Faculty Room
HUH? THE FACULTY ROOM...?
Yeah.
I WAS PICKING UP SOME JOB REQUEST FORMS.
SINCE I'M GOING STRAIGHT INTO THE WORK-FORCE.
I don't want to see it. I don't want to think about it.
Uuuugh...
NO, NO, NO...
BUT THIS... IS A PRETTY BIG COMPANY, ISN'T IT?
IT'S POPULAR, TOO. I DON'T THINK A LOT OF PEOPLE FROM OUR SCHOOL CAN GET INTERVIEWS WITH THEM...
NOPE, APPARENTLY ONLY TWO.
WILL YOU BE OKAY?

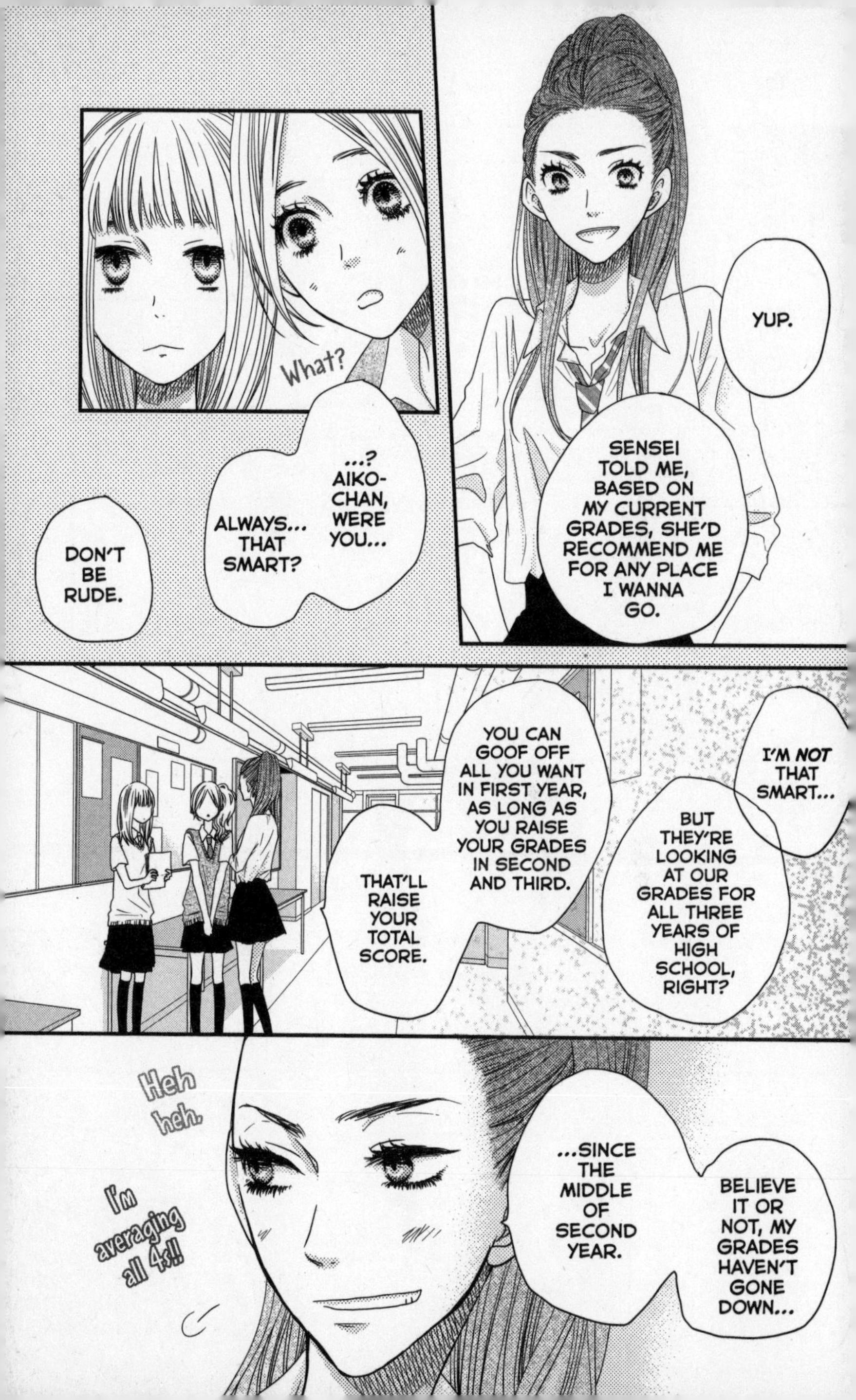
YUP.
SENSEI TOLD ME, BASED ON MY CURRENT GRADES, SHE'D RECOMMEND ME FOR ANY PLACE I WANNA GO.
What?
...? AIKO-CHAN, WERE YOU...
ALWAYS... THAT SMART?
DON'T BE RUDE.
I'M *NOT* THAT SMART...
BUT THEY'RE LOOKING AT OUR GRADES FOR ALL THREE YEARS OF HIGH SCHOOL, RIGHT?
YOU CAN GOOF OFF ALL YOU WANT IN FIRST YEAR, AS LONG AS YOU RAISE YOUR GRADES IN SECOND AND THIRD.
THAT'LL RAISE YOUR TOTAL SCORE.
BELIEVE IT OR NOT, MY GRADES HAVEN'T GONE DOWN...
...SINCE THE MIDDLE OF SECOND YEAR.
Heh heh.
I'm averaging all 4s!!

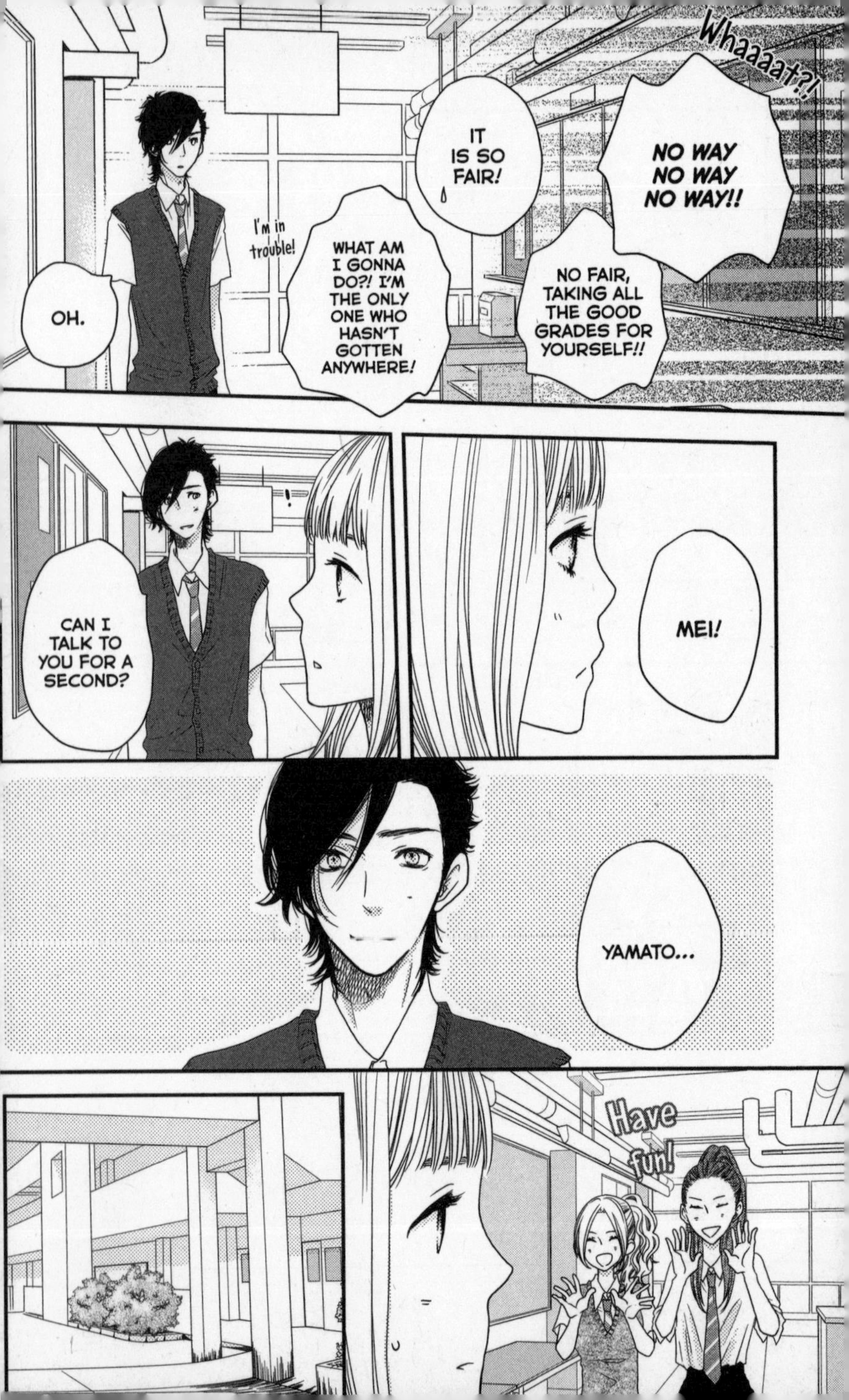
Whaaaaat?!
NO WAY NO WAY NO WAY!!
IT IS SO FAIR!
NO FAIR, TAKING ALL THE GOOD GRADES FOR YOURSELF!!
WHAT AM I GONNA DO?! I'M THE ONLY ONE WHO HASN'T GOTTEN ANYWHERE!
I'm in trouble!
OH.
MEI!
CAN I TALK TO YOU FOR A SECOND?
YAMATO...
Have fun!

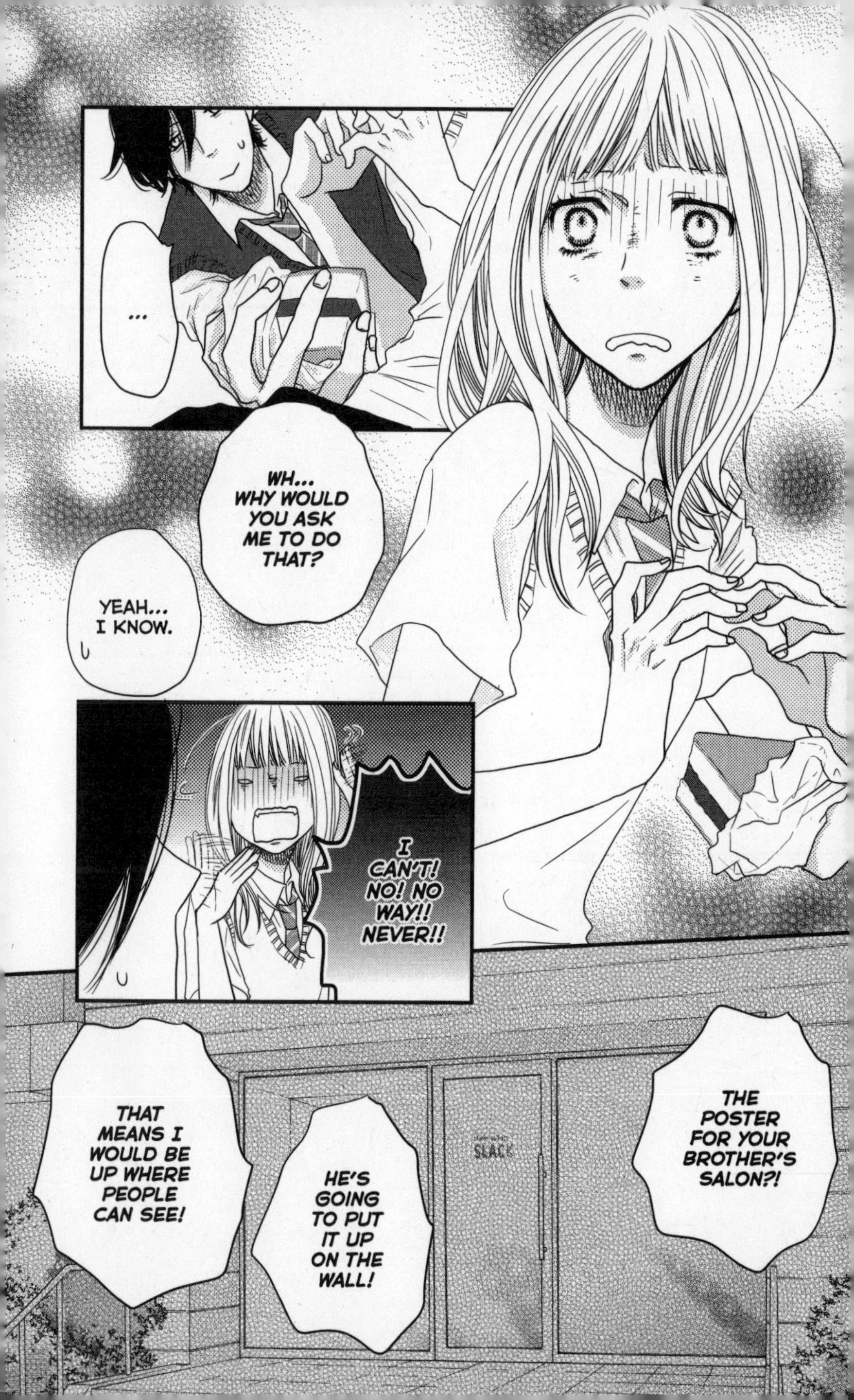
...
WH... WHY WOULD YOU ASK ME TO DO THAT?
YEAH... I KNOW.
I CAN'T! NO! NO WAY!! NEVER!!
THE POSTER FOR YOUR BROTHER'S SALON?!
HE'S GOING TO PUT IT UP ON THE WALL!
THAT MEANS I WOULD BE UP WHERE PEOPLE CAN SEE!
SLACK

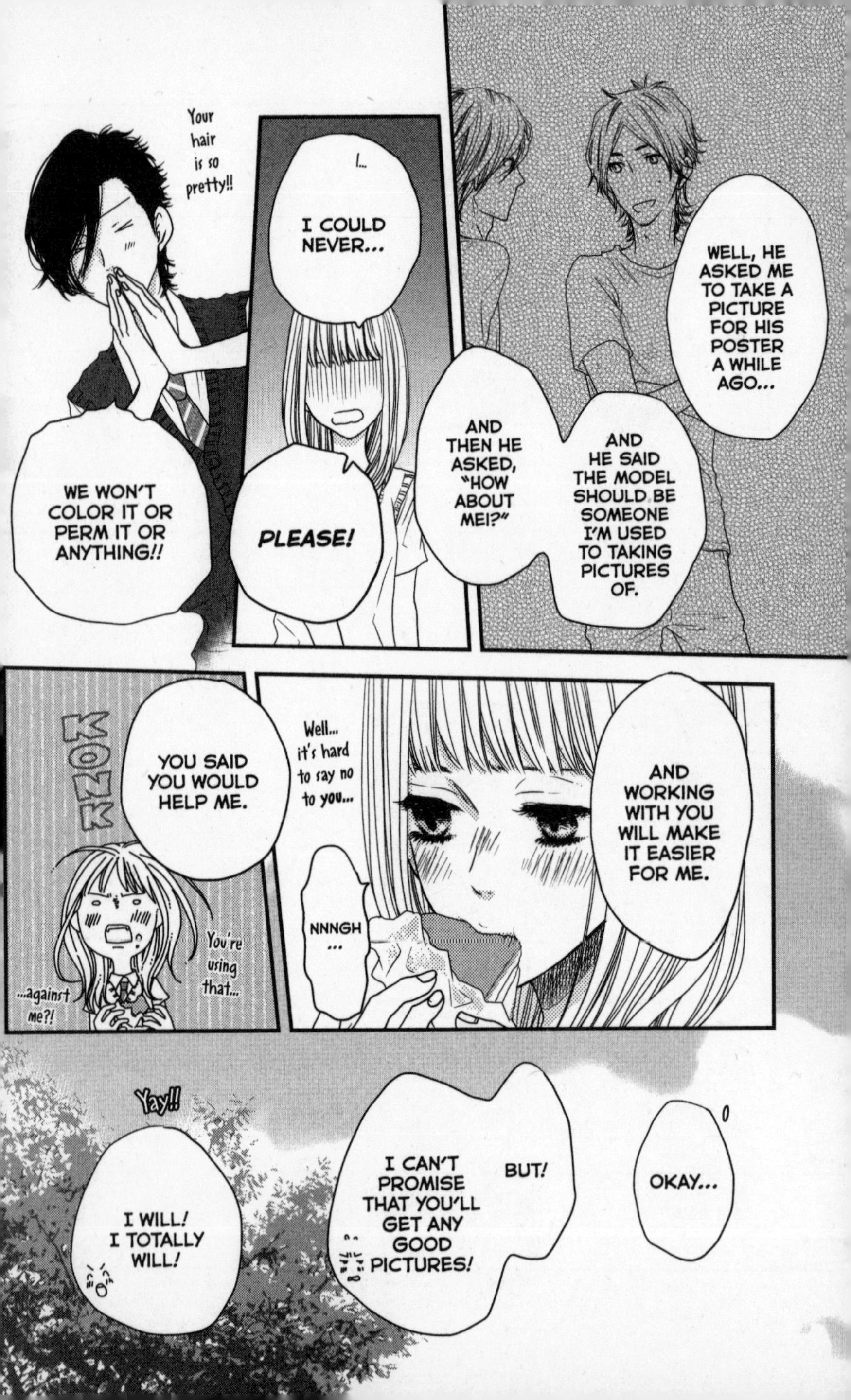
WELL, HE ASKED ME TO TAKE A PICTURE FOR HIS POSTER A WHILE AGO...
AND HE SAID THE MODEL SHOULD BE SOMEONE I'M USED TO TAKING PICTURES OF.
AND THEN HE ASKED, "HOW ABOUT MEI?"
I...
I COULD NEVER...
PLEASE!
Your hair is so pretty!!
WE WON'T COLOR IT OR PERM IT OR ANYTHING!!
AND WORKING WITH YOU WILL MAKE IT EASIER FOR ME.
Well... it's hard to say no to you...
NNNGH...
YOU SAID YOU WOULD HELP ME.
KONK
You're using that...
...against me?!
OKAY...
BUT!
I CAN'T PROMISE THAT YOU'LL GET ANY GOOD PICTURES!
Yay!!
I WILL! I TOTALLY WILL!

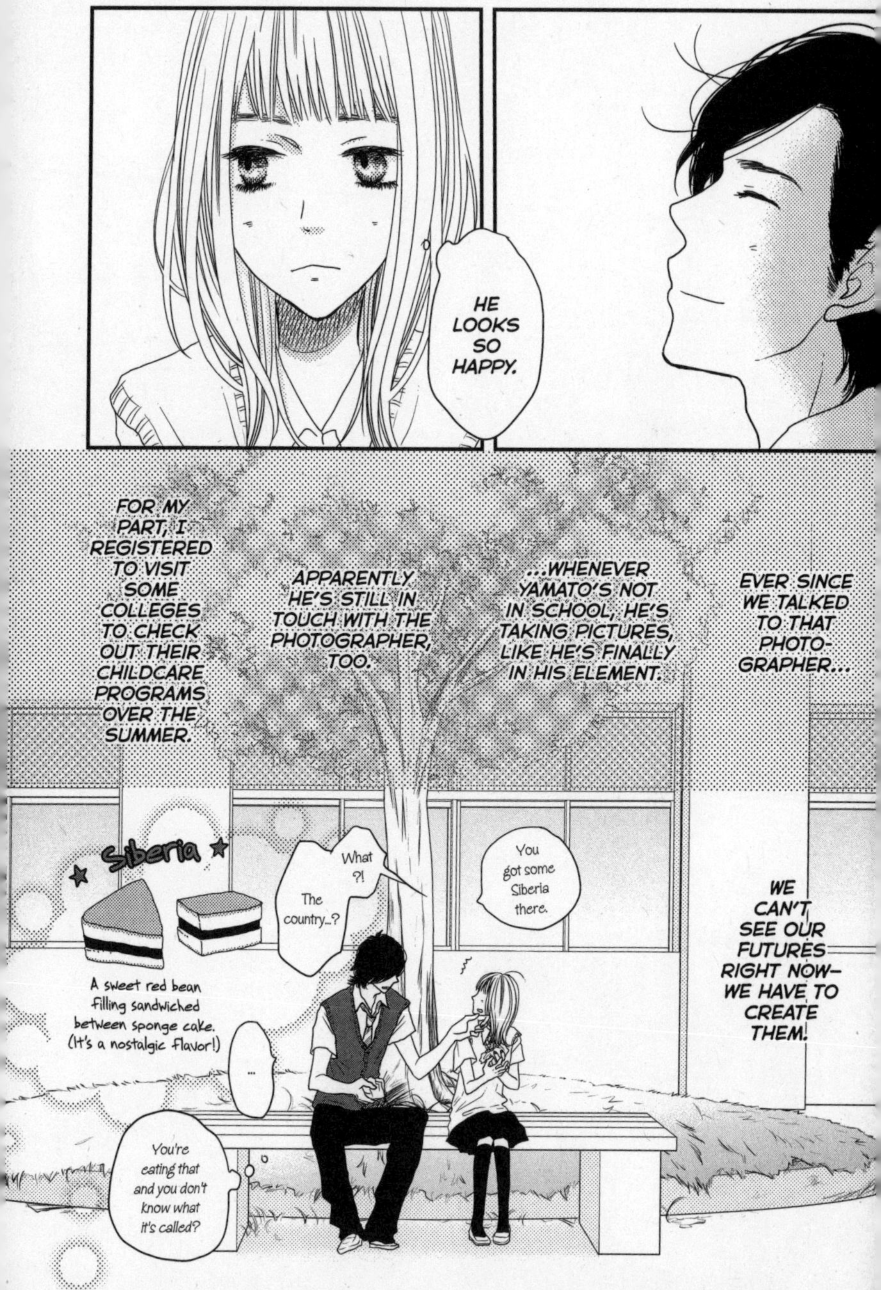
HE LOOKS SO HAPPY.
EVER SINCE WE TALKED TO THAT PHOTO-GRAPHER...
...WHENEVER YAMATO'S NOT IN SCHOOL, HE'S TAKING PICTURES, LIKE HE'S FINALLY IN HIS ELEMENT.
APPARENTLY HE'S STILL IN TOUCH WITH THE PHOTOGRAPHER, TOO.
FOR MY PART, I REGISTERED TO VISIT SOME COLLEGES TO CHECK OUT THEIR CHILDCARE PROGRAMS OVER THE SUMMER.
WE CAN'T SEE OUR FUTURES RIGHT NOW— WE HAVE TO CREATE THEM!
You got some Siberia there.
What?! The country...?
...
You're eating that and you don't know what it's called?
Siberia
A sweet red bean filling sandwiched between sponge cake. (It's a nostalgic flavor!)

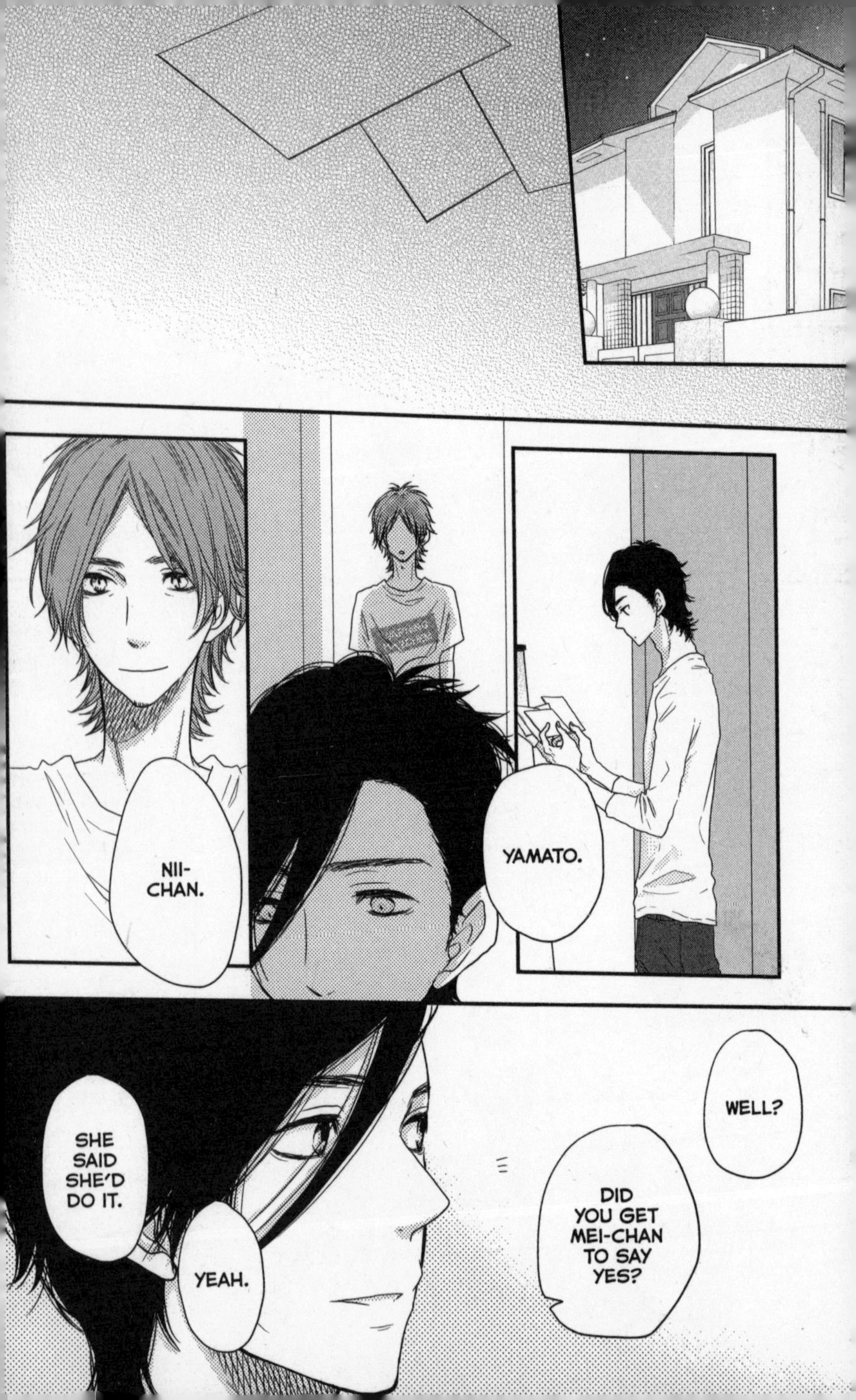
YAMATO.
NII-CHAN.
WELL?
DID YOU GET MEI-CHAN TO SAY YES?
YEAH.
SHE SAID SHE'D DO IT.

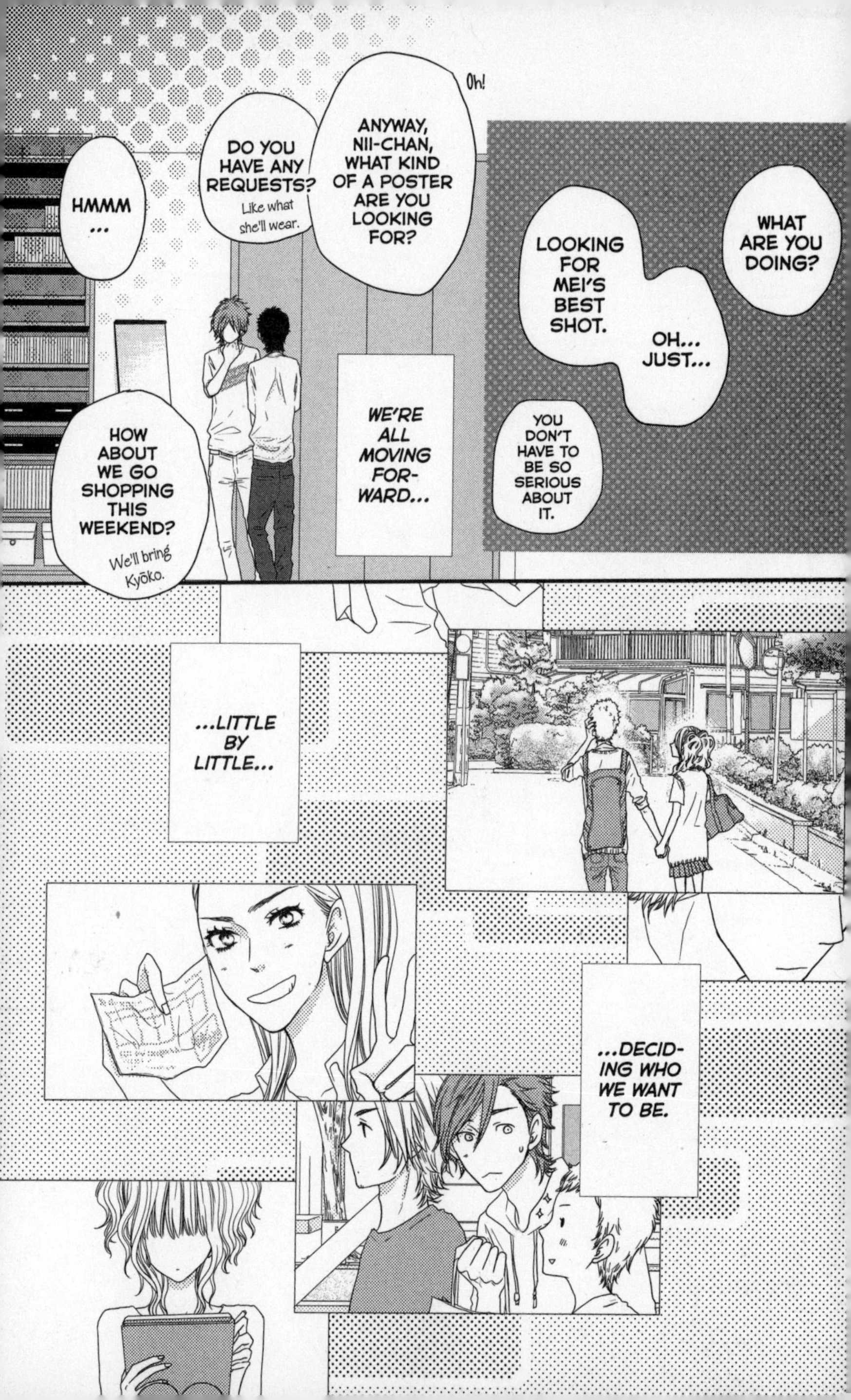
WHAT ARE YOU DOING?
LOOKING FOR MEI'S BEST SHOT.
OH... JUST...
YOU DON'T HAVE TO BE SO SERIOUS ABOUT IT.
Oh!
ANYWAY, NII-CHAN, WHAT KIND OF A POSTER ARE YOU LOOKING FOR?
DO YOU HAVE ANY REQUESTS?
Like what she'll wear.
HMMM ...
WE'RE ALL MOVING FOR-WARD...
HOW ABOUT WE GO SHOPPING THIS WEEKEND?
We'll bring Kyōko.
...LITTLE BY LITTLE...
...DECID-ING WHO WE WANT TO BE.

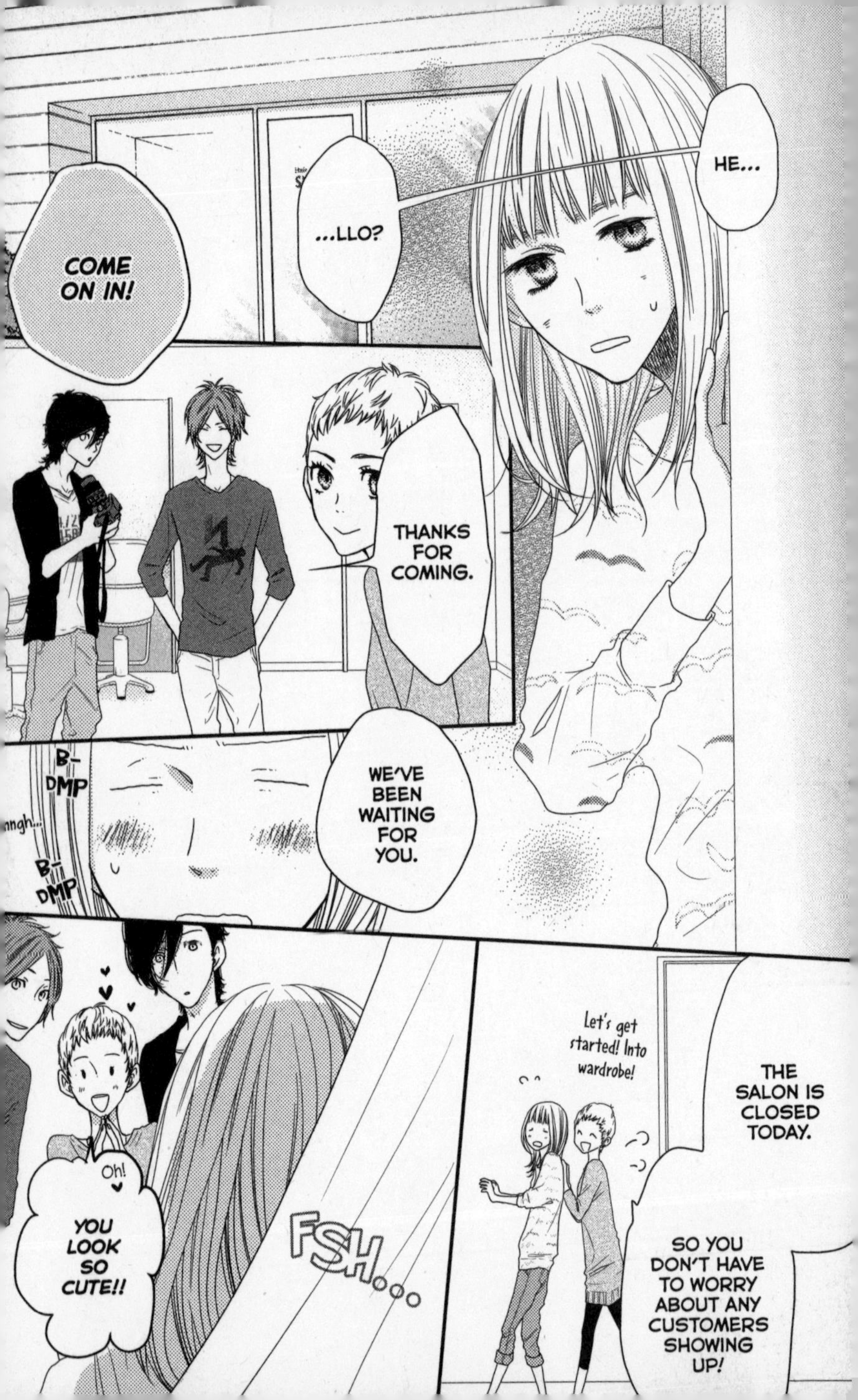
HE...
...LLO?
COME ON IN!
THANKS FOR COMING.
WE'VE BEEN WAITING FOR YOU.
B-DMP
nngh...
B-DMP
THE SALON IS CLOSED TODAY.
SO YOU DON'T HAVE TO WORRY ABOUT ANY CUSTOMERS SHOWING UP!
Let's get started! Into wardrobe!
FSH...
Oh!
YOU LOOK SO CUTE!!

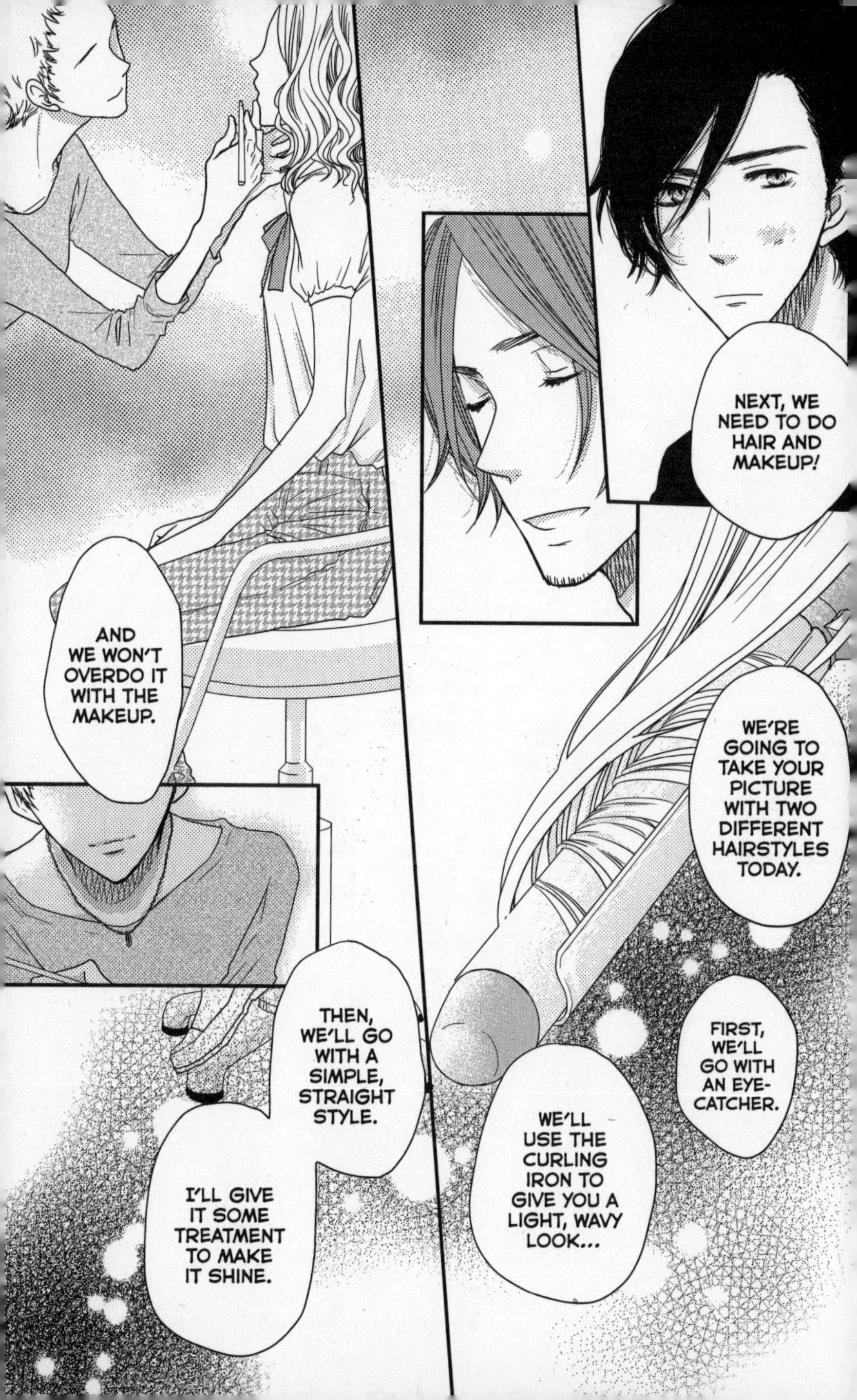
NEXT, WE NEED TO DO HAIR AND MAKEUP!
WE'RE GOING TO TAKE YOUR PICTURE WITH TWO DIFFERENT HAIRSTYLES TODAY.
FIRST, WE'LL GO WITH AN EYE-CATCHER.
WE'LL USE THE CURLING IRON TO GIVE YOU A LIGHT, WAVY LOOK...
AND WE WON'T OVERDO IT WITH THE MAKEUP.
THEN, WE'LL GO WITH A SIMPLE, STRAIGHT STYLE.
I'LL GIVE IT SOME TREATMENT TO MAKE IT SHINE.

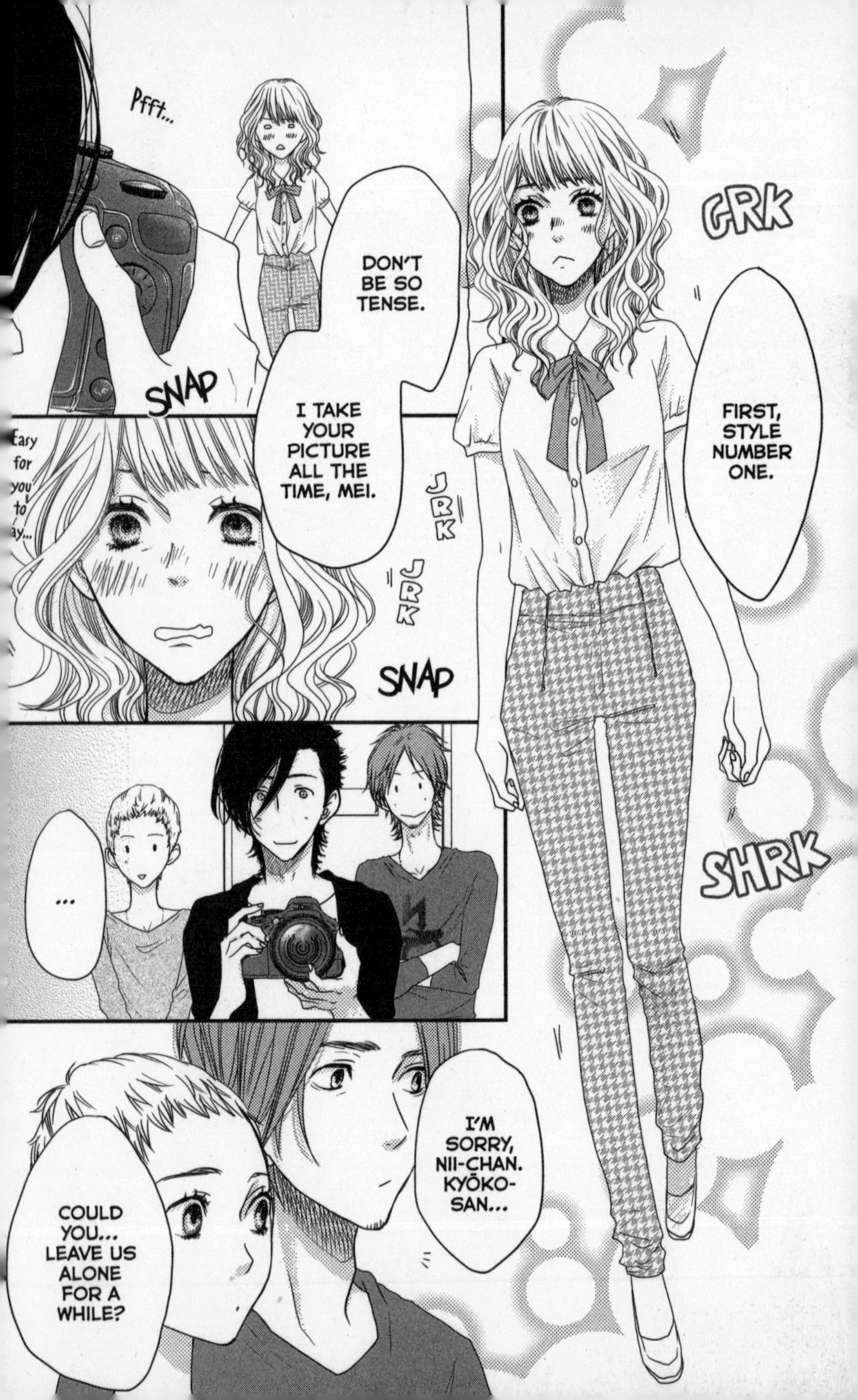
GRK
FIRST, STYLE NUMBER ONE.
SHRK
Pfft...
DON'T BE SO TENSE.
SNAP
I TAKE YOUR PICTURE ALL THE TIME, MEI.
JRK JRK
JRK JRK
SNAP
Easy for you to ay...
...
I'M SORRY, NII-CHAN. KYŌKO-SAN...
COULD YOU... LEAVE US ALONE FOR A WHILE?

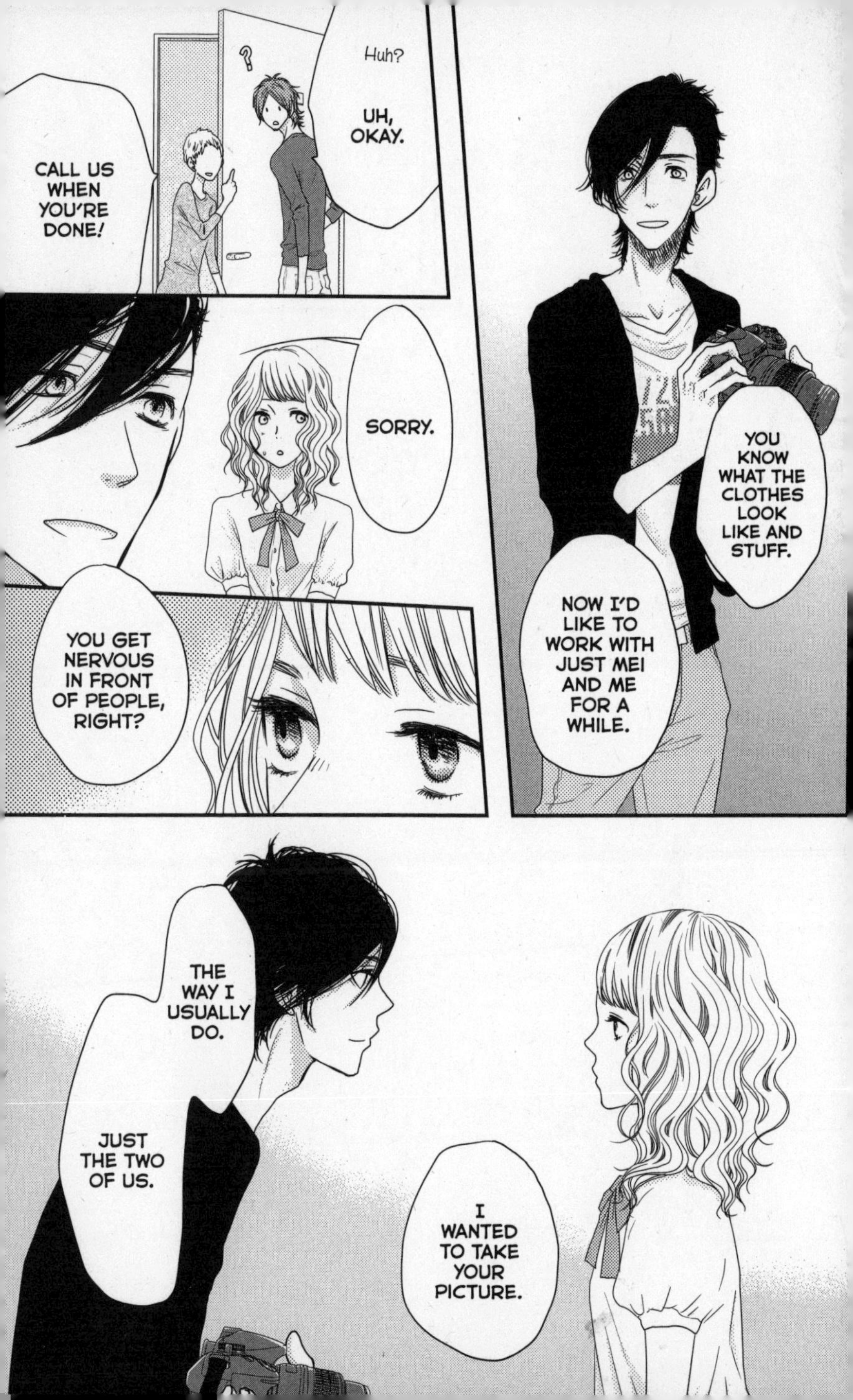
YOU KNOW WHAT THE CLOTHES LOOK LIKE AND STUFF.
NOW I'D LIKE TO WORK WITH JUST MEI AND ME FOR A WHILE.
Huh?
UH, OKAY.
CALL US WHEN YOU'RE DONE!
SORRY.
YOU GET NERVOUS IN FRONT OF PEOPLE, RIGHT?
I WANTED TO TAKE YOUR PICTURE.
THE WAY I USUALLY DO.
JUST THE TWO OF US.

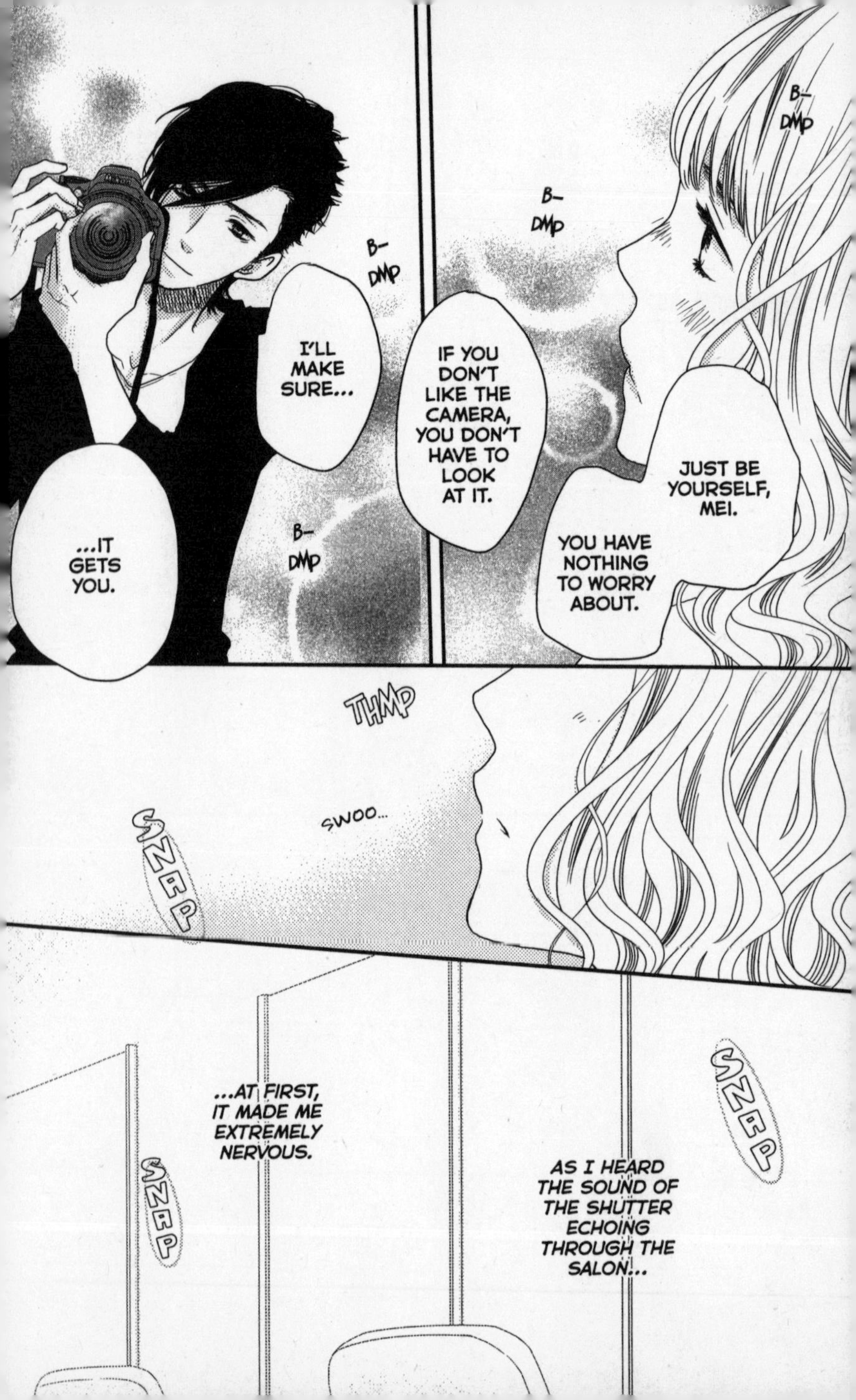
B-DMP
B-DMP
JUST BE YOURSELF, MEI.
YOU HAVE NOTHING TO WORRY ABOUT.
IF YOU DON'T LIKE THE CAMERA, YOU DON'T HAVE TO LOOK AT IT.
B-DMP
I'LL MAKE SURE...
B-DMP
...IT GETS YOU.
THMP
SWOO...
SNAP
SNAP
AS I HEARD THE SOUND OF THE SHUTTER ECHOING THROUGH THE SALON...
...AT FIRST, IT MADE ME EXTREMELY NERVOUS.
SNAP

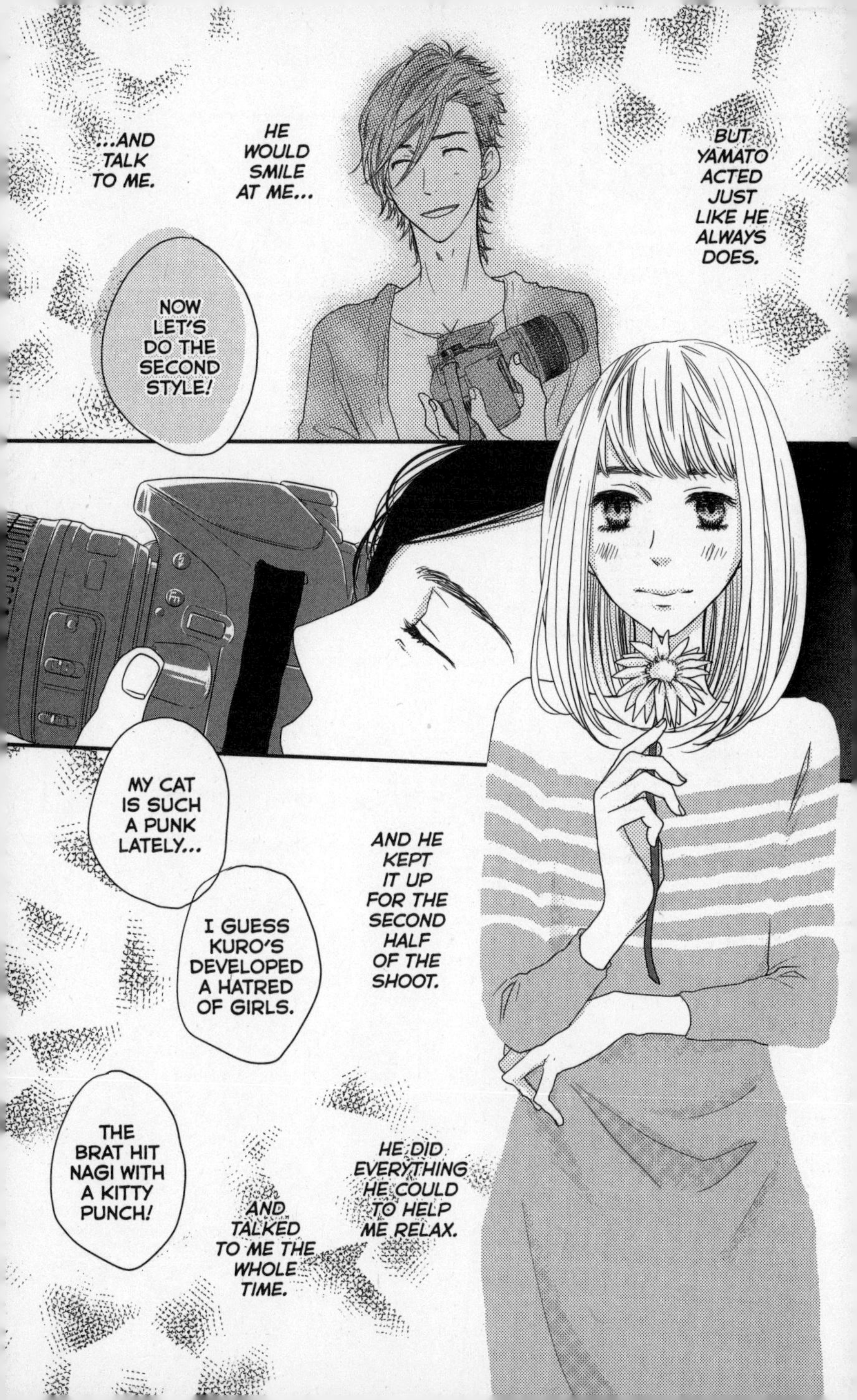
BUT YAMATO ACTED JUST LIKE HE ALWAYS DOES.
HE WOULD SMILE AT ME...
...AND TALK TO ME.
NOW LET'S DO THE SECOND STYLE!
AND HE KEPT IT UP FOR THE SECOND HALF OF THE SHOOT.
MY CAT IS SUCH A PUNK LATELY...
I GUESS KURO'S DEVELOPED A HATRED OF GIRLS.
HE DID EVERYTHING HE COULD TO HELP ME RELAX.
AND TALKED TO ME THE WHOLE TIME.
THE BRAT HIT NAGI WITH A KITTY PUNCH!

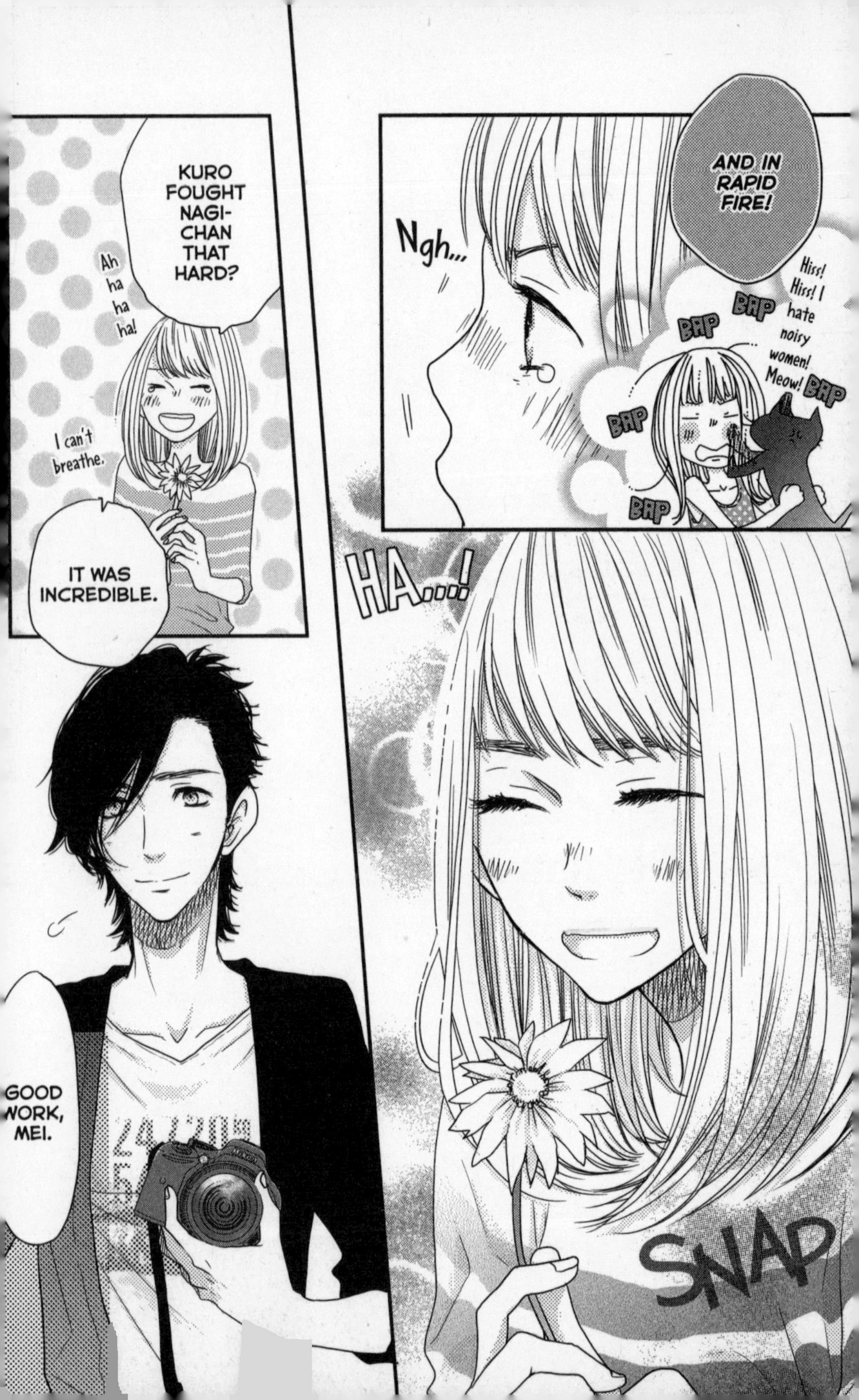
AND IN RAPID FIRE!
Ngh...
Hiss! Hiss! I hate noisy women! Meow!
BAP
BAP
BAP
BAP
BAP
KURO FOUGHT NAGI-CHAN THAT HARD?
Ah ha ha ha!
I can't breathe.
IT WAS INCREDIBLE.
HA...!
SNAP
GOOD WORK, MEI.

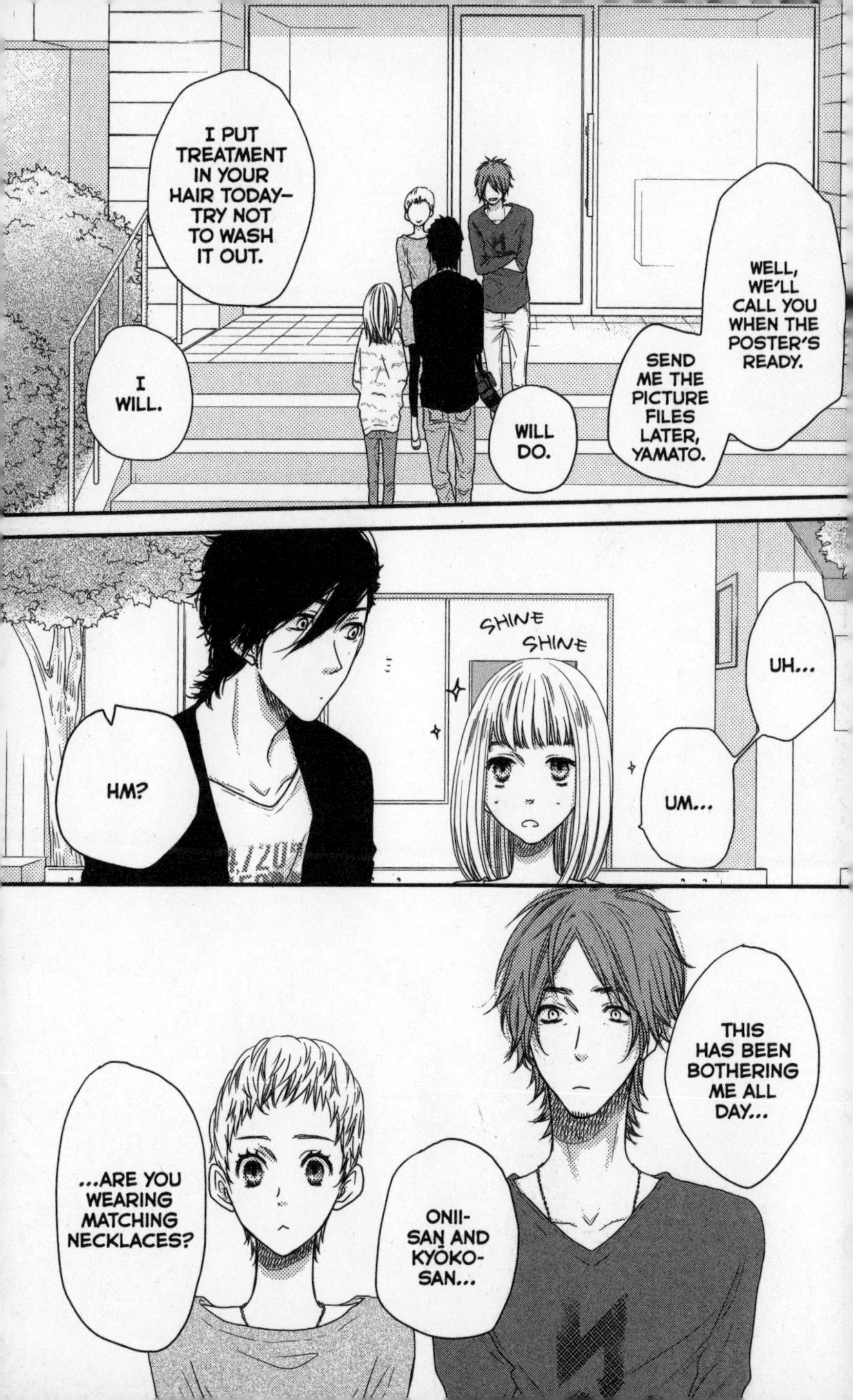
WELL, WE'LL CALL YOU WHEN THE POSTER'S READY.
SEND ME THE PICTURE FILES LATER, YAMATO.
WILL DO.
I PUT TREATMENT IN YOUR HAIR TODAY— TRY NOT TO WASH IT OUT.
I WILL.
SHINE SHINE
UH...
UM...
HM?
THIS HAS BEEN BOTHERING ME ALL DAY...
ONII-SAN AND KYŌKO-SAN...
...ARE YOU WEARING MATCHING NECKLACES?

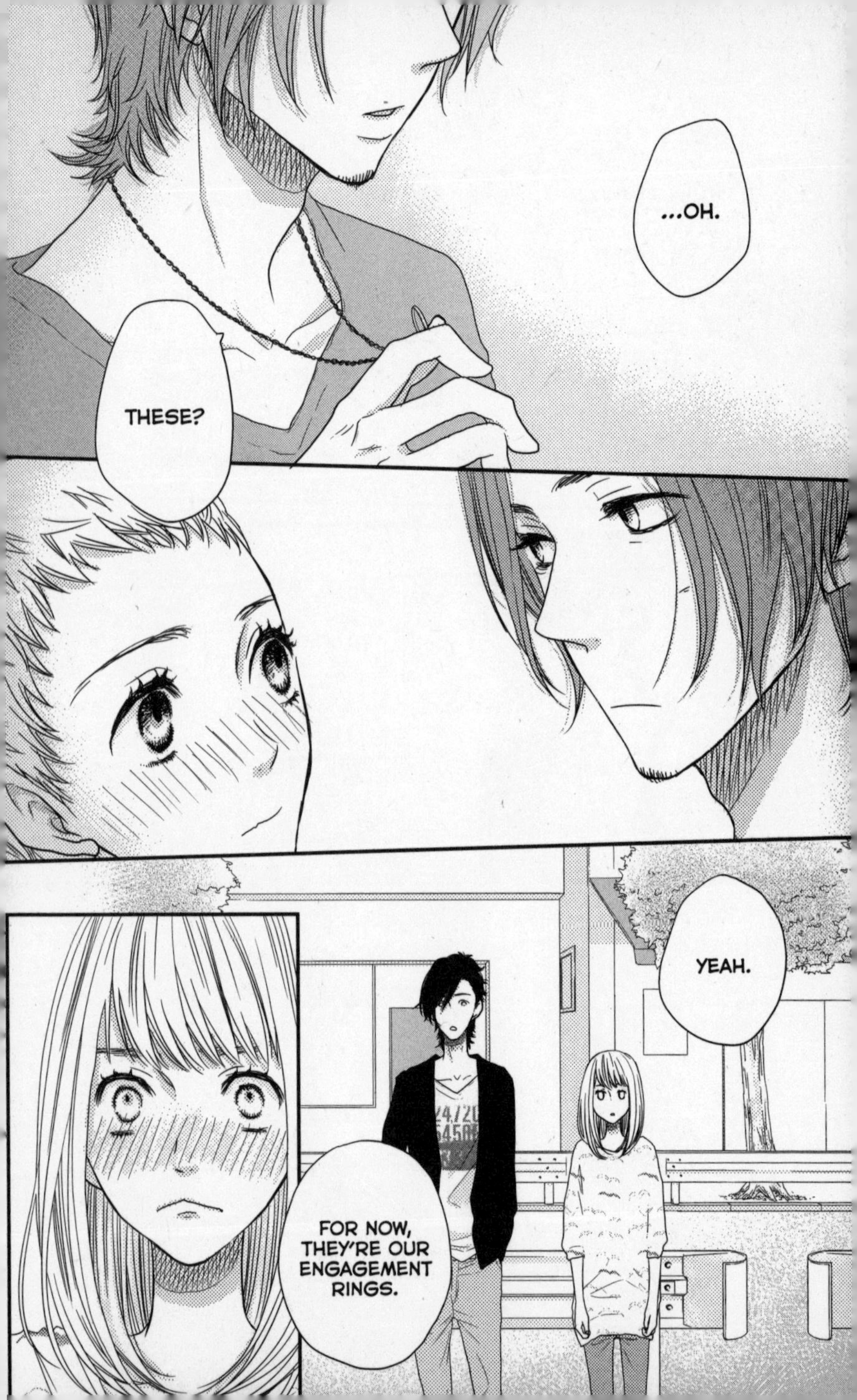
...OH.
THESE?
YEAH.
FOR NOW, THEY'RE OUR ENGAGEMENT RINGS.

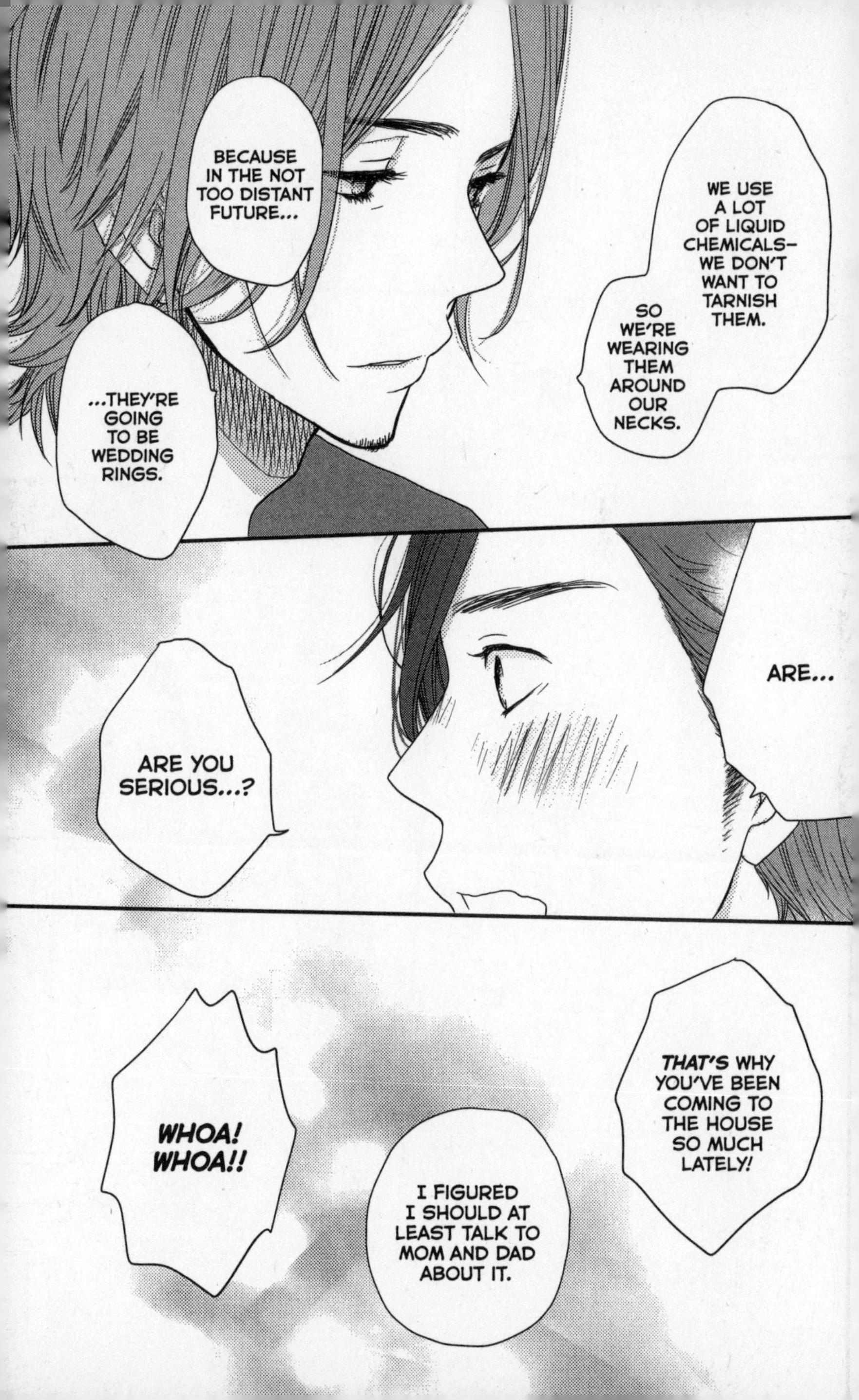
WE USE A LOT OF LIQUID CHEMICALS– WE DON'T WANT TO TARNISH THEM.
SO WE'RE WEARING THEM AROUND OUR NECKS.
BECAUSE IN THE NOT TOO DISTANT FUTURE...
...THEY'RE GOING TO BE WEDDING RINGS.
ARE...
ARE YOU SERIOUS...?
THAT'S WHY YOU'VE BEEN COMING TO THE HOUSE SO MUCH LATELY!
I FIGURED I SHOULD AT LEAST TALK TO MOM AND DAD ABOUT IT.
WHOA! WHOA!!

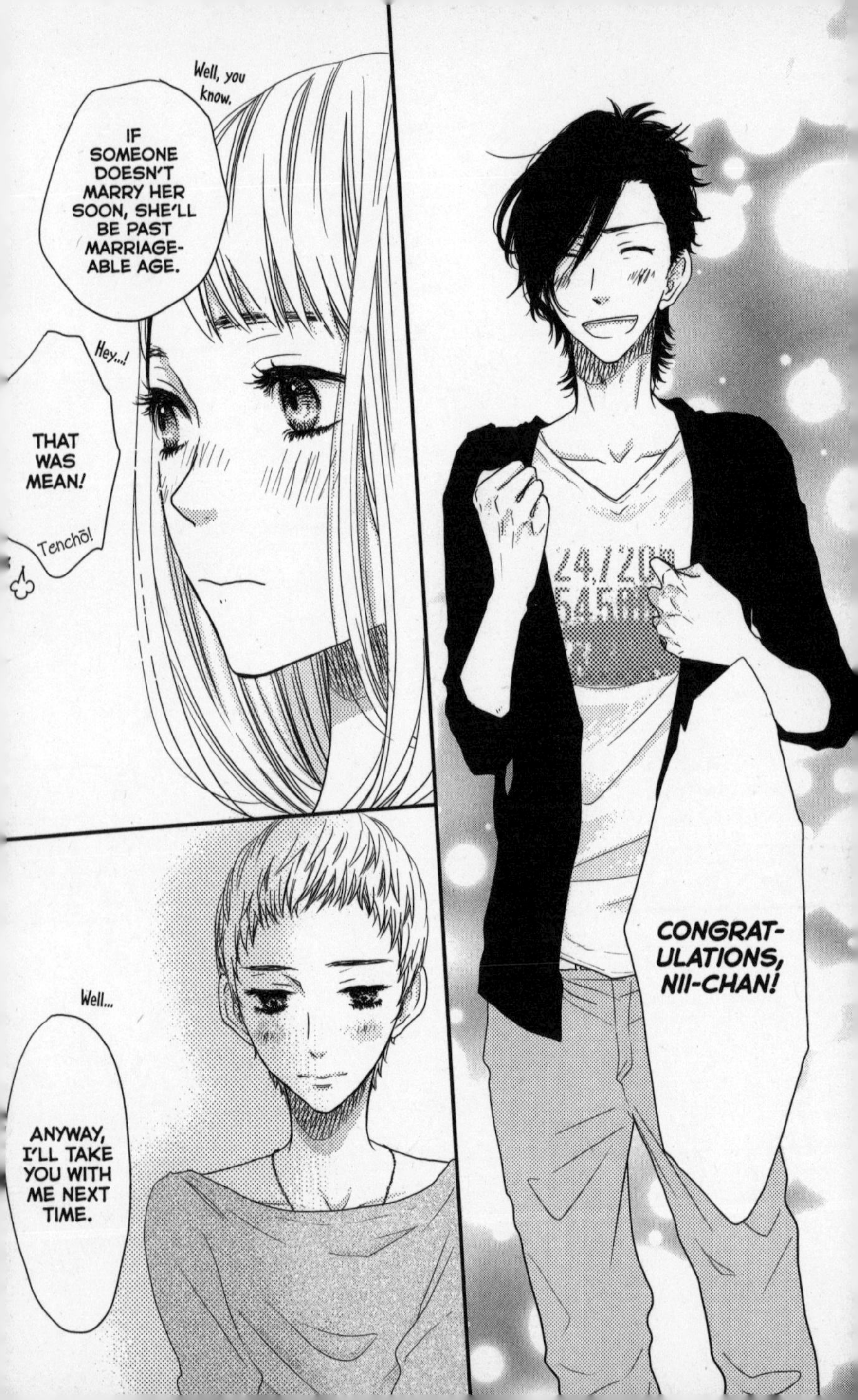
CONGRAT-ULATIONS, NII-CHAN!
Well, you know.
IF SOMEONE DOESN'T MARRY HER SOON, SHE'LL BE PAST MARRIAGE-ABLE AGE.
Hey...!
THAT WAS MEAN!
Tenchō!
Well...
ANYWAY, I'LL TAKE YOU WITH ME NEXT TIME.

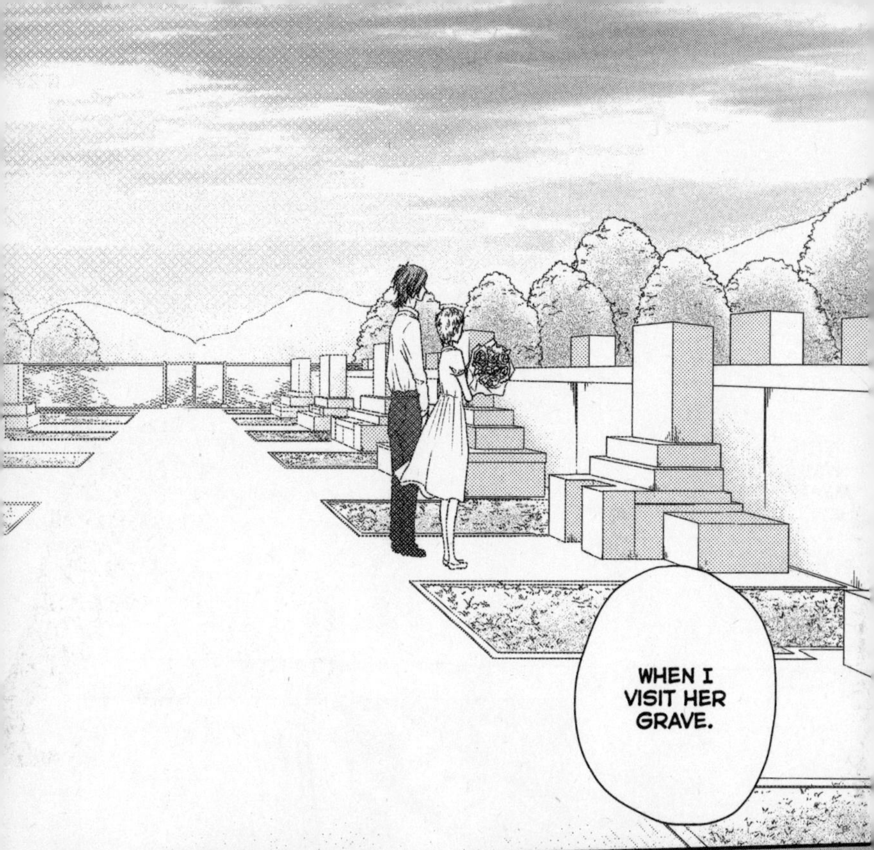
WHEN I VISIT HER GRAVE.
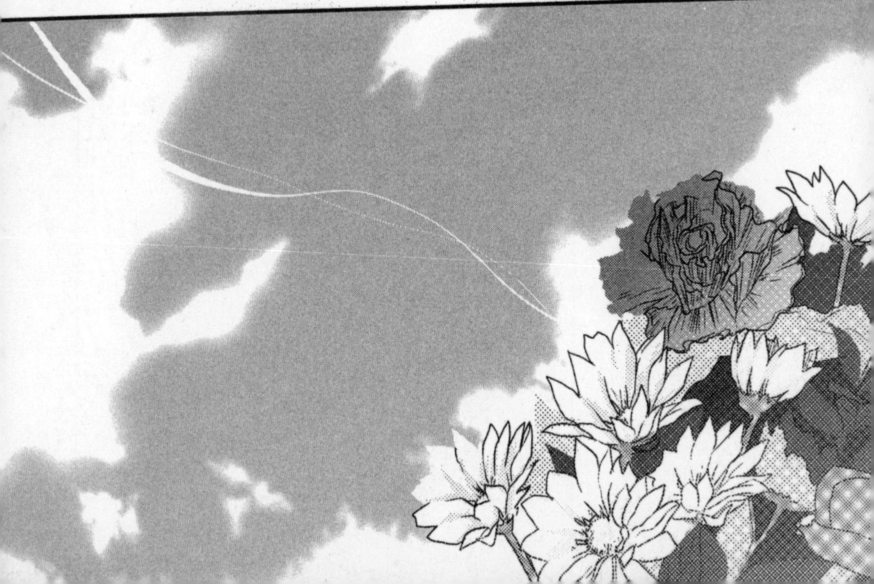

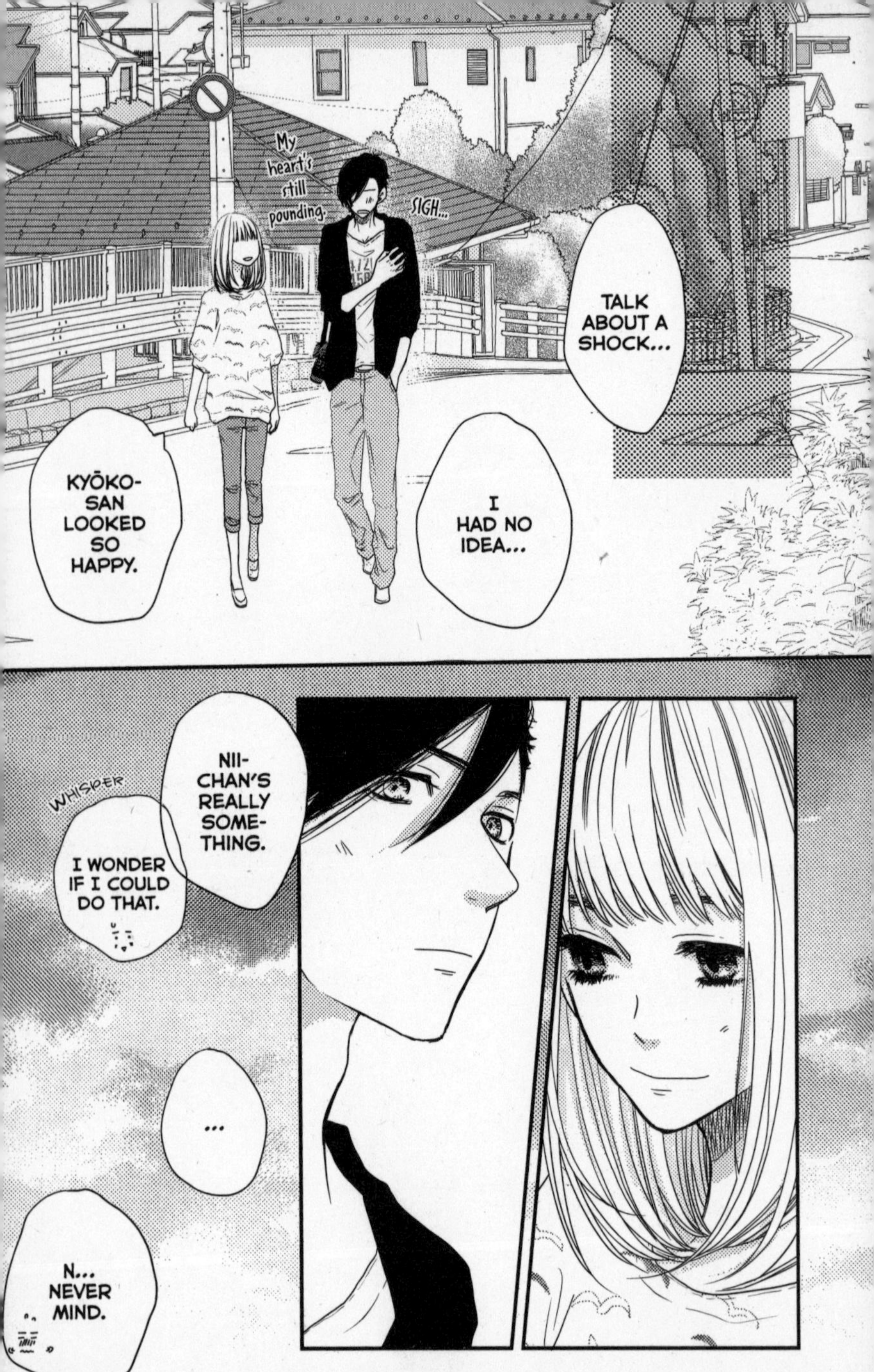
TALK ABOUT A SHOCK...
SIGH...
My heart's still pounding.
I HAD NO IDEA...
KYŌKO-SAN LOOKED SO HAPPY.
NII-CHAN'S REALLY SOMETHING.
WHISPER
I WONDER IF I COULD DO THAT.
...
N... NEVER MIND.

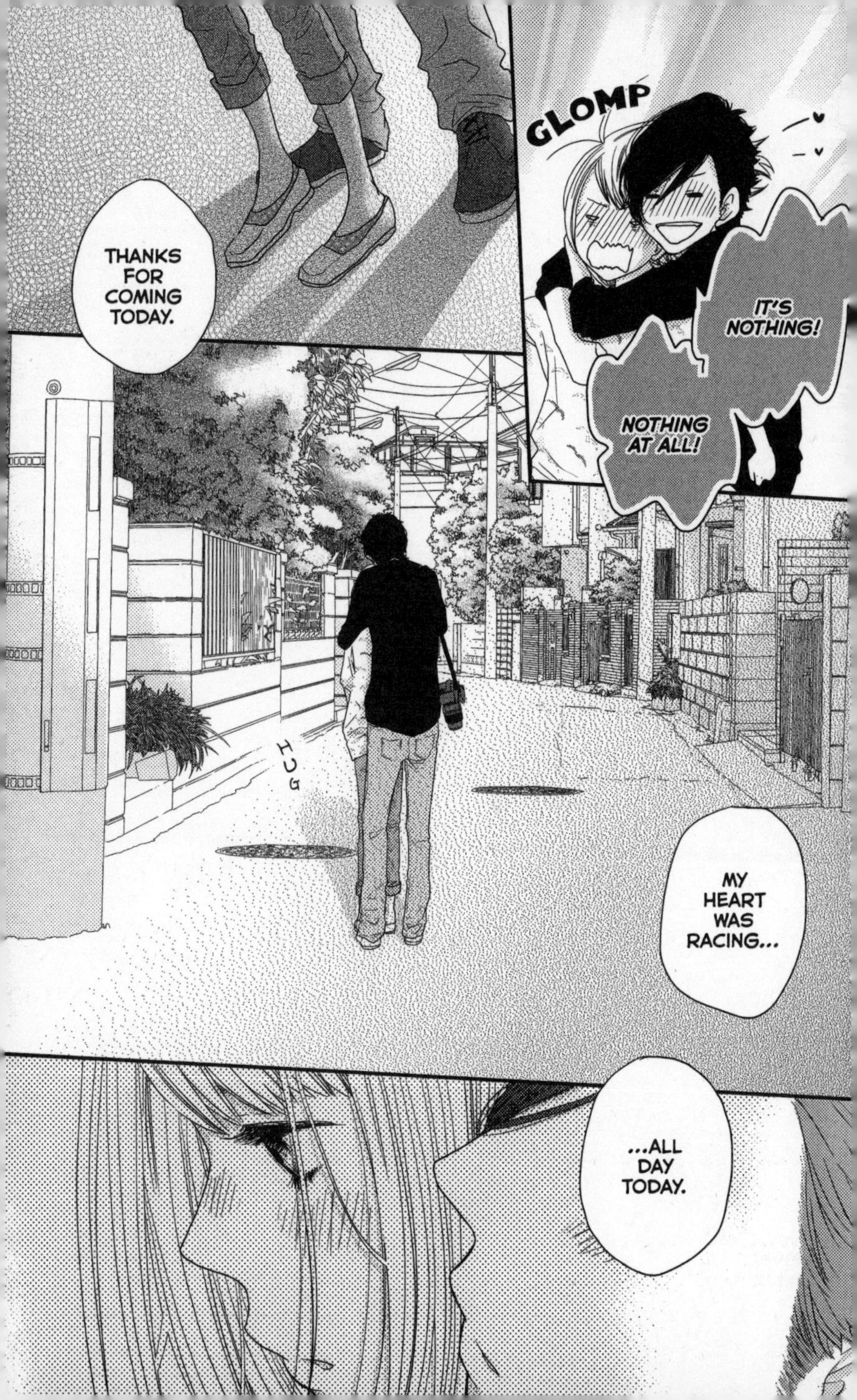
GLOMP
IT'S NOTHING!
NOTHING AT ALL!
THANKS FOR COMING TODAY.
HUG
MY HEART WAS RACING...
...ALL DAY TODAY.

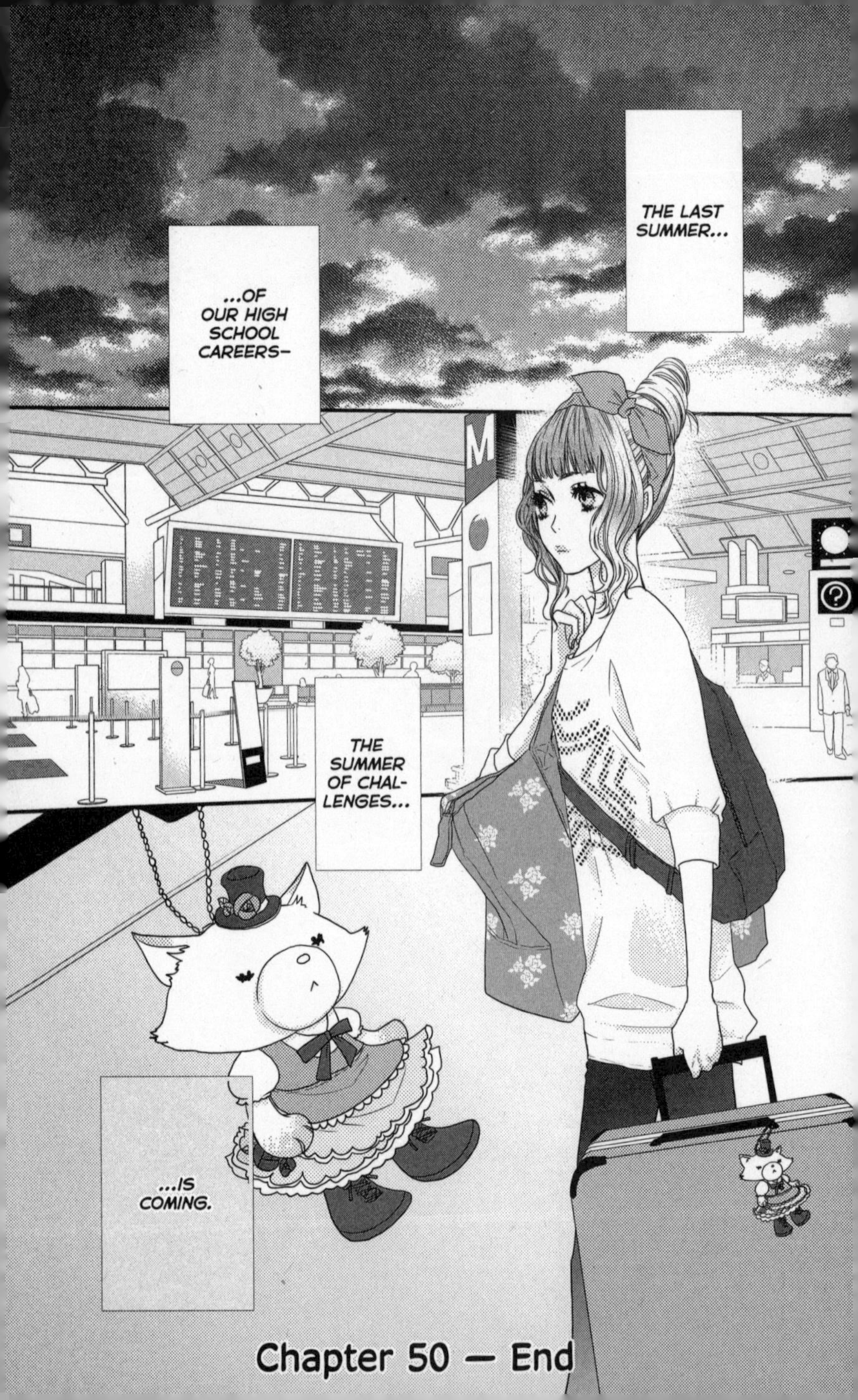
THE LAST SUMMER...
...OF OUR HIGH SCHOOL CAREERS–
THE SUMMER OF CHAL-LENGES...
...IS COMING.
Chapter 50 — End

Say "I love you".

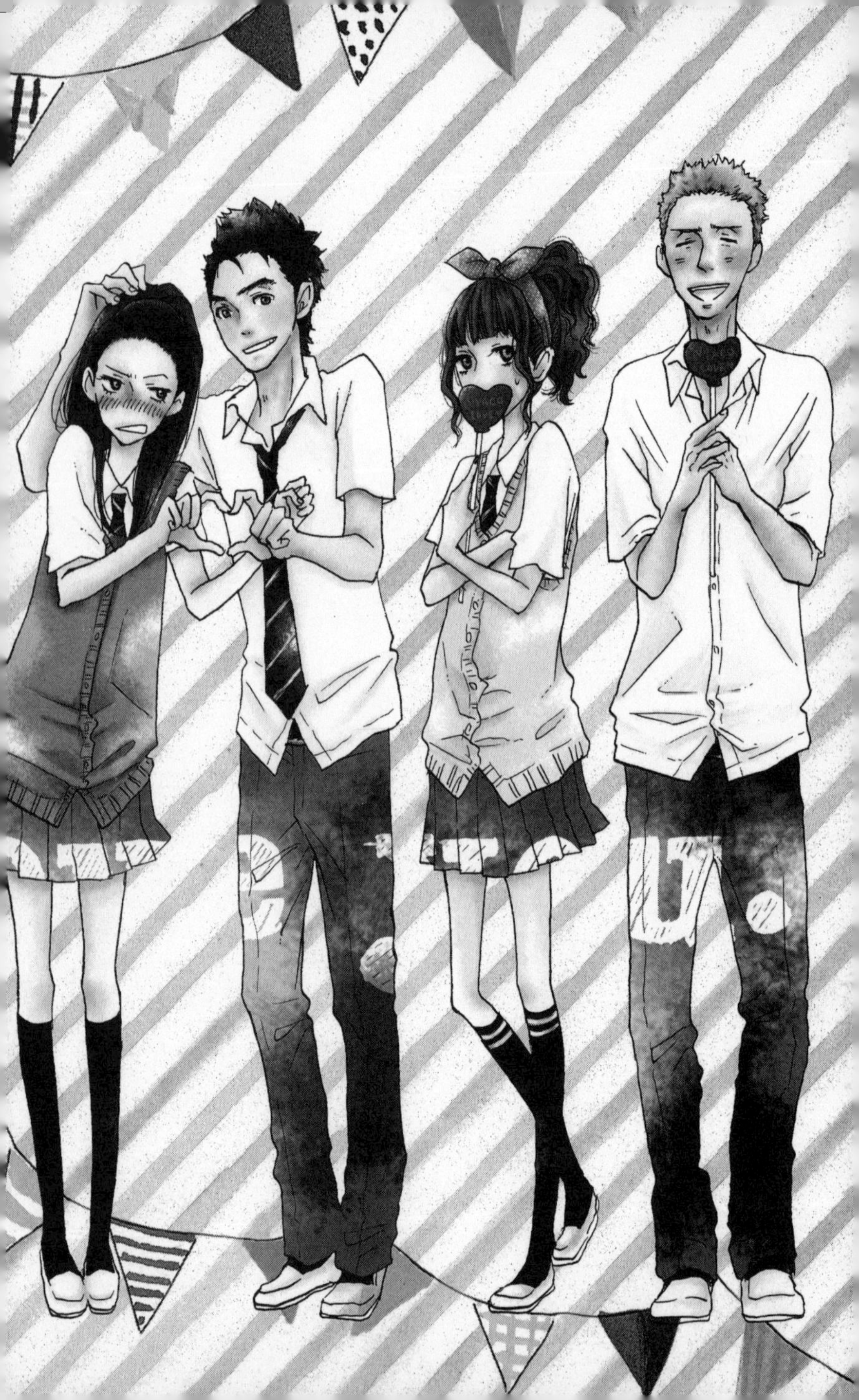

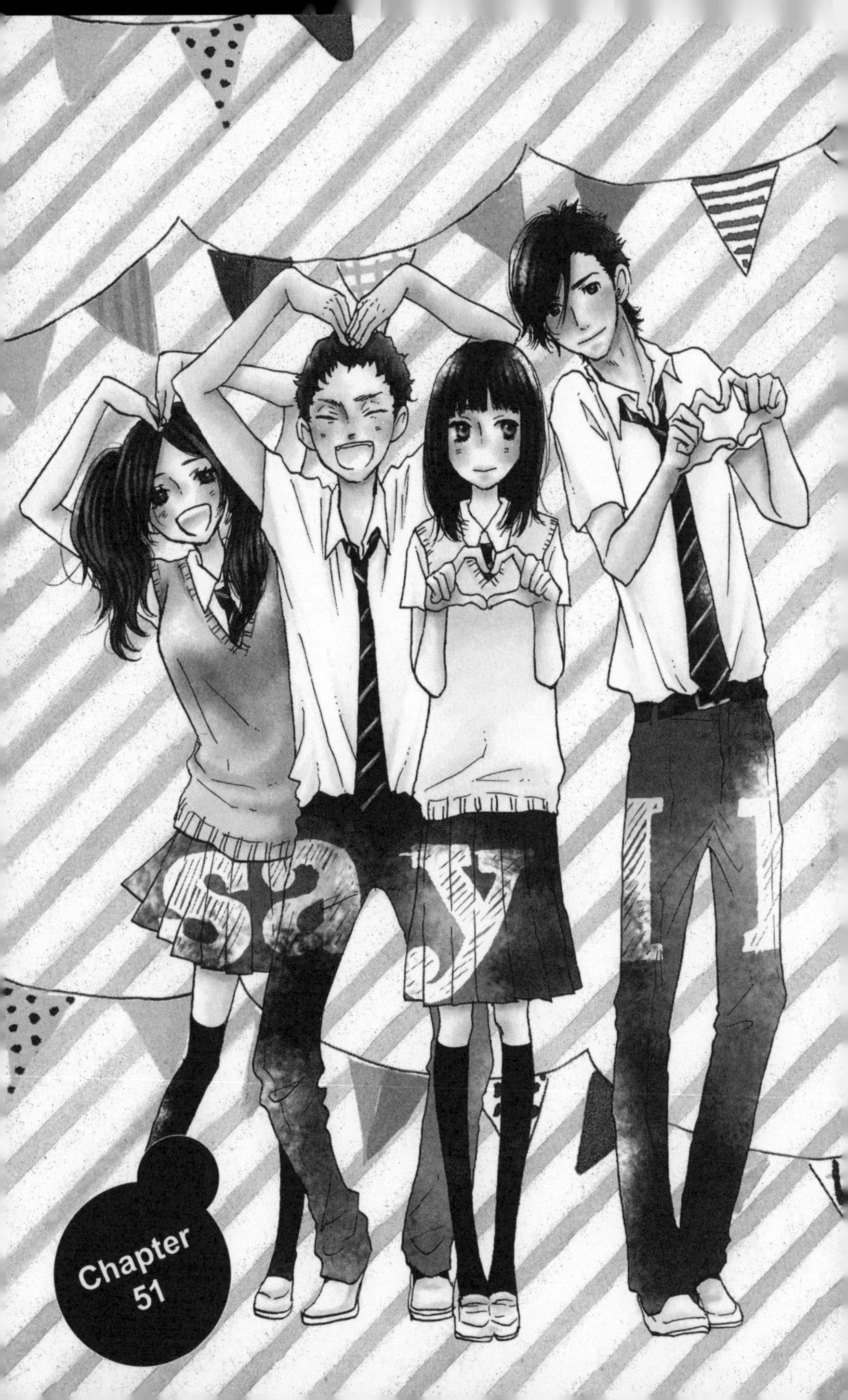
Chapter
51

Say "I love you".

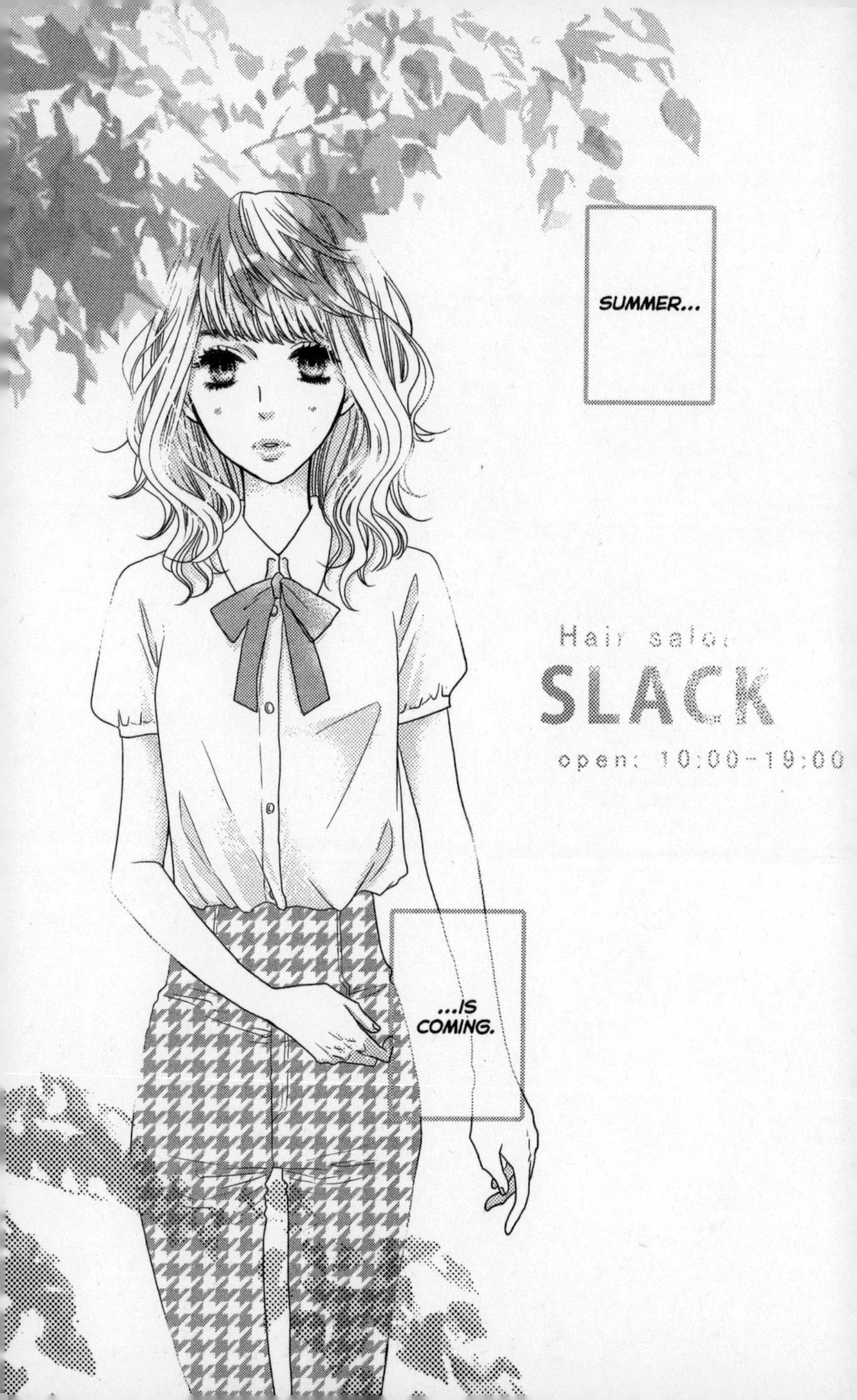
SUMMER...
Hair salo
SLACK
open: 10:00-19:00
...IS COMING.

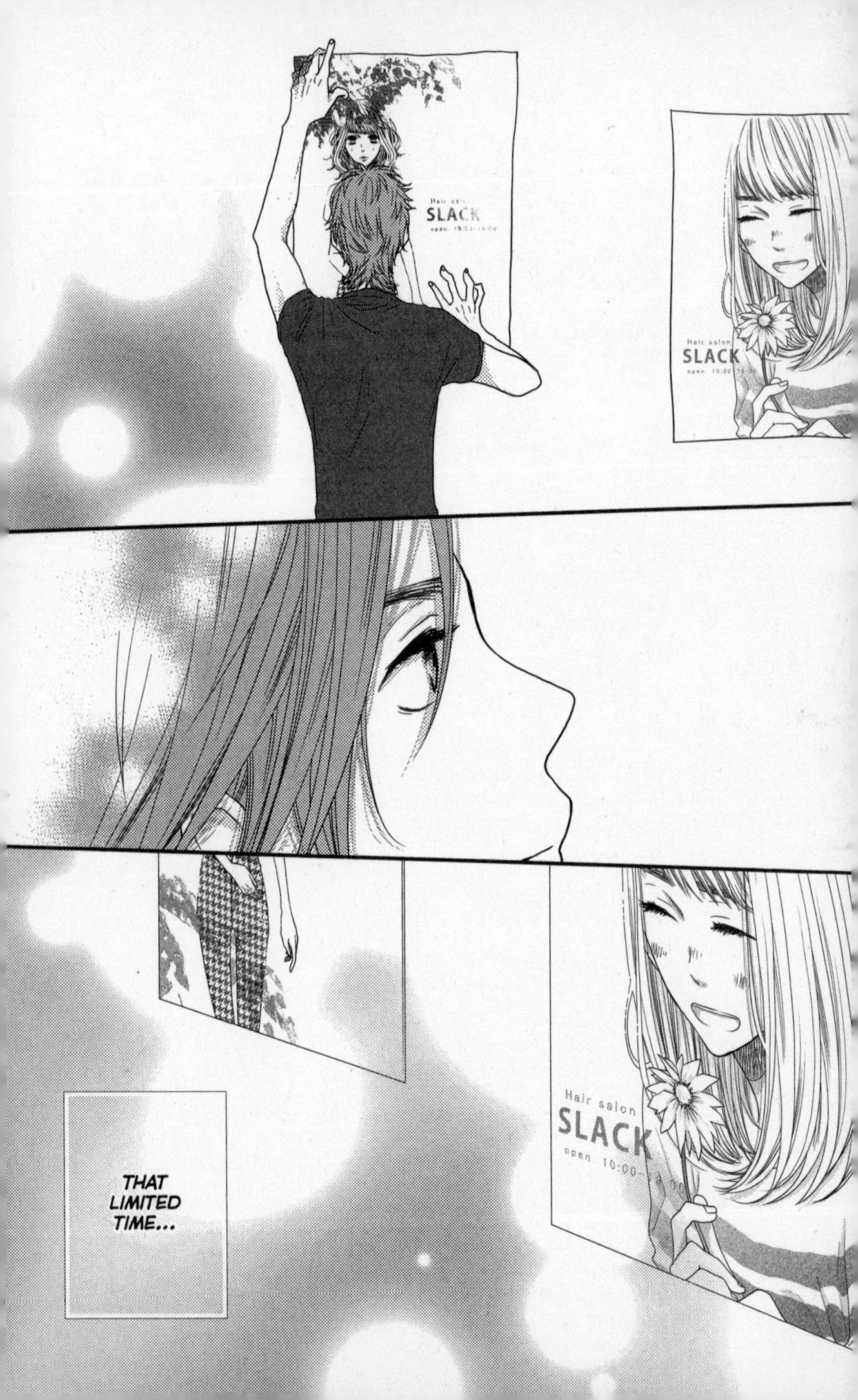
Hair salon
SLACK
SLACK
Hair salon
SLACK
THAT LIMITED TIME...

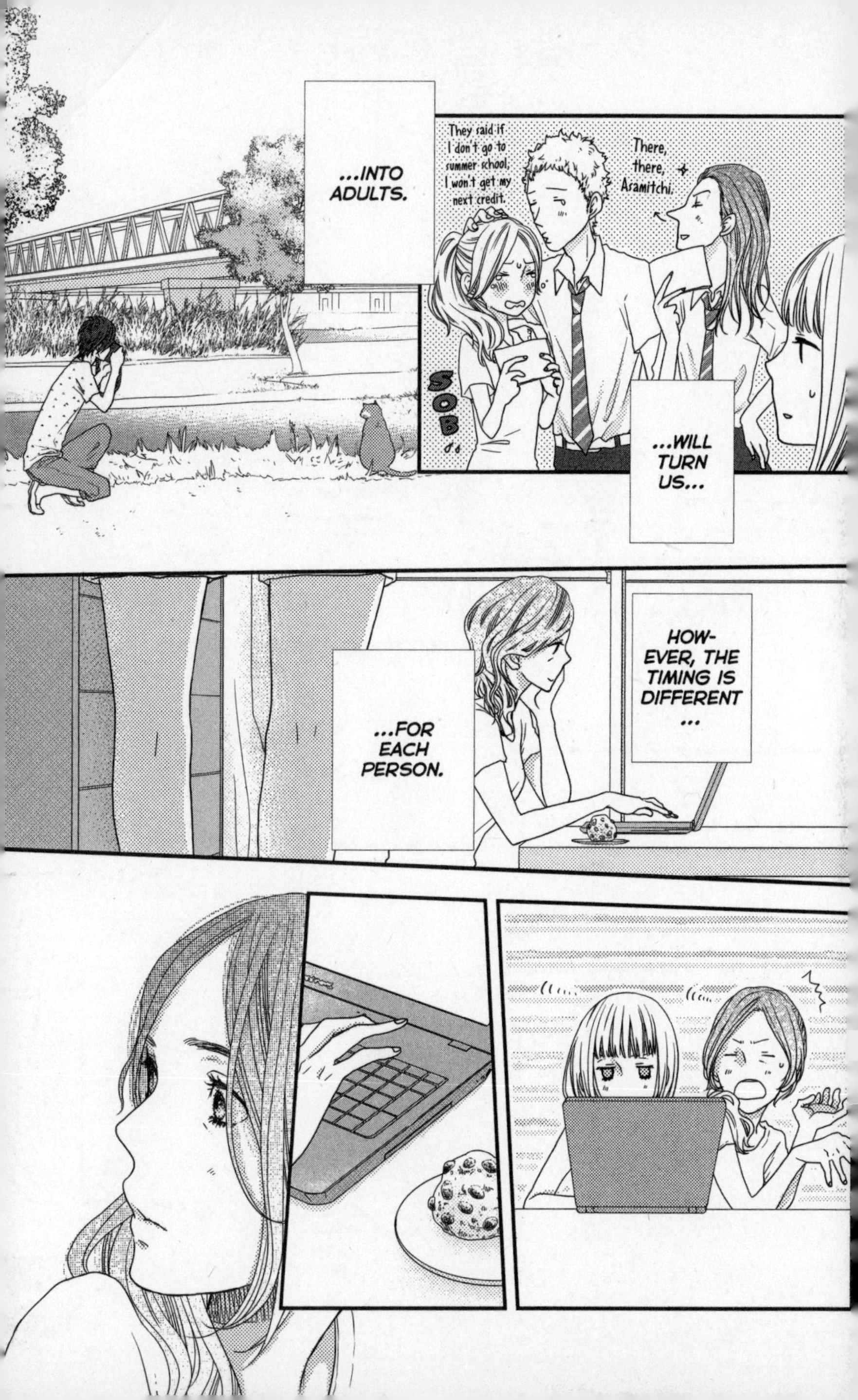
They said if I don't go to summer school, I won't get my next credit.
There, there, Asamitchi.
SOB
...WILL TURN US...
...INTO ADULTS.
HOW-EVER, THE TIMING IS DIFFERENT ...
...FOR EACH PERSON.

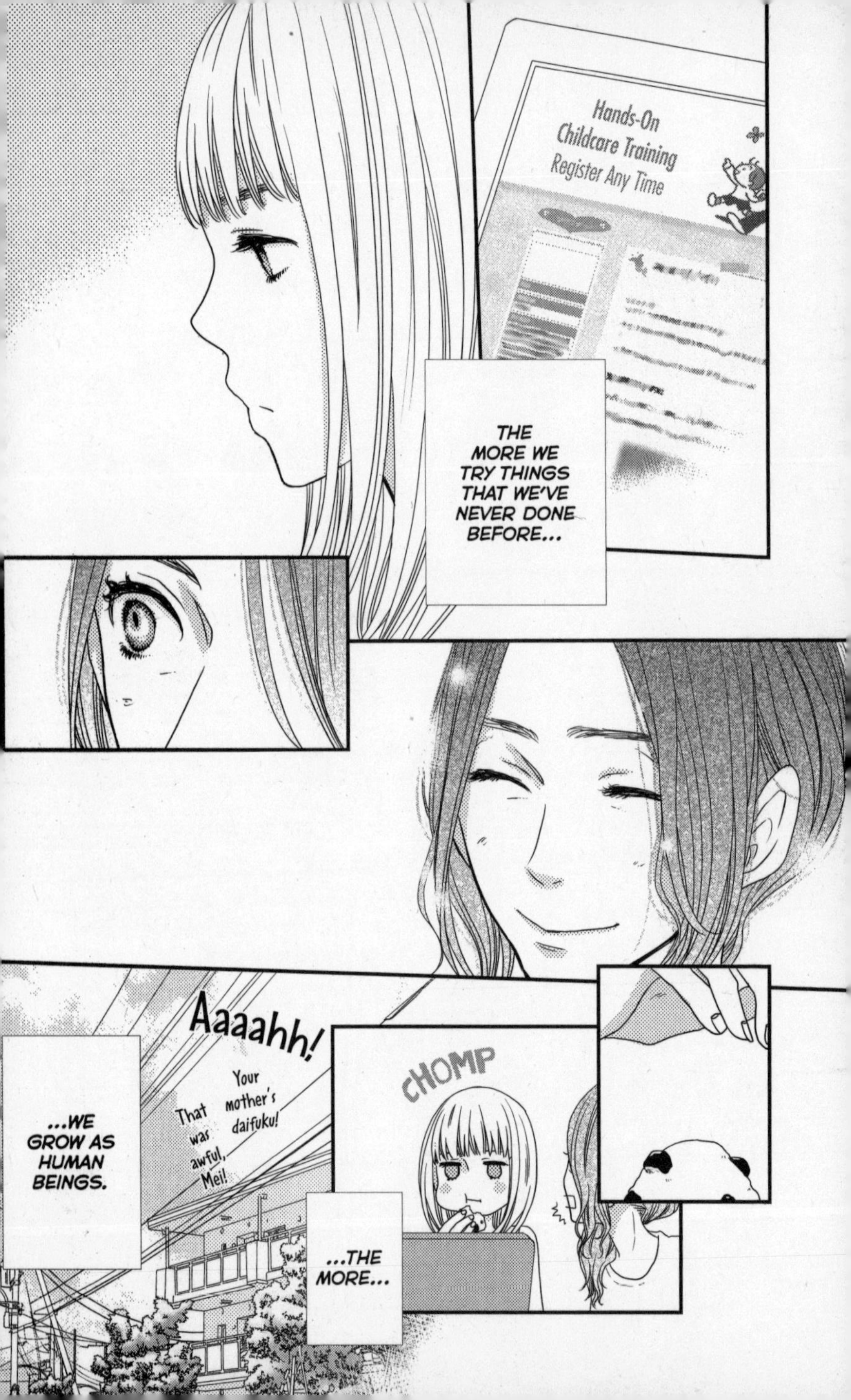
Hands-On
Childcare Training
Register Any Time
THE MORE WE TRY THINGS THAT WE'VE NEVER DONE BEFORE...
CHOMP
...THE MORE...
Aaaahh!
Your mother's daifuku!
That was awful, Mei!
...WE GROW AS HUMAN BEINGS.

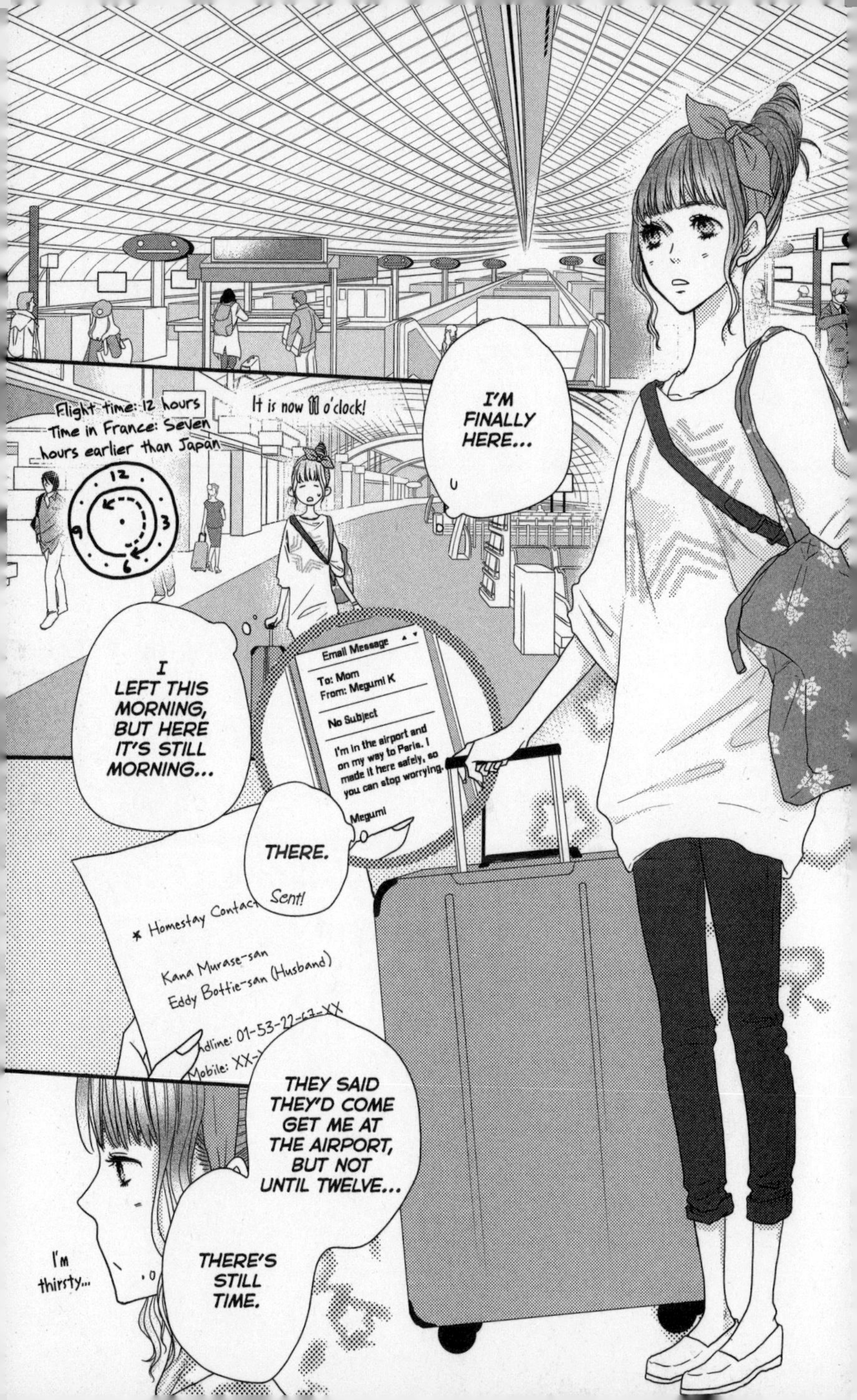
I'M FINALLY HERE...
It is now 11 o'clock!
Flight time: 12 hours
Time in France: Seven hours earlier than Japan
12
3
6
9
I LEFT THIS MORNING, BUT HERE IT'S STILL MORNING...
Email Message
To: Mom
From: Megumi K
No Subject
I'm in the airport and on my way to Paris. I made it here safely, so you can stop worrying.
Megumi
THERE.
Sent!
* Homestay Contact
Kana Murase-san
Eddy Bottie-san (Husband)
ndline: 01-53-22-67-XX
Mobile: XX-
THEY SAID THEY'D COME GET ME AT THE AIRPORT, BUT NOT UNTIL TWELVE...
THERE'S STILL TIME.
I'm thirsty...

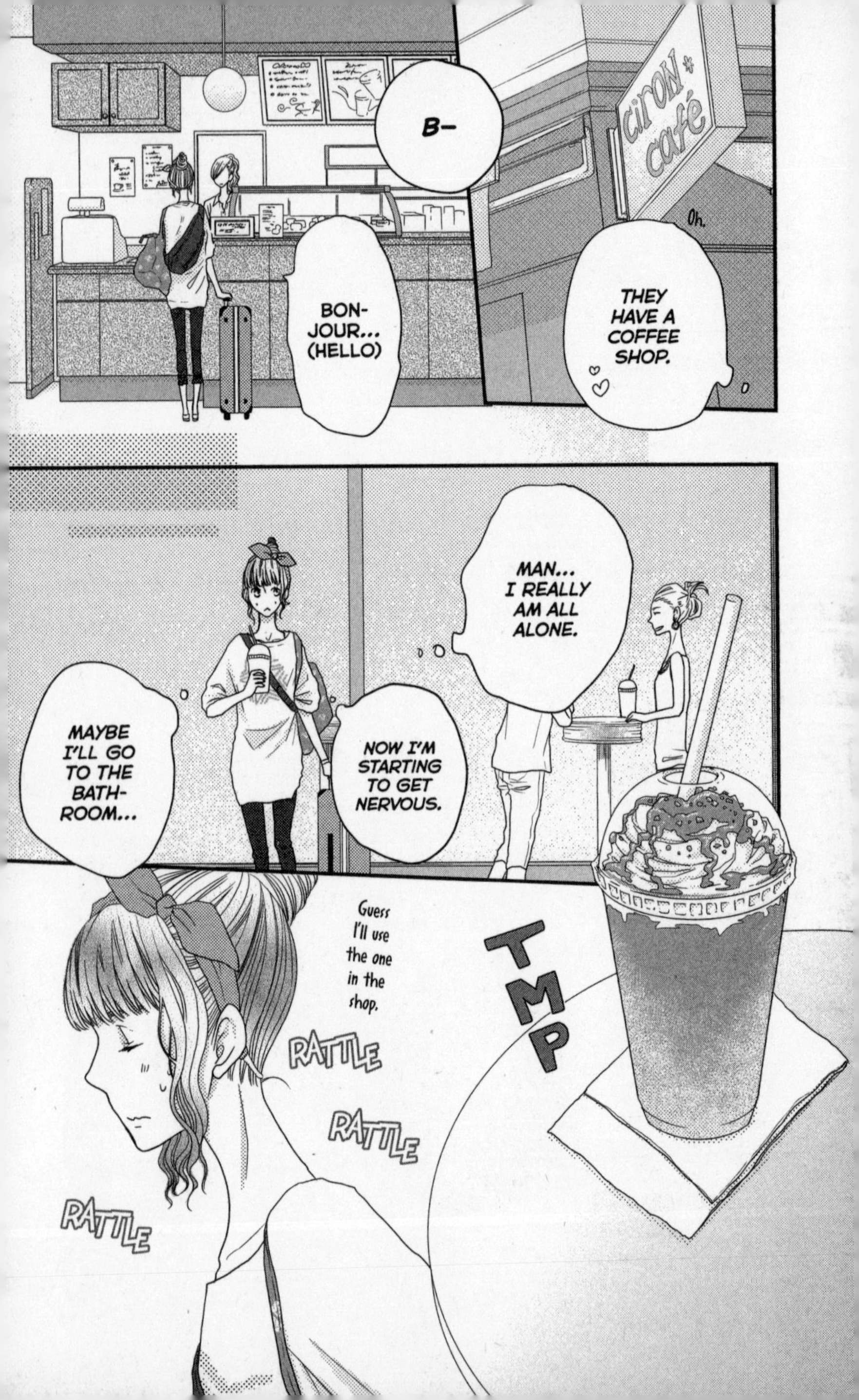
ciron café
Oh.
THEY HAVE A COFFEE SHOP.
B–
BON-JOUR... (HELLO)
MAN... I REALLY AM ALL ALONE.
NOW I'M STARTING TO GET NERVOUS.
MAYBE I'LL GO TO THE BATH-ROOM...
TMP
Guess I'll use the one in the shop.
RATTLE
RATTLE
RATTLE

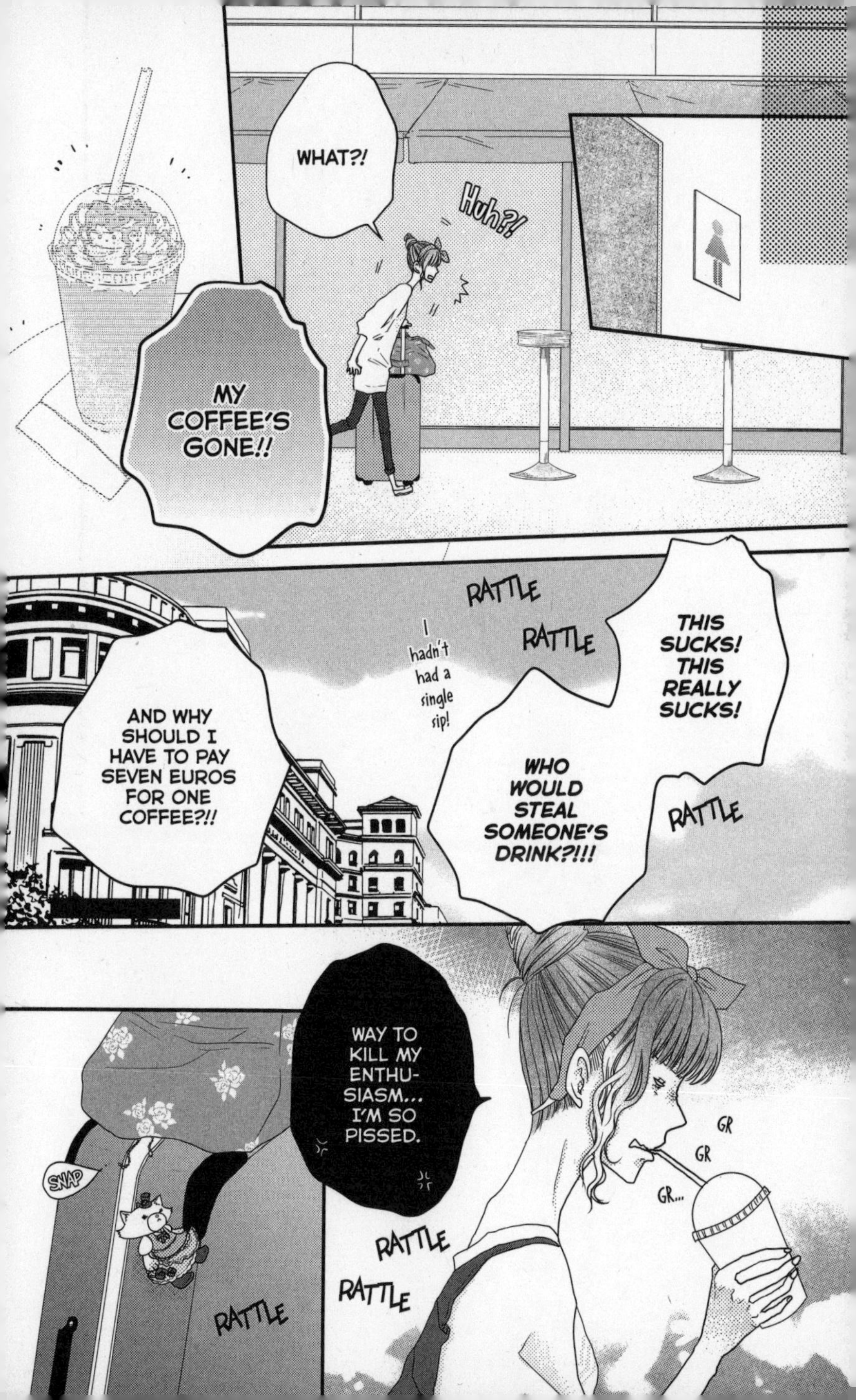
WHAT?!
Huh?!
MY COFFEE'S GONE!!
THIS SUCKS! THIS REALLY SUCKS!
RATTLE
RATTLE
WHO WOULD STEAL SOMEONE'S DRINK?!!!
RATTLE
I hadn't had a single sip!
AND WHY SHOULD I HAVE TO PAY SEVEN EUROS FOR ONE COFFEE?!!
GR
GR
GR...
RATTLE
RATTLE
WAY TO KILL MY ENTHUSIASM... I'M SO PISSED.
SNAP
RATTLE

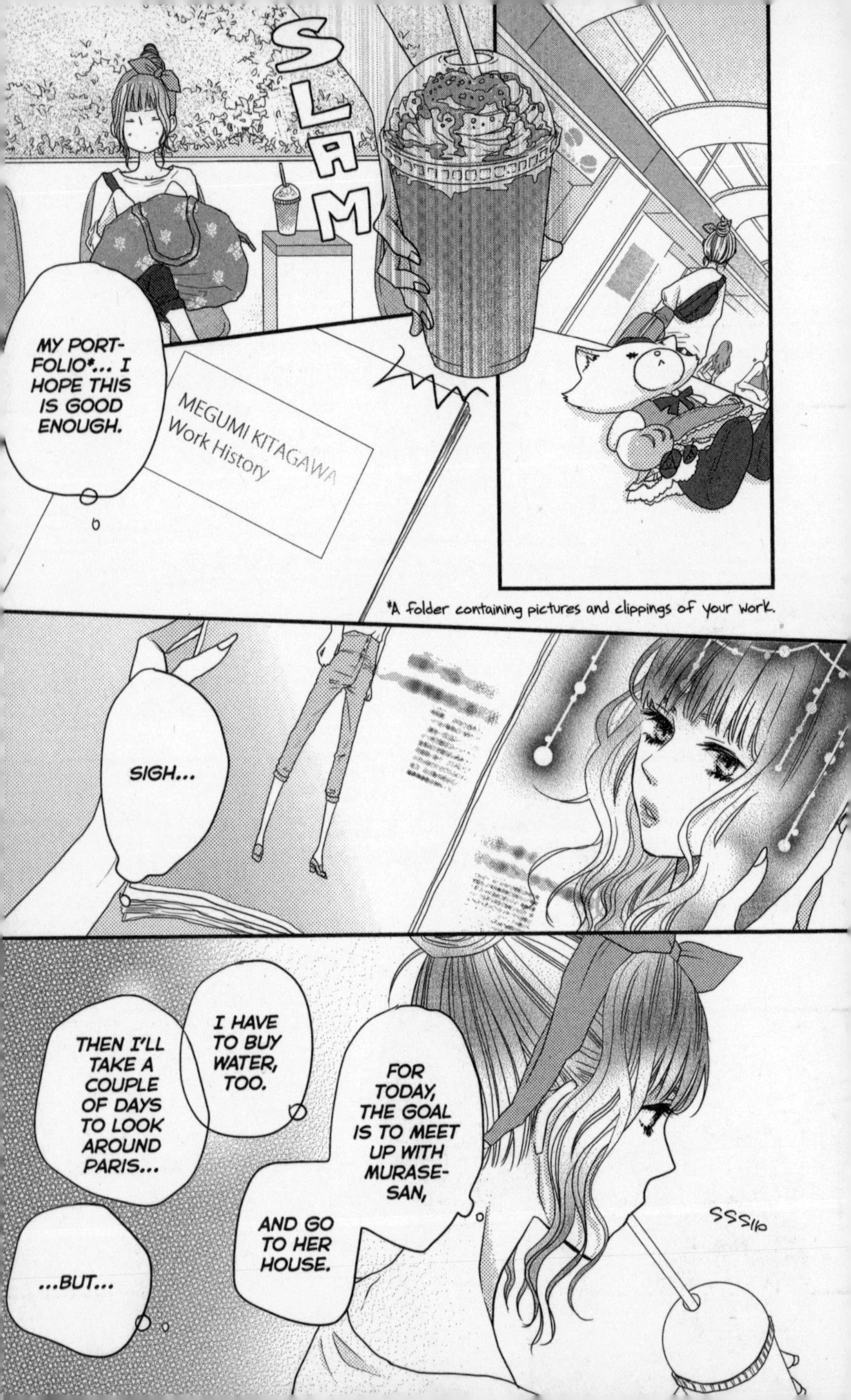
SLAM
MY PORTFOLIO*... I HOPE THIS IS GOOD ENOUGH.
MEGUMI KITAGAWA Work History
*A folder containing pictures and clippings of your work.
SIGH...
SSSIP
FOR TODAY, THE GOAL IS TO MEET UP WITH MURASE-SAN,
AND GO TO HER HOUSE.
I HAVE TO BUY WATER, TOO.
THEN I'LL TAKE A COUPLE OF DAYS TO LOOK AROUND PARIS...
...BUT...

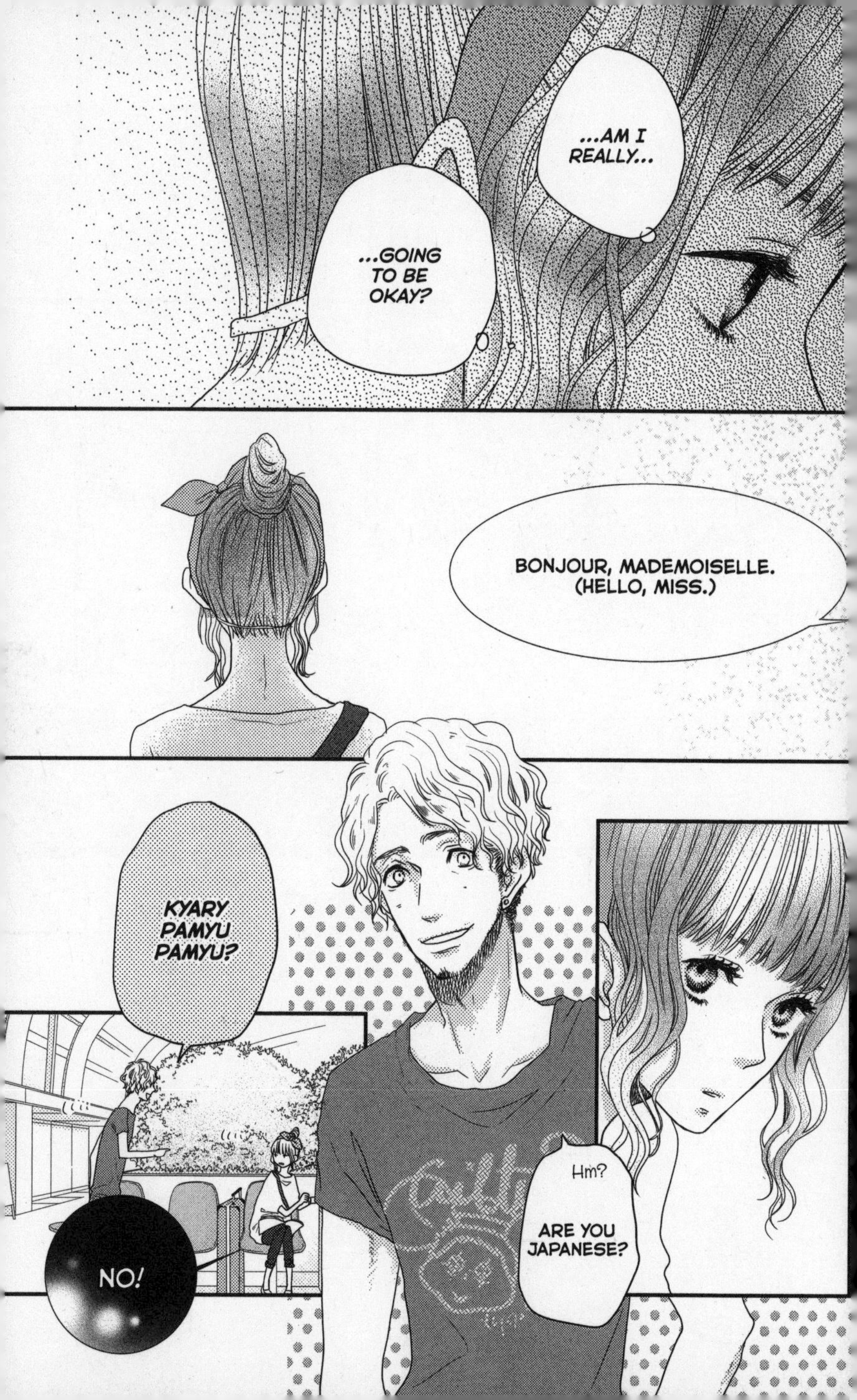
...AM I REALLY...
...GOING TO BE OKAY?
BONJOUR, MADEMOISELLE. (HELLO, MISS.)
Hm?
ARE YOU JAPANESE?
KYARY PAMYU PAMYU?
NO!

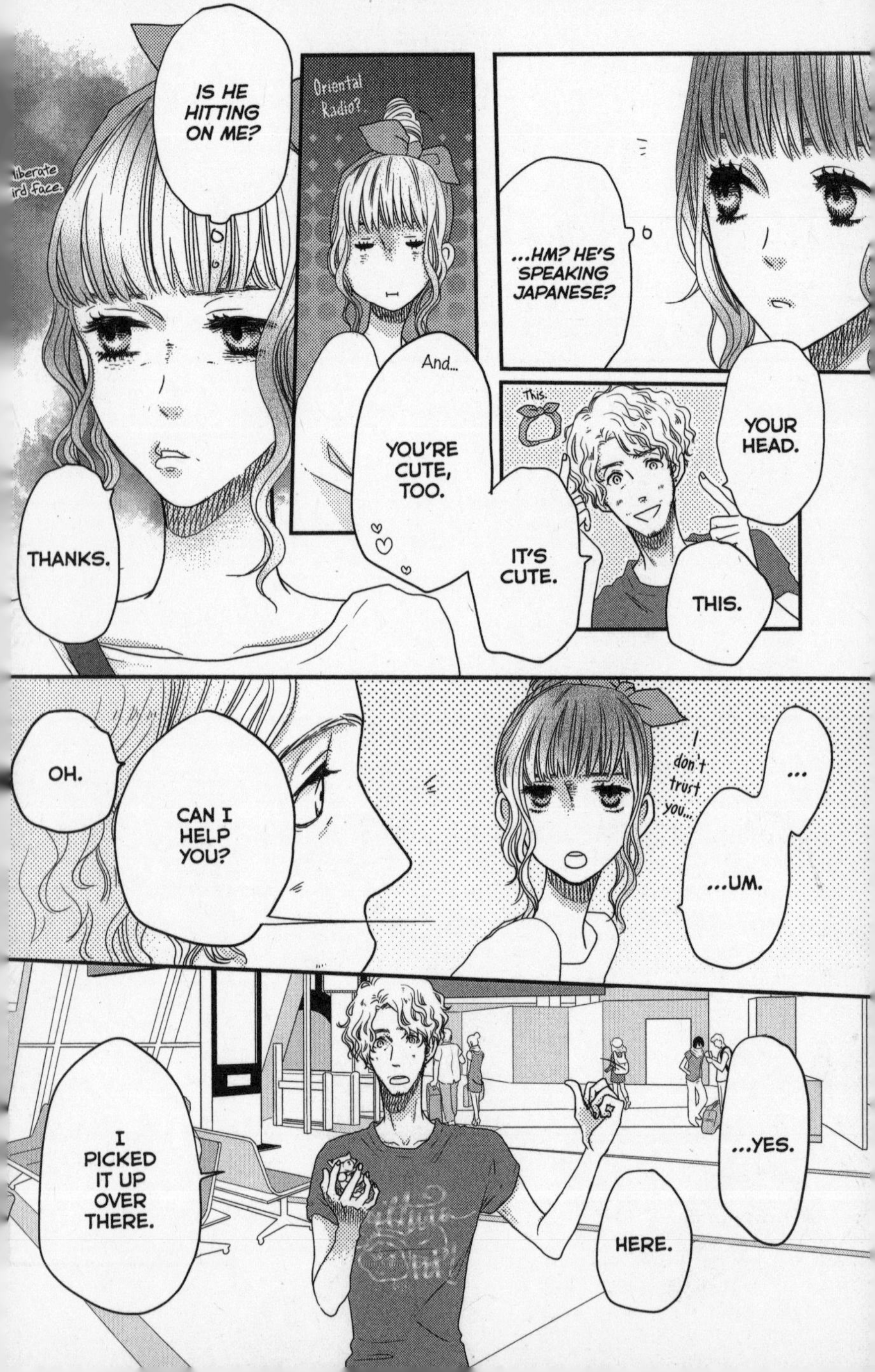
...HM? HE'S SPEAKING JAPANESE?
YOUR HEAD.
THIS.
This.
IT'S CUTE.
Oriental Radio?
And...
YOU'RE CUTE, TOO.
IS HE HITTING ON ME?
THANKS.
...
...UM.
I don't trust you...
CAN I HELP YOU?
OH.
...YES.
HERE.
I PICKED IT UP OVER THERE.

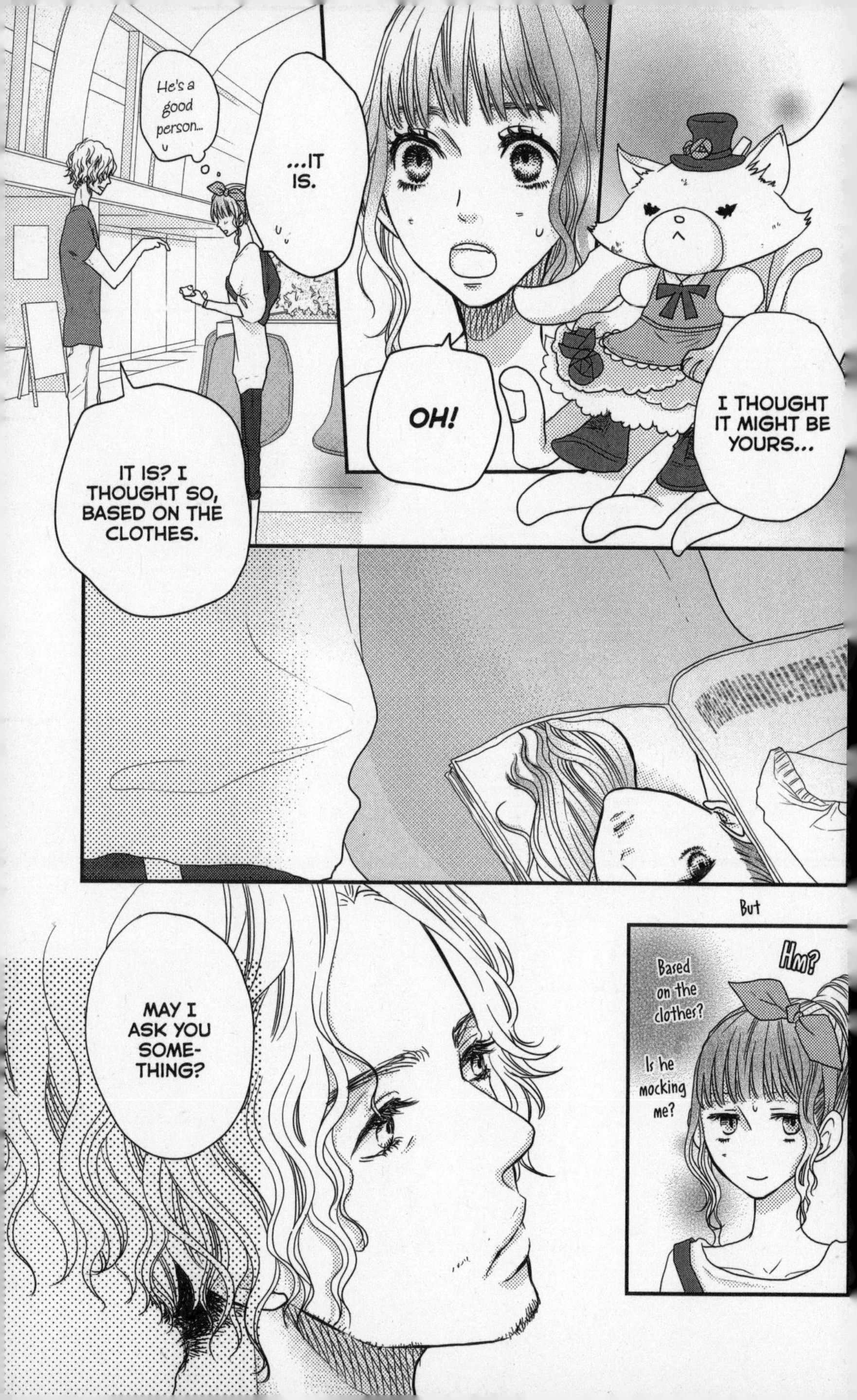
I THOUGHT IT MIGHT BE YOURS...
OH!
...IT IS.
He's a good person...
IT IS? I THOUGHT SO, BASED ON THE CLOTHES.
But
Hm?
Based on the clothes?
Is he mocking me?
MAY I ASK YOU SOMETHING?

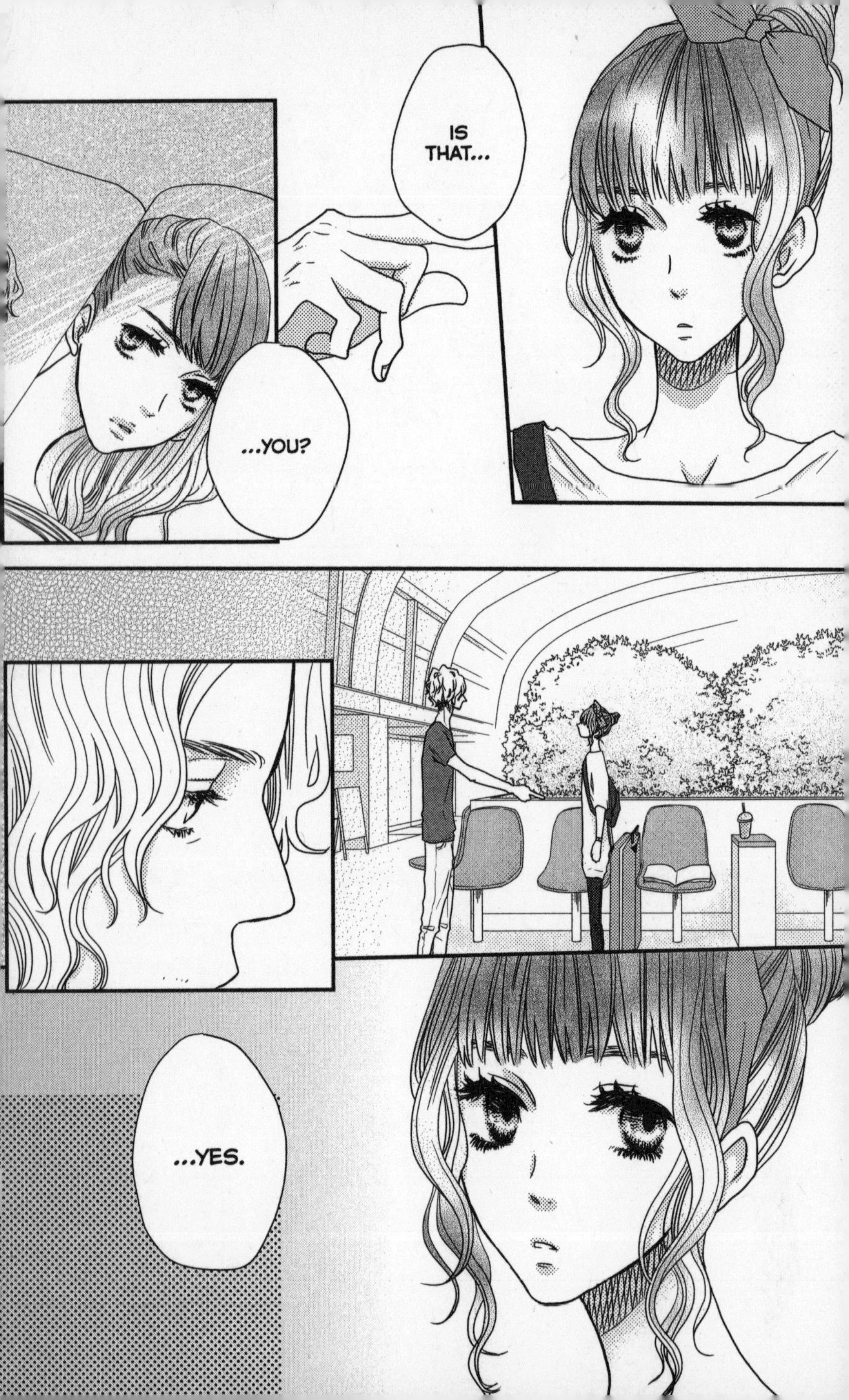
IS THAT...
...YOU?
...YES.

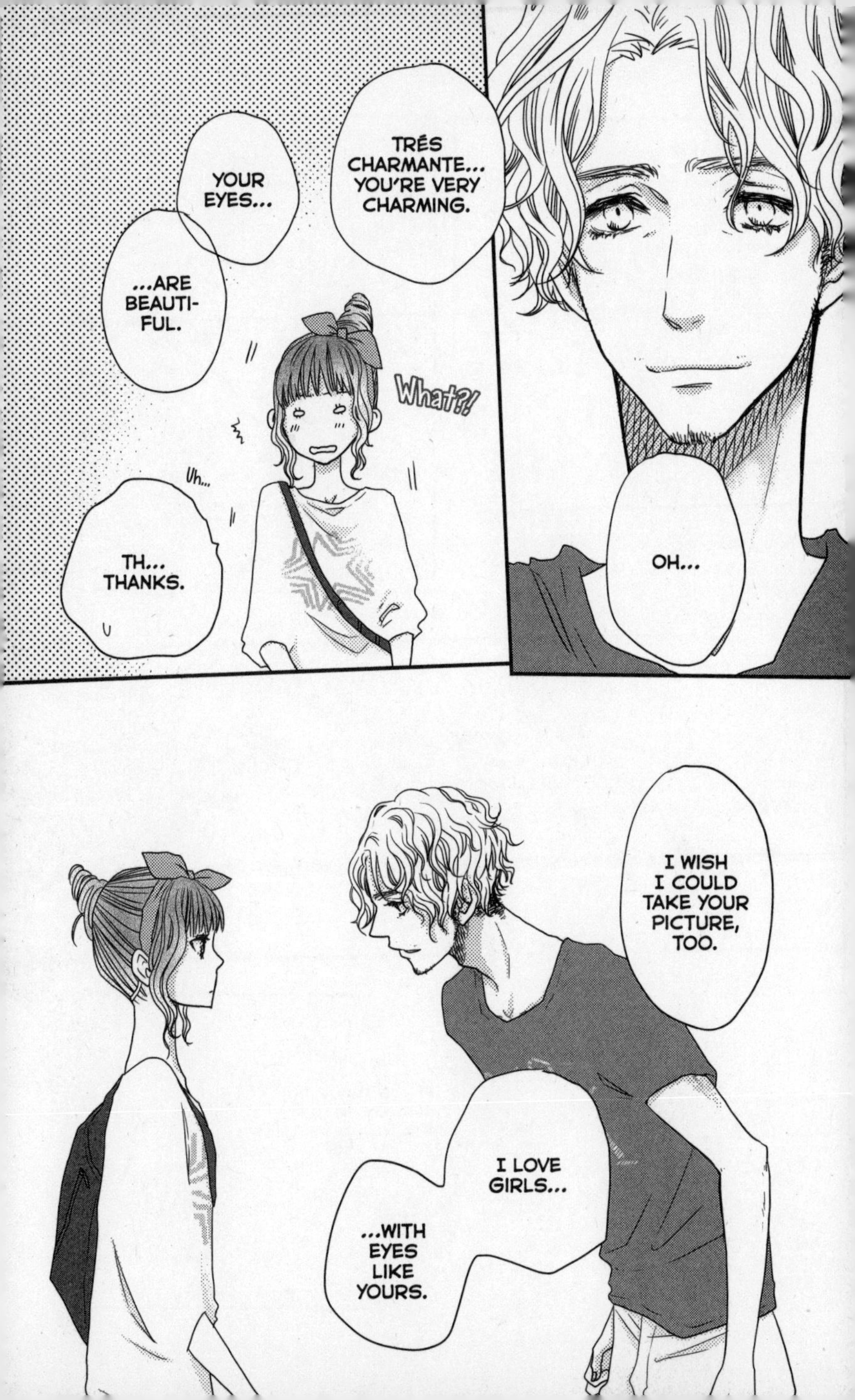
OH...
TRÉS CHARMANTE... YOU'RE VERY CHARMING.
YOUR EYES...
...ARE BEAUTIFUL.
What?!
Uh...
TH... THANKS.
I WISH I COULD TAKE YOUR PICTURE, TOO.
I LOVE GIRLS...
...WITH EYES LIKE YOURS.

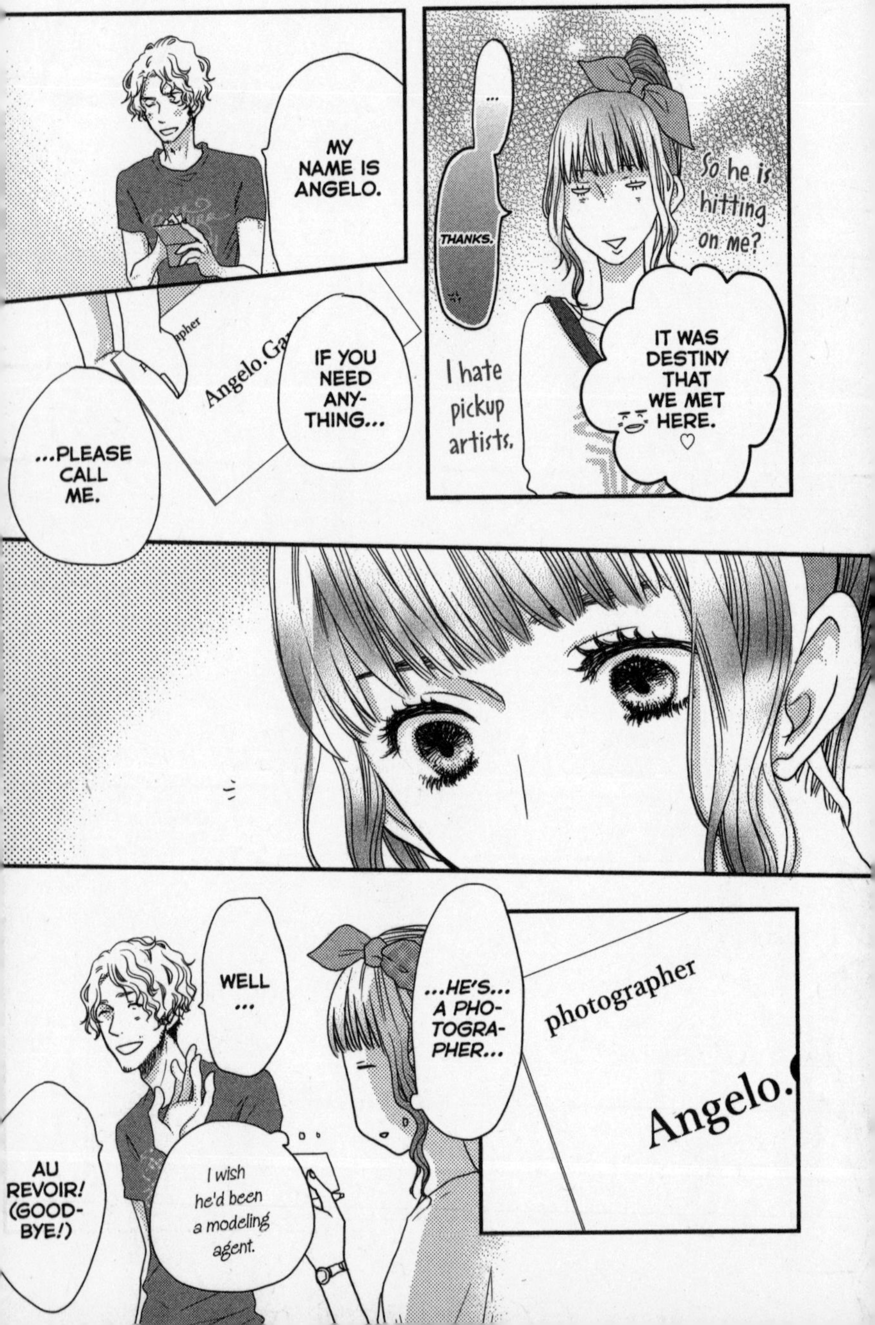
So he is hitting on me?
IT WAS DESTINY THAT WE MET HERE. ♡
...
THANKS.
I hate pickup artists.
MY NAME IS ANGELO.
IF YOU NEED ANY-THING...
...PLEASE CALL ME.
photographer
Angelo.
...HE'S... A PHO-TOGRA-PHER...
WELL ...
I wish he'd been a modeling agent.
AU REVOIR! (GOOD-BYE!)

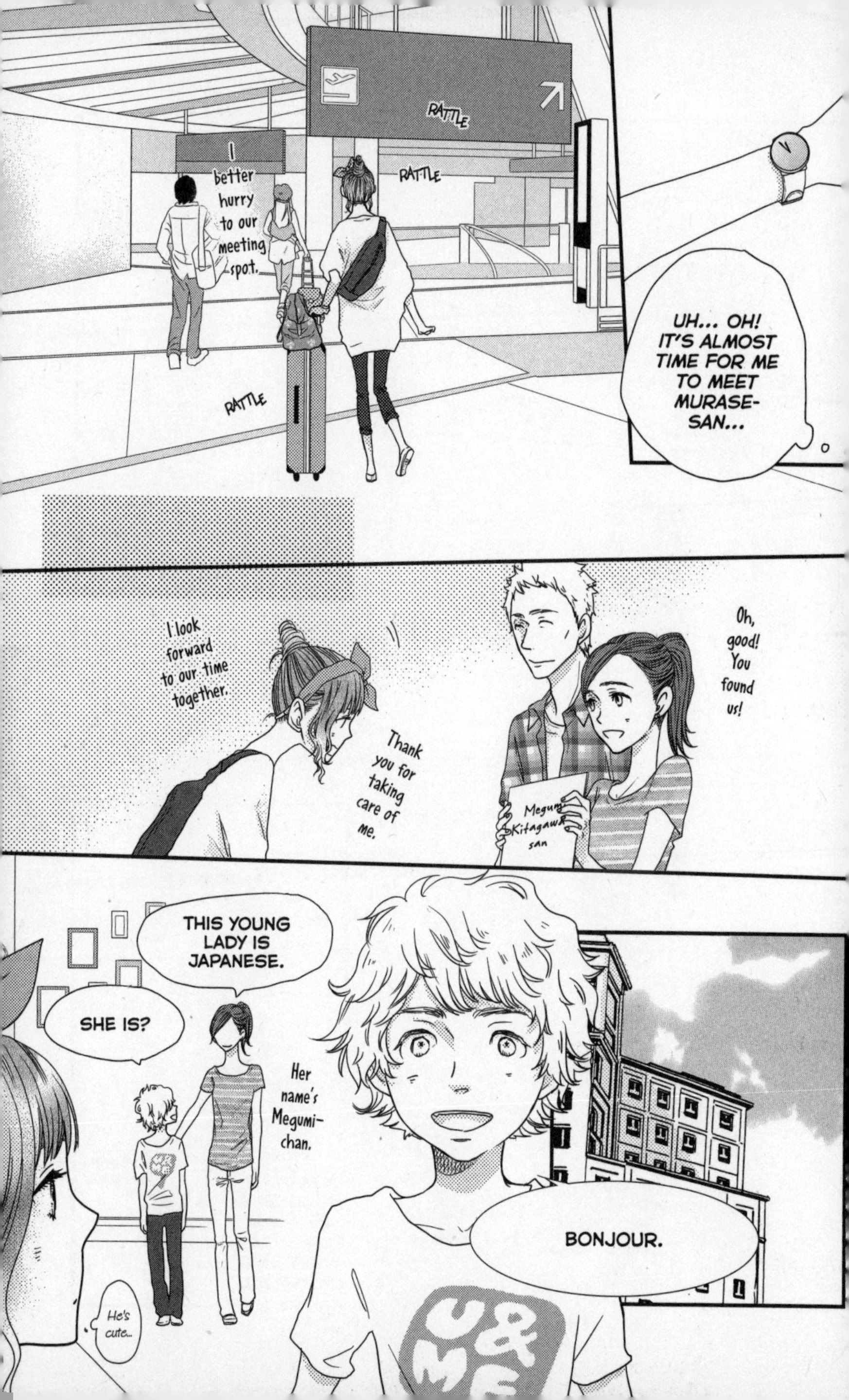
UH... OH! IT'S ALMOST TIME FOR ME TO MEET MURASE-SAN...
RATTLE
RATTLE
I better hurry to our meeting spot.
RATTLE
Oh, good! You found us!
Megumi Kitagawa san
Thank you for taking care of me.
I look forward to our time together.
THIS YOUNG LADY IS JAPANESE.
SHE IS?
Her name's Megumi-chan.
BONJOUR.
He's cute...

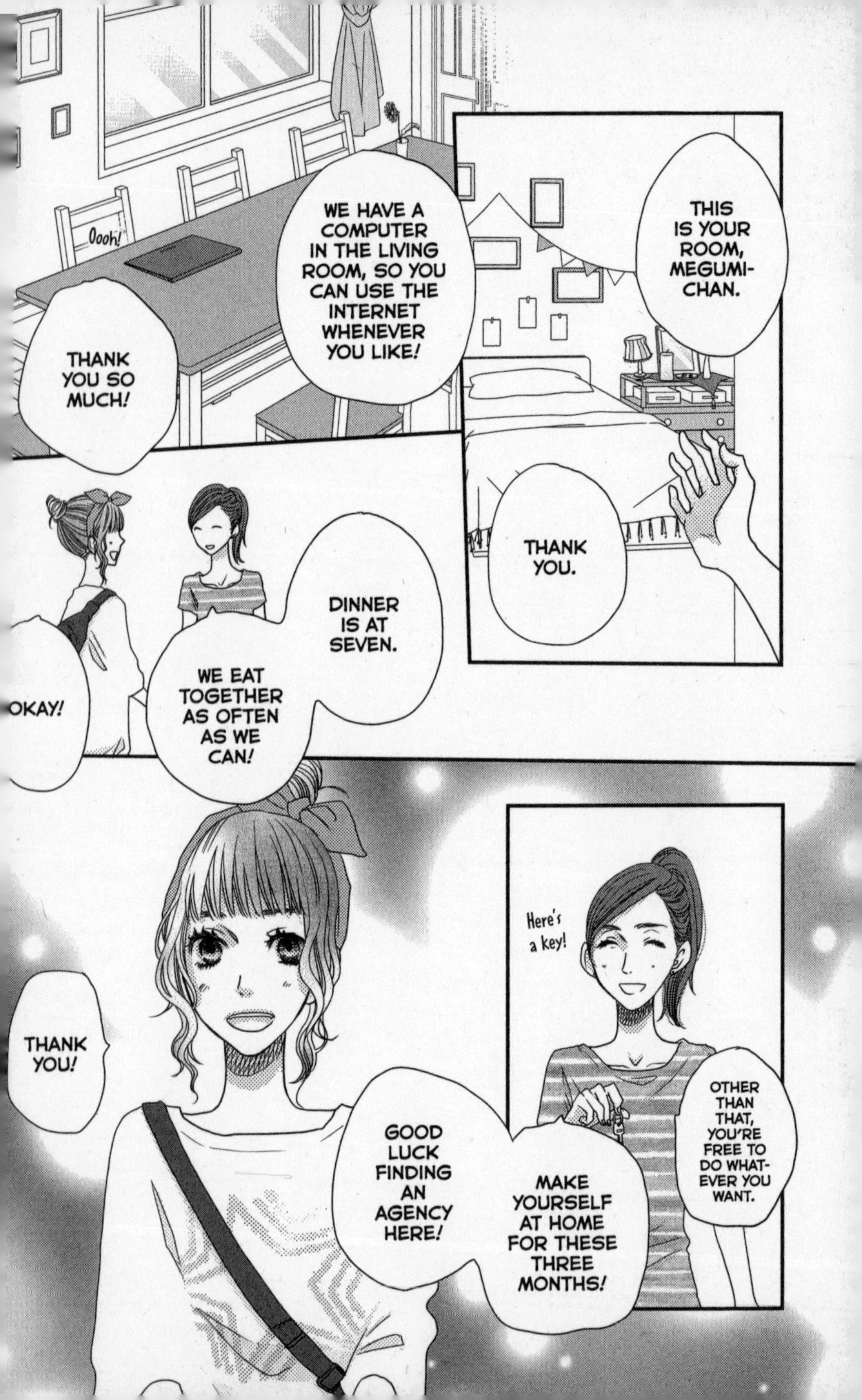
THIS IS YOUR ROOM, MEGUMI-CHAN.
THANK YOU.
WE HAVE A COMPUTER IN THE LIVING ROOM, SO YOU CAN USE THE INTERNET WHENEVER YOU LIKE!
Oooh!
THANK YOU SO MUCH!
DINNER IS AT SEVEN.
WE EAT TOGETHER AS OFTEN AS WE CAN!
OKAY!
Here's a key!
OTHER THAN THAT, YOU'RE FREE TO DO WHATEVER YOU WANT.
MAKE YOURSELF AT HOME FOR THESE THREE MONTHS!
GOOD LUCK FINDING AN AGENCY HERE!
THANK YOU!

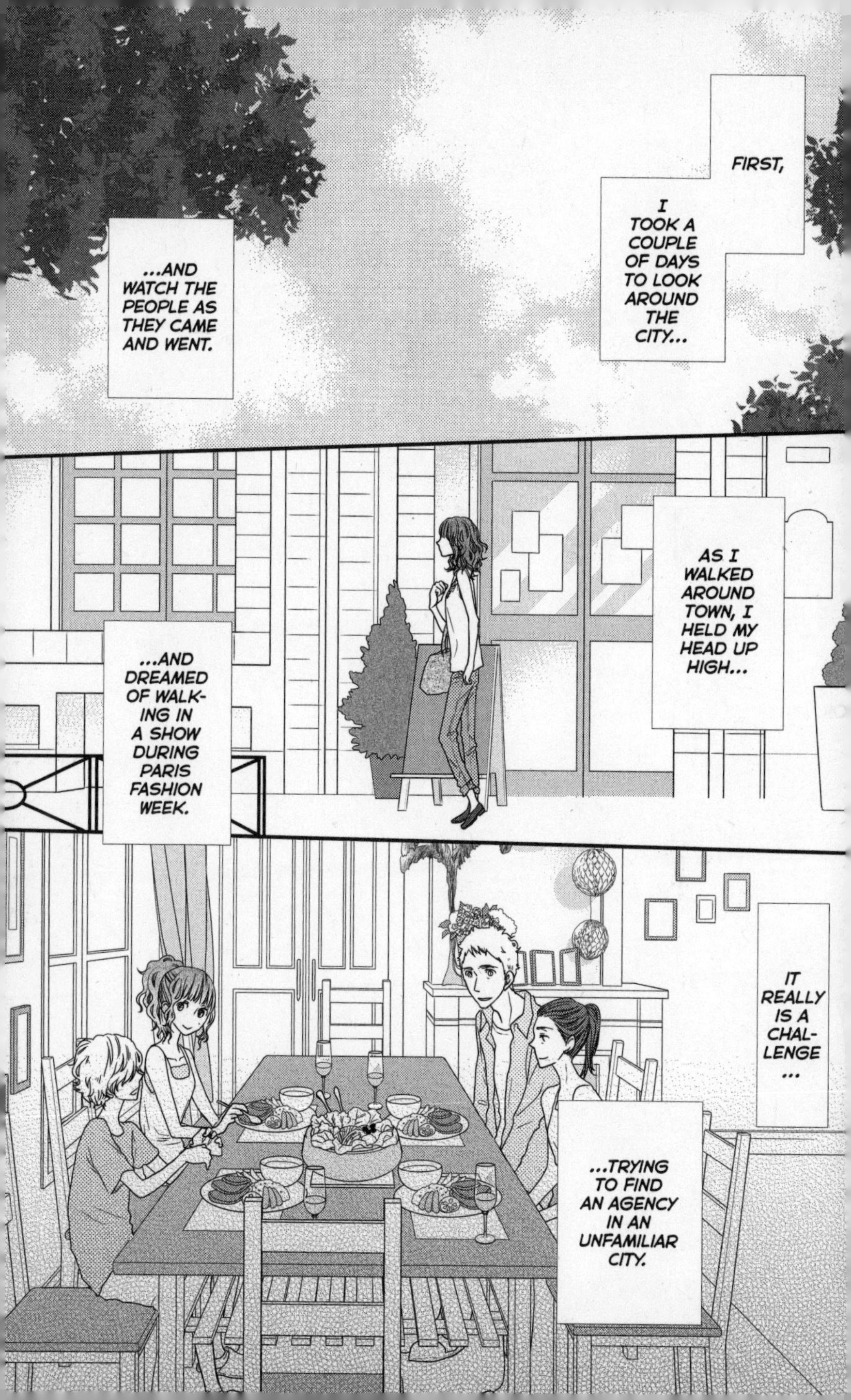
FIRST, I TOOK A COUPLE OF DAYS TO LOOK AROUND THE CITY...
...AND WATCH THE PEOPLE AS THEY CAME AND WENT.
AS I WALKED AROUND TOWN, I HELD MY HEAD UP HIGH...
...AND DREAMED OF WALKING IN A SHOW DURING PARIS FASHION WEEK.
IT REALLY IS A CHALLENGE...
...TRYING TO FIND AN AGENCY IN AN UNFAMILIAR CITY.

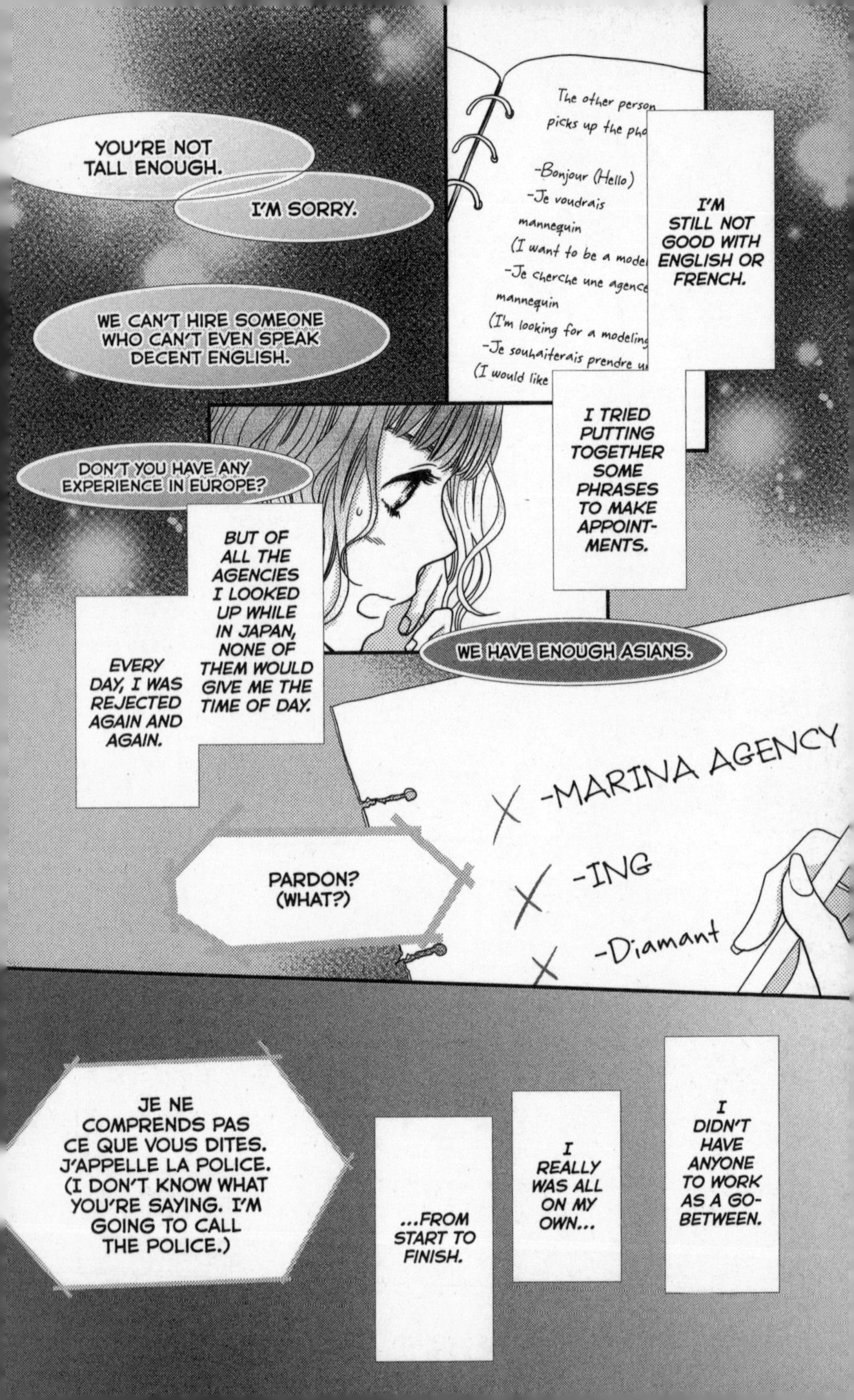
The other person
picks up the pho
-Bonjour (Hello)
-Je voudrais
mannequin
(I want to be a model
-Je cherche une agence
mannequin
(I'm looking for a modeling
-Je souhaiterais prendre u
(I would like
I'M STILL NOT GOOD WITH ENGLISH OR FRENCH.
I TRIED PUTTING TOGETHER SOME PHRASES TO MAKE APPOINT-MENTS.
YOU'RE NOT TALL ENOUGH.
I'M SORRY.
WE CAN'T HIRE SOMEONE WHO CAN'T EVEN SPEAK DECENT ENGLISH.
DON'T YOU HAVE ANY EXPERIENCE IN EUROPE?
BUT OF ALL THE AGENCIES I LOOKED UP WHILE IN JAPAN, NONE OF THEM WOULD GIVE ME THE TIME OF DAY.
EVERY DAY, I WAS REJECTED AGAIN AND AGAIN.
WE HAVE ENOUGH ASIANS.
X -MARINA AGENCY
X -ING
X -Diamant
PARDON? (WHAT?)
I DIDN'T HAVE ANYONE TO WORK AS A GO-BETWEEN.
I REALLY WAS ALL ON MY OWN...
...FROM START TO FINISH.
JE NE COMPRENDS PAS CE QUE VOUS DITES. J'APPELLE LA POLICE. (I DON'T KNOW WHAT YOU'RE SAYING. I'M GOING TO CALL THE POLICE.)

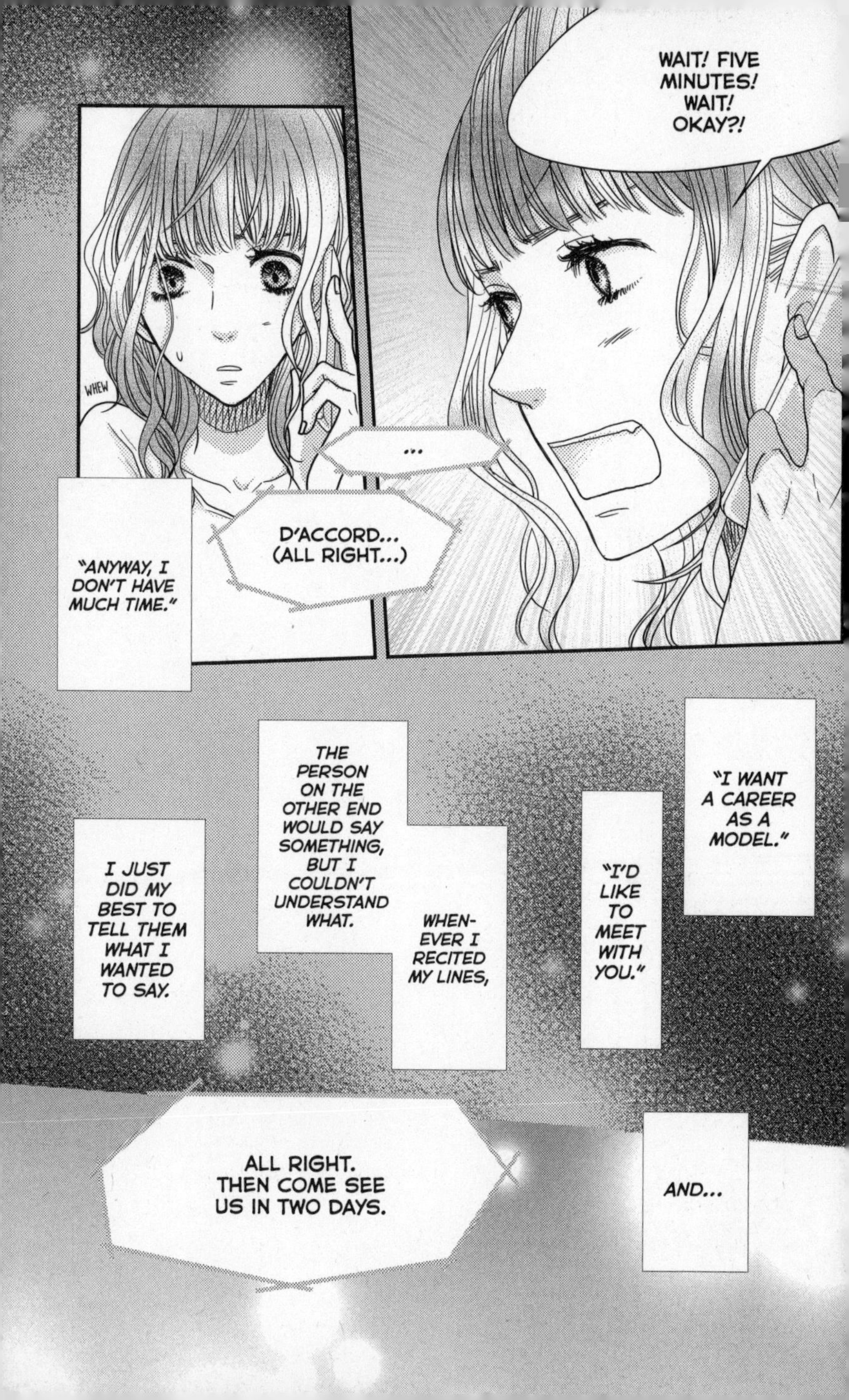
WAIT! FIVE MINUTES! WAIT! OKAY?!
...
WHEW
D'ACCORD... (ALL RIGHT...)
"ANYWAY, I DON'T HAVE MUCH TIME."
"I WANT A CAREER AS A MODEL."
"I'D LIKE TO MEET WITH YOU."
WHEN-EVER I RECITED MY LINES,
THE PERSON ON THE OTHER END WOULD SAY SOMETHING, BUT I COULDN'T UNDERSTAND WHAT.
I JUST DID MY BEST TO TELL THEM WHAT I WANTED TO SAY.
AND...
ALL RIGHT. THEN COME SEE US IN TWO DAYS.

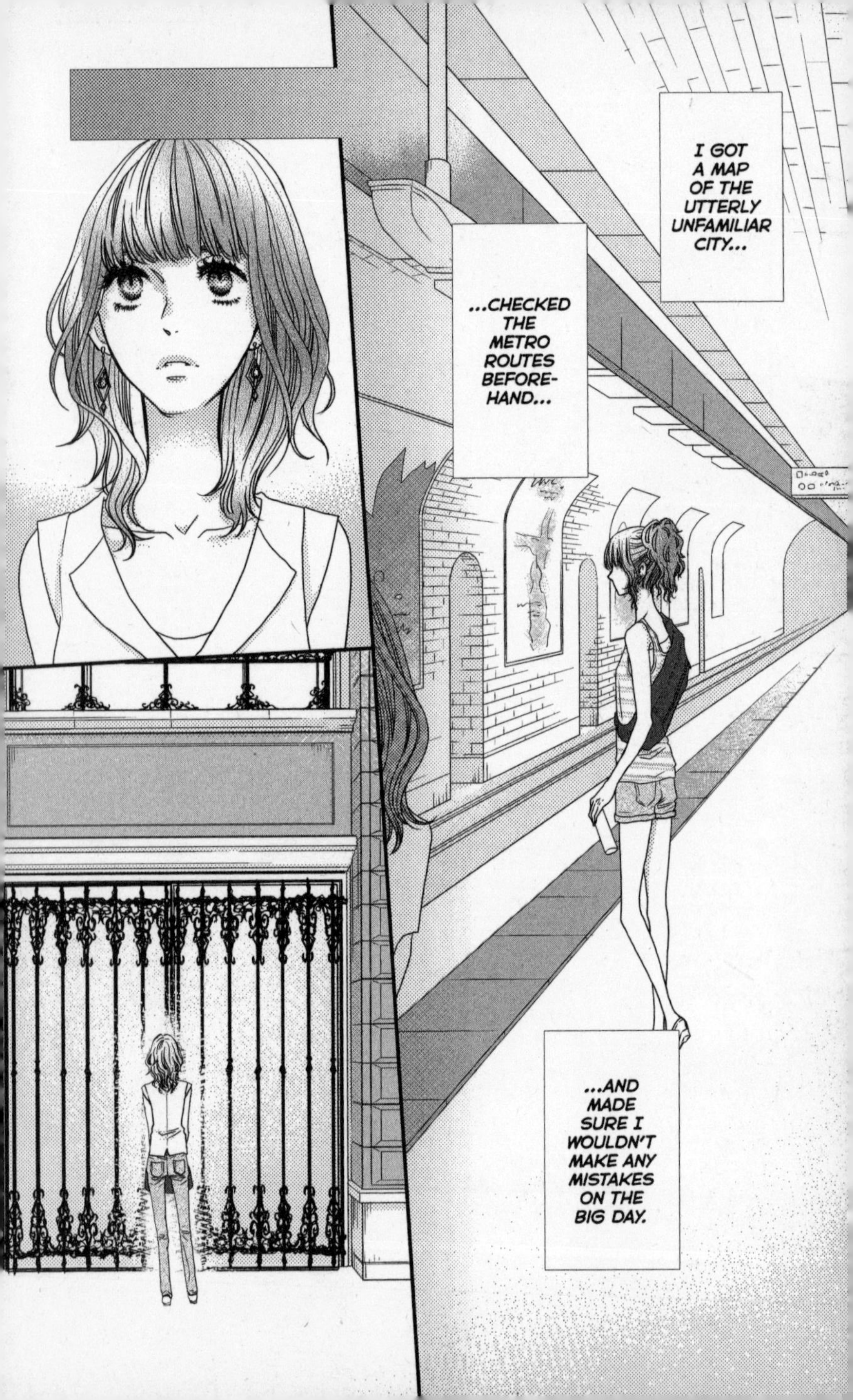
I GOT A MAP OF THE UTTERLY UNFAMILIAR CITY...
...CHECKED THE METRO ROUTES BEFORE-HAND...
...AND MADE SURE I WOULDN'T MAKE ANY MISTAKES ON THE BIG DAY.

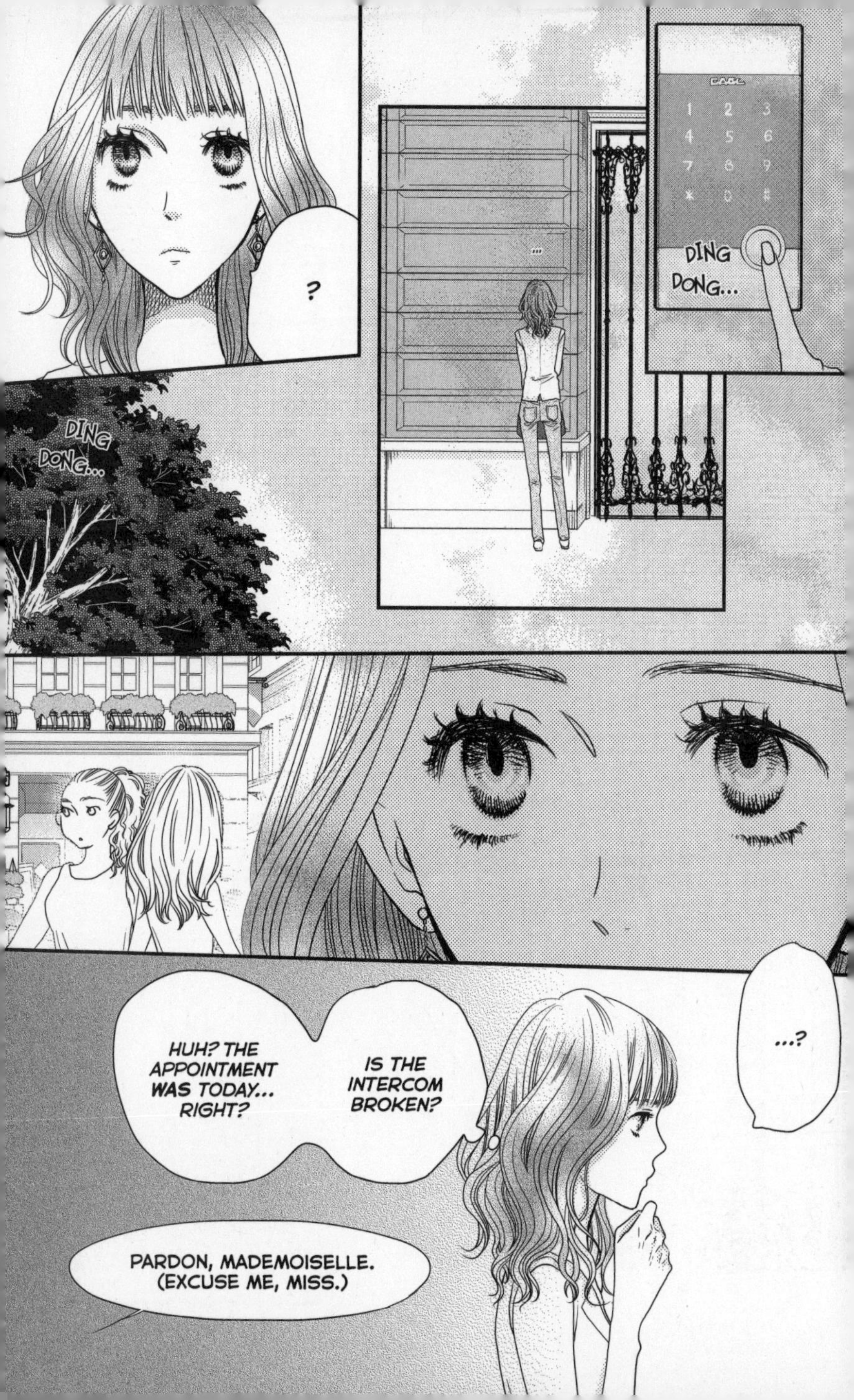
DING DONG...
...
?
DING DONG...
...?
IS THE INTERCOM BROKEN?
HUH? THE APPOINTMENT WAS TODAY... RIGHT?
PARDON, MADEMOISELLE. (EXCUSE ME, MISS.)

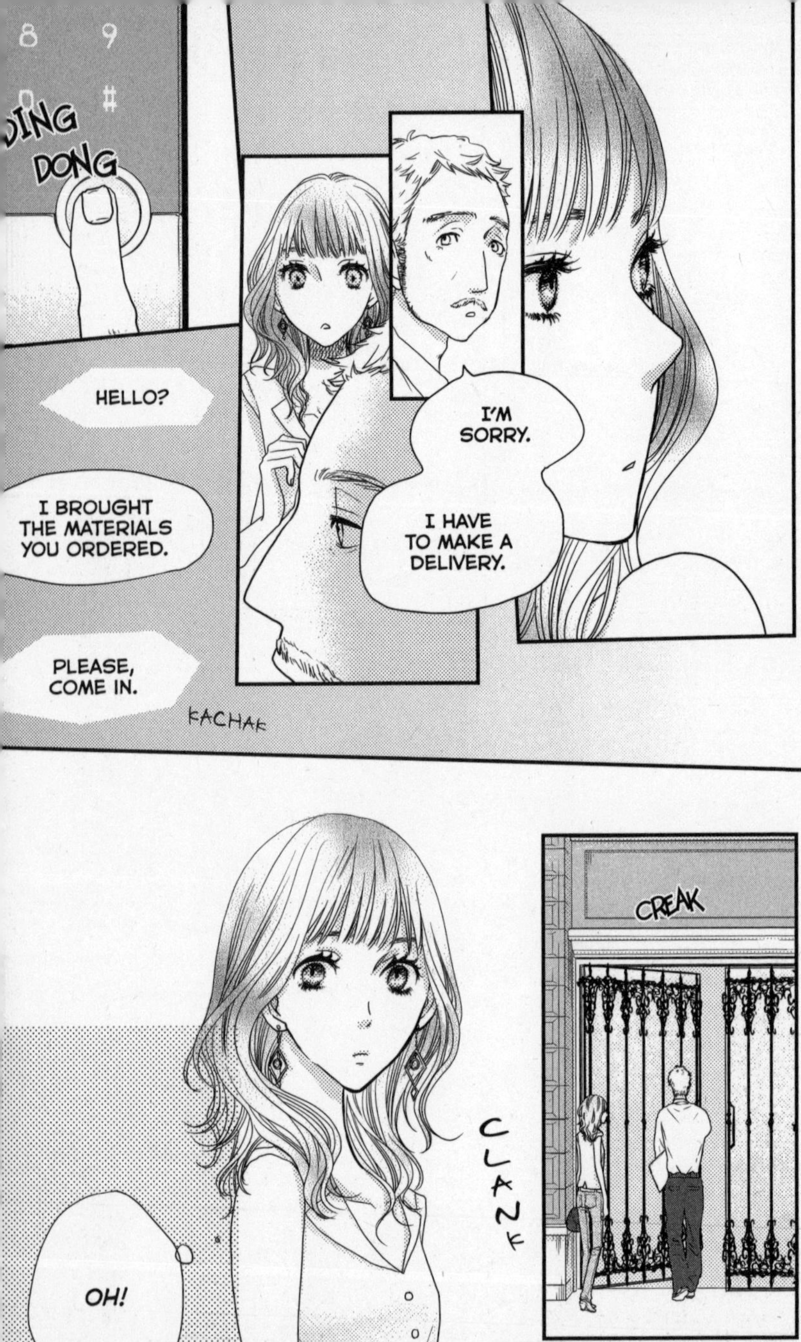
I'M SORRY.
I HAVE TO MAKE A DELIVERY.
DING DONG
HELLO?
I BROUGHT THE MATERIALS YOU ORDERED.
PLEASE, COME IN.
KACHAK
CREAK
CLANK
OH!

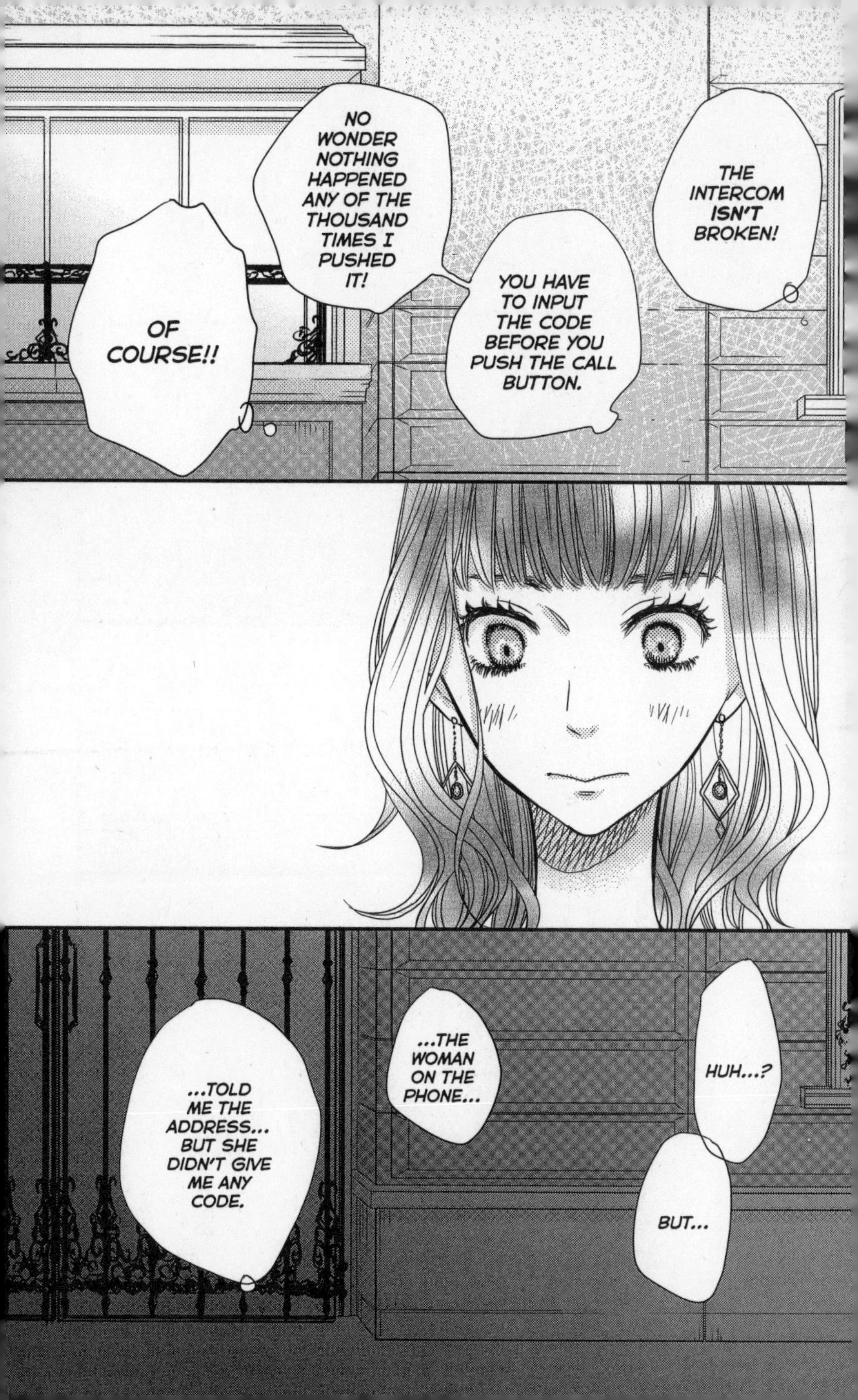
THE INTERCOM ISN'T BROKEN!
YOU HAVE TO INPUT THE CODE BEFORE YOU PUSH THE CALL BUTTON.
NO WONDER NOTHING HAPPENED ANY OF THE THOUSAND TIMES I PUSHED IT!
OF COURSE!!
HUH...?
BUT...
...THE WOMAN ON THE PHONE...
...TOLD ME THE ADDRESS... BUT SHE DIDN'T GIVE ME ANY CODE.

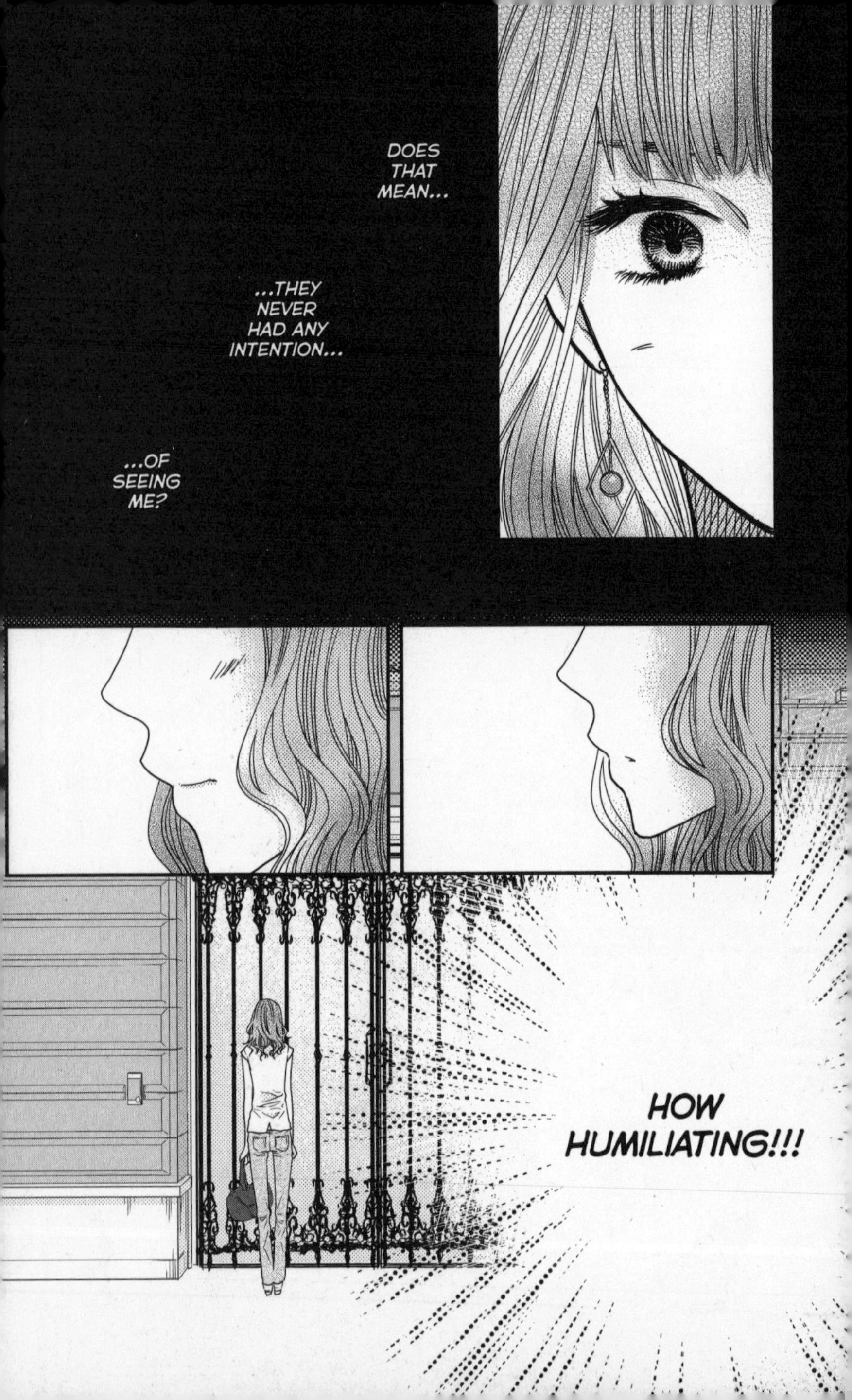
DOES THAT MEAN...
...THEY NEVER HAD ANY INTENTION...
...OF SEEING ME?
HOW HUMILIATING!!!

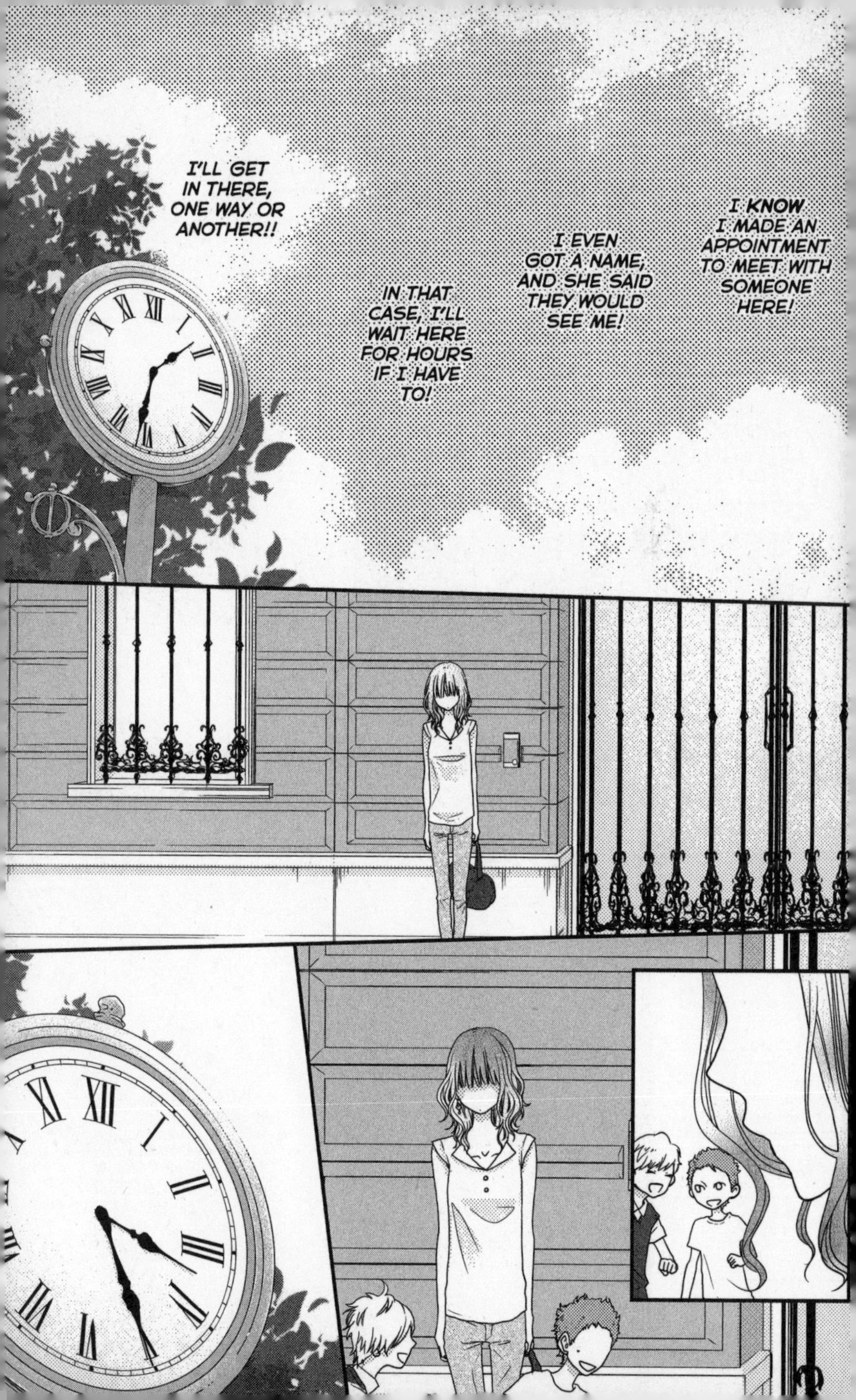
I KNOW I MADE AN APPOINTMENT TO MEET WITH SOMEONE HERE!
I EVEN GOT A NAME, AND SHE SAID THEY WOULD SEE ME!
IN THAT CASE, I'LL WAIT HERE FOR HOURS IF I HAVE TO!
I'LL GET IN THERE, ONE WAY OR ANOTHER!!

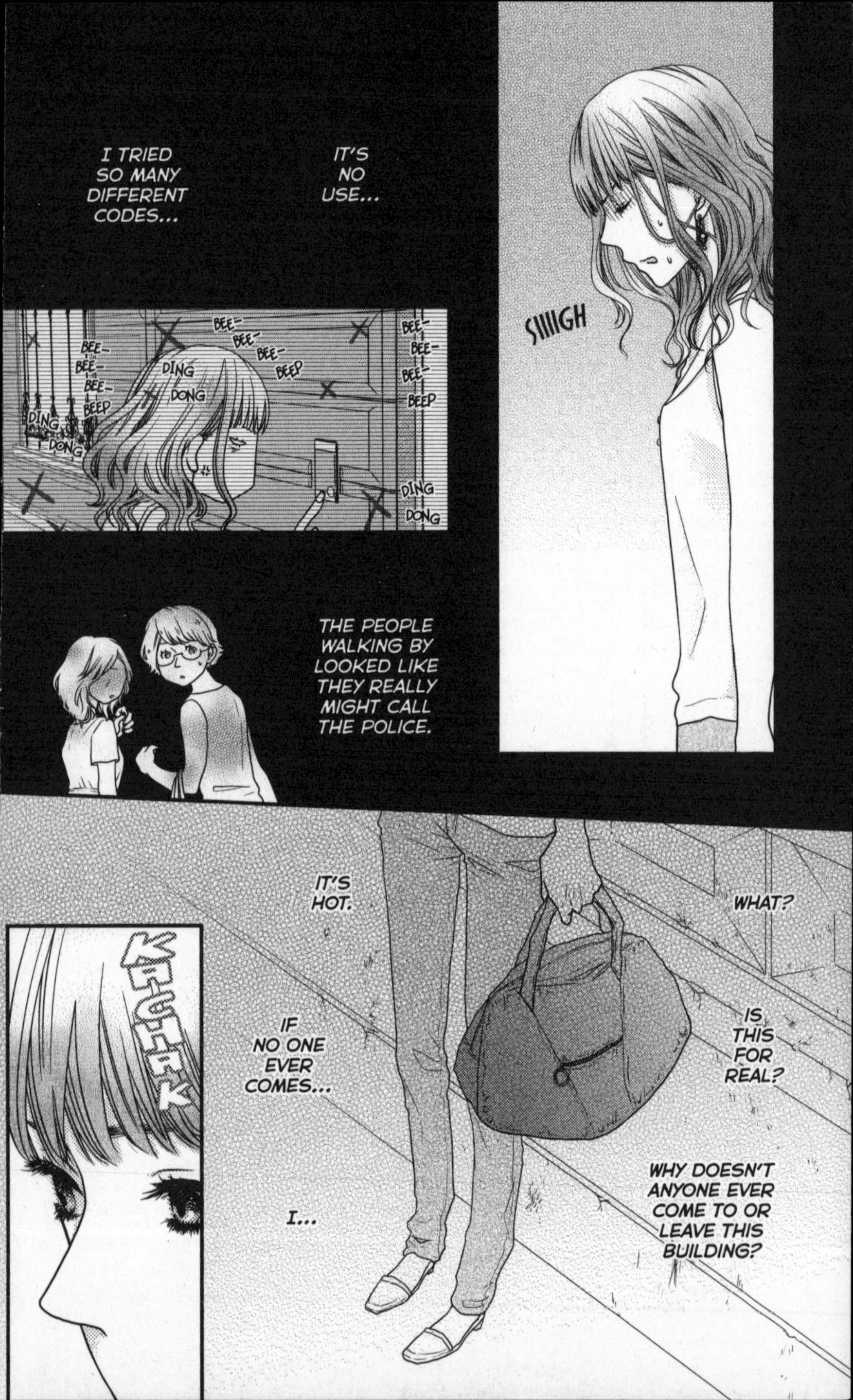
SIIIGH
IT'S NO USE...
I TRIED SO MANY DIFFERENT CODES...
BEE- BEE- BEE- BEEP
BEE- BEE- BEE- BEEP
DING DONG
BEE- BEE- BEE- BEEP
DING DONG
BEE- BEE- BEE- BEEP
DING DONG
THE PEOPLE WALKING BY LOOKED LIKE THEY REALLY MIGHT CALL THE POLICE.
WHAT?
IS THIS FOR REAL?
WHY DOESN'T ANYONE EVER COME TO OR LEAVE THIS BUILDING?
IT'S HOT.
IF NO ONE EVER COMES...
I...
KACHAK

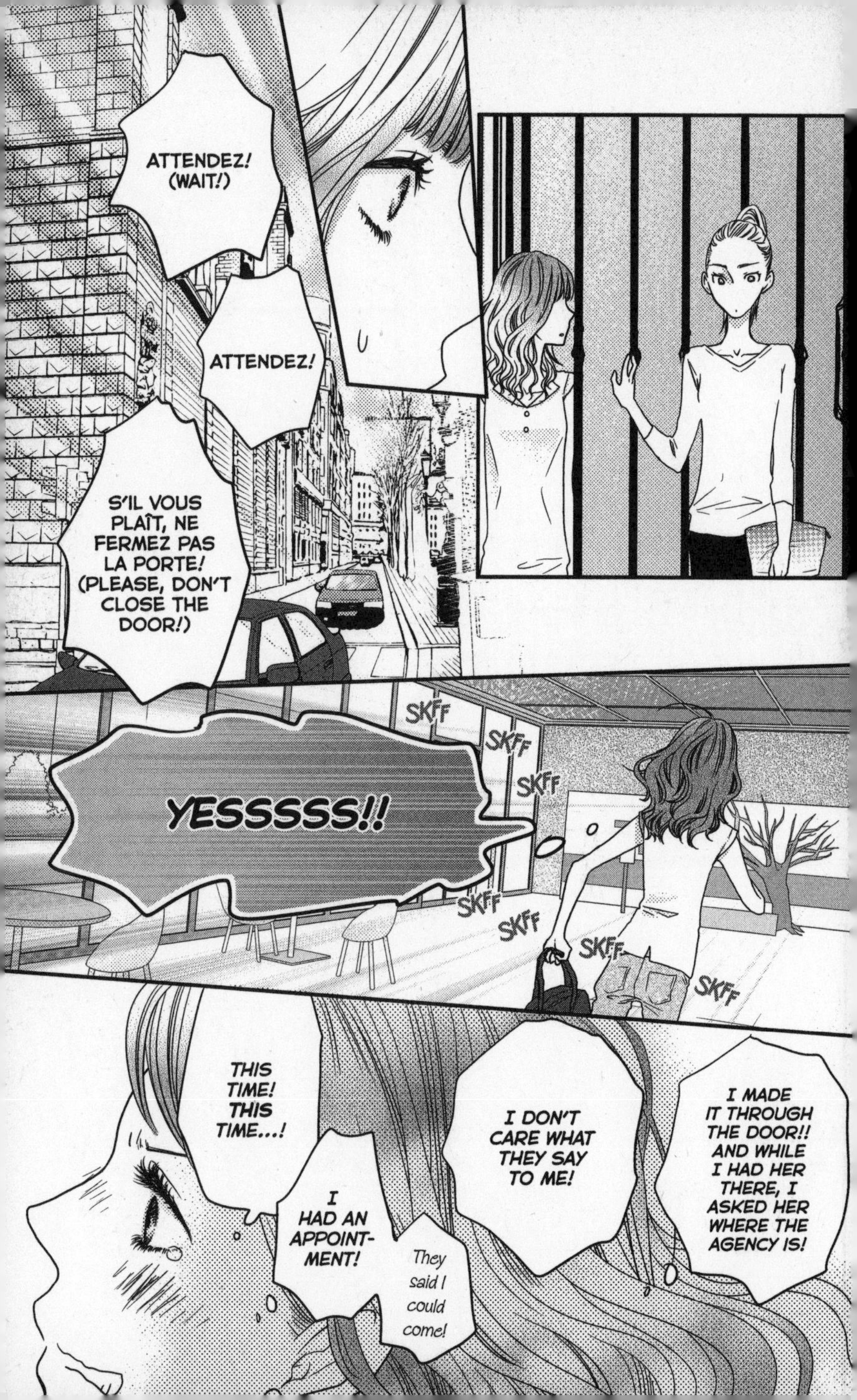
ATTENDEZ! (WAIT!)
ATTENDEZ!
S'IL VOUS PLAÎT, NE FERMEZ PAS LA PORTE! (PLEASE, DON'T CLOSE THE DOOR!)
SKFF
SKFF
SKFF
YESSSSS!!
SKFF
SKFF
SKFF
SKFF
I MADE IT THROUGH THE DOOR!! AND WHILE I HAD HER THERE, I ASKED HER WHERE THE AGENCY IS!
I DON'T CARE WHAT THEY SAY TO ME!
THIS TIME! THIS TIME...!
I HAD AN APPOINT-MENT!
They said I could come!

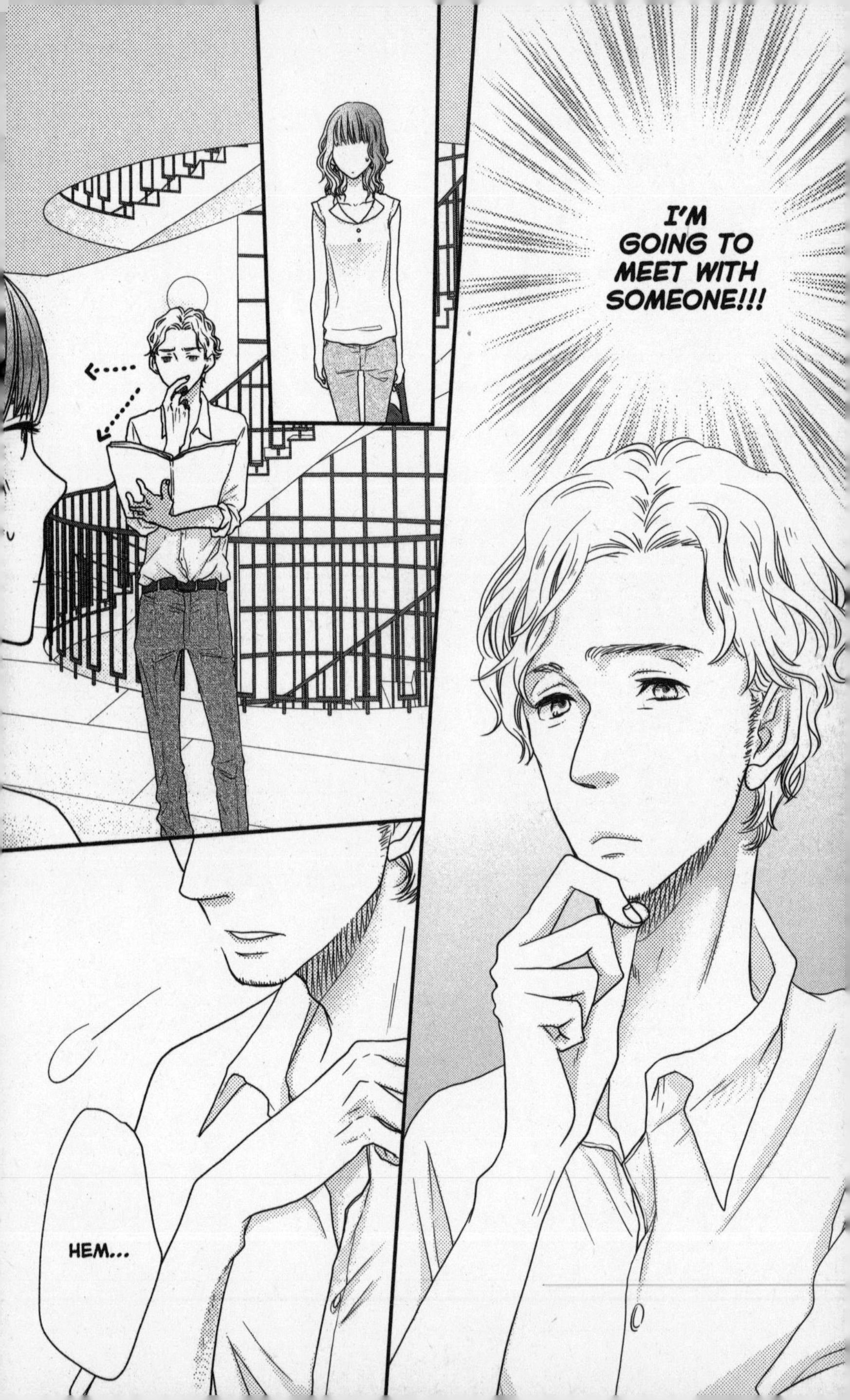
I'M GOING TO MEET WITH SOMEONE!!!
HEM...

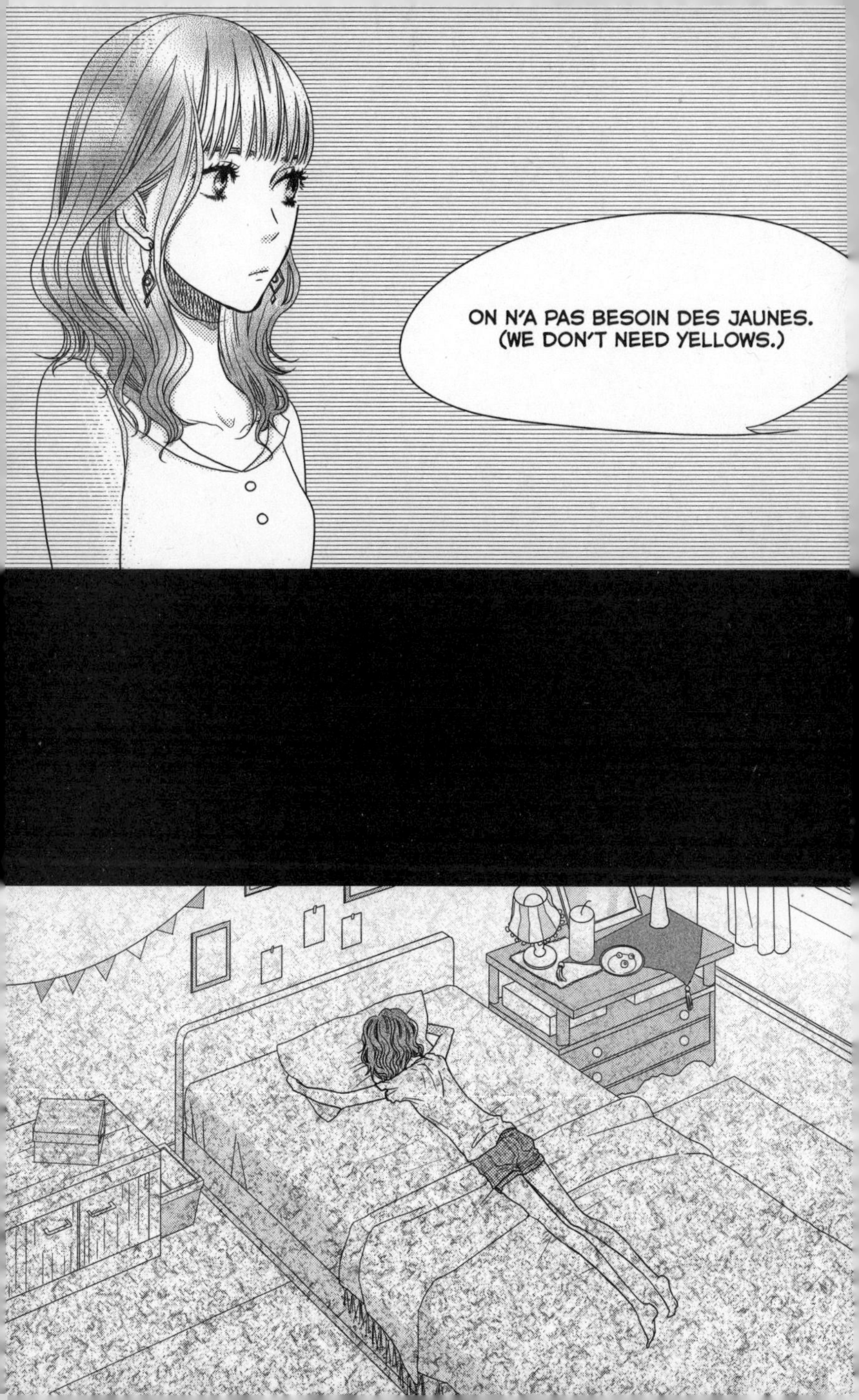
ON N'A PAS BESOIN DES JAUNES. (WE DON'T NEED YELLOWS.)

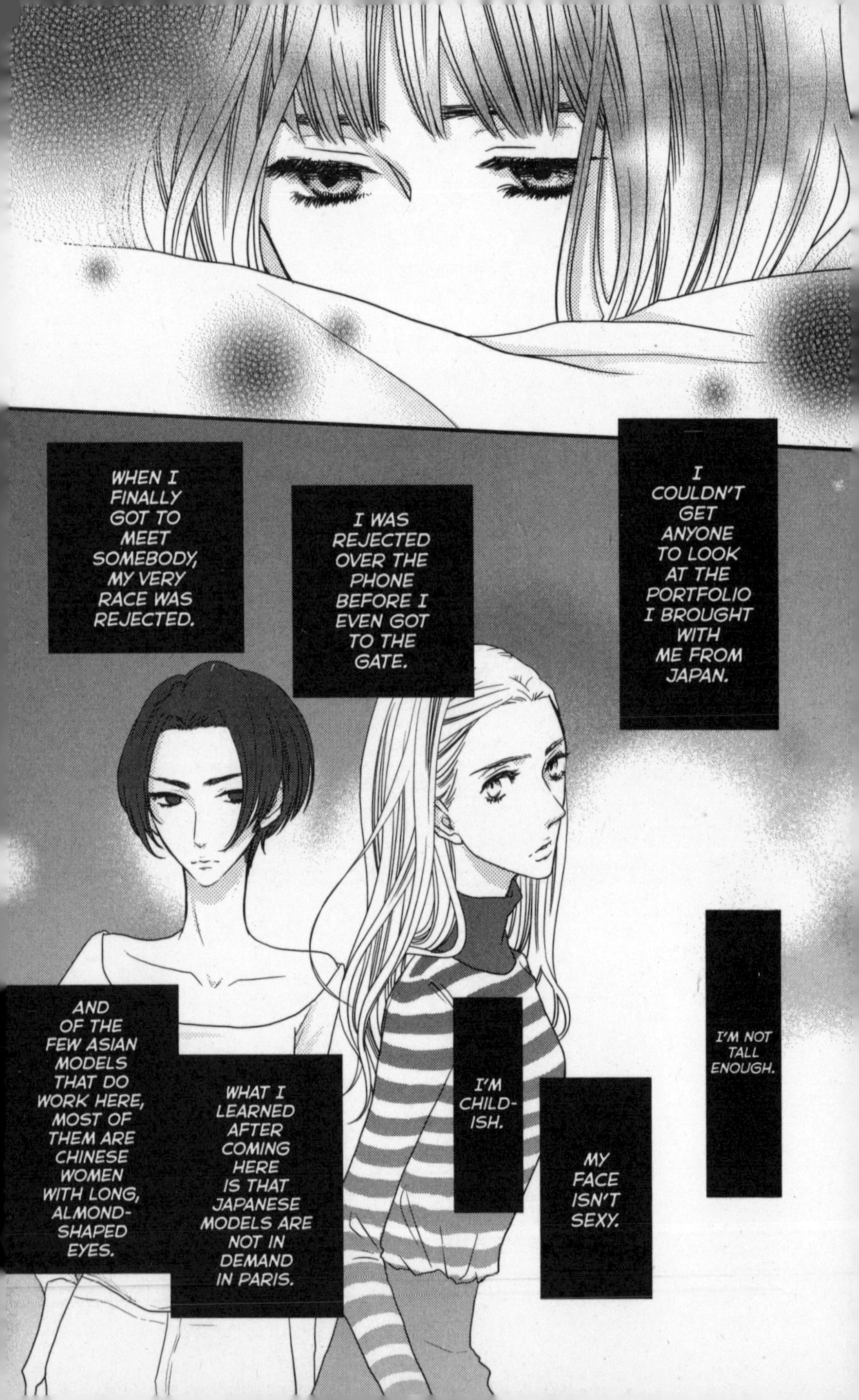
I COULDN'T GET ANYONE TO LOOK AT THE PORTFOLIO I BROUGHT WITH ME FROM JAPAN.
I WAS REJECTED OVER THE PHONE BEFORE I EVEN GOT TO THE GATE.
WHEN I FINALLY GOT TO MEET SOMEBODY, MY VERY RACE WAS REJECTED.
I'M NOT TALL ENOUGH.
MY FACE ISN'T SEXY.
I'M CHILD-ISH.
WHAT I LEARNED AFTER COMING HERE IS THAT JAPANESE MODELS ARE NOT IN DEMAND IN PARIS.
AND OF THE FEW ASIAN MODELS THAT DO WORK HERE, MOST OF THEM ARE CHINESE WOMEN WITH LONG, ALMOND-SHAPED EYES.

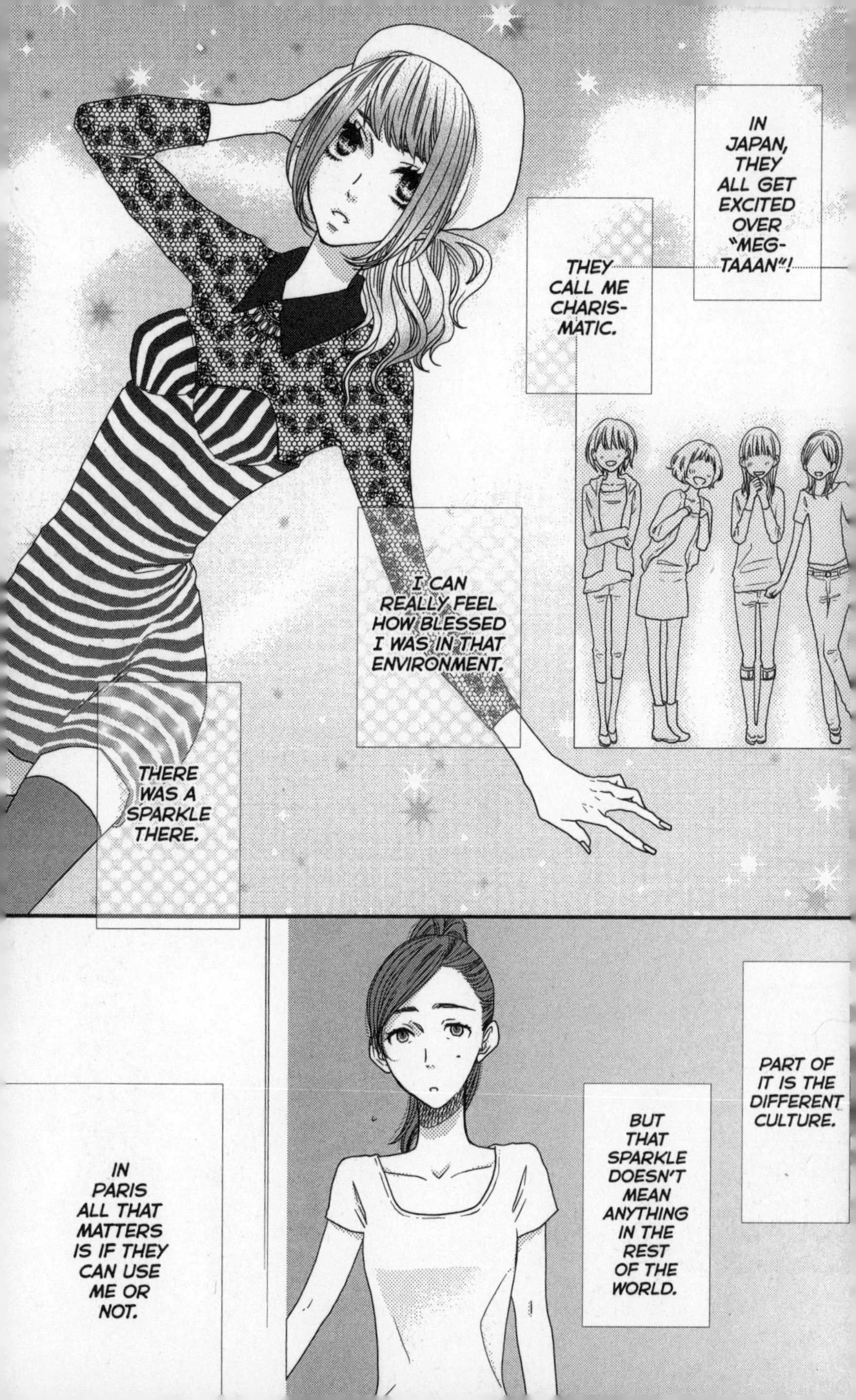
IN JAPAN, THEY ALL GET EXCITED OVER "MEG-TAAAN"!
THEY CALL ME CHARISMATIC.
I CAN REALLY FEEL HOW BLESSED I WAS IN THAT ENVIRONMENT.
THERE WAS A SPARKLE THERE.
PART OF IT IS THE DIFFERENT CULTURE.
BUT THAT SPARKLE DOESN'T MEAN ANYTHING IN THE REST OF THE WORLD.
IN PARIS ALL THAT MATTERS IS IF THEY CAN USE ME OR NOT.

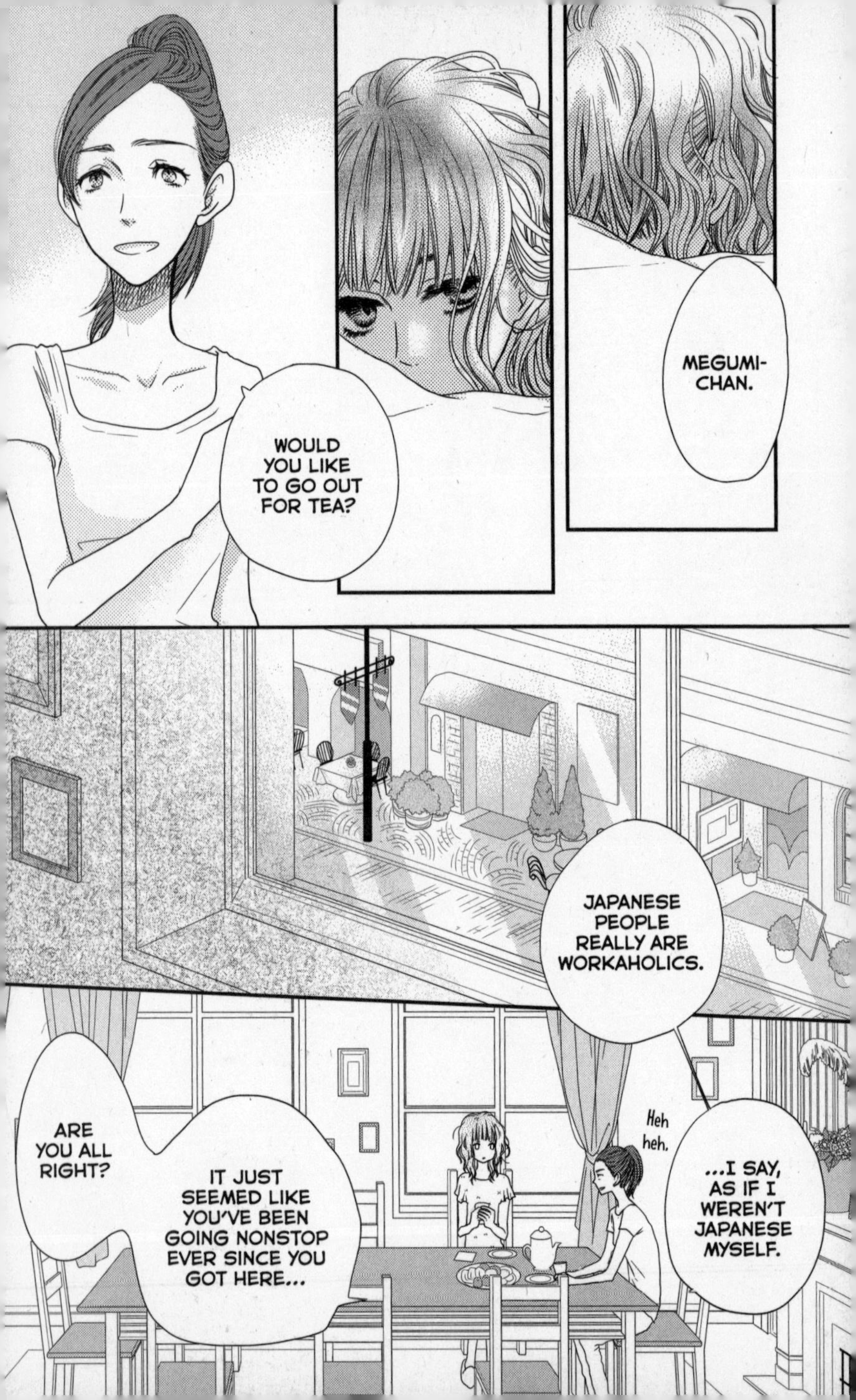
MEGUMI-CHAN.
WOULD YOU LIKE TO GO OUT FOR TEA?
JAPANESE PEOPLE REALLY ARE WORKAHOLICS.
...I SAY, AS IF I WEREN'T JAPANESE MYSELF.
Heh heh.
ARE YOU ALL RIGHT?
IT JUST SEEMED LIKE YOU'VE BEEN GOING NONSTOP EVER SINCE YOU GOT HERE...

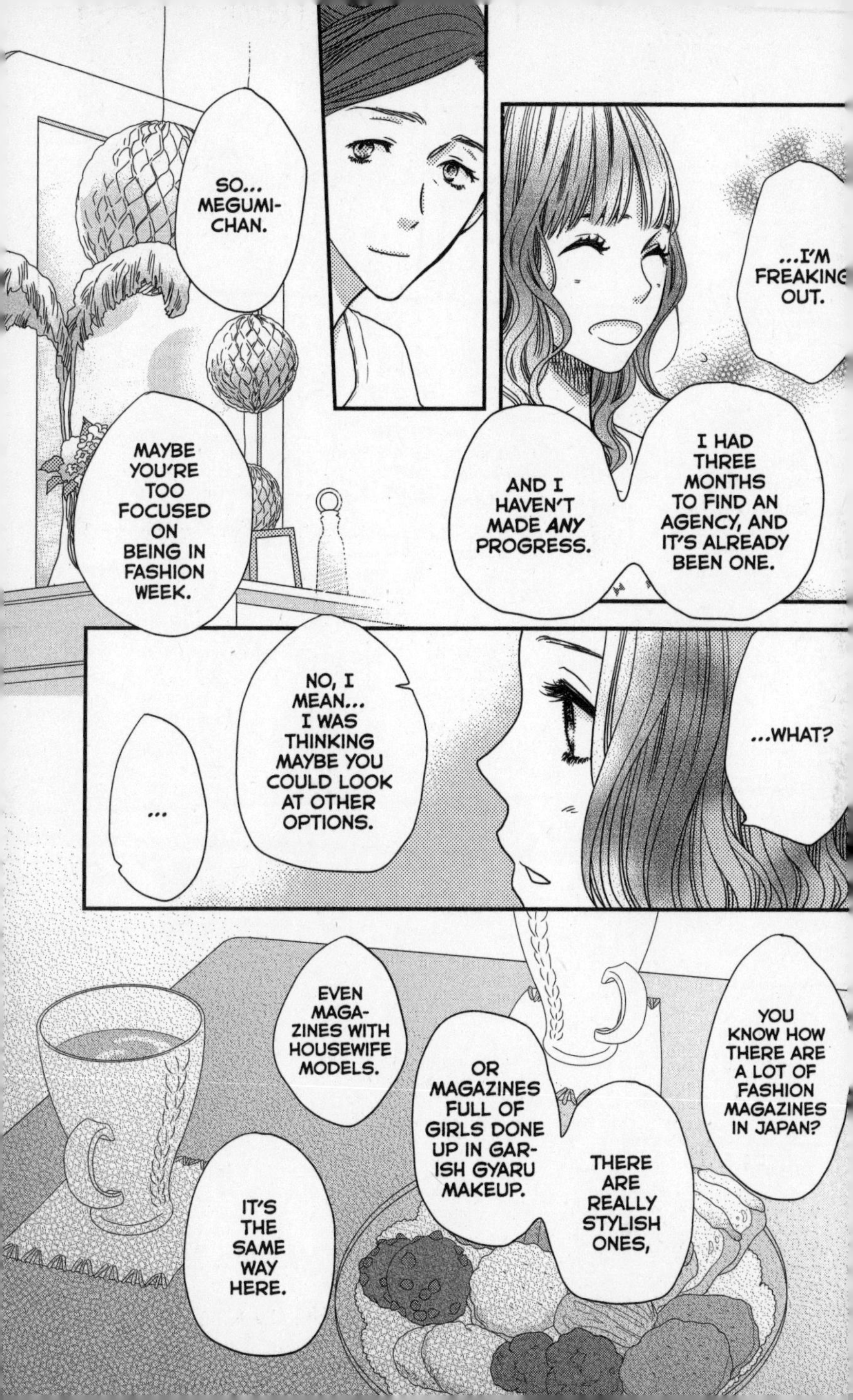
...I'M FREAKING OUT.
I HAD THREE MONTHS TO FIND AN AGENCY, AND IT'S ALREADY BEEN ONE.
AND I HAVEN'T MADE *ANY* PROGRESS.
SO... MEGUMI-CHAN.
MAYBE YOU'RE TOO FOCUSED ON BEING IN FASHION WEEK.
...WHAT?
NO, I MEAN... I WAS THINKING MAYBE YOU COULD LOOK AT OTHER OPTIONS.
...
YOU KNOW HOW THERE ARE A LOT OF FASHION MAGAZINES IN JAPAN?
THERE ARE REALLY STYLISH ONES,
OR MAGAZINES FULL OF GIRLS DONE UP IN GAR-ISH GYARU MAKEUP.
EVEN MAGA-ZINES WITH HOUSEWIFE MODELS.
IT'S THE SAME WAY HERE.

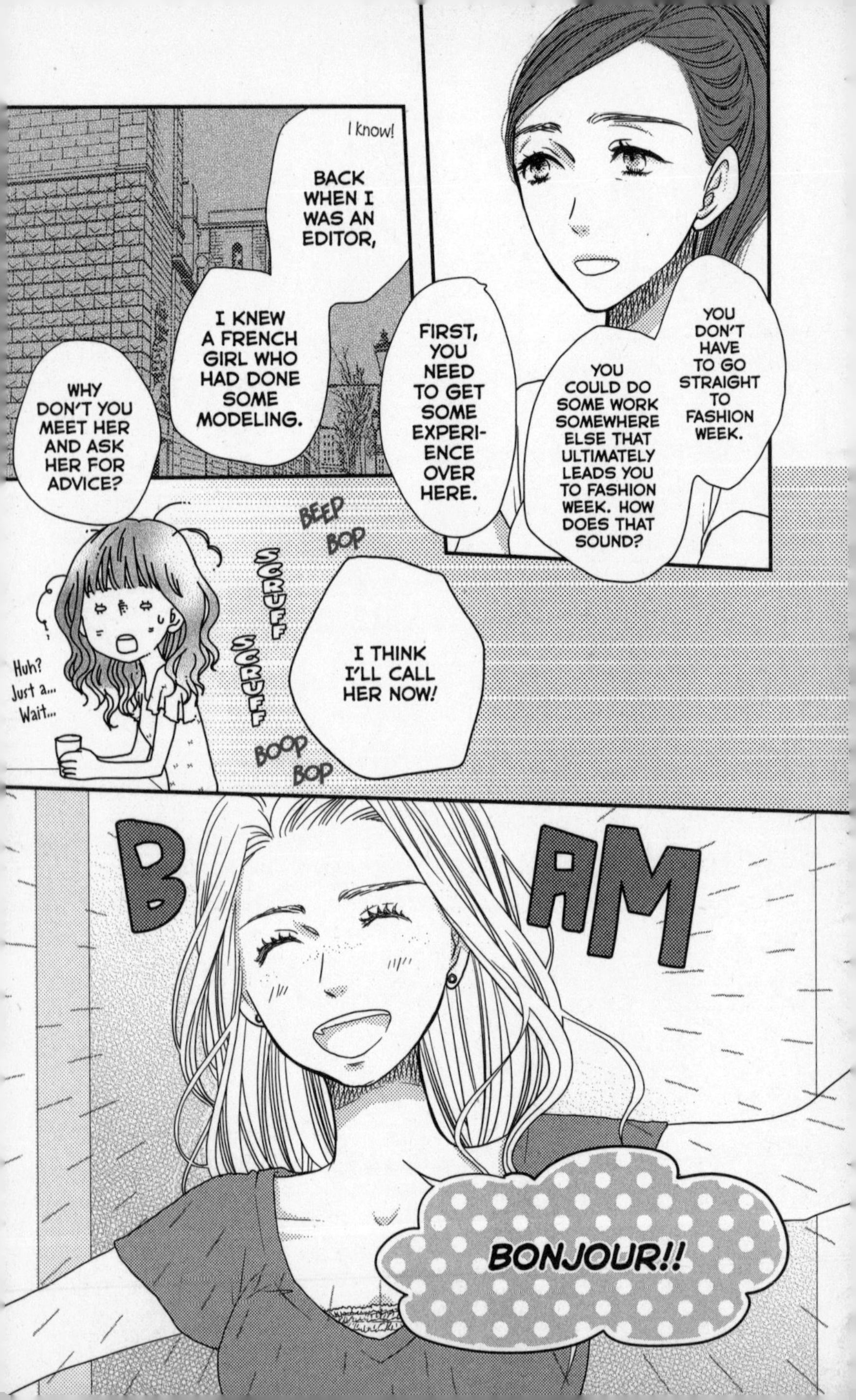
YOU DON'T HAVE TO GO STRAIGHT TO FASHION WEEK.
YOU COULD DO SOME WORK SOMEWHERE ELSE THAT ULTIMATELY LEADS YOU TO FASHION WEEK. HOW DOES THAT SOUND?
FIRST, YOU NEED TO GET SOME EXPERIENCE OVER HERE.
I know!
BACK WHEN I WAS AN EDITOR,
I KNEW A FRENCH GIRL WHO HAD DONE SOME MODELING.
WHY DON'T YOU MEET HER AND ASK HER FOR ADVICE?
BEEP
BOP
I THINK I'LL CALL HER NOW!
SCRUFF
SCRUFF
BOOP
BOP
Huh? Just a... Wait...
BAM
BONJOUR!!

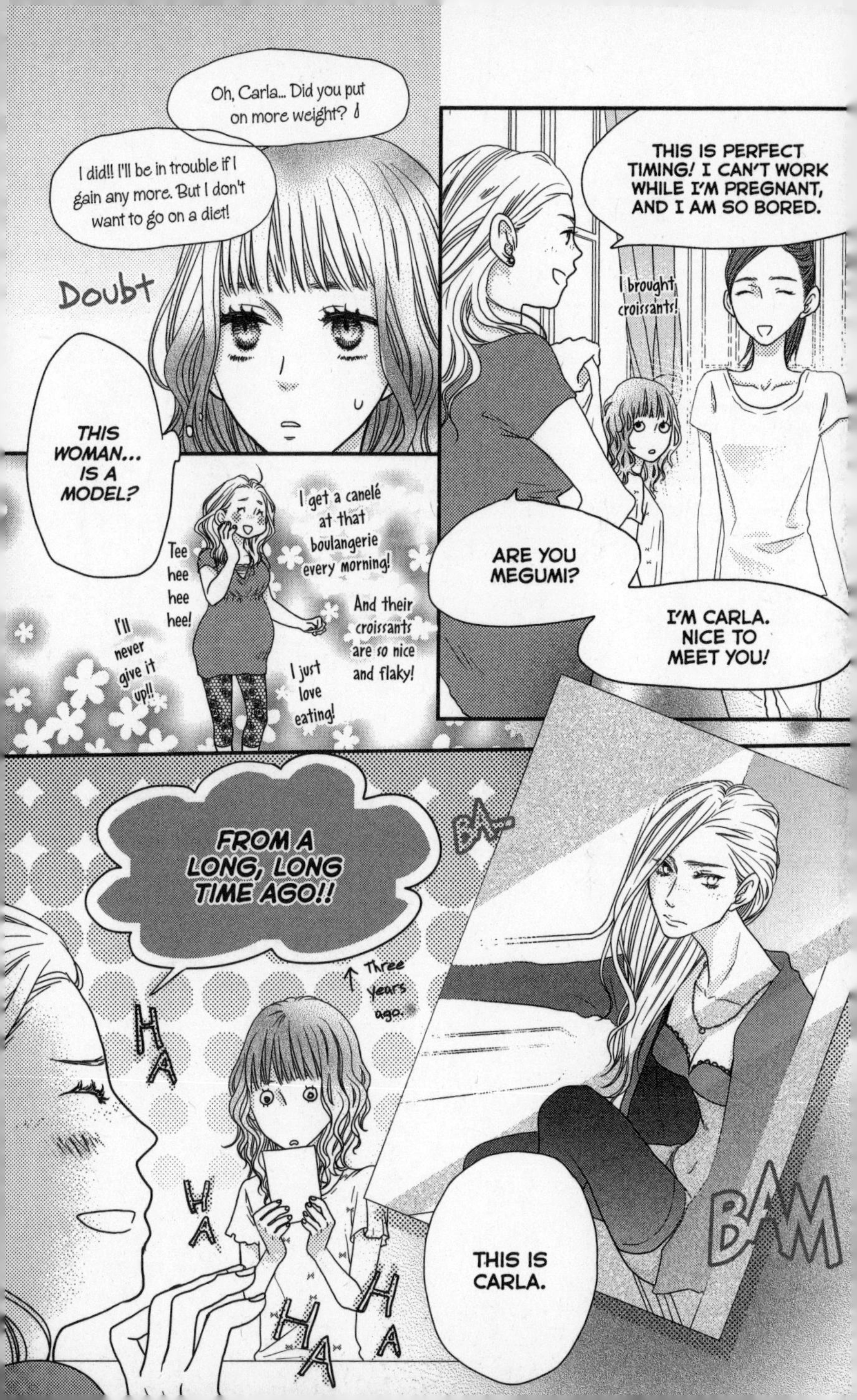

THIS IS PERFECT TIMING! I CAN'T WORK WHILE I'M PREGNANT, AND I AM SO BORED.
I brought croissants!
ARE YOU MEGUMI?
I'M CARLA. NICE TO MEET YOU!
Oh, Carla... Did you put on more weight? ♪
I did!! I'll be in trouble if I gain any more. But I don't want to go on a diet!
Doubt
THIS WOMAN... IS A MODEL?
I get a canelé at that boulangerie every morning!
And their croissants are so nice and flaky!
I just love eating!
Tee hee hee hee!
I'll never give it up!!
BA-
BAM
THIS IS CARLA.
FROM A LONG, LONG TIME AGO!!
Three years ago.
HA
HA
HA
HA
HA
HA

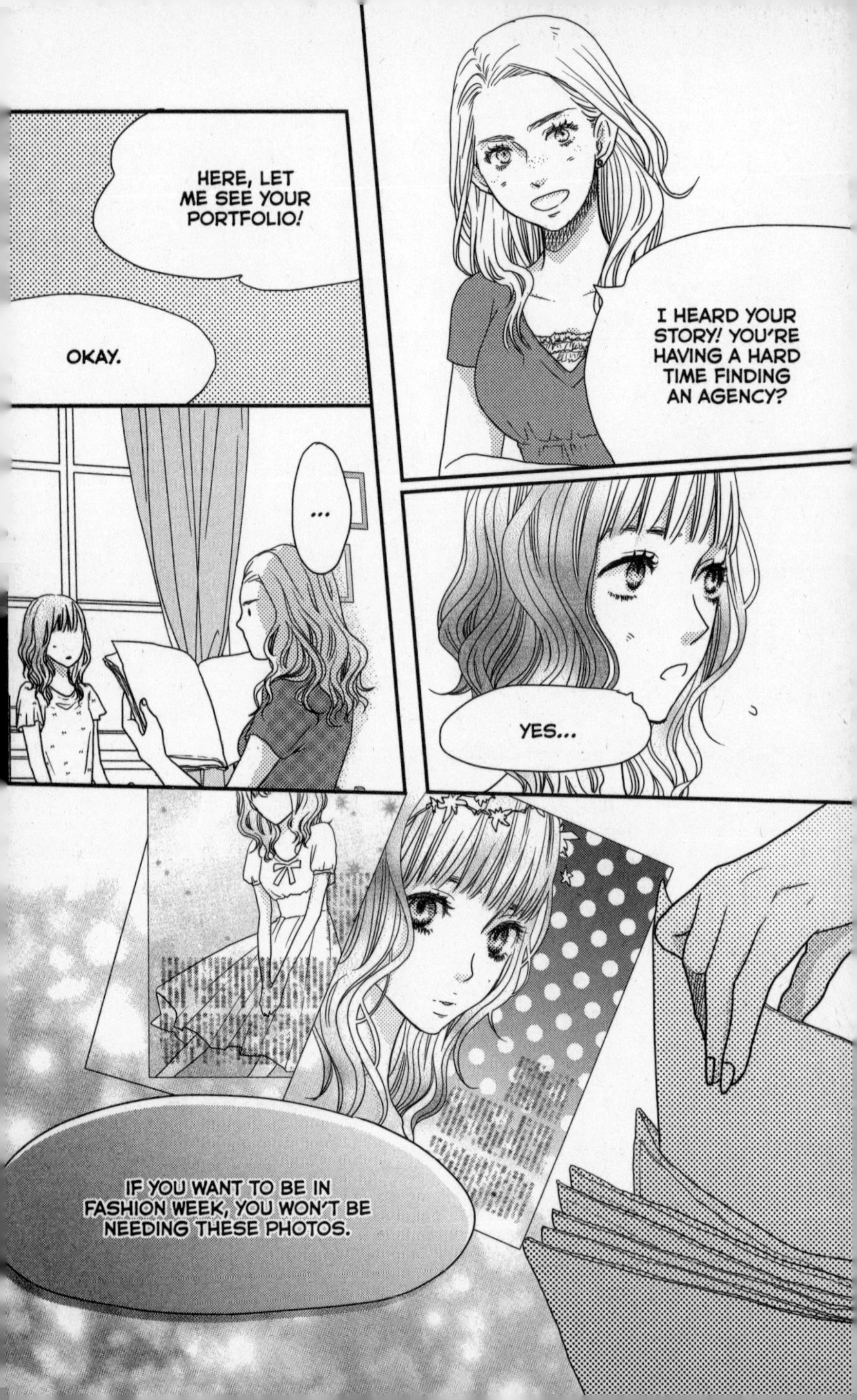
I HEARD YOUR STORY! YOU'RE HAVING A HARD TIME FINDING AN AGENCY?
HERE, LET ME SEE YOUR PORTFOLIO!
OKAY.
YES...
...
IF YOU WANT TO BE IN FASHION WEEK, YOU WON'T BE NEEDING THESE PHOTOS.

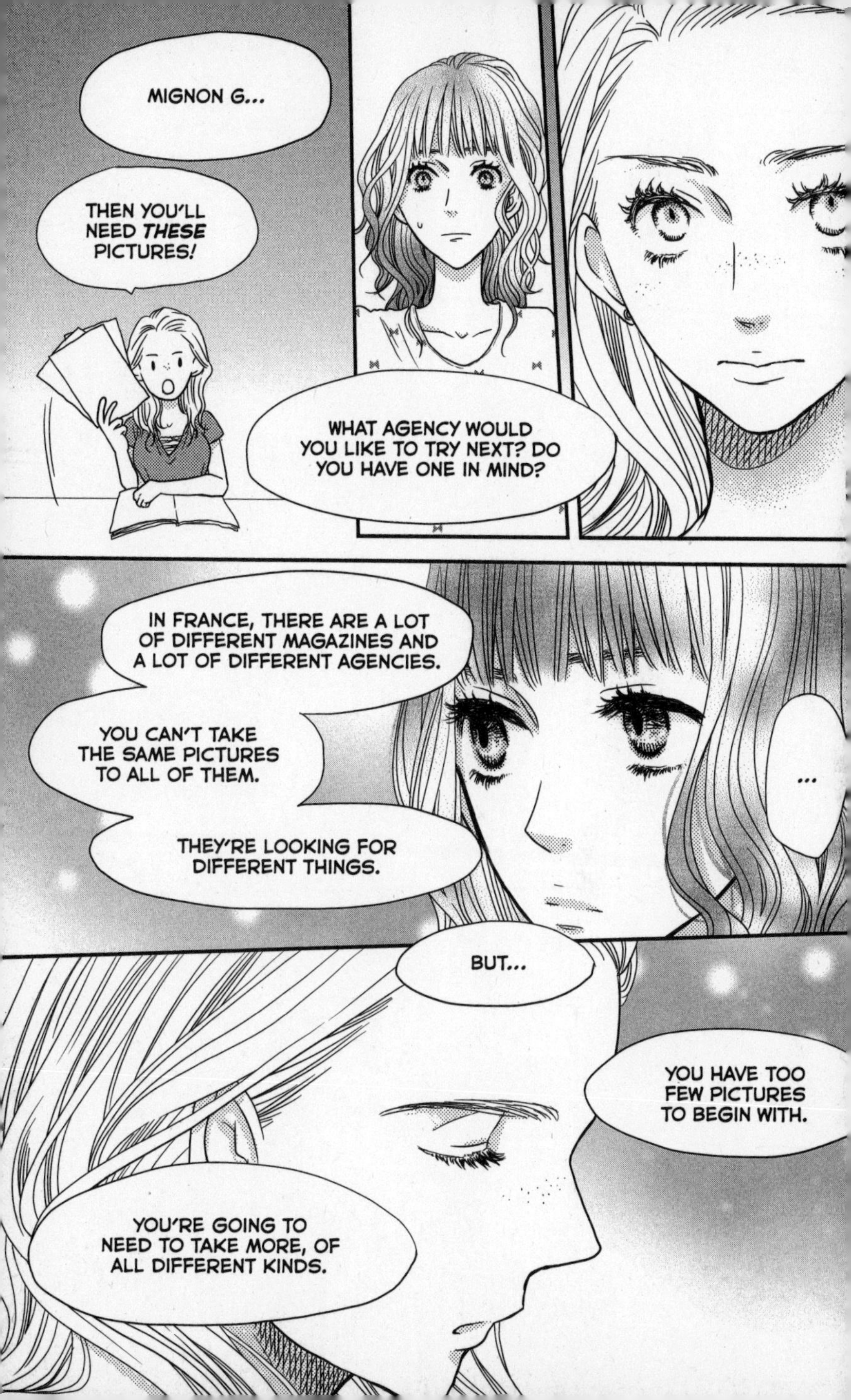
WHAT AGENCY WOULD YOU LIKE TO TRY NEXT? DO YOU HAVE ONE IN MIND?
MIGNON G...
THEN YOU'LL NEED *THESE* PICTURES!
...
IN FRANCE, THERE ARE A LOT OF DIFFERENT MAGAZINES AND A LOT OF DIFFERENT AGENCIES.
YOU CAN'T TAKE THE SAME PICTURES TO ALL OF THEM.
THEY'RE LOOKING FOR DIFFERENT THINGS.
BUT...
YOU HAVE TOO FEW PICTURES TO BEGIN WITH.
YOU'RE GOING TO NEED TO TAKE MORE, OF ALL DIFFERENT KINDS.

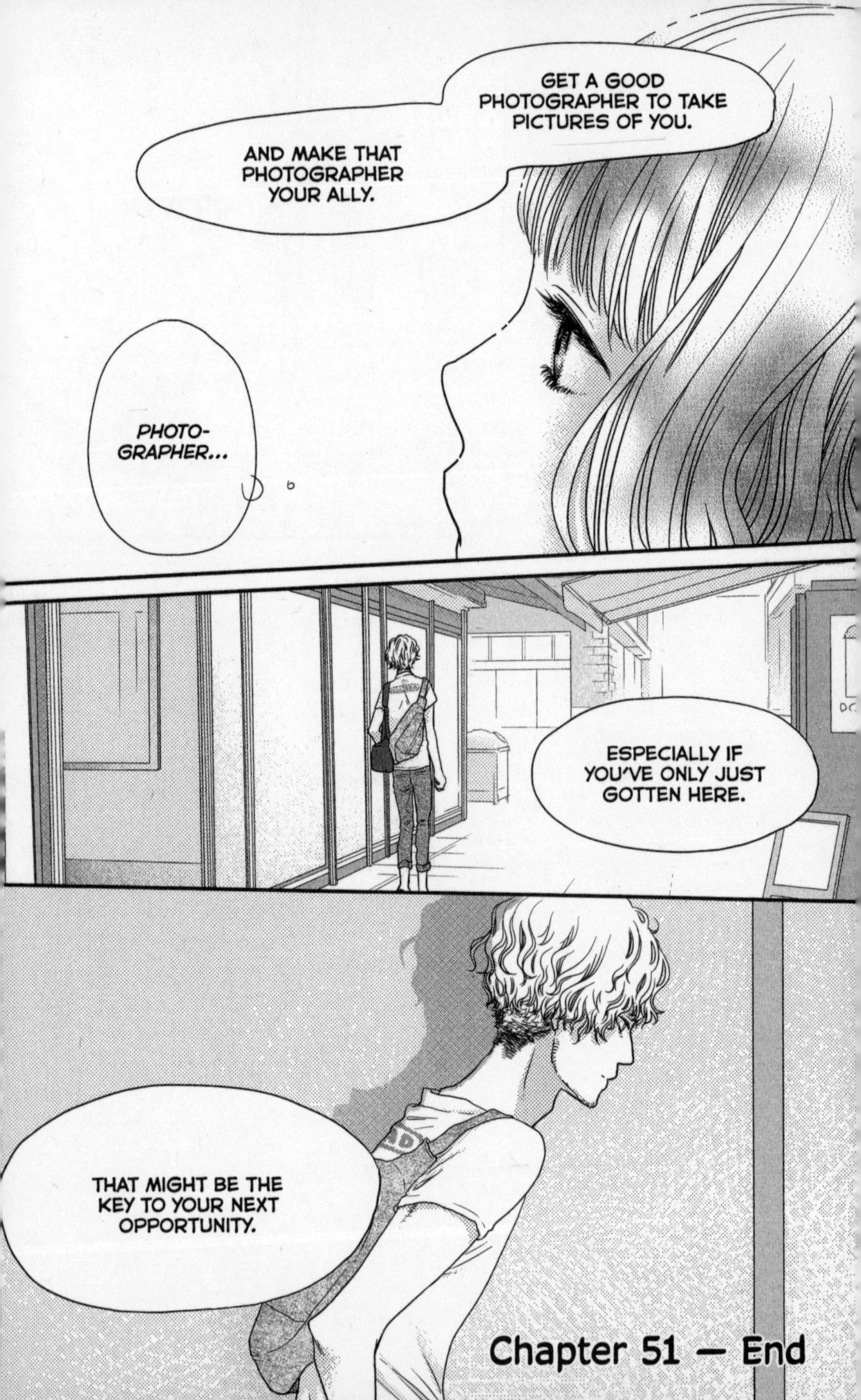
GET A GOOD PHOTOGRAPHER TO TAKE PICTURES OF YOU.
AND MAKE THAT PHOTOGRAPHER YOUR ALLY.
PHOTO-GRAPHER...
ESPECIALLY IF YOU'VE ONLY JUST GOTTEN HERE.
THAT MIGHT BE THE KEY TO YOUR NEXT OPPORTUNITY.
Chapter 51 — End

Say "I love you".

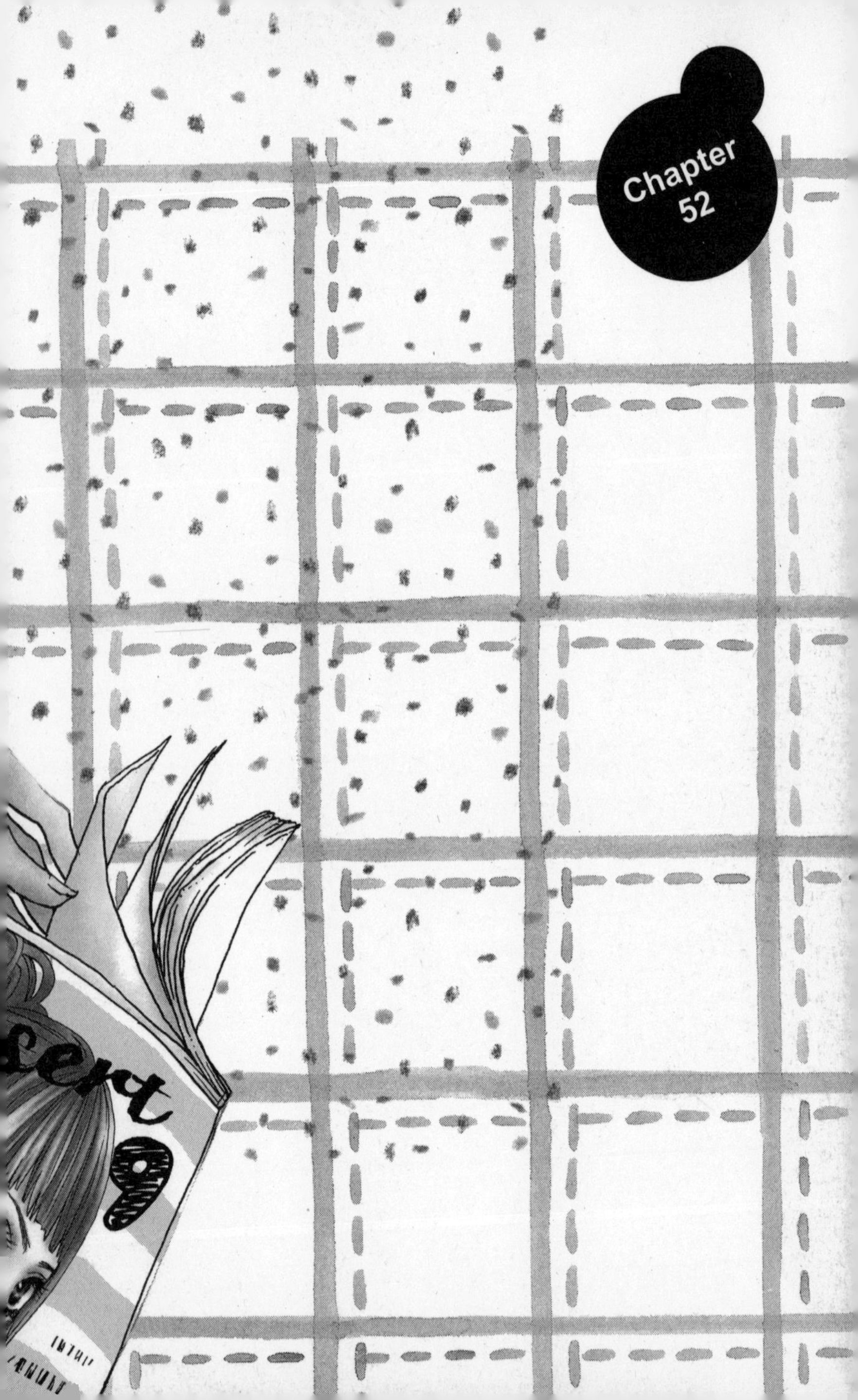
Chapter
52

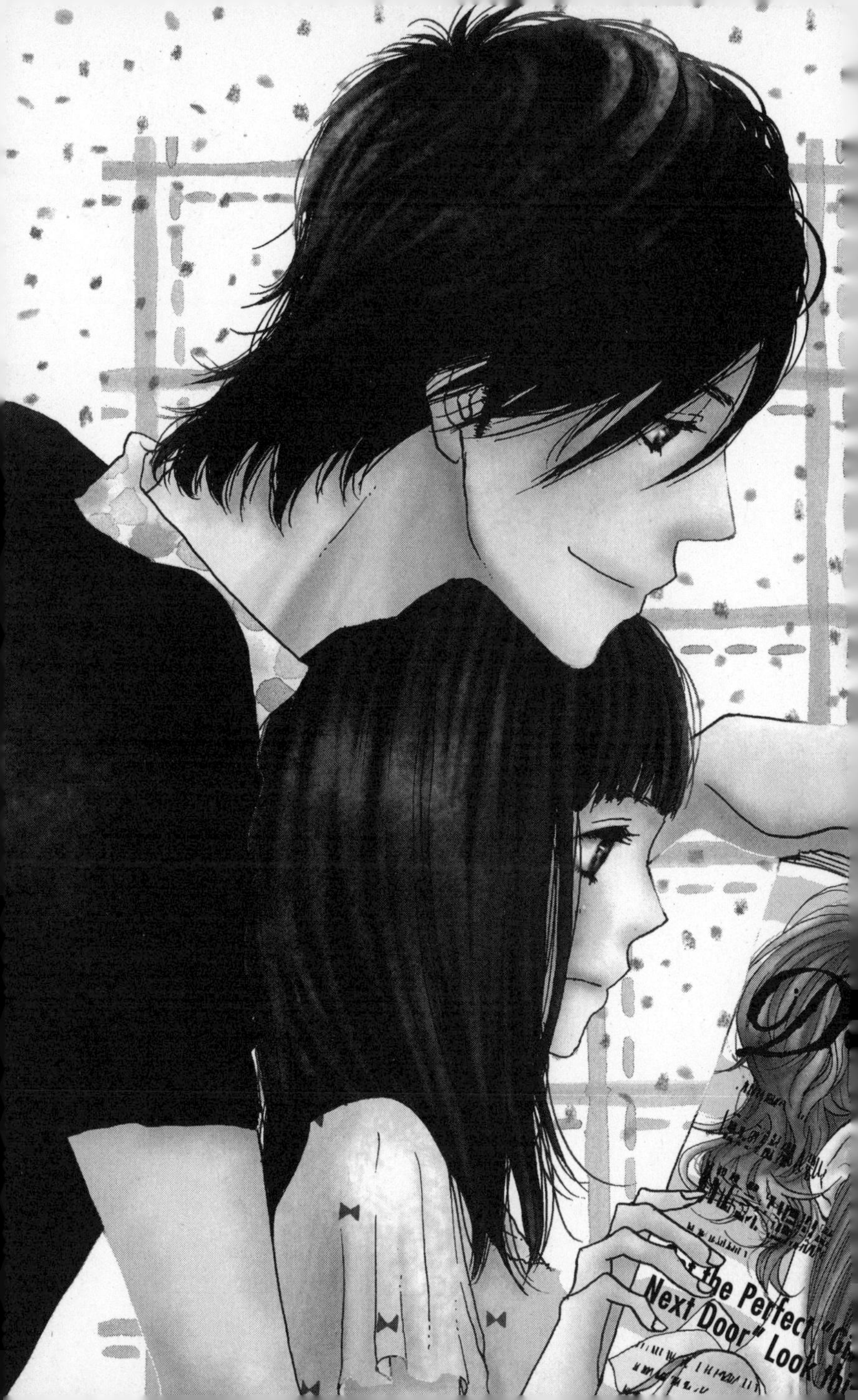
the Perfect "Gi
Next Door" Look thi

Say "I love you".

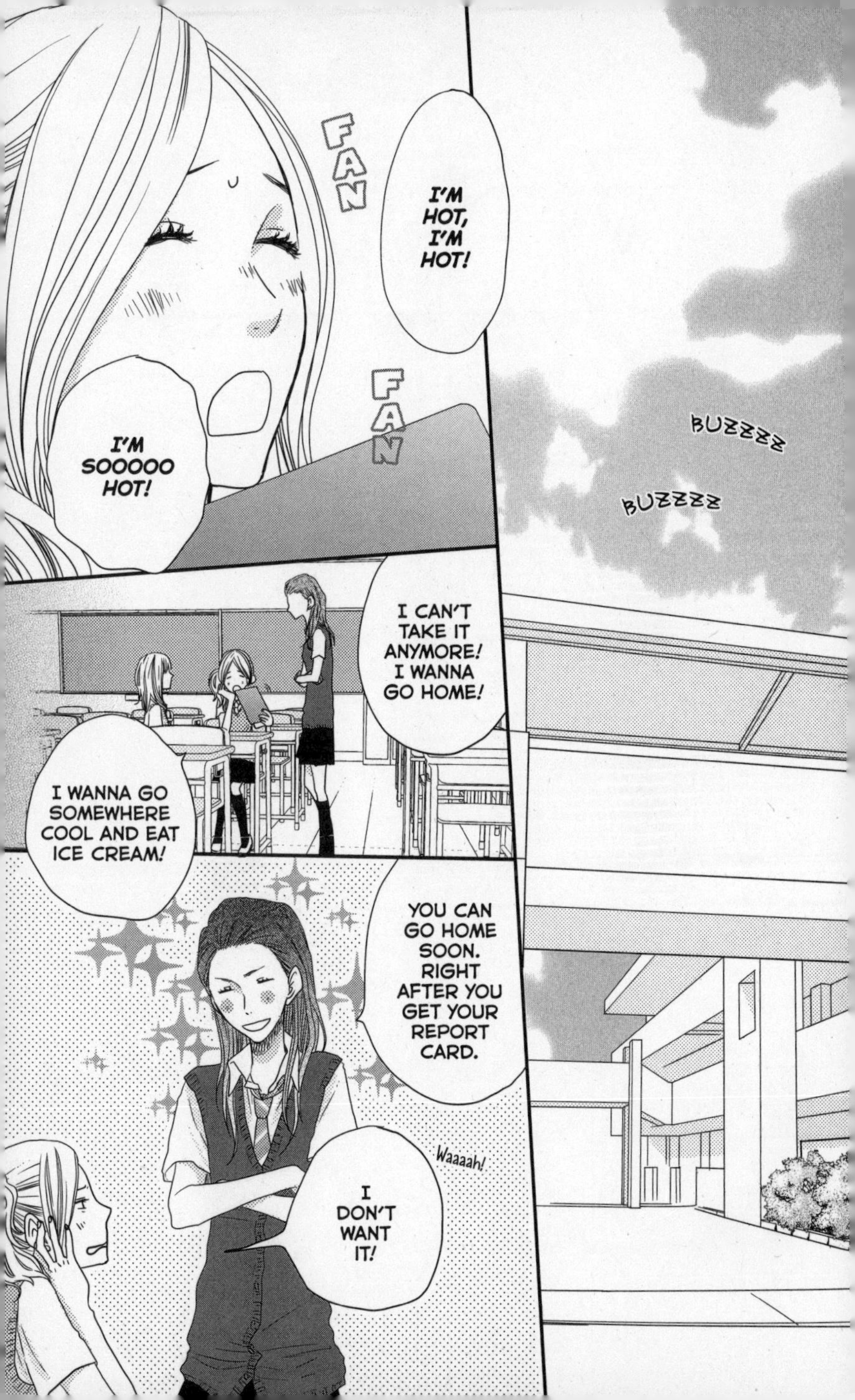
BUZZZZZ
BUZZZZ
I'M HOT, I'M HOT!
FAN
FAN
I'M SOOOOO HOT!
I CAN'T TAKE IT ANYMORE! I WANNA GO HOME!
I WANNA GO SOMEWHERE COOL AND EAT ICE CREAM!
YOU CAN GO HOME SOON. RIGHT AFTER YOU GET YOUR REPORT CARD.
Waaaah!
I DON'T WANT IT!

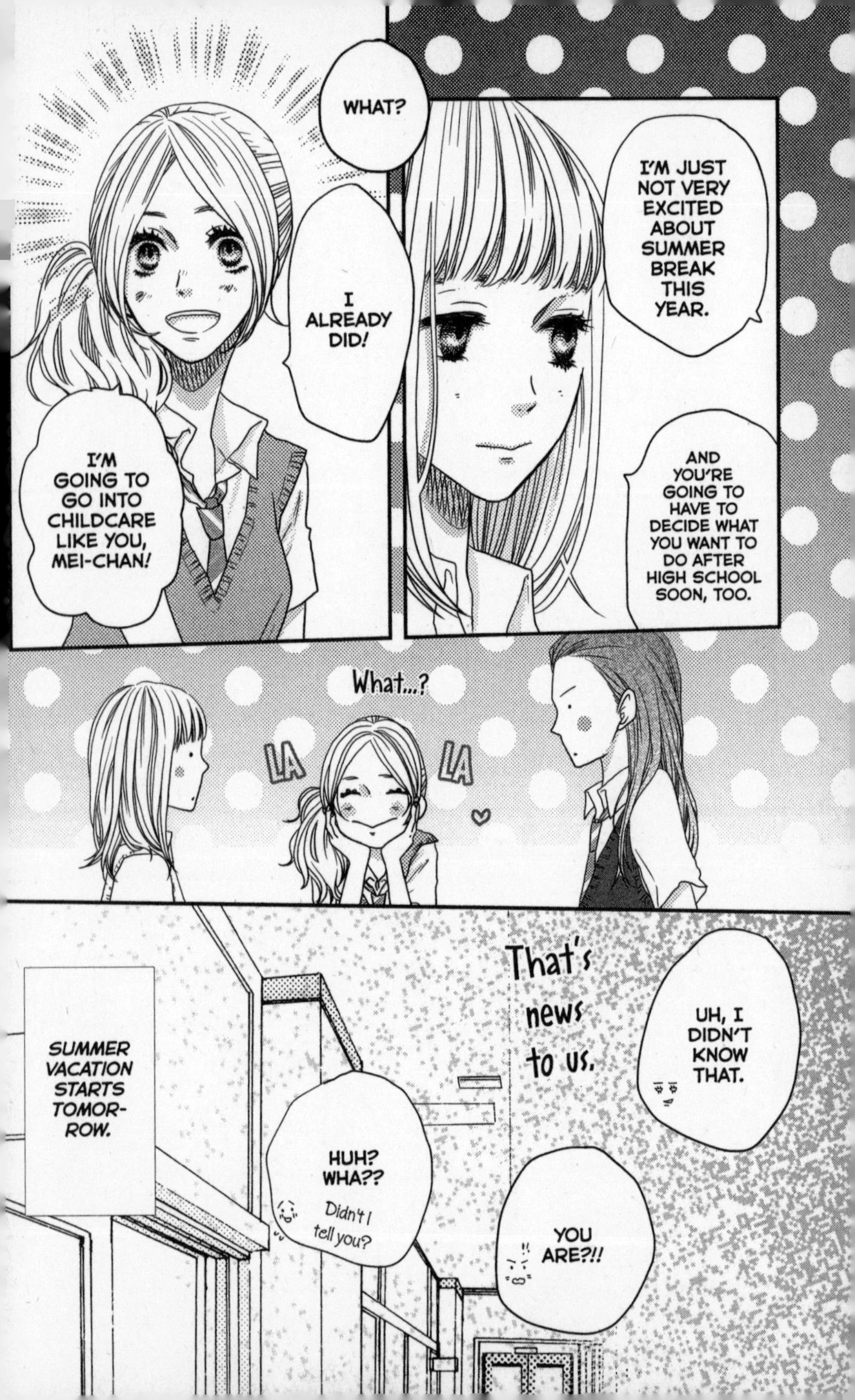

I'M JUST NOT VERY EXCITED ABOUT SUMMER BREAK THIS YEAR.
AND YOU'RE GOING TO HAVE TO DECIDE WHAT YOU WANT TO DO AFTER HIGH SCHOOL SOON, TOO.
WHAT?
I ALREADY DID!
I'M GOING TO GO INTO CHILDCARE LIKE YOU, MEI-CHAN!
What...?
LA
LA
UH, I DIDN'T KNOW THAT.
That's news to us.
YOU ARE?!!
HUH? WHA??
Didn't I tell you?
SUMMER VACATION STARTS TOMORROW.

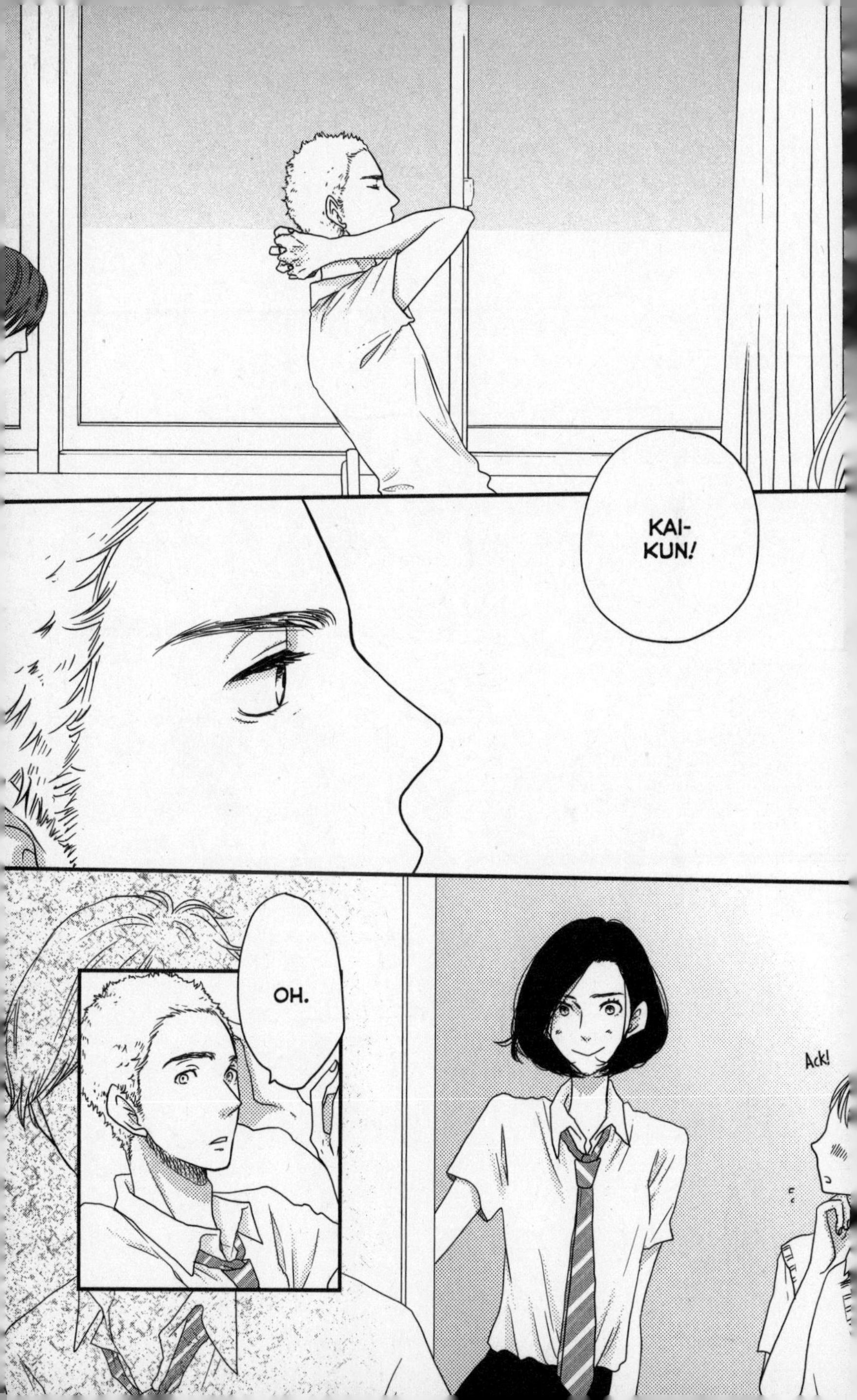
KAI-KUN!
OH.
Ack!

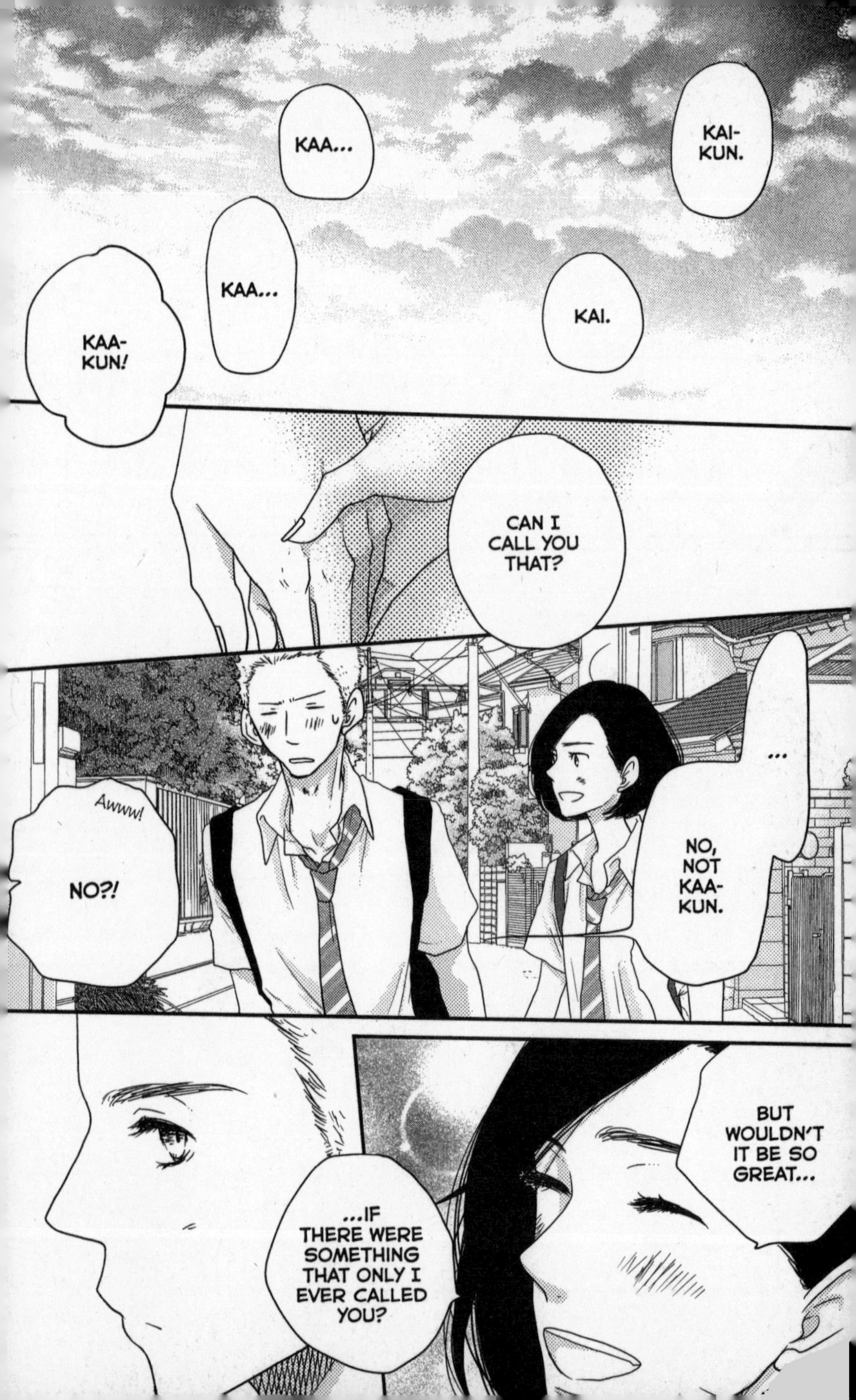
KAI-KUN.
KAI.
KAA...
KAA...
KAA-KUN!
CAN I CALL YOU THAT?
...
NO, NOT KAA-KUN.
Awww!
NO?!
BUT WOULDN'T IT BE SO GREAT...
...IF THERE WERE SOMETHING THAT ONLY I EVER CALLED YOU?

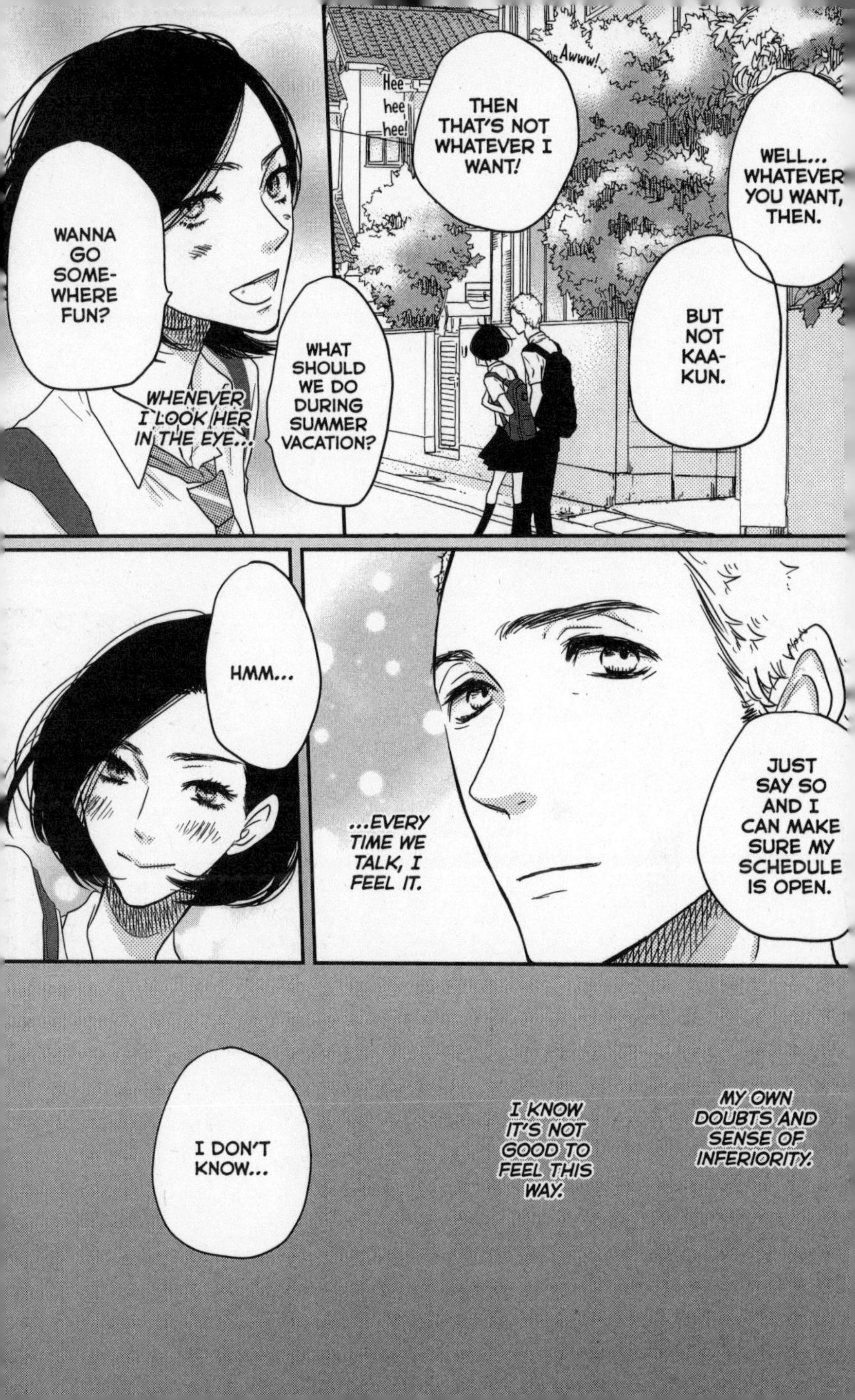
WELL... WHATEVER YOU WANT, THEN.
BUT NOT KAA-KUN.
THEN THAT'S NOT WHATEVER I WANT!
Awww!
Hee hee hee!
WHAT SHOULD WE DO DURING SUMMER VACATION?
WANNA GO SOMEWHERE FUN?
WHENEVER I LOOK HER IN THE EYE...
JUST SAY SO AND I CAN MAKE SURE MY SCHEDULE IS OPEN.
...EVERY TIME WE TALK, I FEEL IT.
HMM...
MY OWN DOUBTS AND SENSE OF INFERIORITY.
I KNOW IT'S NOT GOOD TO FEEL THIS WAY.
I DON'T KNOW...

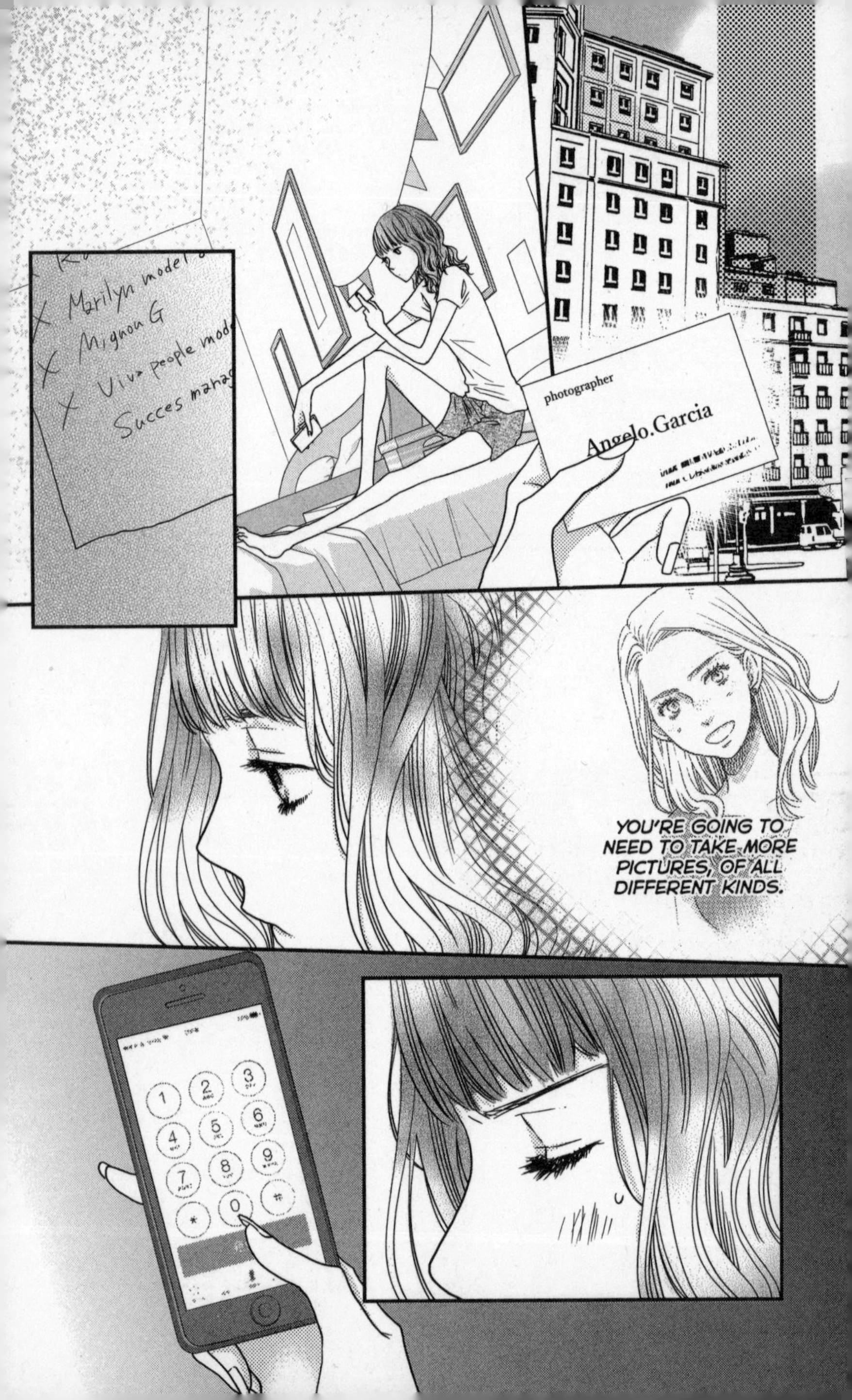
photographer
Angelo.Garcia
Marilyn model
Mignon G
Viva people mod
Succes manag
YOU'RE GOING TO NEED TO TAKE MORE PICTURES, OF ALL DIFFERENT KINDS.

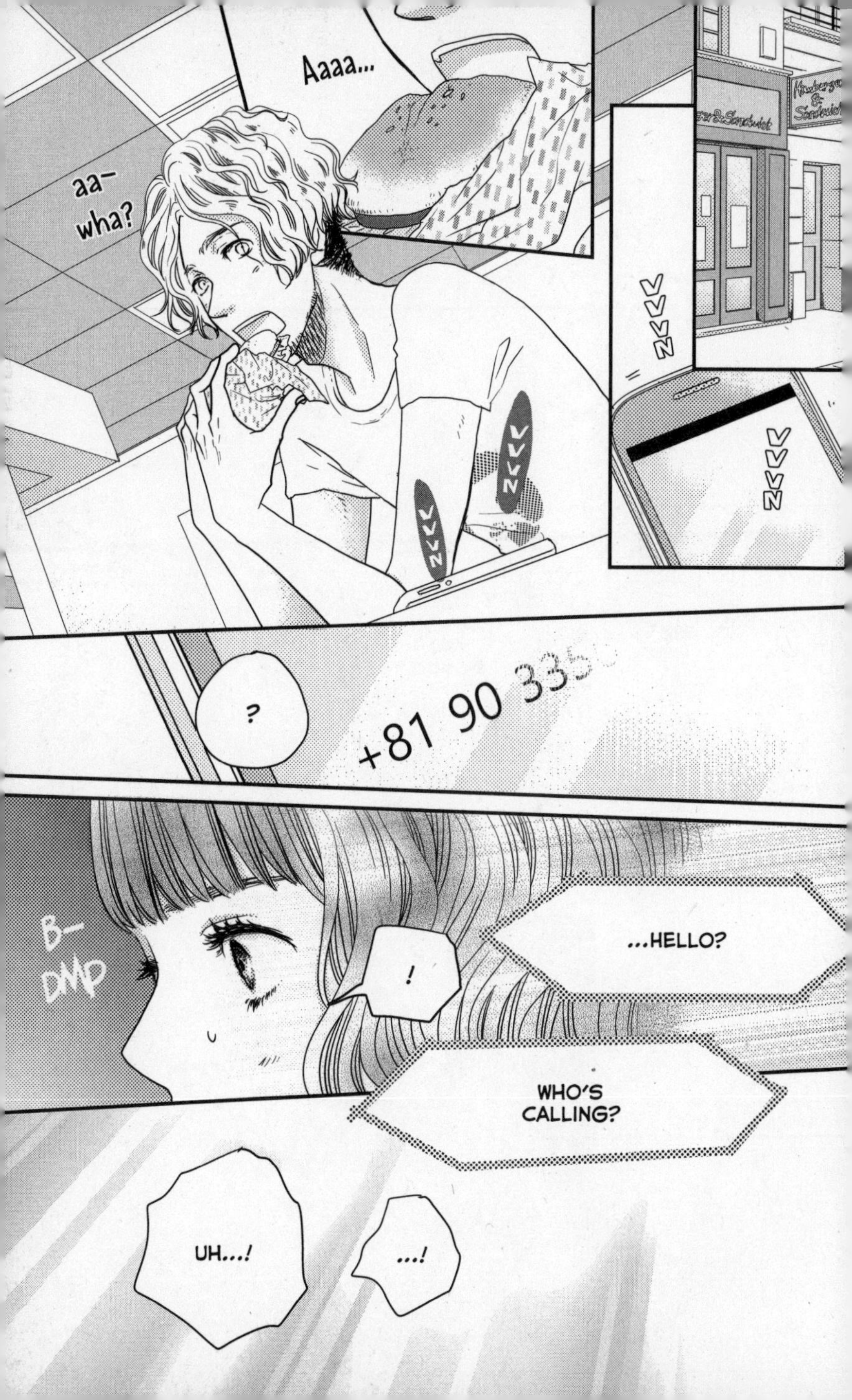
VVVN
VVVN
Aaaa...
aa-wha?
VVVN
VVVN
?
+81 90 335
...HELLO?
!
B-DMP
WHO'S CALLING?
...!
UH...!

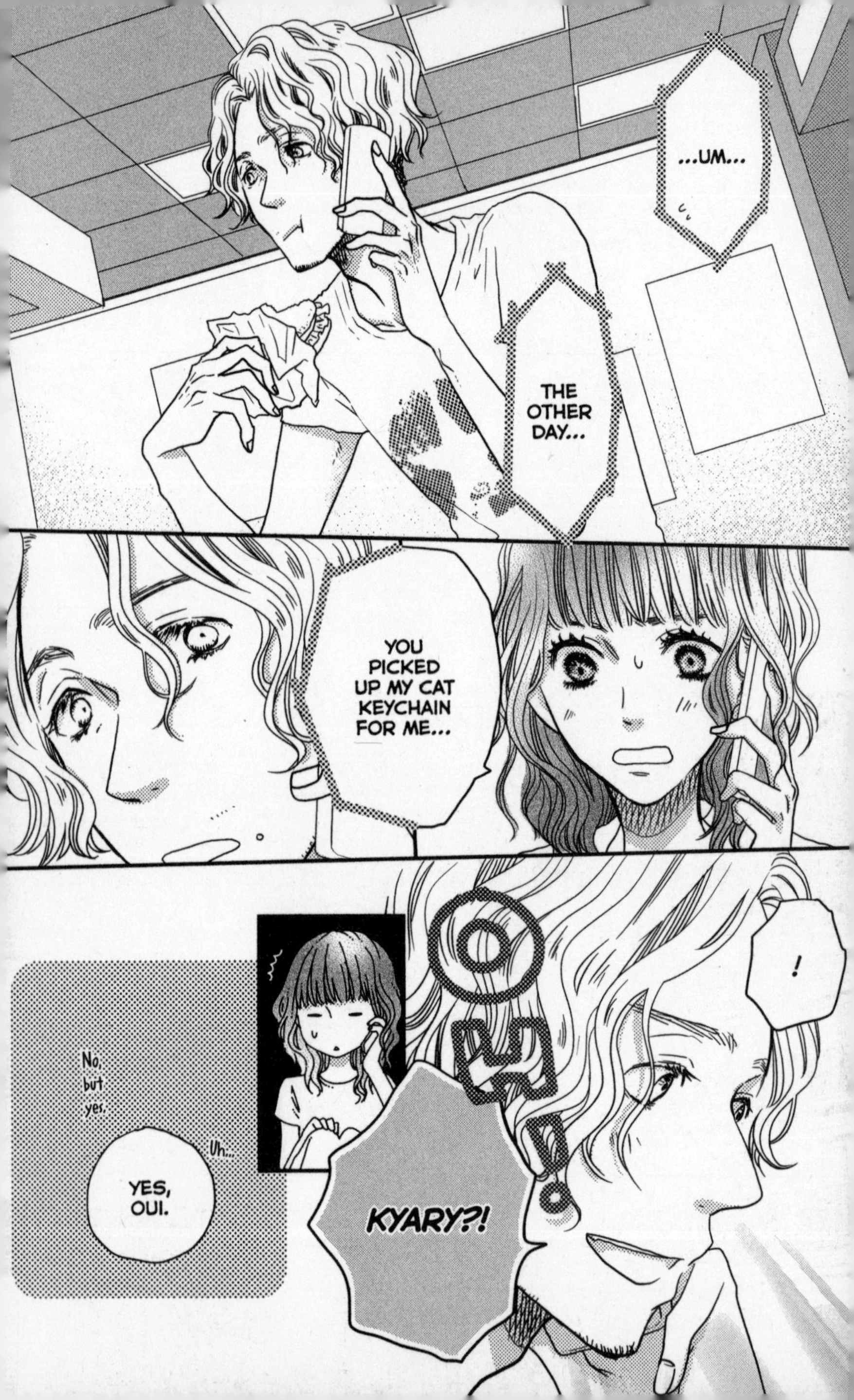
...UM...
THE OTHER DAY...
YOU PICKED UP MY CAT KEYCHAIN FOR ME...
!
KYARY?!
Uh...
YES, OUI.
No, but yes.

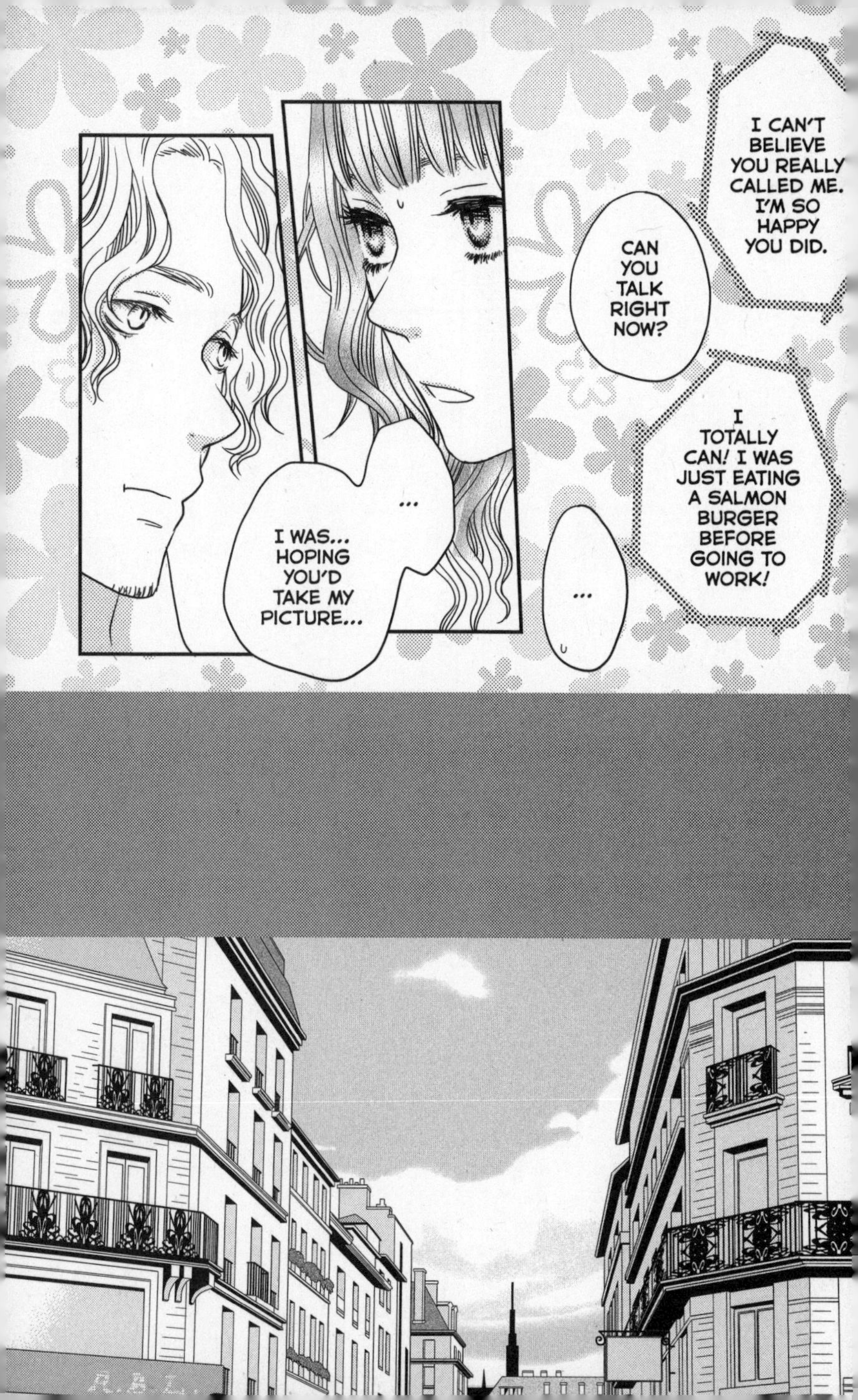
I CAN'T BELIEVE YOU REALLY CALLED ME. I'M SO HAPPY YOU DID.
CAN YOU TALK RIGHT NOW?
I TOTALLY CAN! I WAS JUST EATING A SALMON BURGER BEFORE GOING TO WORK!
...
...
I WAS... HOPING YOU'D TAKE MY PICTURE...

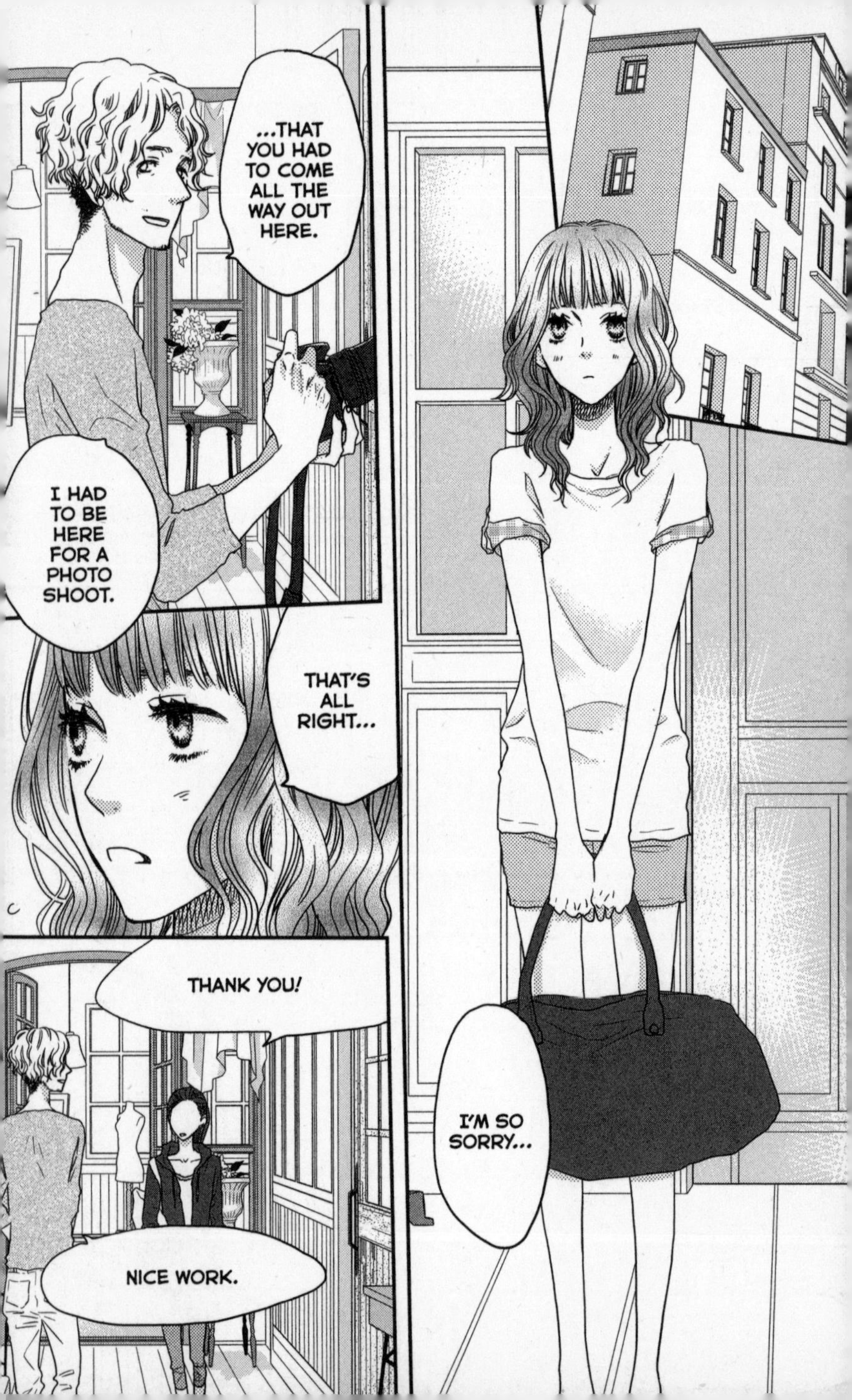
I'M SO SORRY...
...THAT YOU HAD TO COME ALL THE WAY OUT HERE.
I HAD TO BE HERE FOR A PHOTO SHOOT.
THAT'S ALL RIGHT...
THANK YOU!
NICE WORK.

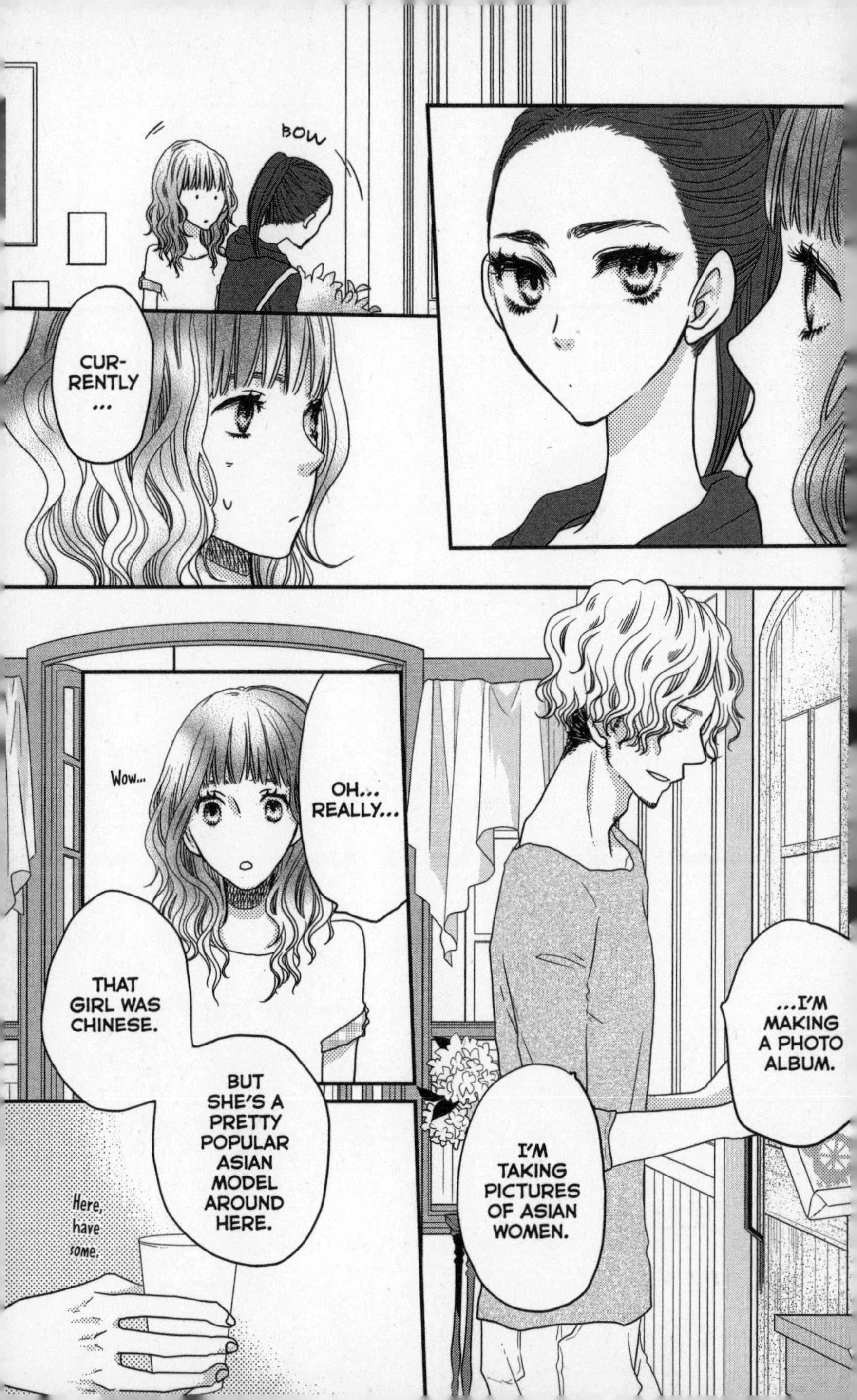
BOW
CUR-RENTLY...
...I'M MAKING A PHOTO ALBUM.
I'M TAKING PICTURES OF ASIAN WOMEN.
OH... REALLY...
Wow...
THAT GIRL WAS CHINESE.
BUT SHE'S A PRETTY POPULAR ASIAN MODEL AROUND HERE.
Here, have some.

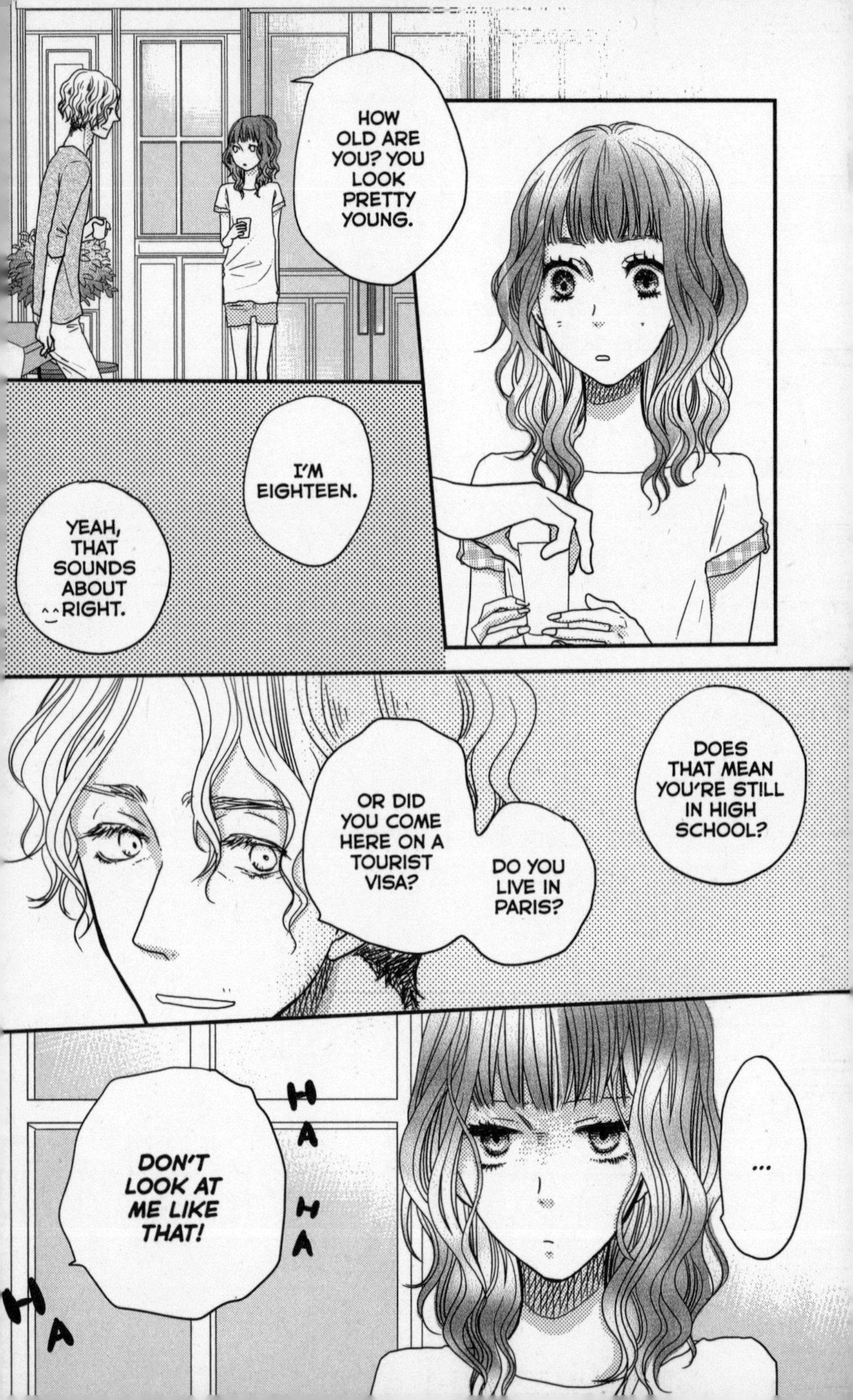
HOW OLD ARE YOU? YOU LOOK PRETTY YOUNG.
I'M EIGHTEEN.
YEAH, THAT SOUNDS ABOUT RIGHT.
DOES THAT MEAN YOU'RE STILL IN HIGH SCHOOL?
DO YOU LIVE IN PARIS?
OR DID YOU COME HERE ON A TOURIST VISA?
...
HA HA
DON'T LOOK AT ME LIKE THAT!
HA HA

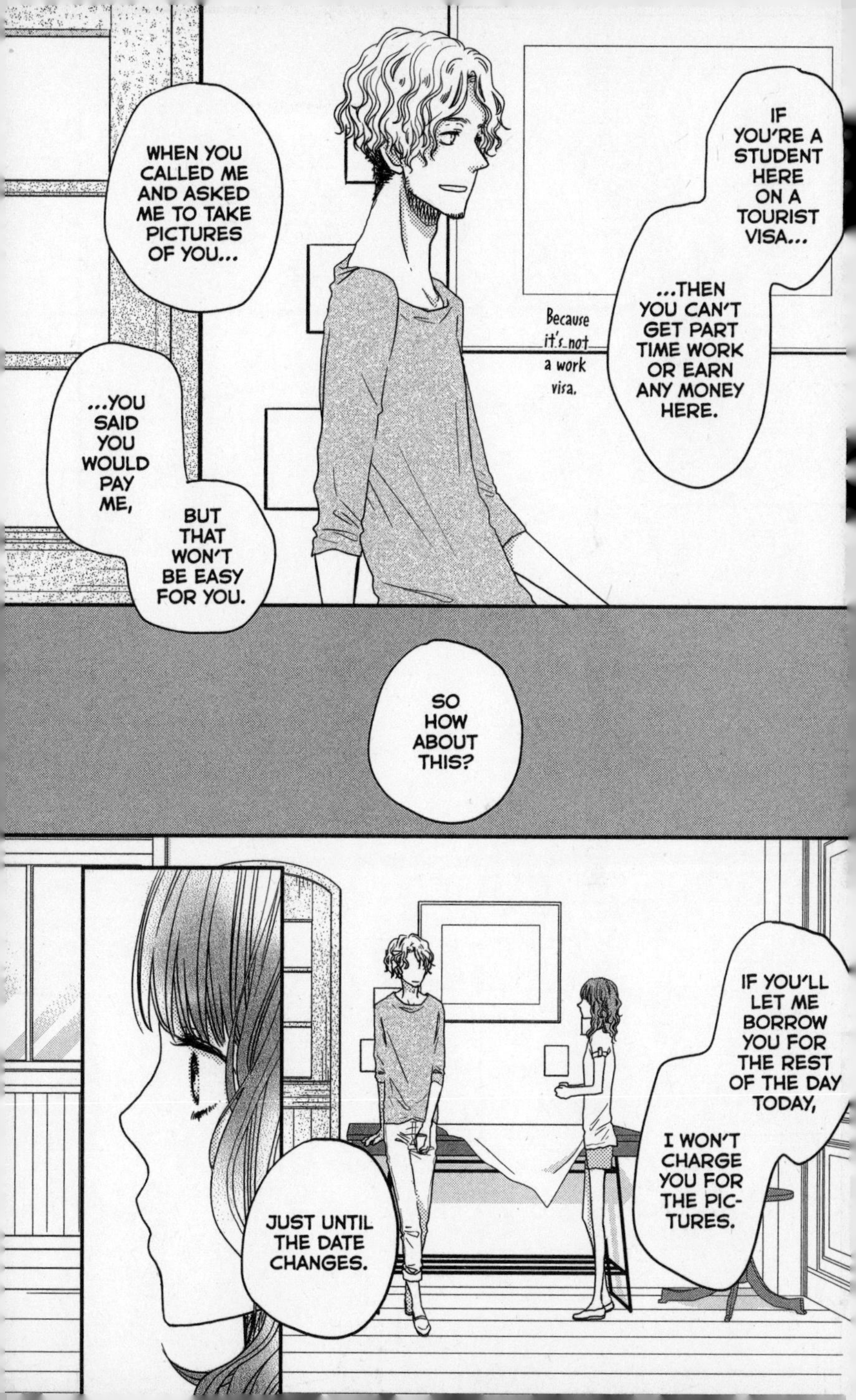
IF YOU'RE A STUDENT HERE ON A TOURIST VISA...
...THEN YOU CAN'T GET PART TIME WORK OR EARN ANY MONEY HERE.
Because it's not a work visa.
WHEN YOU CALLED ME AND ASKED ME TO TAKE PICTURES OF YOU...
...YOU SAID YOU WOULD PAY ME,
BUT THAT WON'T BE EASY FOR YOU.
SO HOW ABOUT THIS?
IF YOU'LL LET ME BORROW YOU FOR THE REST OF THE DAY TODAY,
I WON'T CHARGE YOU FOR THE PICTURES.
JUST UNTIL THE DATE CHANGES.

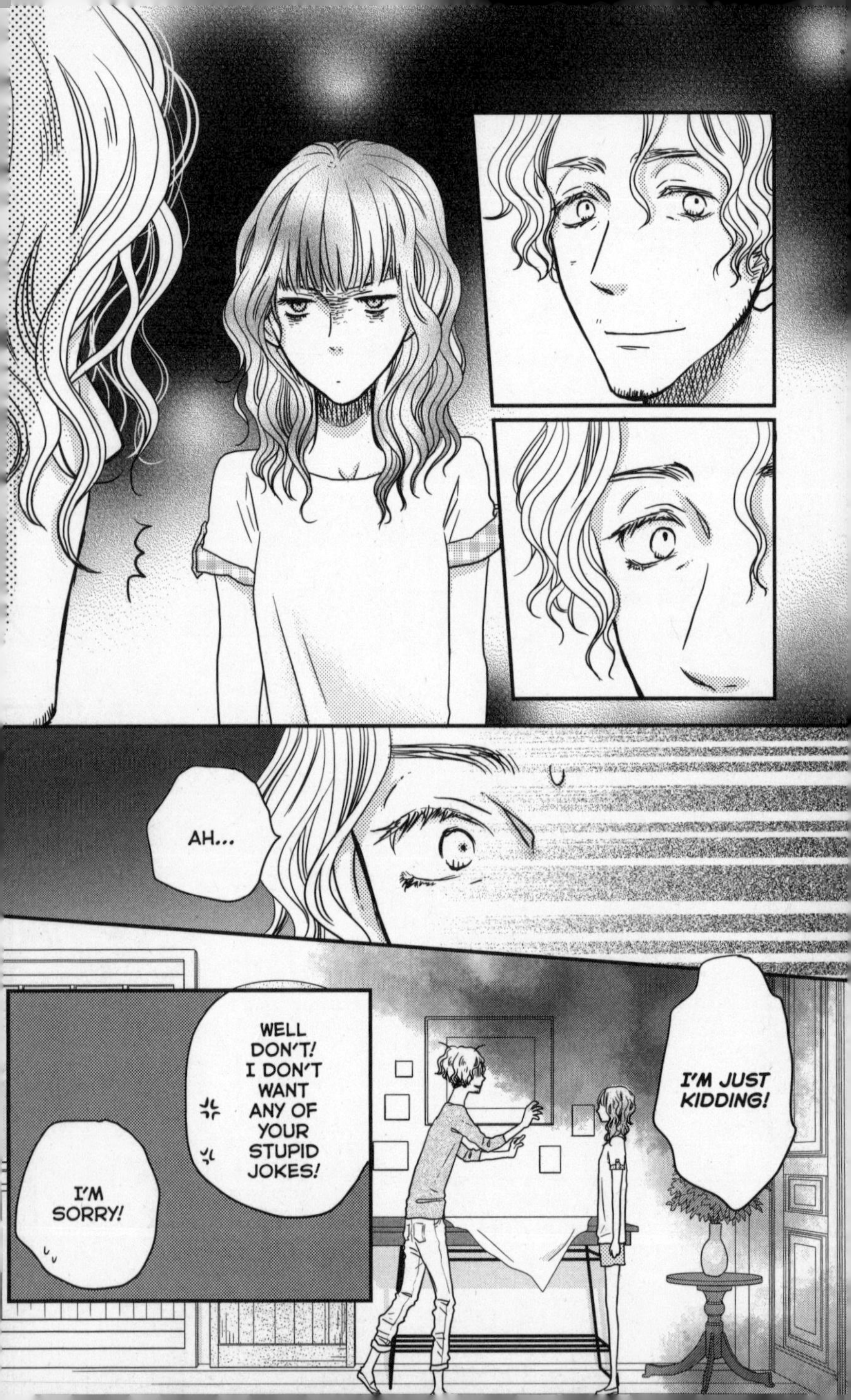
AH...
I'M JUST KIDDING!
WELL DON'T! I DON'T WANT ANY OF YOUR STUPID JOKES!
I'M SORRY!

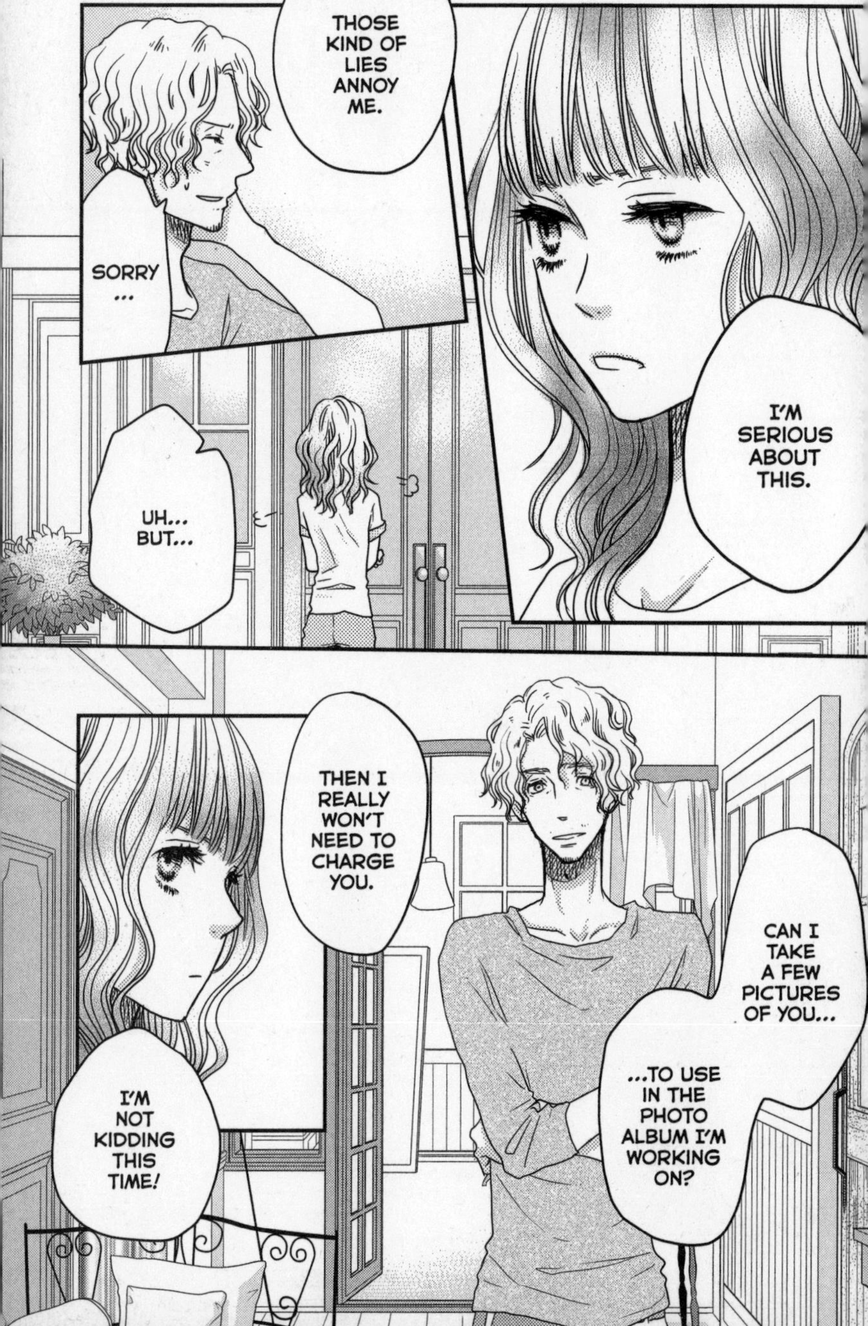
I'M SERIOUS ABOUT THIS.
THOSE KIND OF LIES ANNOY ME.
SORRY ...
UH... BUT...
CAN I TAKE A FEW PICTURES OF YOU...
...TO USE IN THE PHOTO ALBUM I'M WORKING ON?
THEN I REALLY WON'T NEED TO CHARGE YOU.
I'M NOT KIDDING THIS TIME!

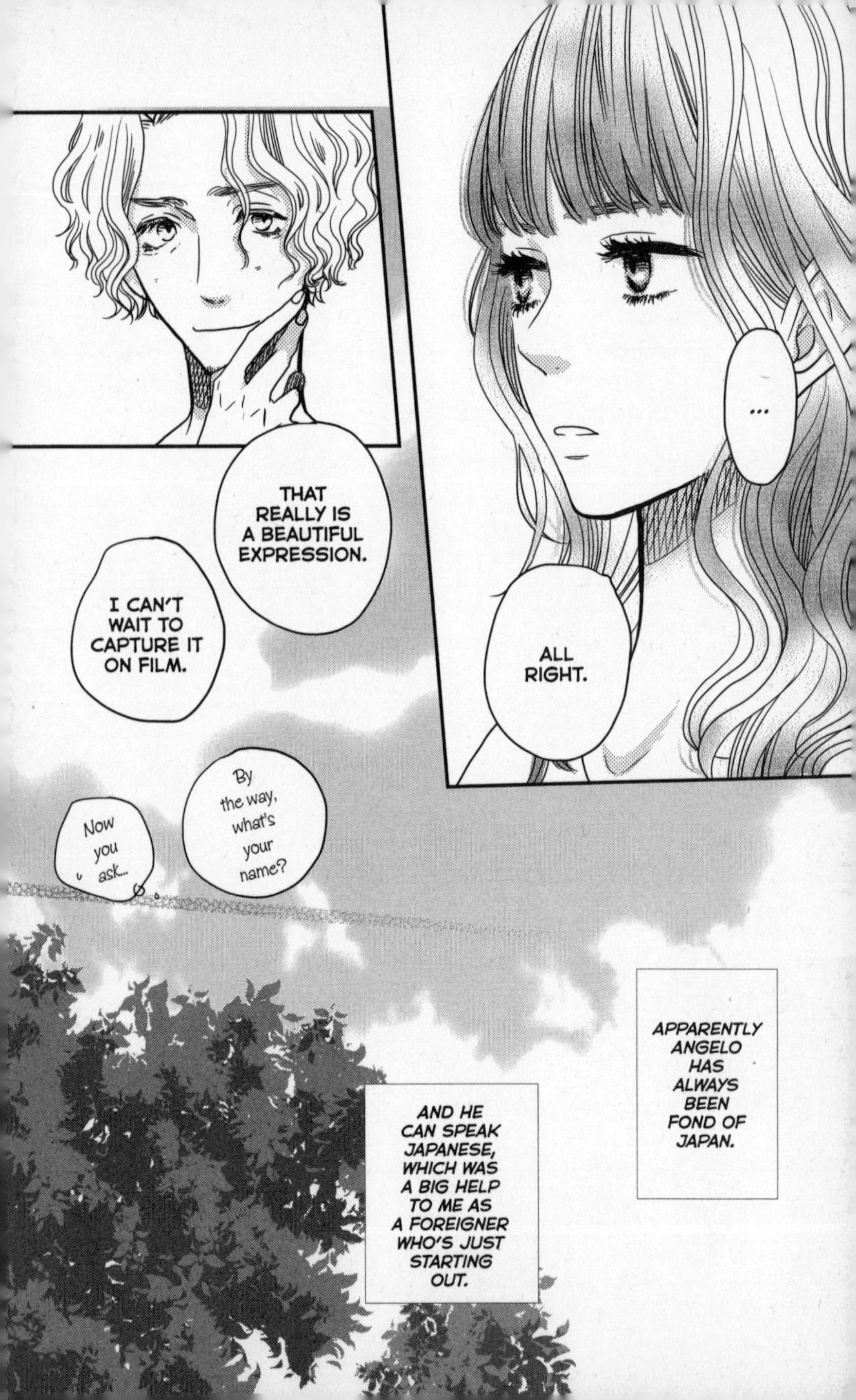
...
ALL RIGHT.
THAT REALLY IS A BEAUTIFUL EXPRESSION.
I CAN'T WAIT TO CAPTURE IT ON FILM.
By the way, what's your name?
Now you ask...
APPARENTLY ANGELO HAS ALWAYS BEEN FOND OF JAPAN.
AND HE CAN SPEAK JAPANESE, WHICH WAS A BIG HELP TO ME AS A FOREIGNER WHO'S JUST STARTING OUT.

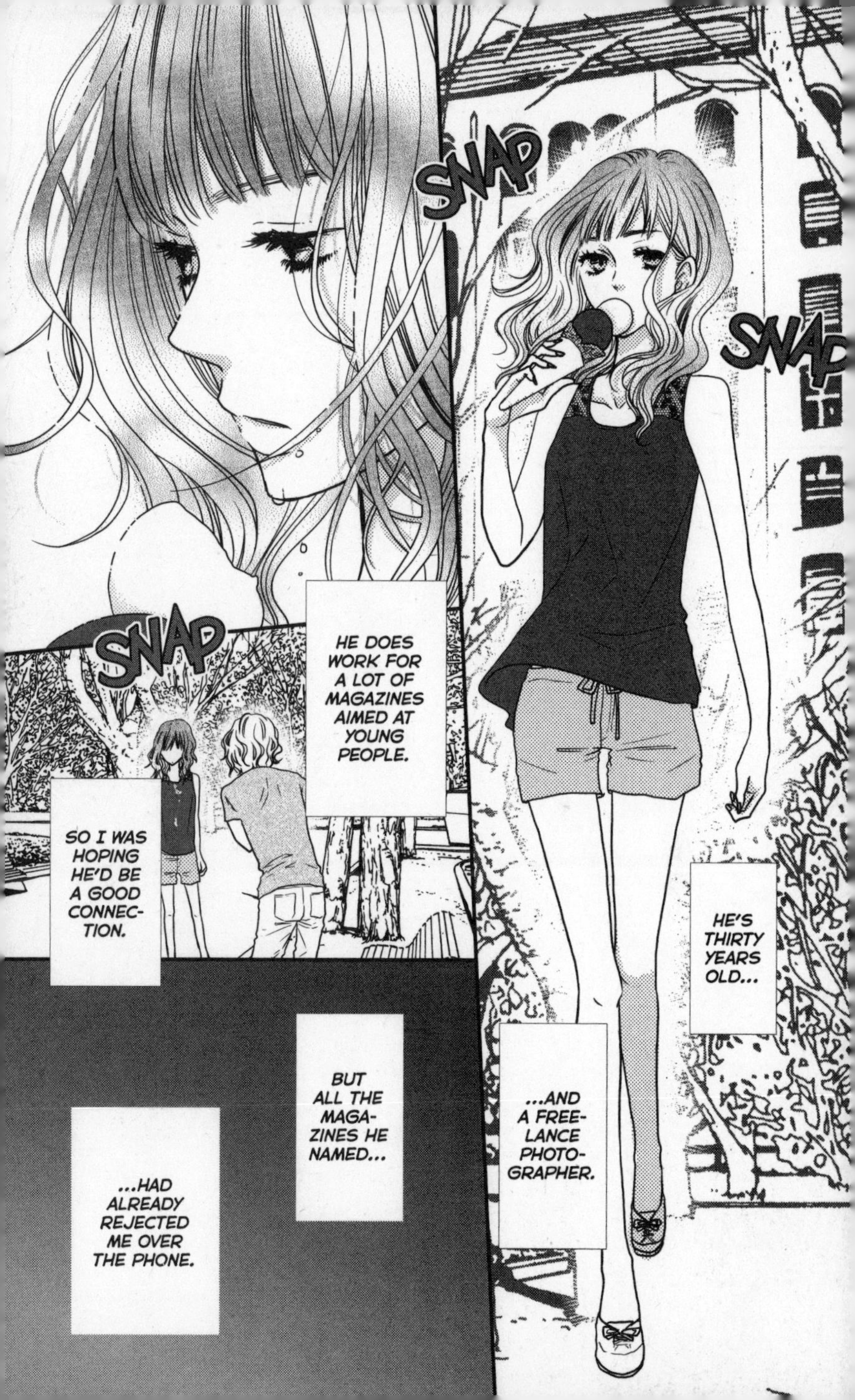
SNAP
SNAP
HE'S THIRTY YEARS OLD...
...AND A FREE-LANCE PHOTO-GRAPHER.
HE DOES WORK FOR A LOT OF MAGAZINES AIMED AT YOUNG PEOPLE.
SNAP
SO I WAS HOPING HE'D BE A GOOD CONNEC-TION.
BUT ALL THE MAGA-ZINES HE NAMED...
...HAD ALREADY REJECTED ME OVER THE PHONE.

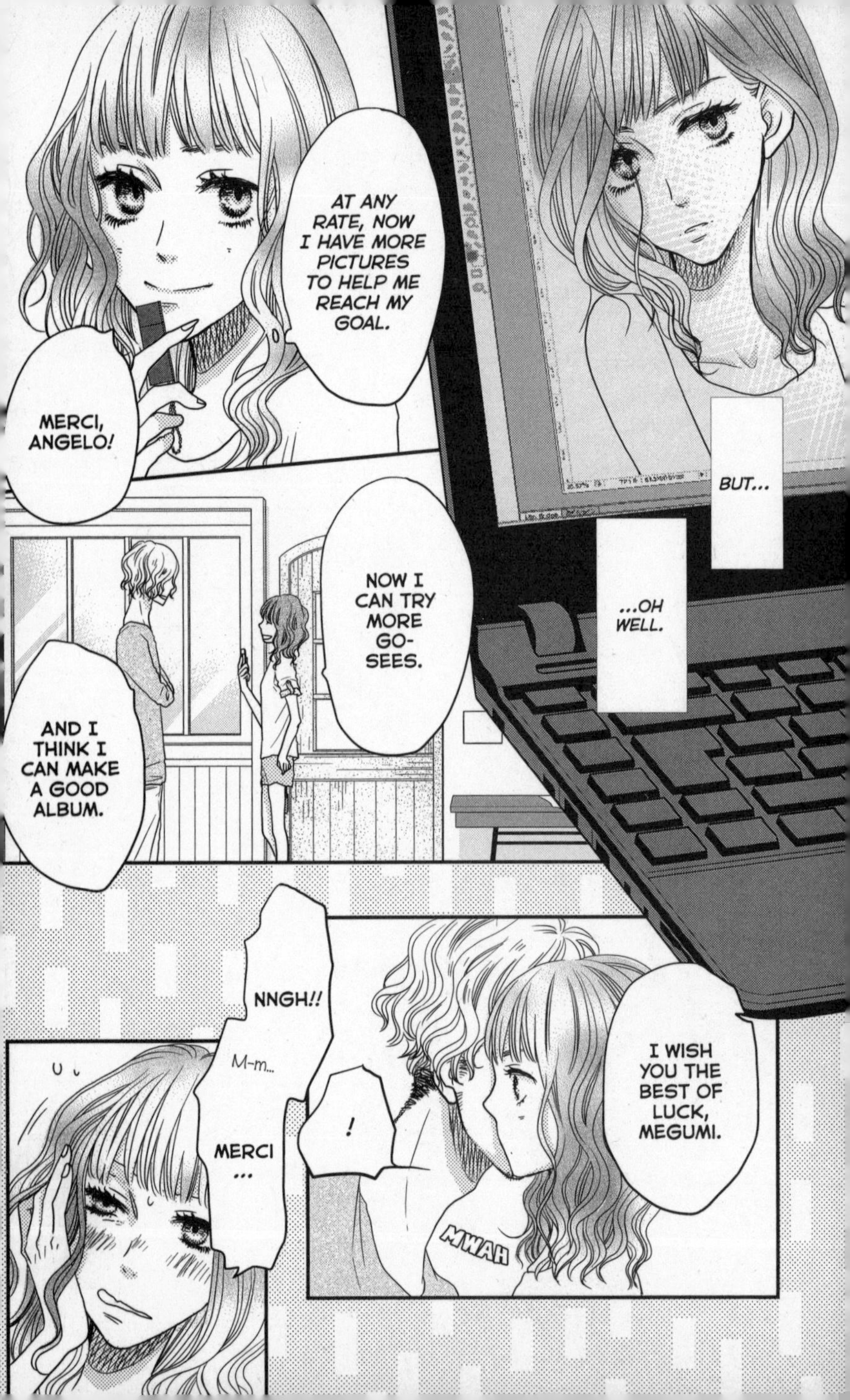

BUT...
...OH WELL.
AT ANY RATE, NOW I HAVE MORE PICTURES TO HELP ME REACH MY GOAL.
MERCI, ANGELO!
NOW I CAN TRY MORE GO-SEES.
AND I THINK I CAN MAKE A GOOD ALBUM.
I WISH YOU THE BEST OF LUCK, MEGUMI.
!
MWAH
NNGH!!
M-m...
MERCI ...

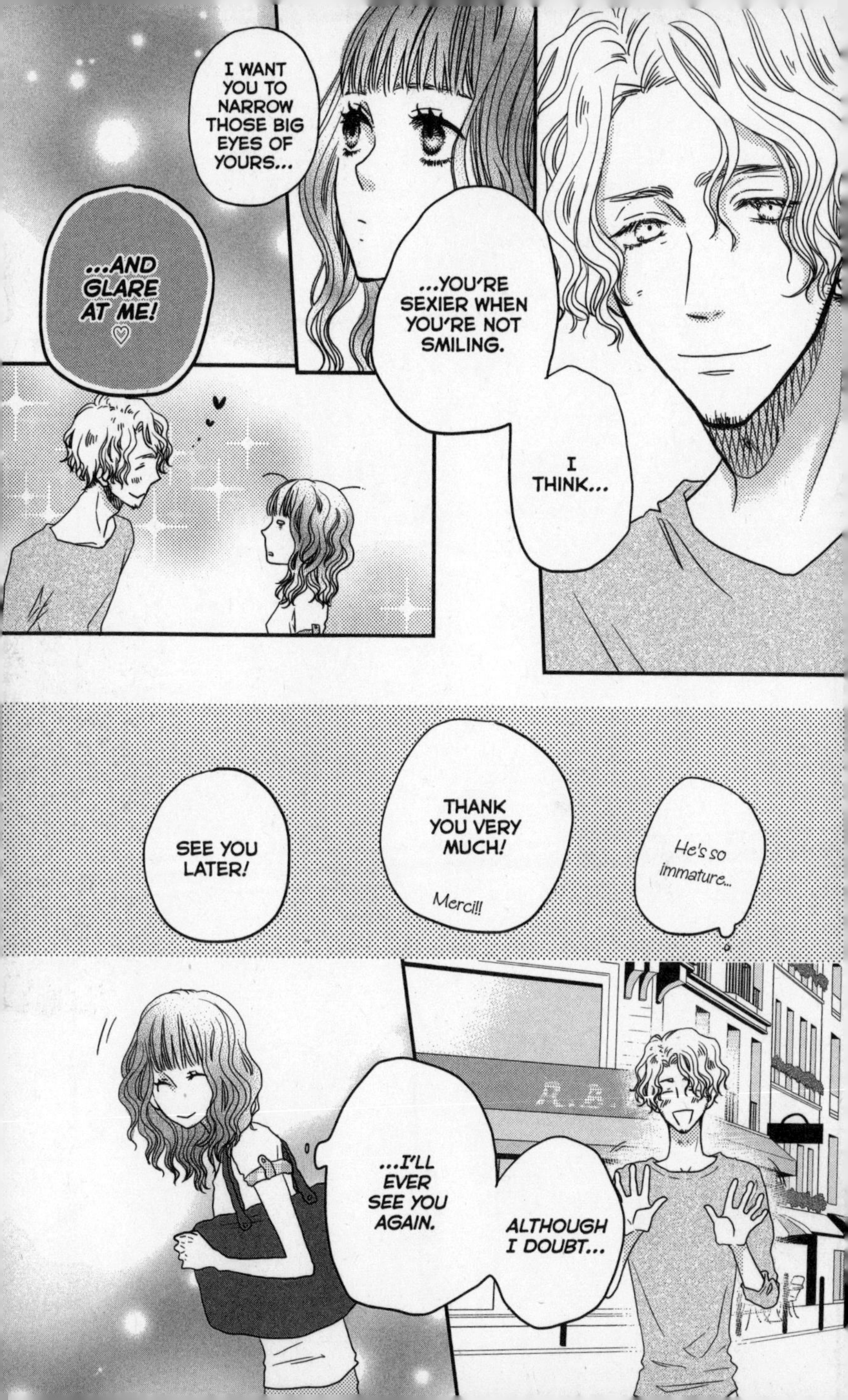
...YOU'RE SEXIER WHEN YOU'RE NOT SMILING.
I THINK...
I WANT YOU TO NARROW THOSE BIG EYES OF YOURS...
...AND GLARE AT ME! ♡
He's so immature...
THANK YOU VERY MUCH!
Merci!!
SEE YOU LATER!
ALTHOUGH I DOUBT...
...I'LL EVER SEE YOU AGAIN.

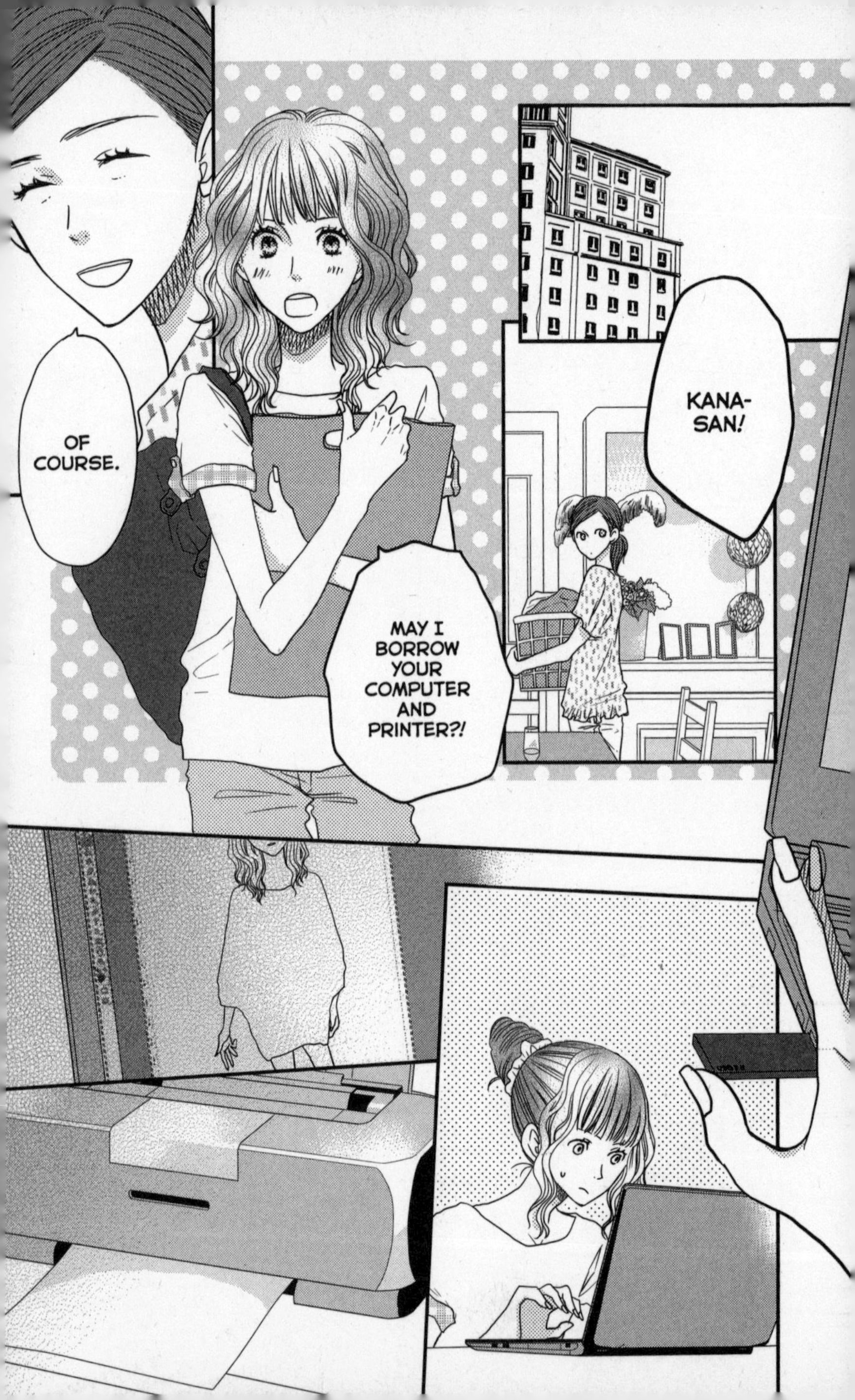
KANA-SAN!
MAY I BORROW YOUR COMPUTER AND PRINTER?!
OF COURSE.

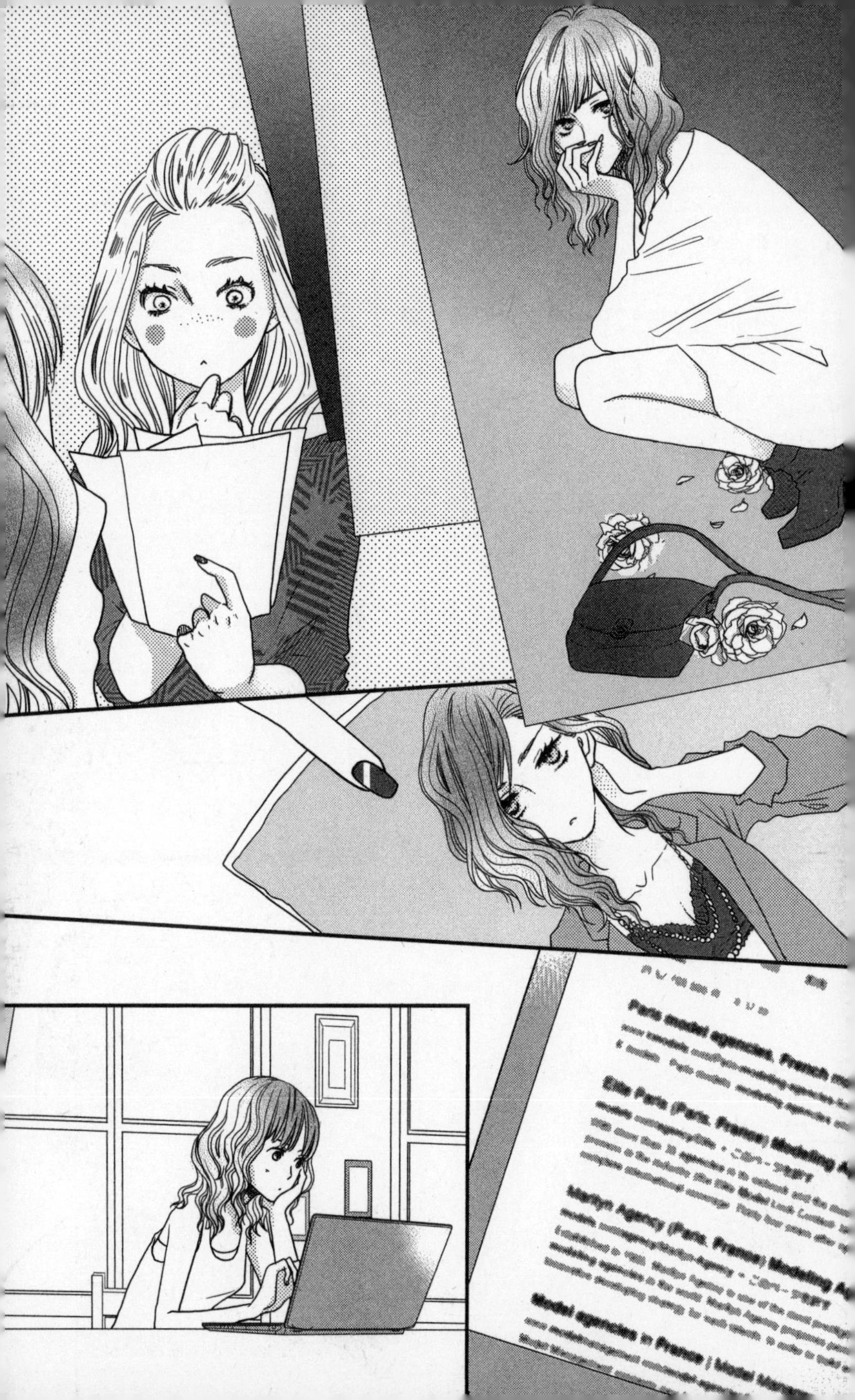

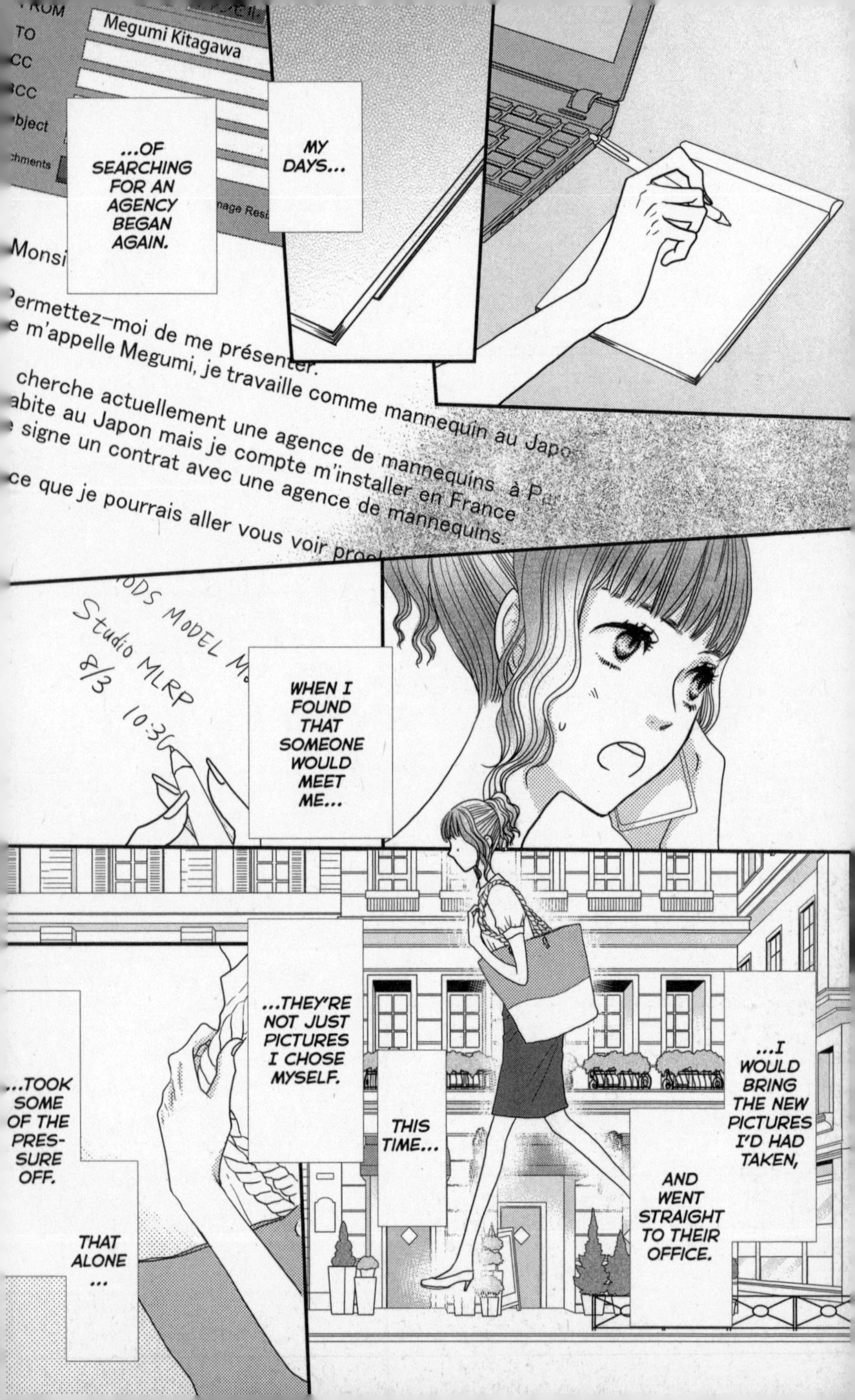
MY DAYS...
...OF SEARCHING FOR AN AGENCY BEGAN AGAIN.
TO
CC
BCC
bject
chments
mage Resi
Megumi Kitagawa
Monsi
Permettez-moi de me présenter.
e m'appelle Megumi, je travaille comme mannequin au Japo
cherche actuellement une agence de mannequins à P
abite au Japon mais je compte m'installer en France
e signe un contrat avec une agence de mannequins.
ce que je pourrais aller vous voir proc
WHEN I FOUND THAT SOMEONE WOULD MEET ME...
ODS MODEL M
Studio MLRP
8/3 10:3
...I WOULD BRING THE NEW PICTURES I'D HAD TAKEN,
AND WENT STRAIGHT TO THEIR OFFICE.
THIS TIME...
...THEY'RE NOT JUST PICTURES I CHOSE MYSELF.
THAT ALONE...
...TOOK SOME OF THE PRES-SURE OFF.

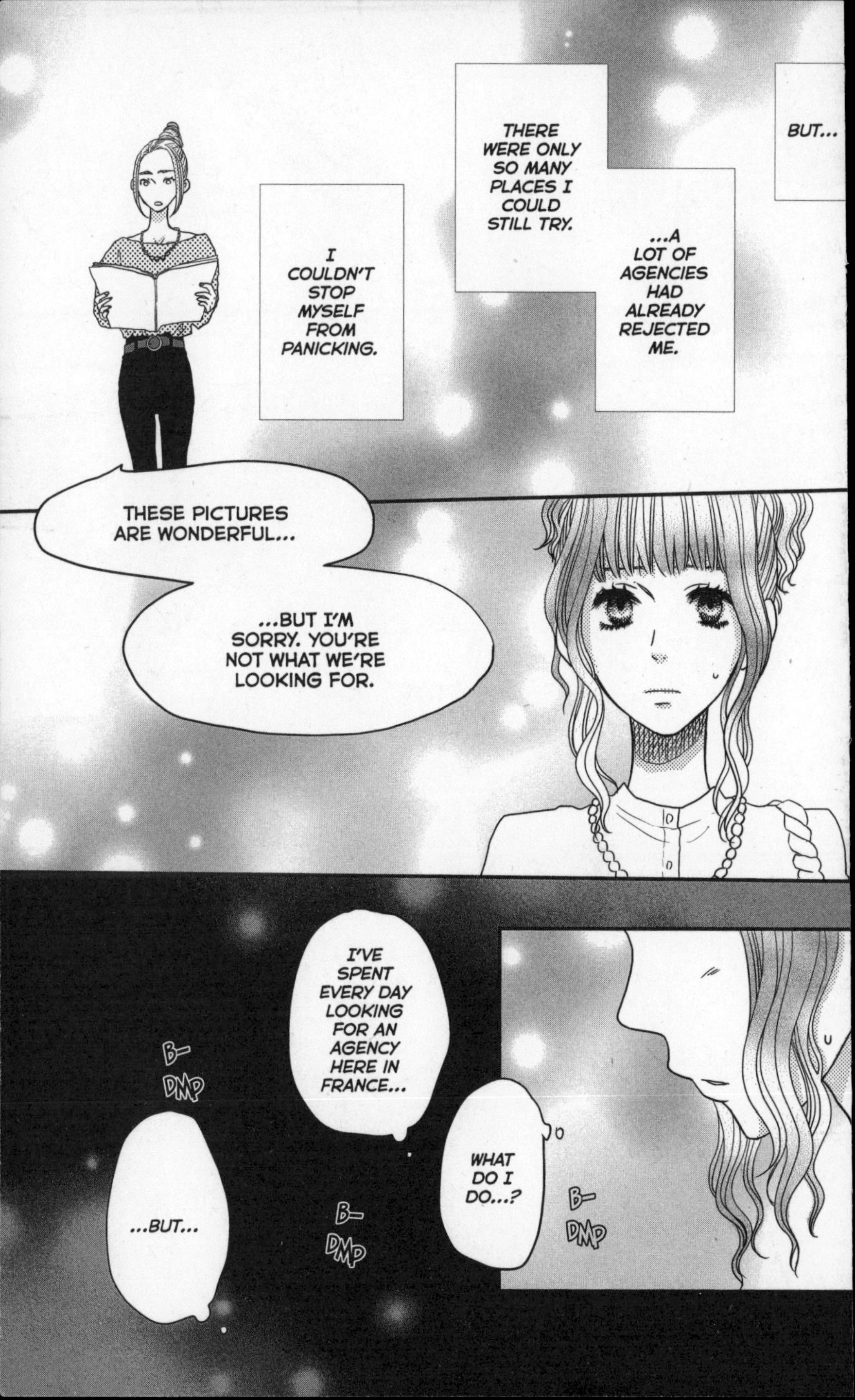
BUT...
THERE WERE ONLY SO MANY PLACES I COULD STILL TRY.
...A LOT OF AGENCIES HAD ALREADY REJECTED ME.
I COULDN'T STOP MYSELF FROM PANICKING.
THESE PICTURES ARE WONDERFUL...
...BUT I'M SORRY. YOU'RE NOT WHAT WE'RE LOOKING FOR.
WHAT DO I DO...?
B-DMP
I'VE SPENT EVERY DAY LOOKING FOR AN AGENCY HERE IN FRANCE...
B-DMP
B-DMP
...BUT...

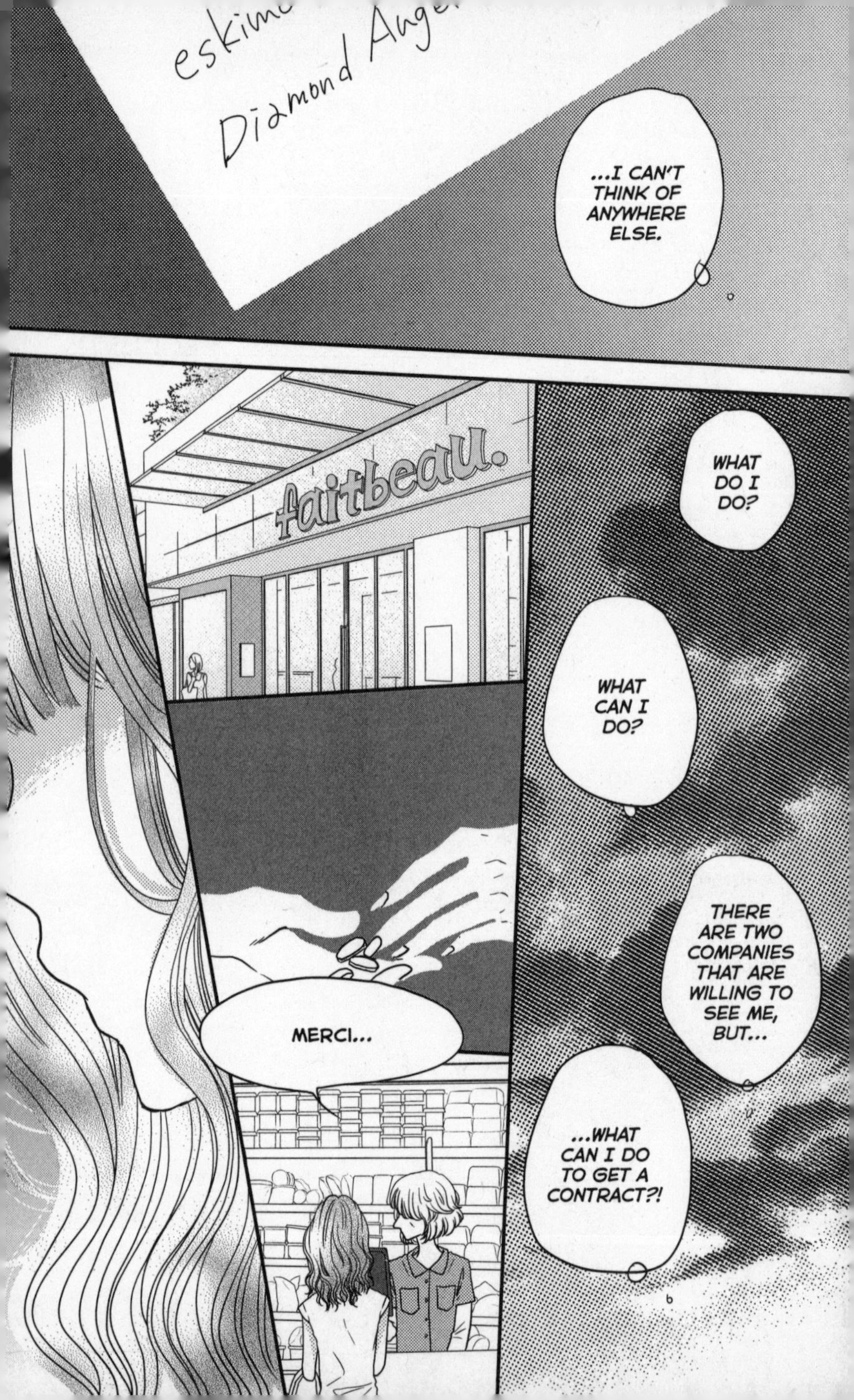
Diamond
...I CAN'T THINK OF ANYWHERE ELSE.
WHAT DO I DO?
WHAT CAN I DO?
THERE ARE TWO COMPANIES THAT ARE WILLING TO SEE ME, BUT...
...WHAT CAN I DO TO GET A CONTRACT?!
faitbeau.
MERCI...

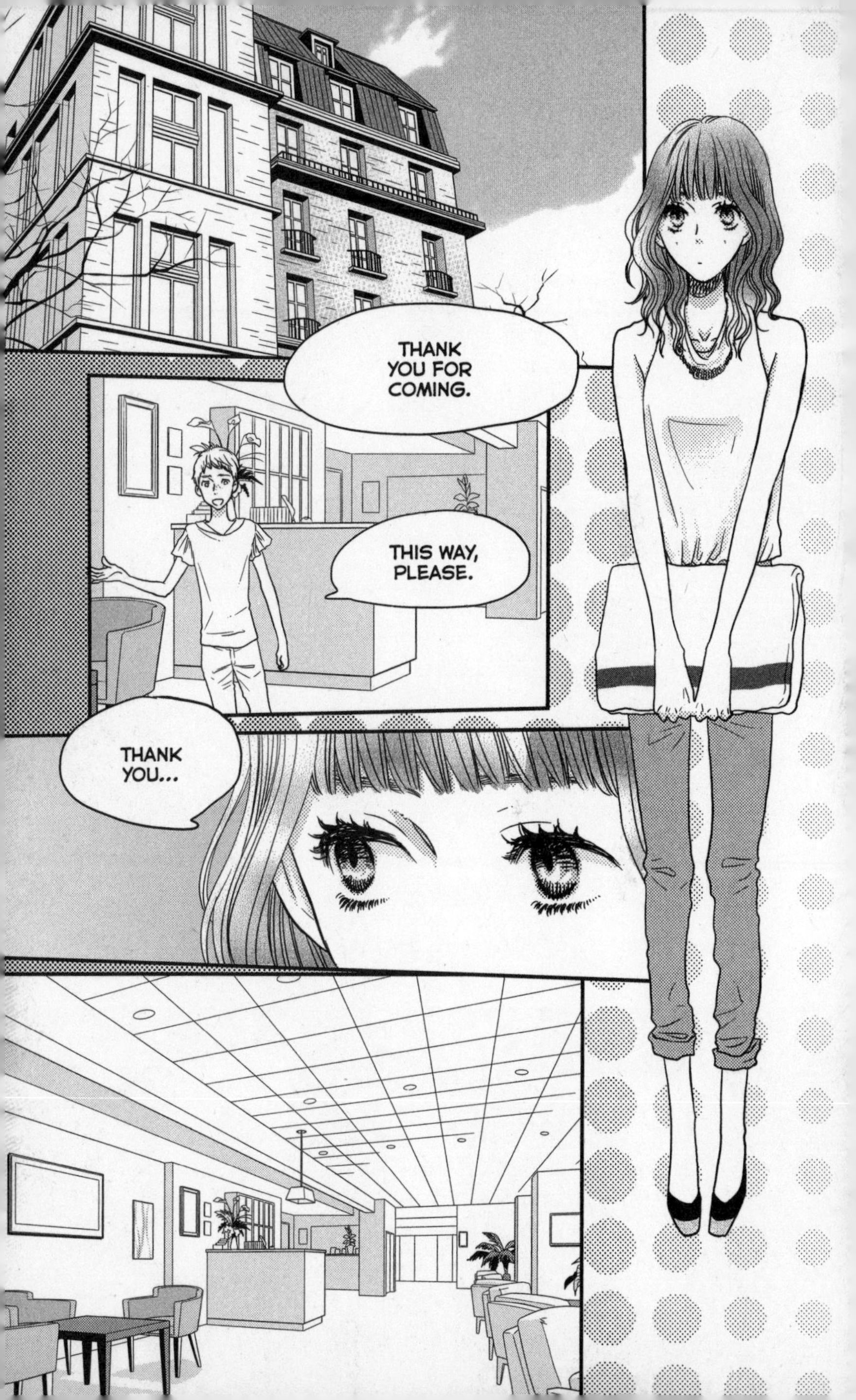
THANK YOU FOR COMING.
THIS WAY, PLEASE.
THANK YOU...

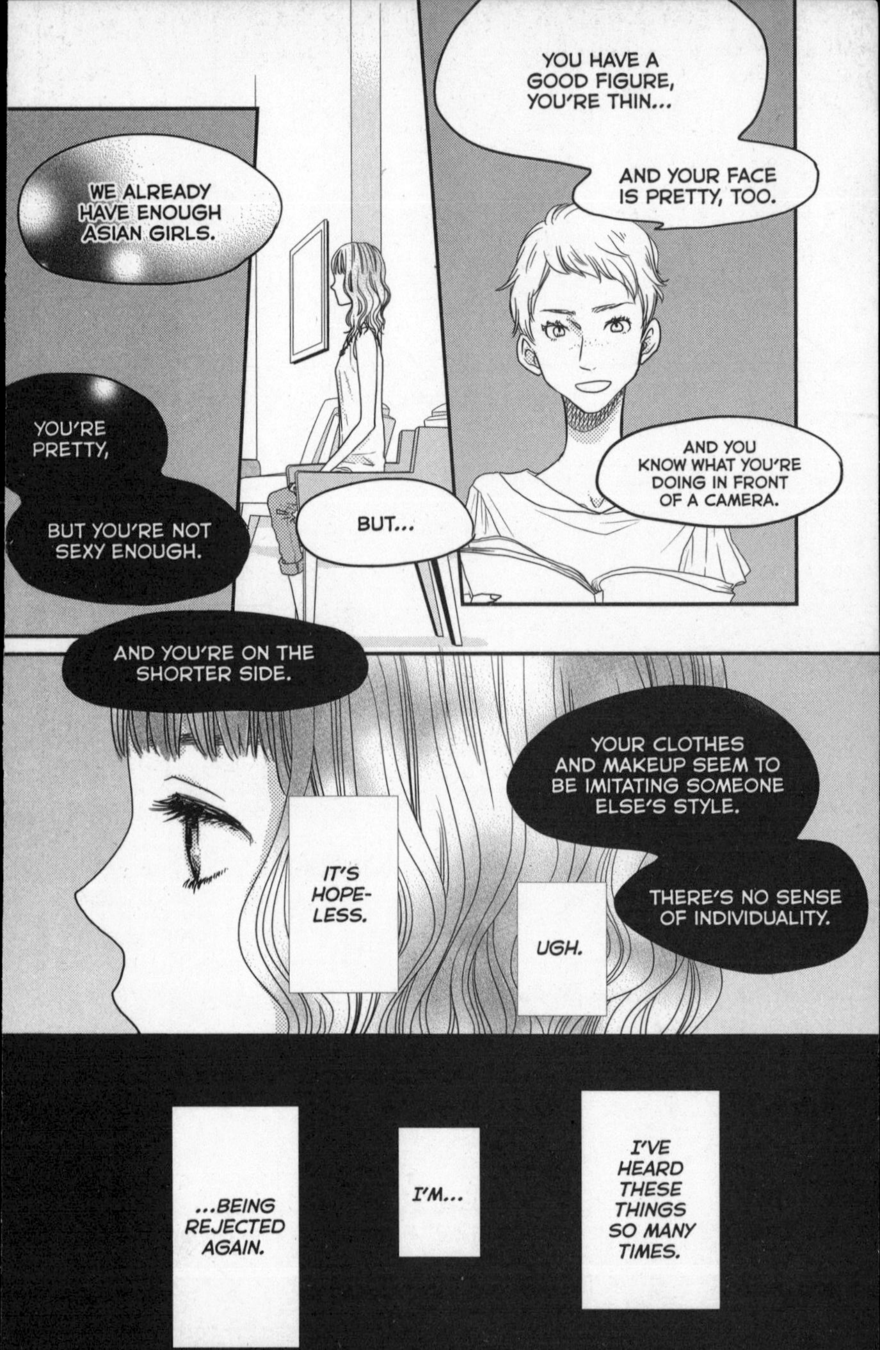
YOU HAVE A GOOD FIGURE, YOU'RE THIN...
AND YOUR FACE IS PRETTY, TOO.
AND YOU KNOW WHAT YOU'RE DOING IN FRONT OF A CAMERA.
BUT...
WE ALREADY HAVE ENOUGH ASIAN GIRLS.
YOU'RE PRETTY,
BUT YOU'RE NOT SEXY ENOUGH.
AND YOU'RE ON THE SHORTER SIDE.
YOUR CLOTHES AND MAKEUP SEEM TO BE IMITATING SOMEONE ELSE'S STYLE.
THERE'S NO SENSE OF INDIVIDUALITY.
UGH.
IT'S HOPE-LESS.
I'VE HEARD THESE THINGS SO MANY TIMES.
I'M...
...BEING REJECTED AGAIN.

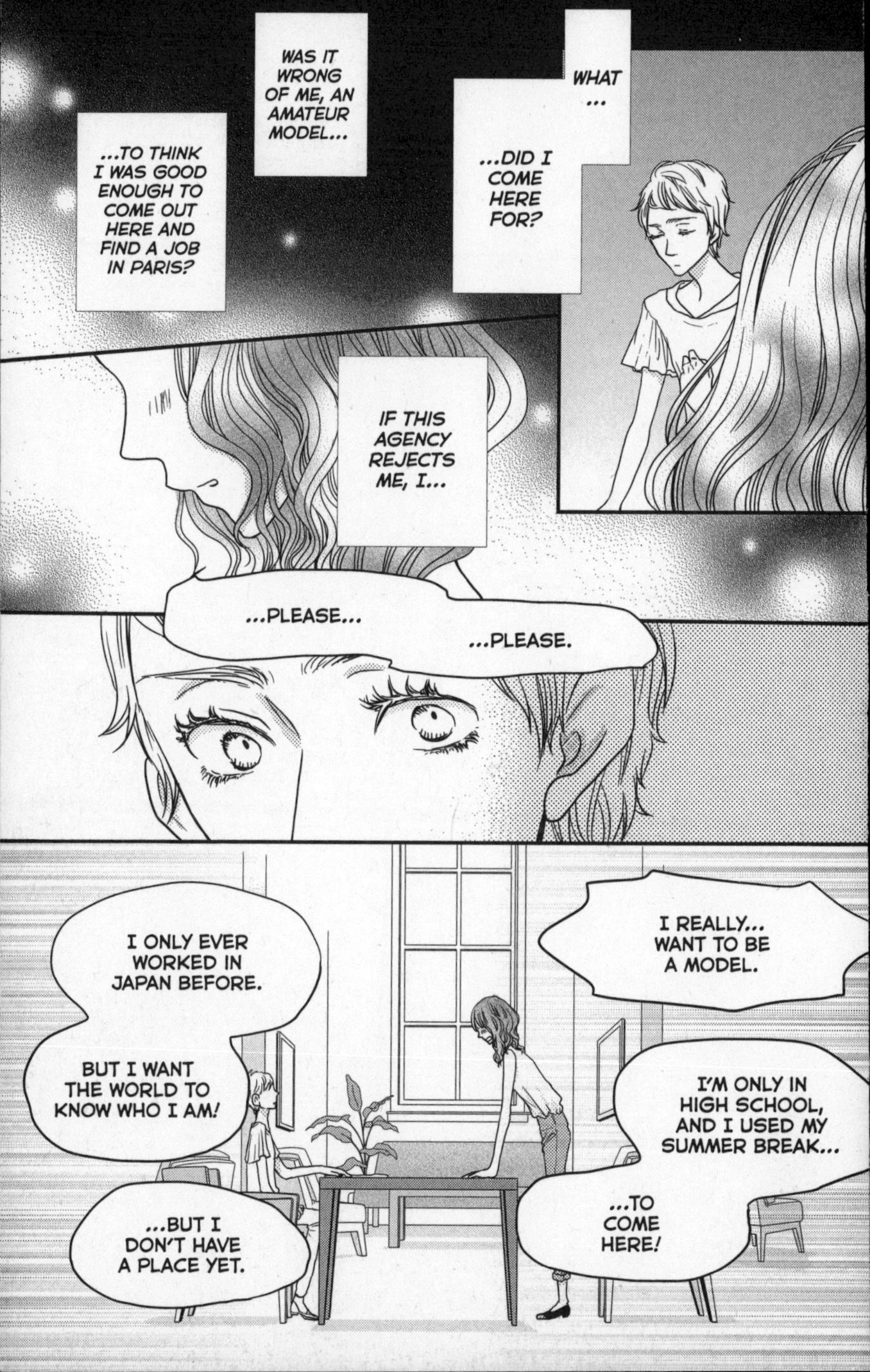
WHAT ...
...DID I COME HERE FOR?
WAS IT WRONG OF ME, AN AMATEUR MODEL...
...TO THINK I WAS GOOD ENOUGH TO COME OUT HERE AND FIND A JOB IN PARIS?
IF THIS AGENCY REJECTS ME, I...
...PLEASE...
...PLEASE.
I REALLY... WANT TO BE A MODEL.
I'M ONLY IN HIGH SCHOOL, AND I USED MY SUMMER BREAK...
...TO COME HERE!
I ONLY EVER WORKED IN JAPAN BEFORE.
BUT I WANT THE WORLD TO KNOW WHO I AM!
...BUT I DON'T HAVE A PLACE YET.

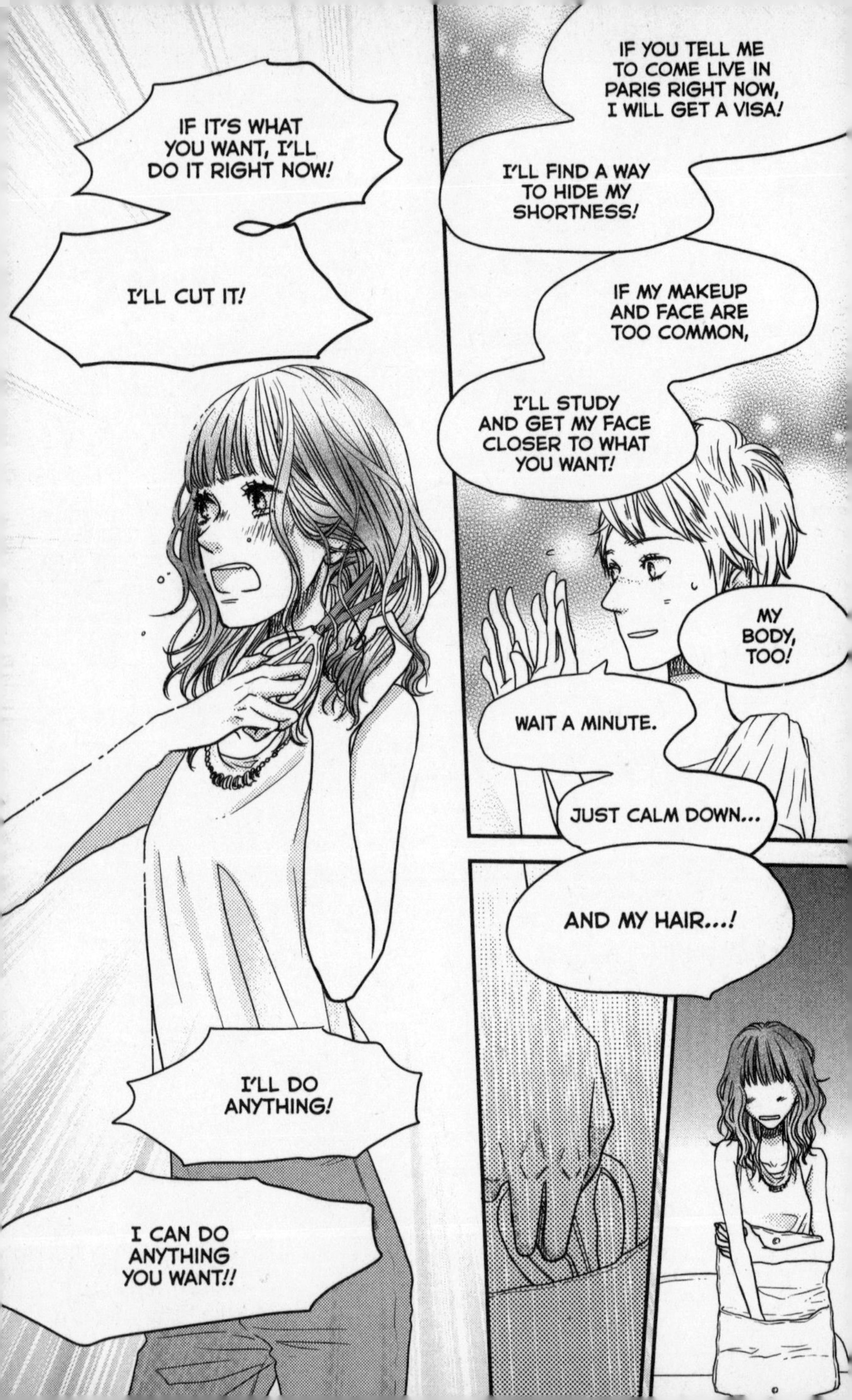
IF YOU TELL ME TO COME LIVE IN PARIS RIGHT NOW, I WILL GET A VISA!
I'LL FIND A WAY TO HIDE MY SHORTNESS!
IF MY MAKEUP AND FACE ARE TOO COMMON,
I'LL STUDY AND GET MY FACE CLOSER TO WHAT YOU WANT!
MY BODY, TOO!
WAIT A MINUTE.
JUST CALM DOWN...
AND MY HAIR...!
IF IT'S WHAT YOU WANT, I'LL DO IT RIGHT NOW!
I'LL CUT IT!
I'LL DO ANYTHING!
I CAN DO ANYTHING YOU WANT!!

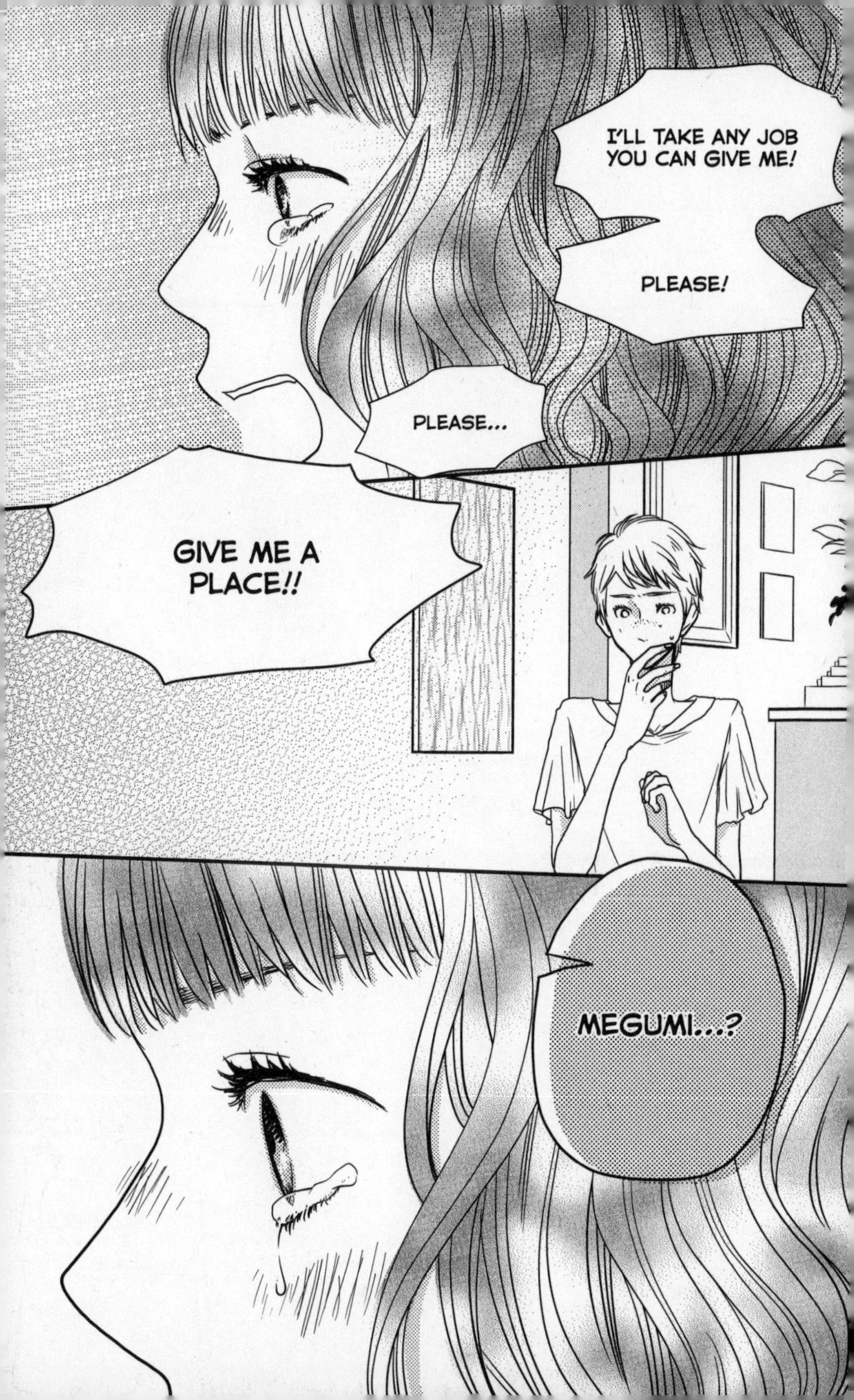
I'LL TAKE ANY JOB YOU CAN GIVE ME!
PLEASE!
PLEASE...
GIVE ME A PLACE!!
MEGUMI...?

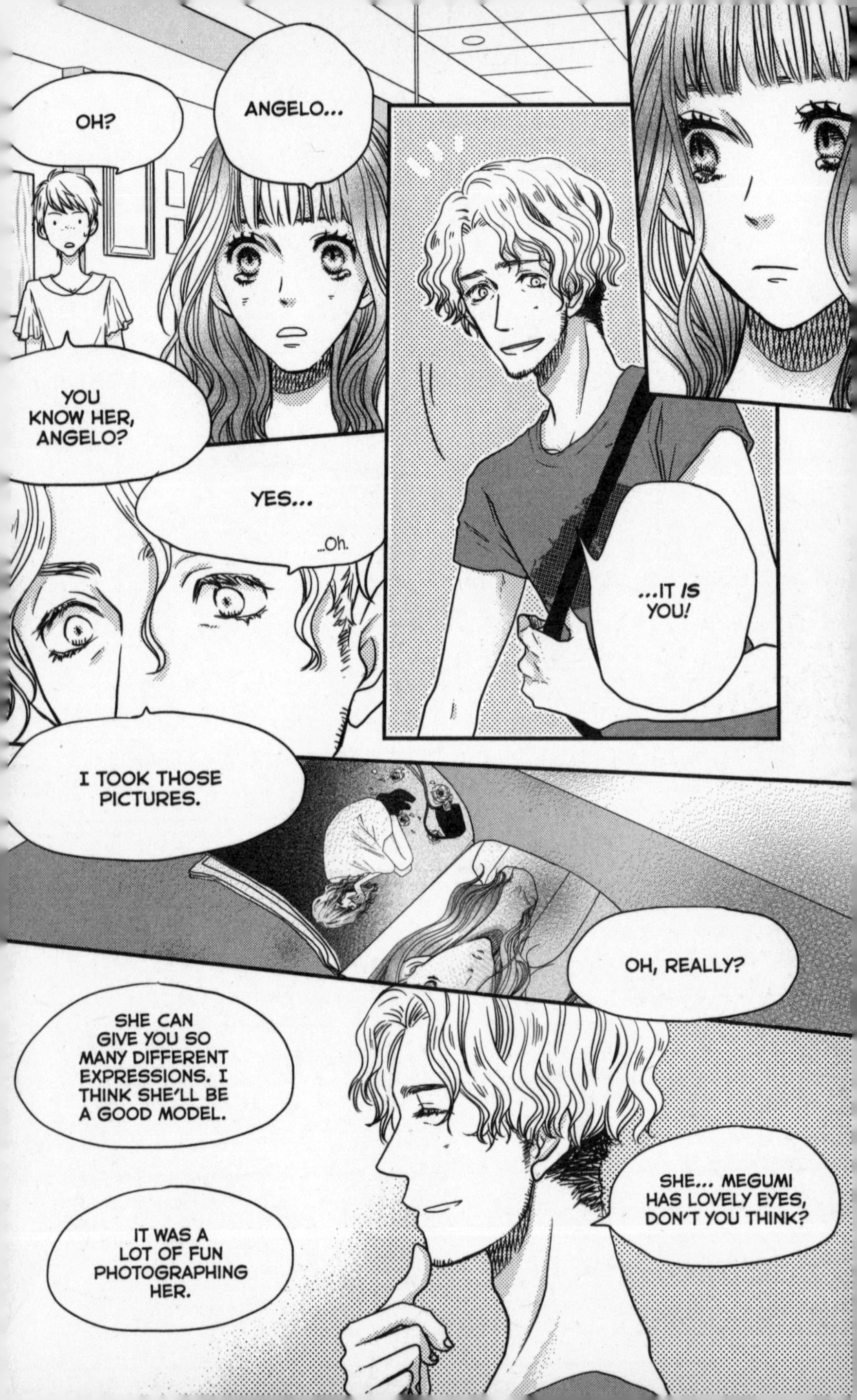
...IT IS YOU!
ANGELO...
OH?
YOU KNOW HER, ANGELO?
YES...
...Oh.
I TOOK THOSE PICTURES.
OH, REALLY?
SHE... MEGUMI HAS LOVELY EYES, DON'T YOU THINK?
SHE CAN GIVE YOU SO MANY DIFFERENT EXPRESSIONS. I THINK SHE'LL BE A GOOD MODEL.
IT WAS A LOT OF FUN PHOTOGRAPHING HER.

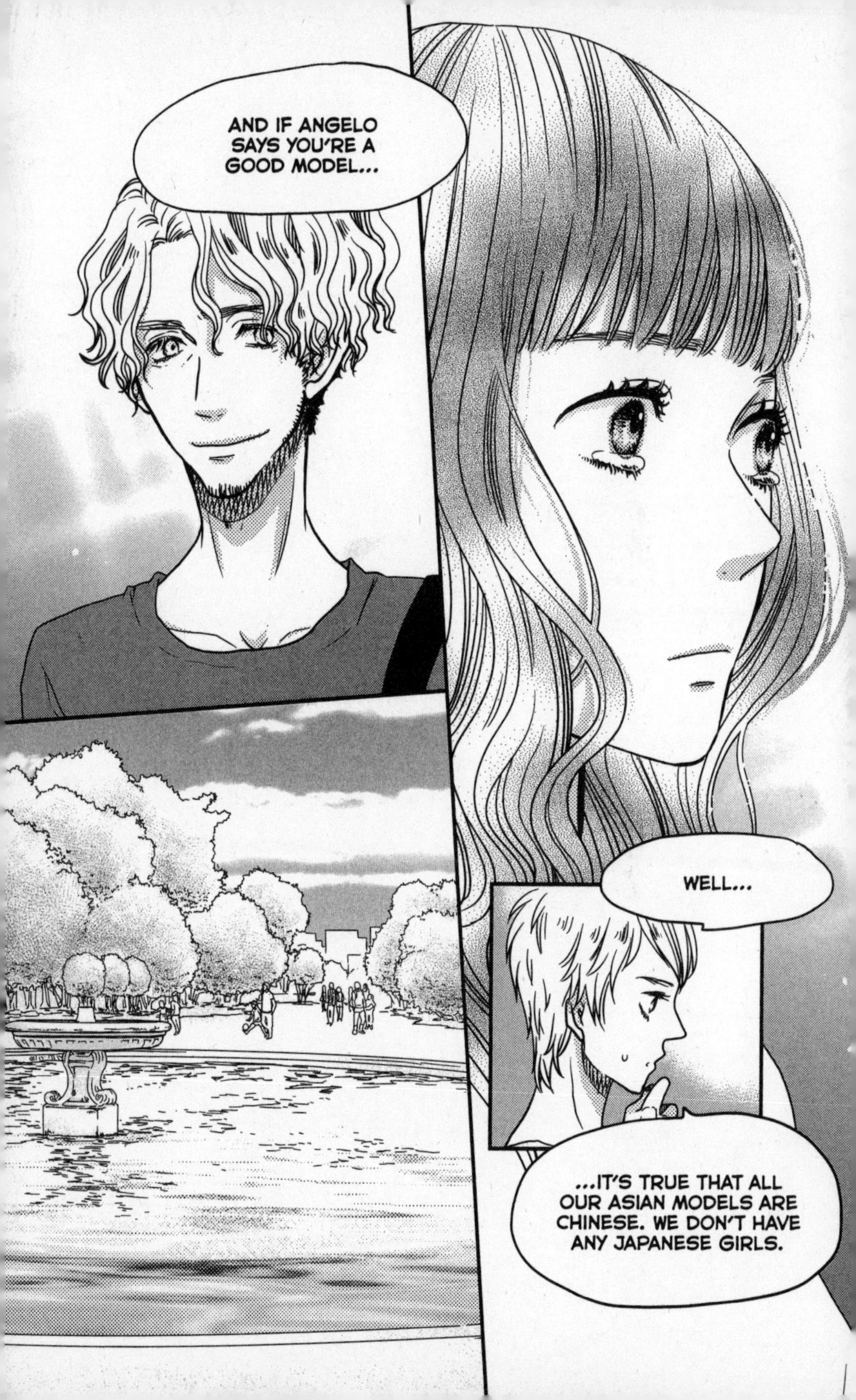
AND IF ANGELO SAYS YOU'RE A GOOD MODEL...
WELL...
...IT'S TRUE THAT ALL OUR ASIAN MODELS ARE CHINESE. WE DON'T HAVE ANY JAPANESE GIRLS.

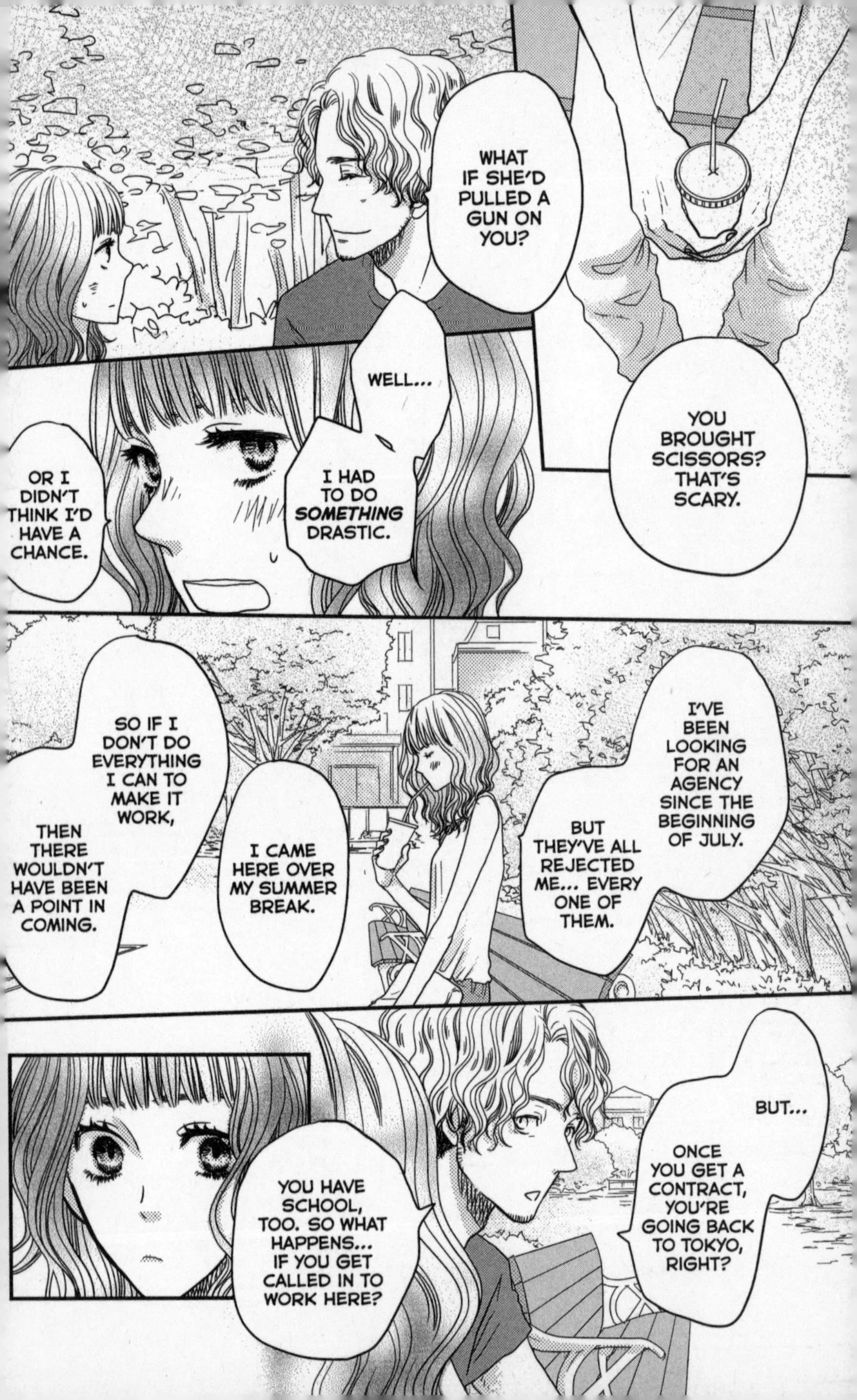
YOU BROUGHT SCISSORS? THAT'S SCARY.
WHAT IF SHE'D PULLED A GUN ON YOU?
WELL...
I HAD TO DO *SOMETHING* DRASTIC.
OR I DIDN'T THINK I'D HAVE A CHANCE.
I'VE BEEN LOOKING FOR AN AGENCY SINCE THE BEGINNING OF JULY.
BUT THEY'VE ALL REJECTED ME... EVERY ONE OF THEM.
I CAME HERE OVER MY SUMMER BREAK.
SO IF I DON'T DO EVERYTHING I CAN TO MAKE IT WORK,
THEN THERE WOULDN'T HAVE BEEN A POINT IN COMING.
BUT...
ONCE YOU GET A CONTRACT, YOU'RE GOING BACK TO TOKYO, RIGHT?
YOU HAVE SCHOOL, TOO. SO WHAT HAPPENS... IF YOU GET CALLED IN TO WORK HERE?

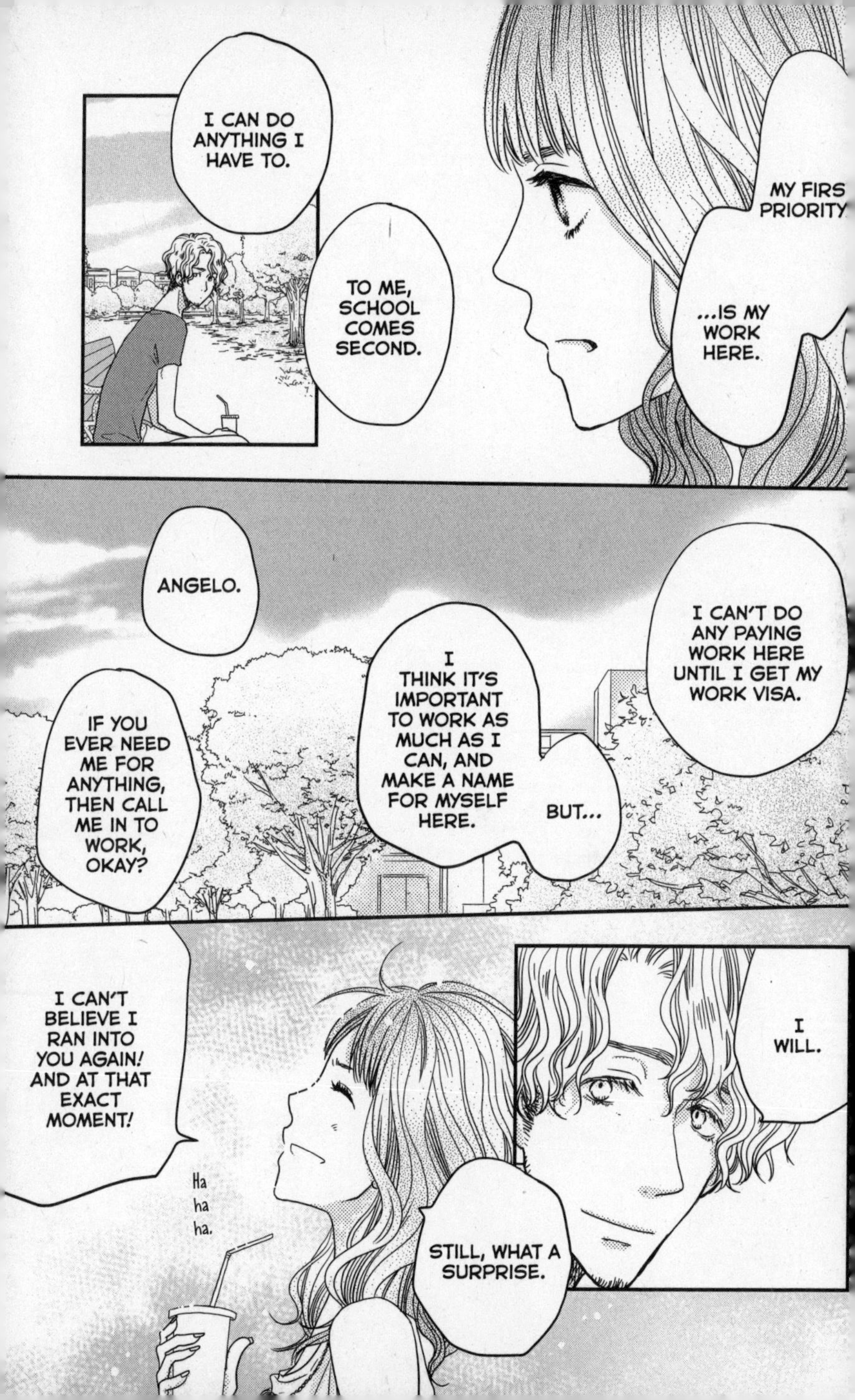
MY FIRS PRIORITY
...IS MY WORK HERE.
TO ME, SCHOOL COMES SECOND.
I CAN DO ANYTHING I HAVE TO.
I CAN'T DO ANY PAYING WORK HERE UNTIL I GET MY WORK VISA.
I THINK IT'S IMPORTANT TO WORK AS MUCH AS I CAN, AND MAKE A NAME FOR MYSELF HERE.
BUT...
ANGELO.
IF YOU EVER NEED ME FOR ANYTHING, THEN CALL ME IN TO WORK, OKAY?
I WILL.
STILL, WHAT A SURPRISE.
I CAN'T BELIEVE I RAN INTO YOU AGAIN! AND AT THAT EXACT MOMENT!
Ha ha ha.

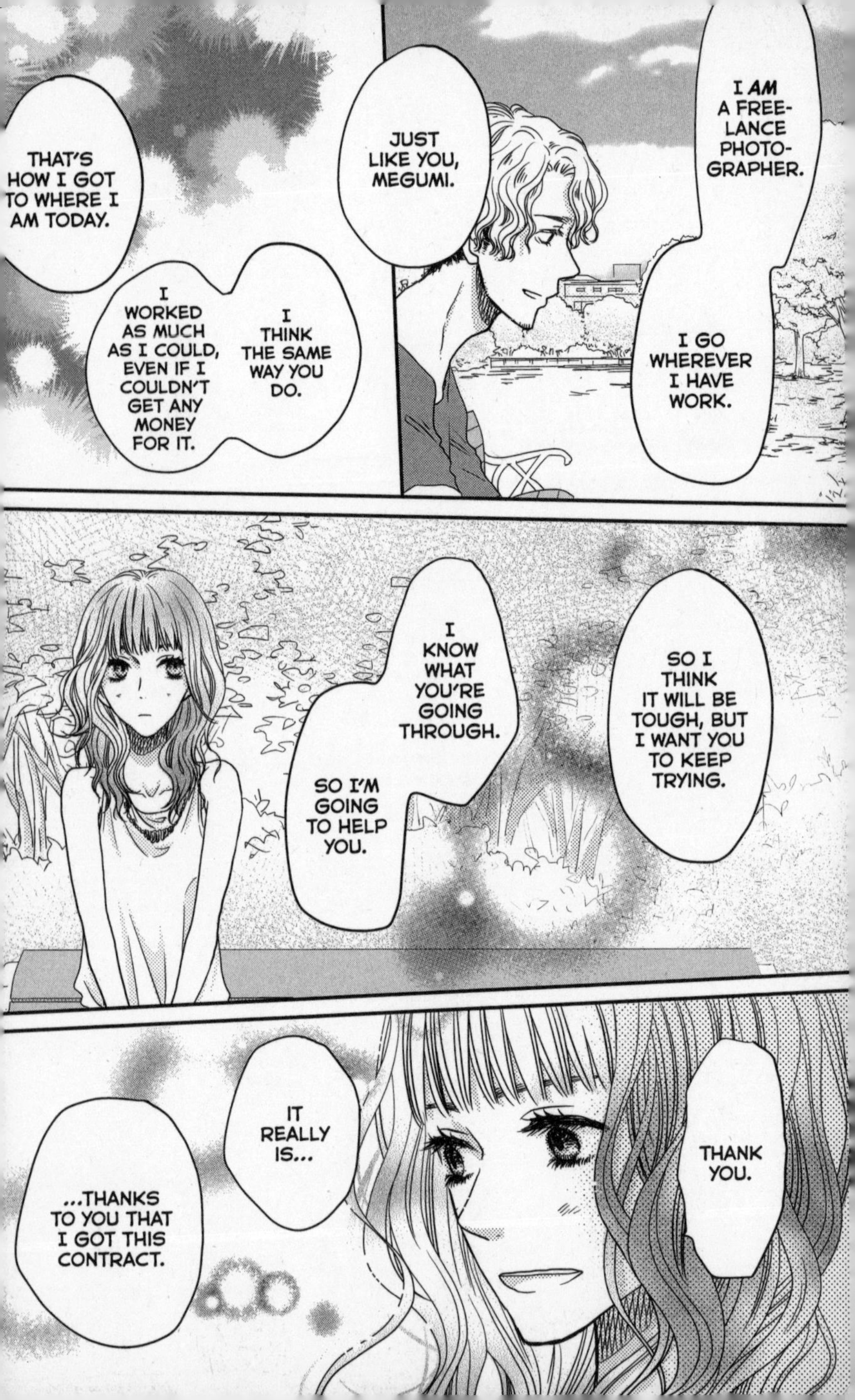
I *AM* A FREELANCE PHOTOGRAPHER.
I GO WHEREVER I HAVE WORK.
JUST LIKE YOU, MEGUMI.
I THINK THE SAME WAY YOU DO.
I WORKED AS MUCH AS I COULD, EVEN IF I COULDN'T GET ANY MONEY FOR IT.
THAT'S HOW I GOT TO WHERE I AM TODAY.
SO I THINK IT WILL BE TOUGH, BUT I WANT YOU TO KEEP TRYING.
I KNOW WHAT YOU'RE GOING THROUGH.
SO I'M GOING TO HELP YOU.
THANK YOU.
IT REALLY IS...
...THANKS TO YOU THAT I GOT THIS CONTRACT.

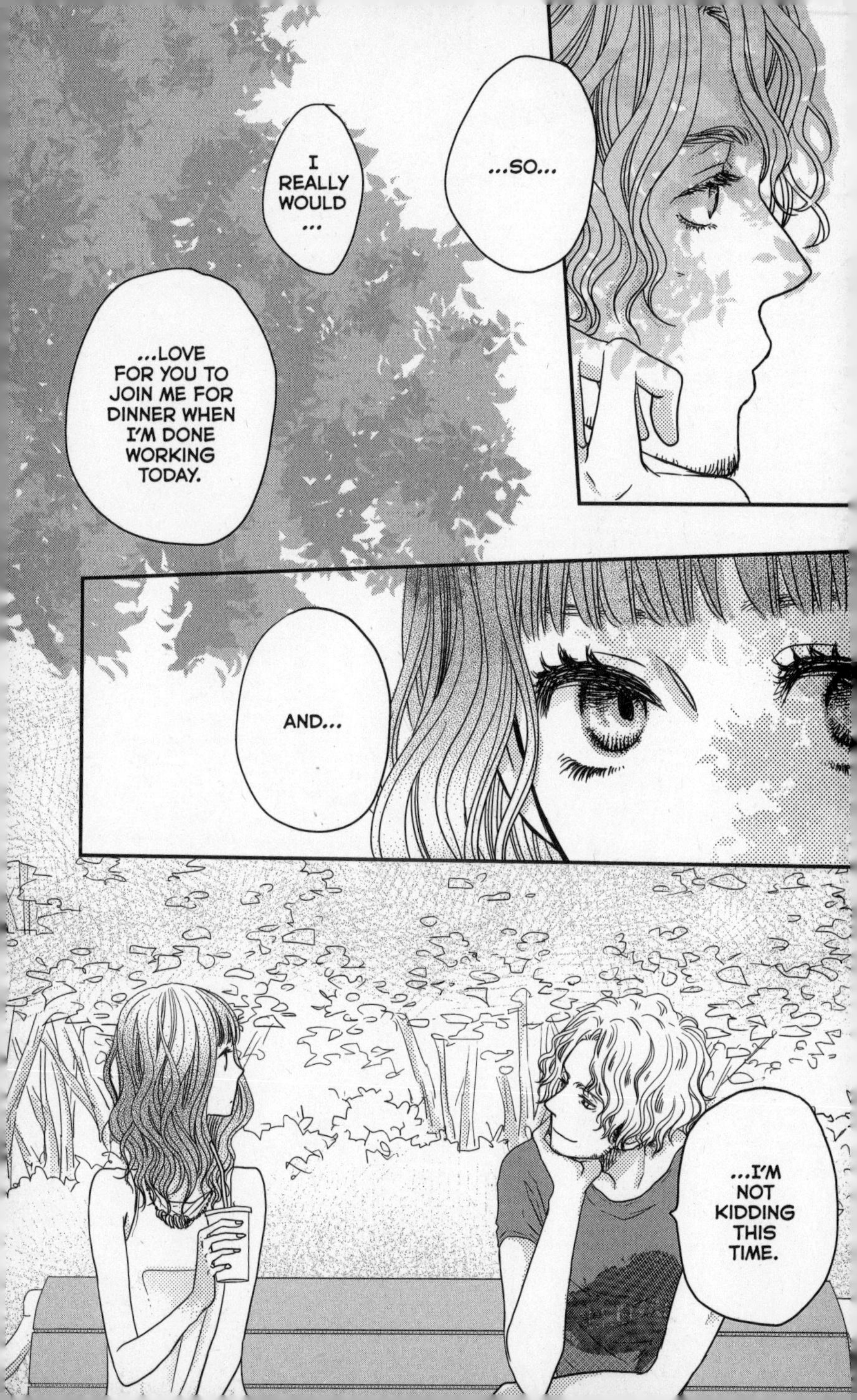
...SO...
I REALLY WOULD ...
...LOVE FOR YOU TO JOIN ME FOR DINNER WHEN I'M DONE WORKING TODAY.
AND...
...I'M NOT KIDDING THIS TIME.

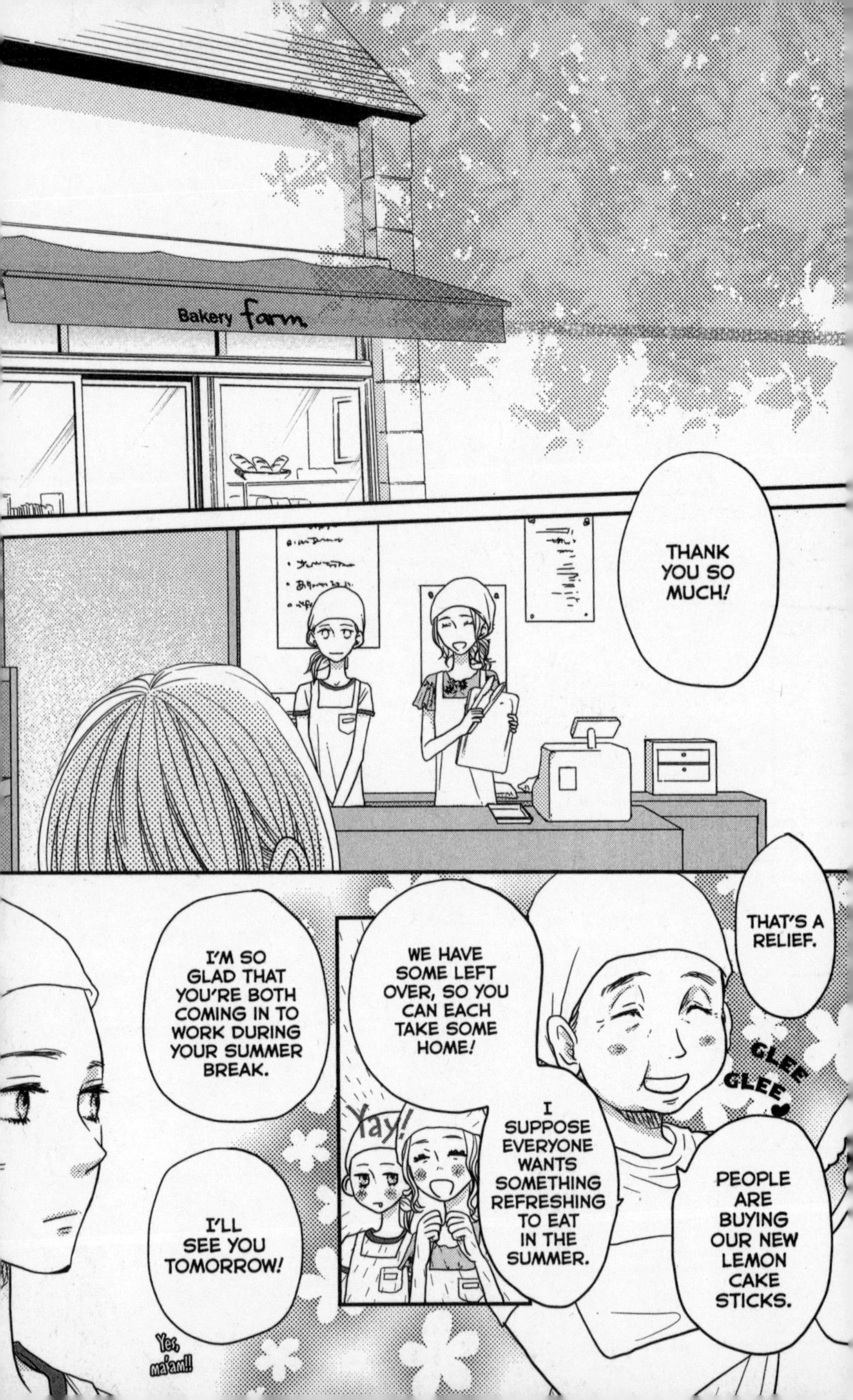

Bakery farm
THANK YOU SO MUCH!
THAT'S A RELIEF.
GLEE GLEE
PEOPLE ARE BUYING OUR NEW LEMON CAKE STICKS.
I SUPPOSE EVERYONE WANTS SOMETHING REFRESHING TO EAT IN THE SUMMER.
WE HAVE SOME LEFT OVER, SO YOU CAN EACH TAKE SOME HOME!
Yay!
I'M SO GLAD THAT YOU'RE BOTH COMING IN TO WORK DURING YOUR SUMMER BREAK.
I'LL SEE YOU TOMORROW!
Yes, ma'am!!

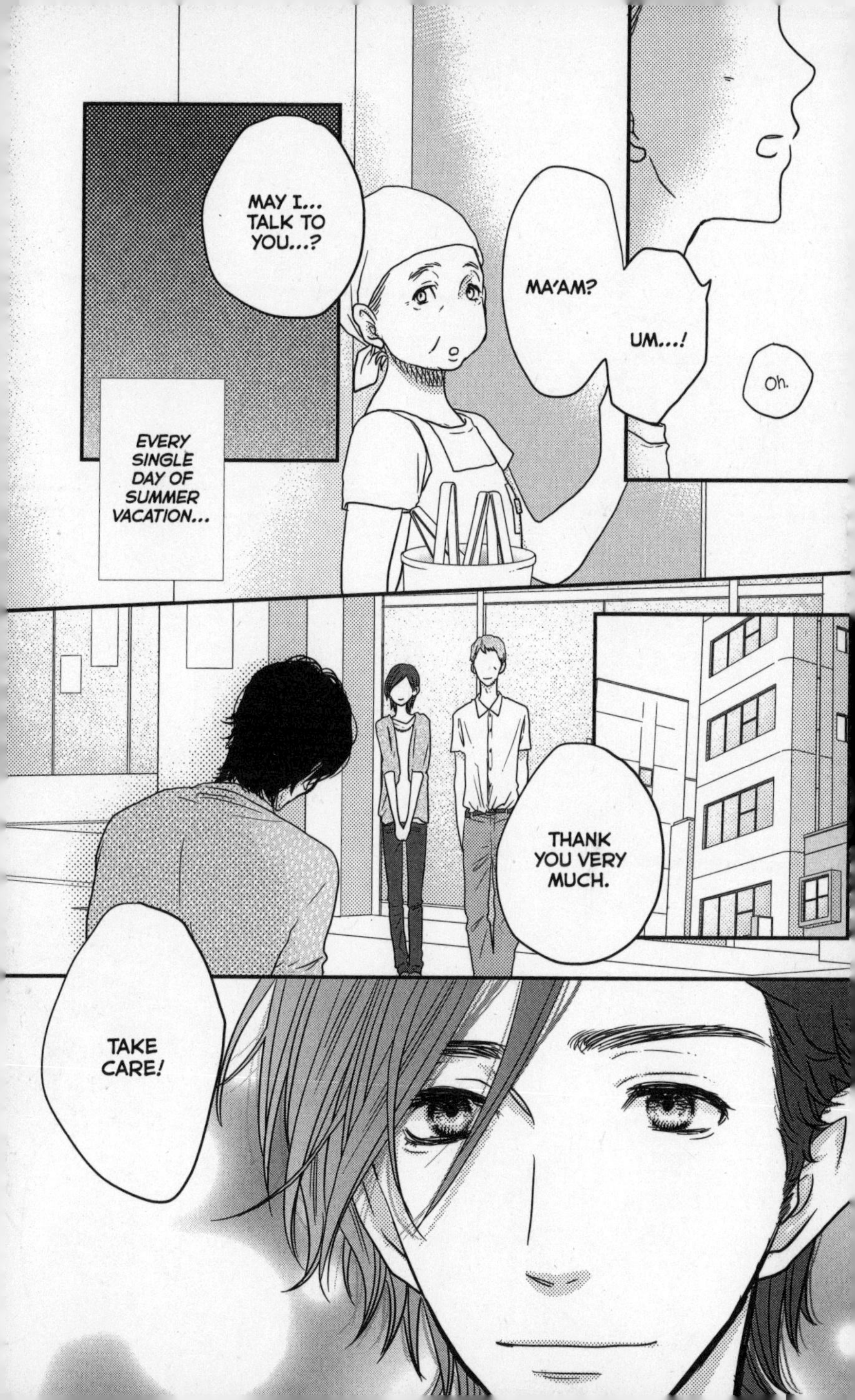
Oh.
MA'AM? UM...!
MAY I... TALK TO YOU...?
EVERY SINGLE DAY OF SUMMER VACATION...
THANK YOU VERY MUCH.
TAKE CARE!

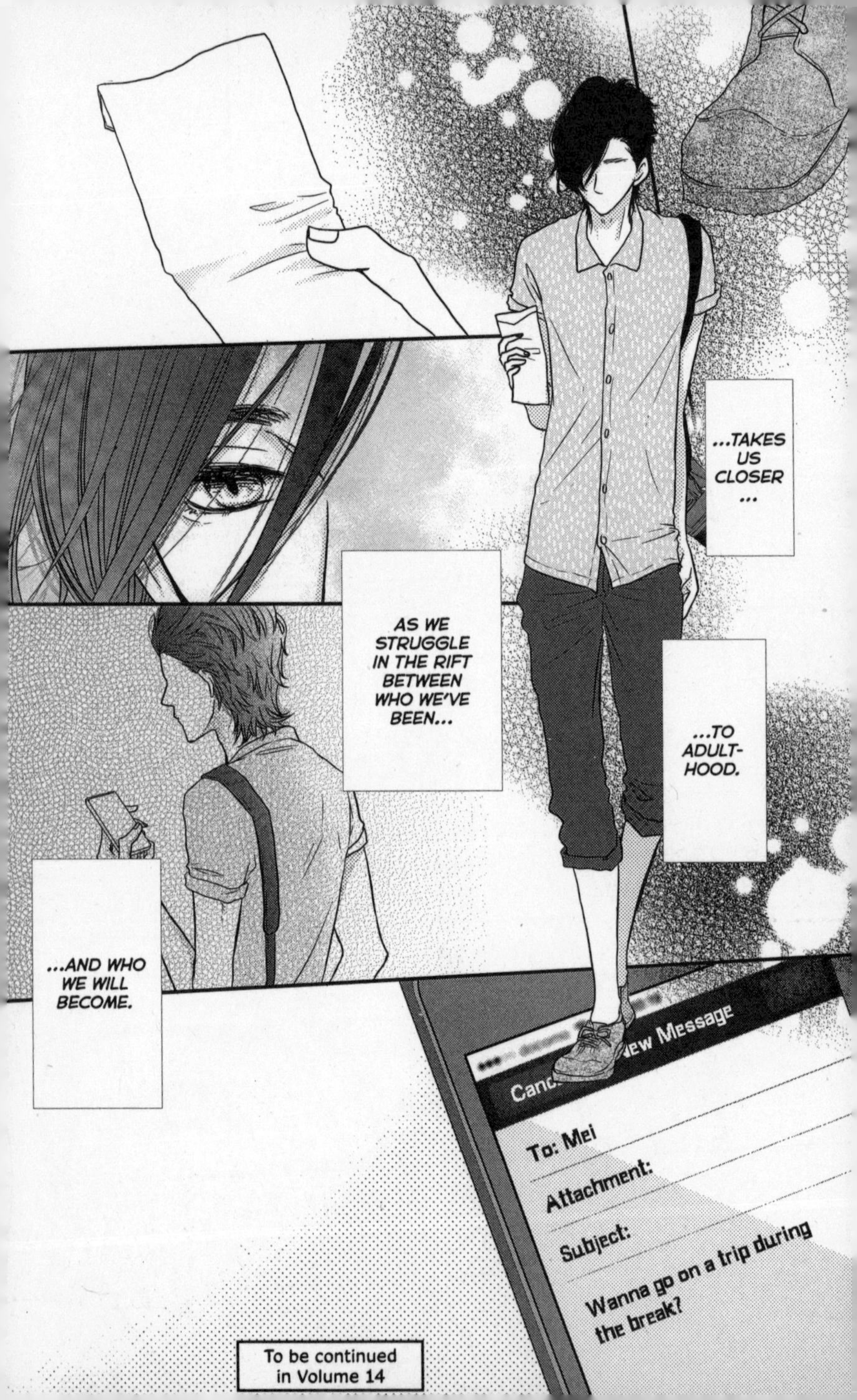
...TAKES US CLOSER ...
...TO ADULT-HOOD.
AS WE STRUGGLE IN THE RIFT BETWEEN WHO WE'VE BEEN...
...AND WHO WE WILL BECOME.
New Message
To: Mei
Attachment:
Subject:
Wanna go on a trip during the break?
To be continued in Volume 14

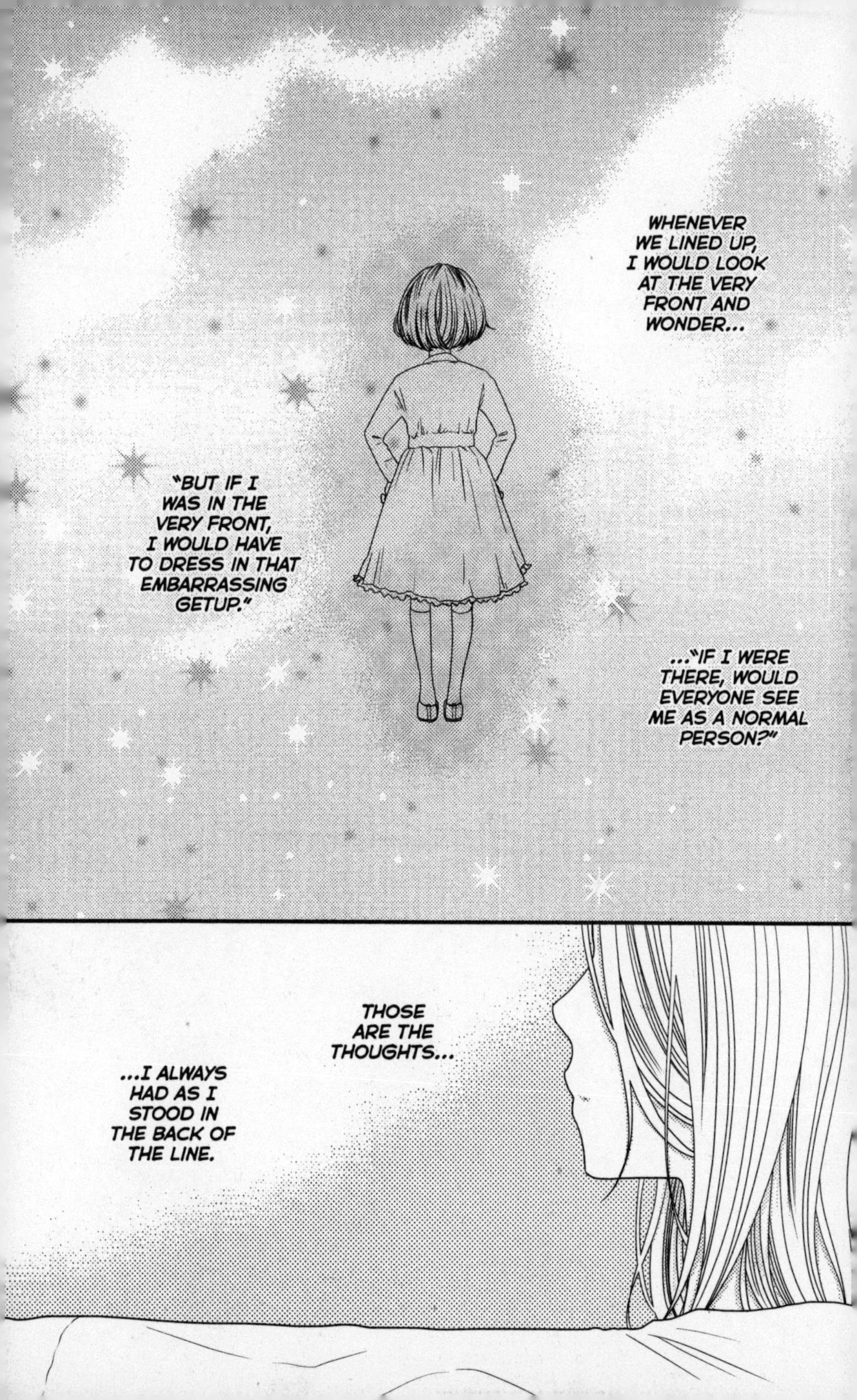
WHENEVER WE LINED UP, I WOULD LOOK AT THE VERY FRONT AND WONDER...
..."IF I WERE THERE, WOULD EVERYONE SEE ME AS A NORMAL PERSON?"
"BUT IF I WAS IN THE VERY FRONT, I WOULD HAVE TO DRESS IN THAT EMBARRASSING GETUP."
THOSE ARE THE THOUGHTS...
...I ALWAYS HAD AS I STOOD IN THE BACK OF THE LINE.

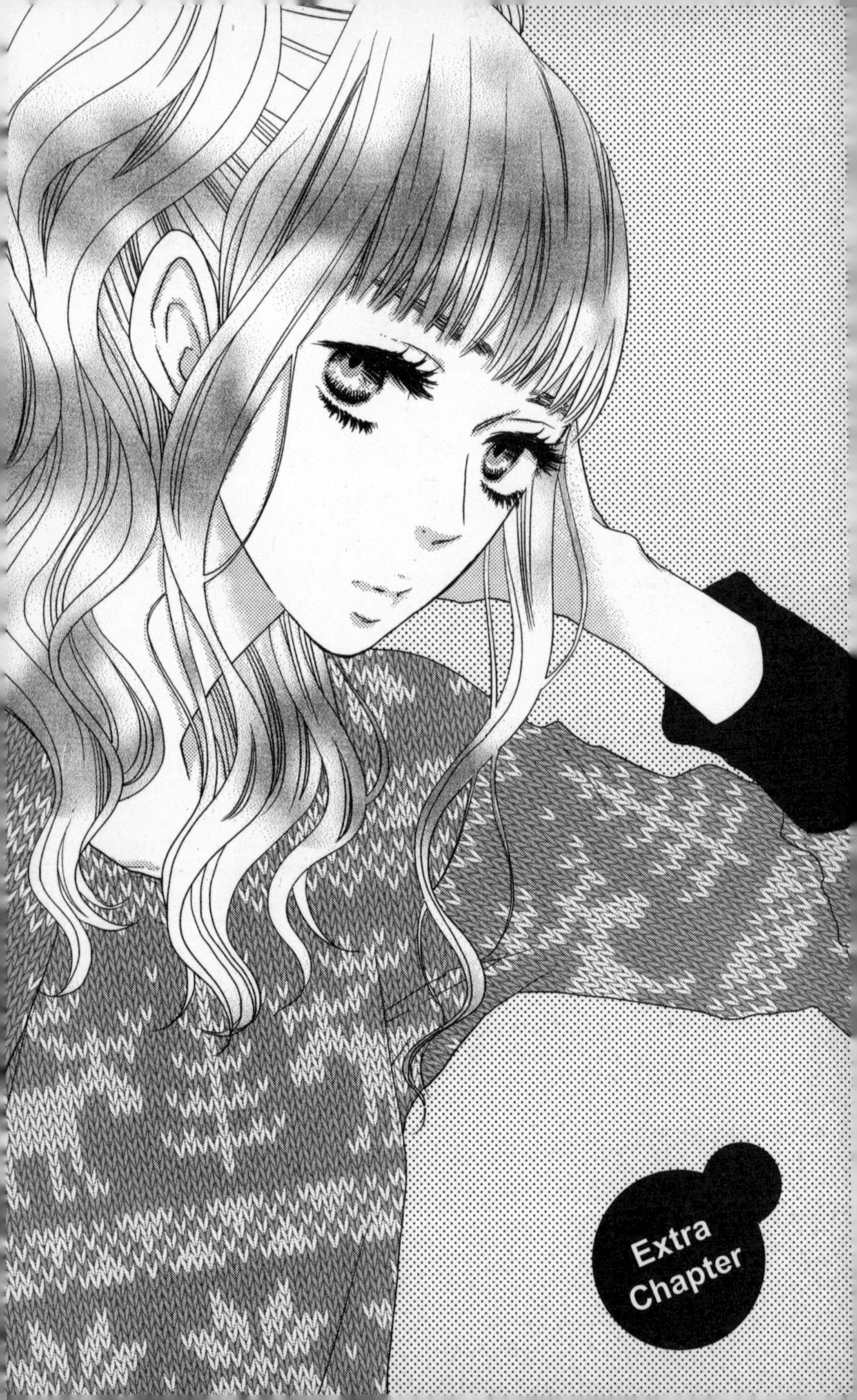
Extra Chapter

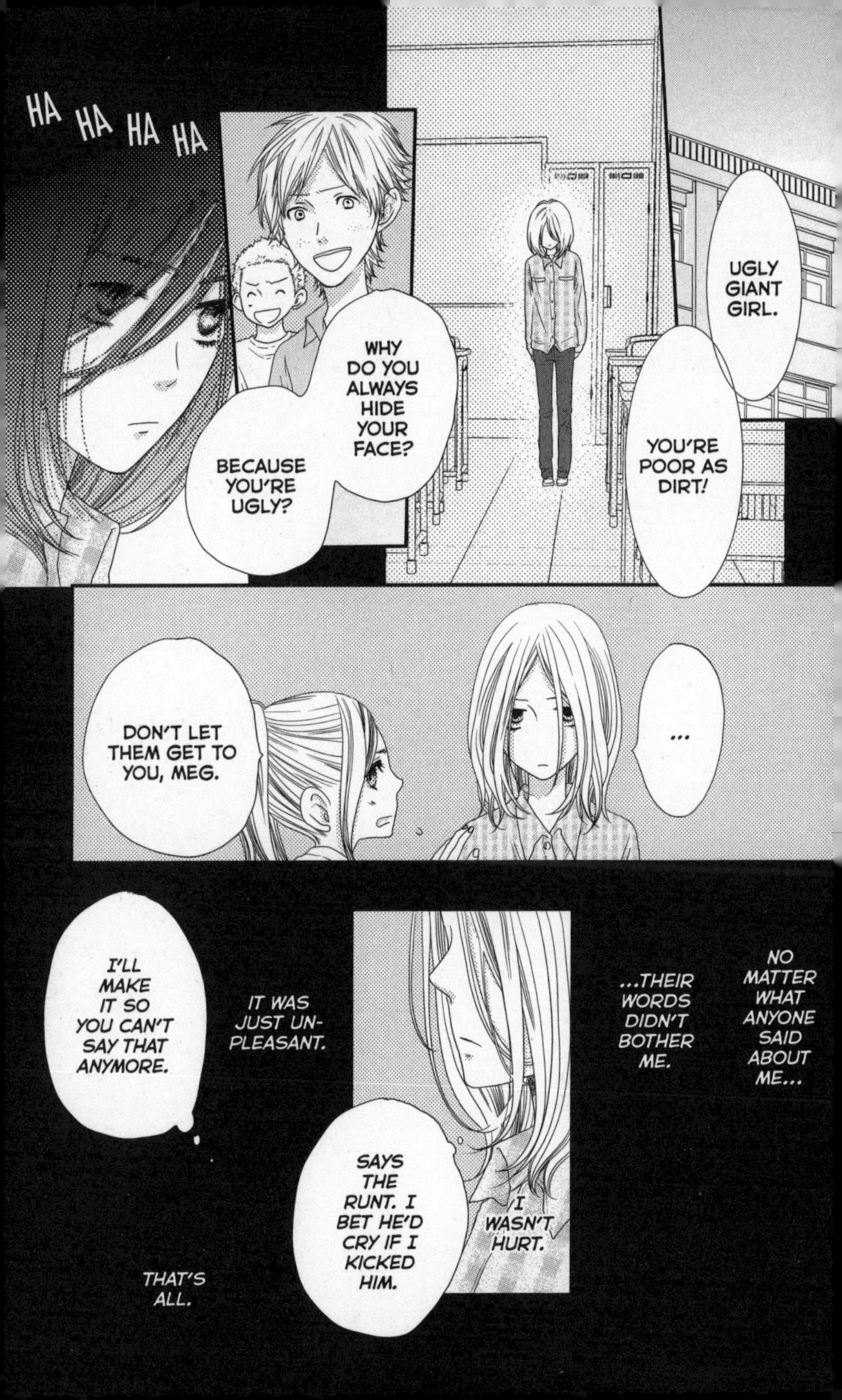
UGLY GIANT GIRL.
YOU'RE POOR AS DIRT!
WHY DO YOU ALWAYS HIDE YOUR FACE?
BECAUSE YOU'RE UGLY?
HA HA HA HA
...
DON'T LET THEM GET TO YOU, MEG.
NO MATTER WHAT ANYONE SAID ABOUT ME...
...THEIR WORDS DIDN'T BOTHER ME.
I WASN'T HURT.
SAYS THE RUNT. I BET HE'D CRY IF I KICKED HIM.
IT WAS JUST UN-PLEASANT.
I'LL MAKE IT SO YOU CAN'T SAY THAT ANYMORE.
THAT'S ALL.

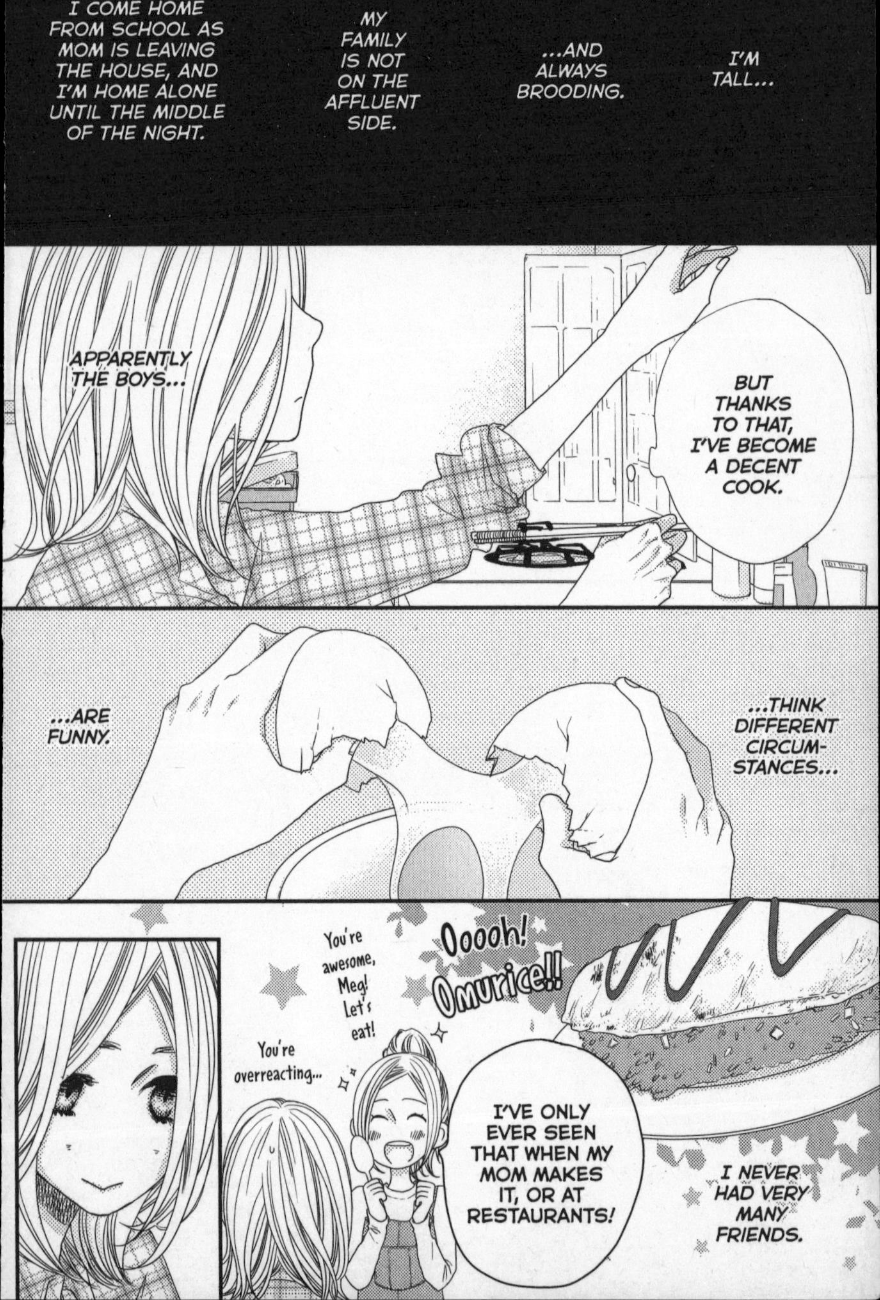
I'M TALL...
...AND ALWAYS BROODING.
MY FAMILY IS NOT ON THE AFFLUENT SIDE.
I COME HOME FROM SCHOOL AS MOM IS LEAVING THE HOUSE, AND I'M HOME ALONE UNTIL THE MIDDLE OF THE NIGHT.
BUT THANKS TO THAT, I'VE BECOME A DECENT COOK.
APPARENTLY THE BOYS...
...THINK DIFFERENT CIRCUM-STANCES...
...ARE FUNNY.
I NEVER HAD VERY MANY FRIENDS.
Ooooh! Omurice!!
I'VE ONLY EVER SEEN THAT WHEN MY MOM MAKES IT, OR AT RESTAURANTS!
You're awesome, Meg! Let's eat!
You're overreacting...

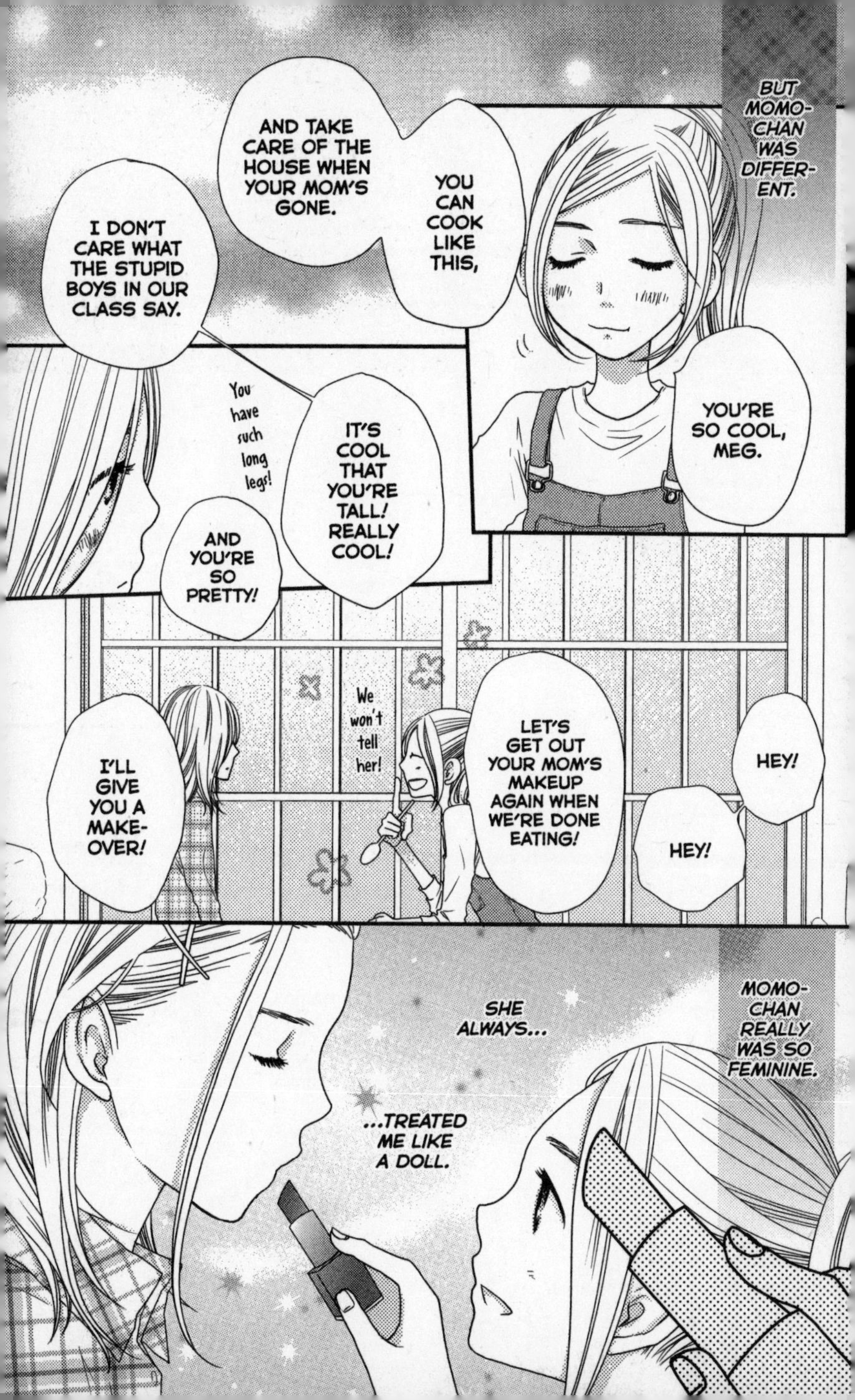
BUT MOMO-CHAN WAS DIFFERENT.
YOU CAN COOK LIKE THIS,
AND TAKE CARE OF THE HOUSE WHEN YOUR MOM'S GONE.
YOU'RE SO COOL, MEG.
I DON'T CARE WHAT THE STUPID BOYS IN OUR CLASS SAY.
IT'S COOL THAT YOU'RE TALL! REALLY COOL!
You have such long legs!
AND YOU'RE SO PRETTY!
HEY!
HEY!
LET'S GET OUT YOUR MOM'S MAKEUP AGAIN WHEN WE'RE DONE EATING!
We won't tell her!
I'LL GIVE YOU A MAKE-OVER!
MOMO-CHAN REALLY WAS SO FEMININE.
SHE ALWAYS...
...TREATED ME LIKE A DOLL.

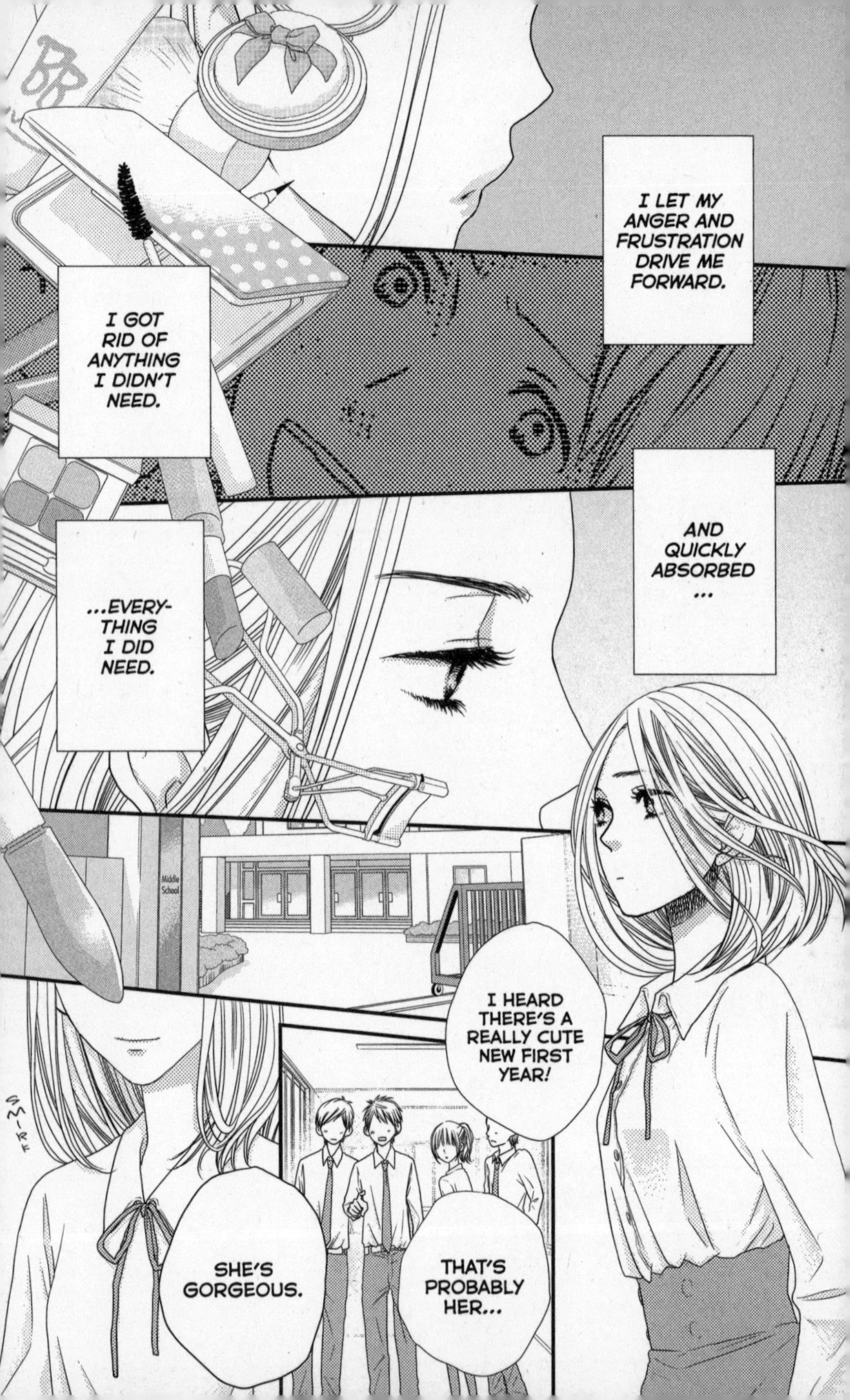
I LET MY ANGER AND FRUSTRATION DRIVE ME FORWARD.
I GOT RID OF ANYTHING I DIDN'T NEED.
AND QUICKLY ABSORBED ...
...EVERY-THING I DID NEED.
Middle School
I HEARD THERE'S A REALLY CUTE NEW FIRST YEAR!
THAT'S PROBABLY HER...
SHE'S GORGEOUS.
SMIRK

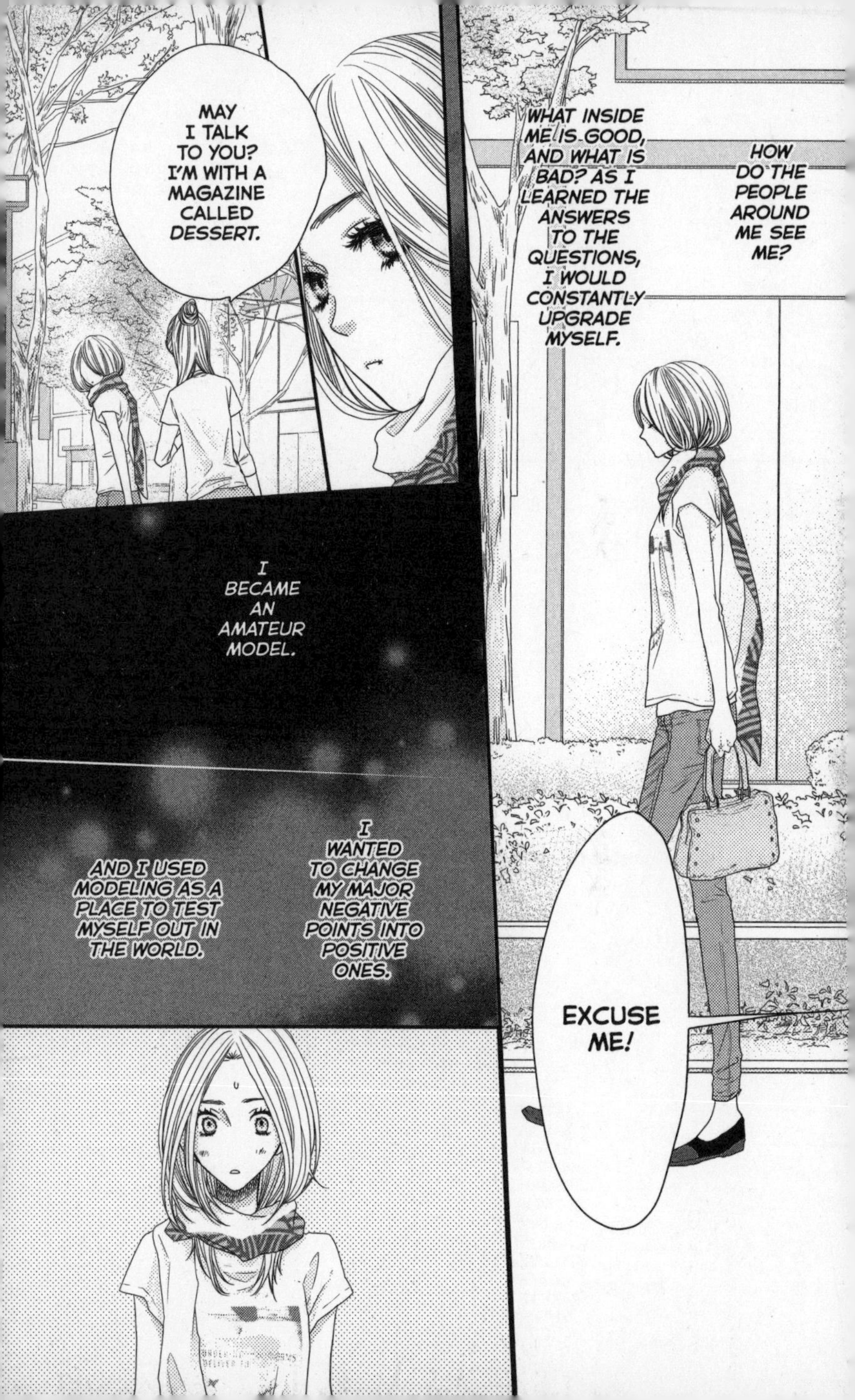
HOW DO THE PEOPLE AROUND ME SEE ME?
WHAT INSIDE ME IS GOOD, AND WHAT IS BAD? AS I LEARNED THE ANSWERS TO THE QUESTIONS, I WOULD CONSTANTLY UPGRADE MYSELF.
EXCUSE ME!
MAY I TALK TO YOU? I'M WITH A MAGAZINE CALLED DESSERT.
I BECAME AN AMATEUR MODEL.
I WANTED TO CHANGE MY MAJOR NEGATIVE POINTS INTO POSITIVE ONES.
AND I USED MODELING AS A PLACE TO TEST MYSELF OUT IN THE WORLD.

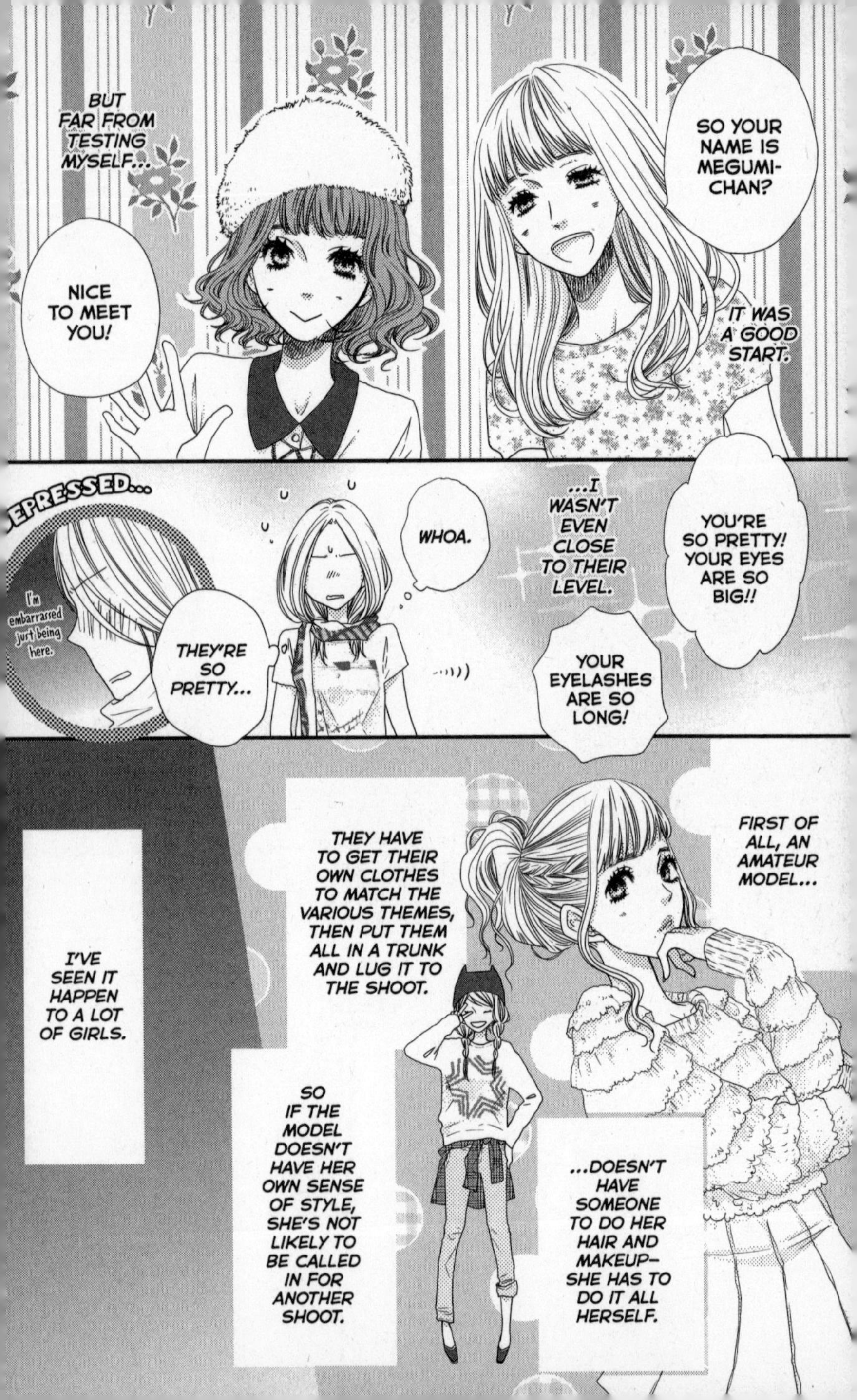

SO YOUR NAME IS MEGUMI-CHAN?
NICE TO MEET YOU!
IT WAS A GOOD START.
BUT FAR FROM TESTING MYSELF...
YOU'RE SO PRETTY! YOUR EYES ARE SO BIG!!
YOUR EYELASHES ARE SO LONG!
...I WASN'T EVEN CLOSE TO THEIR LEVEL.
WHOA.
THEY'RE SO PRETTY...
DEPRESSED...
I'm embarrassed just being here.
FIRST OF ALL, AN AMATEUR MODEL...
...DOESN'T HAVE SOMEONE TO DO HER HAIR AND MAKEUP— SHE HAS TO DO IT ALL HERSELF.
THEY HAVE TO GET THEIR OWN CLOTHES TO MATCH THE VARIOUS THEMES, THEN PUT THEM ALL IN A TRUNK AND LUG IT TO THE SHOOT.
SO IF THE MODEL DOESN'T HAVE HER OWN SENSE OF STYLE, SHE'S NOT LIKELY TO BE CALLED IN FOR ANOTHER SHOOT.
I'VE SEEN IT HAPPEN TO A LOT OF GIRLS.

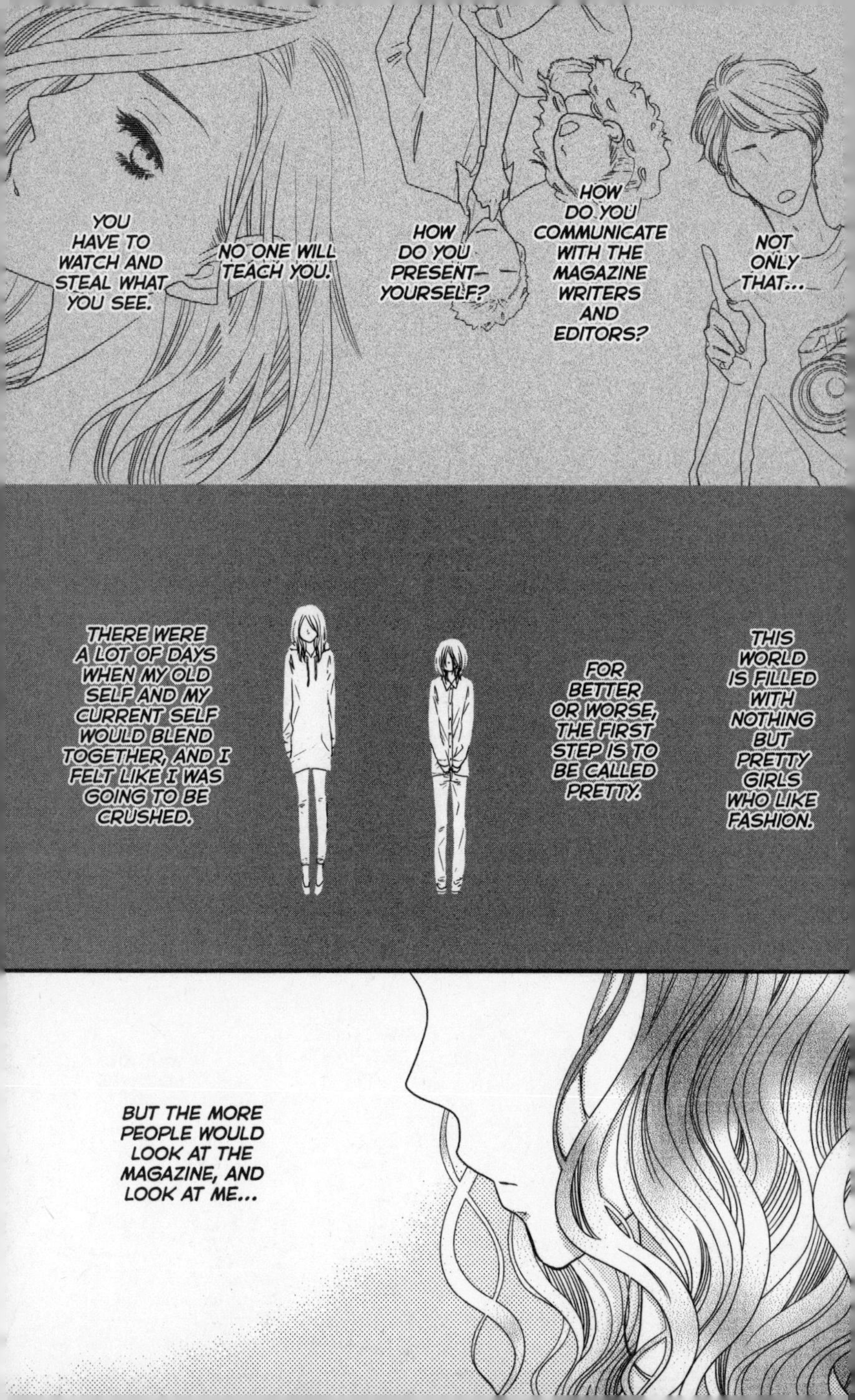
NOT ONLY THAT...
HOW DO YOU COMMUNICATE WITH THE MAGAZINE WRITERS AND EDITORS?
HOW DO YOU PRESENT YOURSELF?
NO ONE WILL TEACH YOU.
YOU HAVE TO WATCH AND STEAL WHAT YOU SEE.
THIS WORLD IS FILLED WITH NOTHING BUT PRETTY GIRLS WHO LIKE FASHION.
FOR BETTER OR WORSE, THE FIRST STEP IS TO BE CALLED PRETTY.
THERE WERE A LOT OF DAYS WHEN MY OLD SELF AND MY CURRENT SELF WOULD BLEND TOGETHER, AND I FELT LIKE I WAS GOING TO BE CRUSHED.
BUT THE MORE PEOPLE WOULD LOOK AT THE MAGAZINE, AND LOOK AT ME...

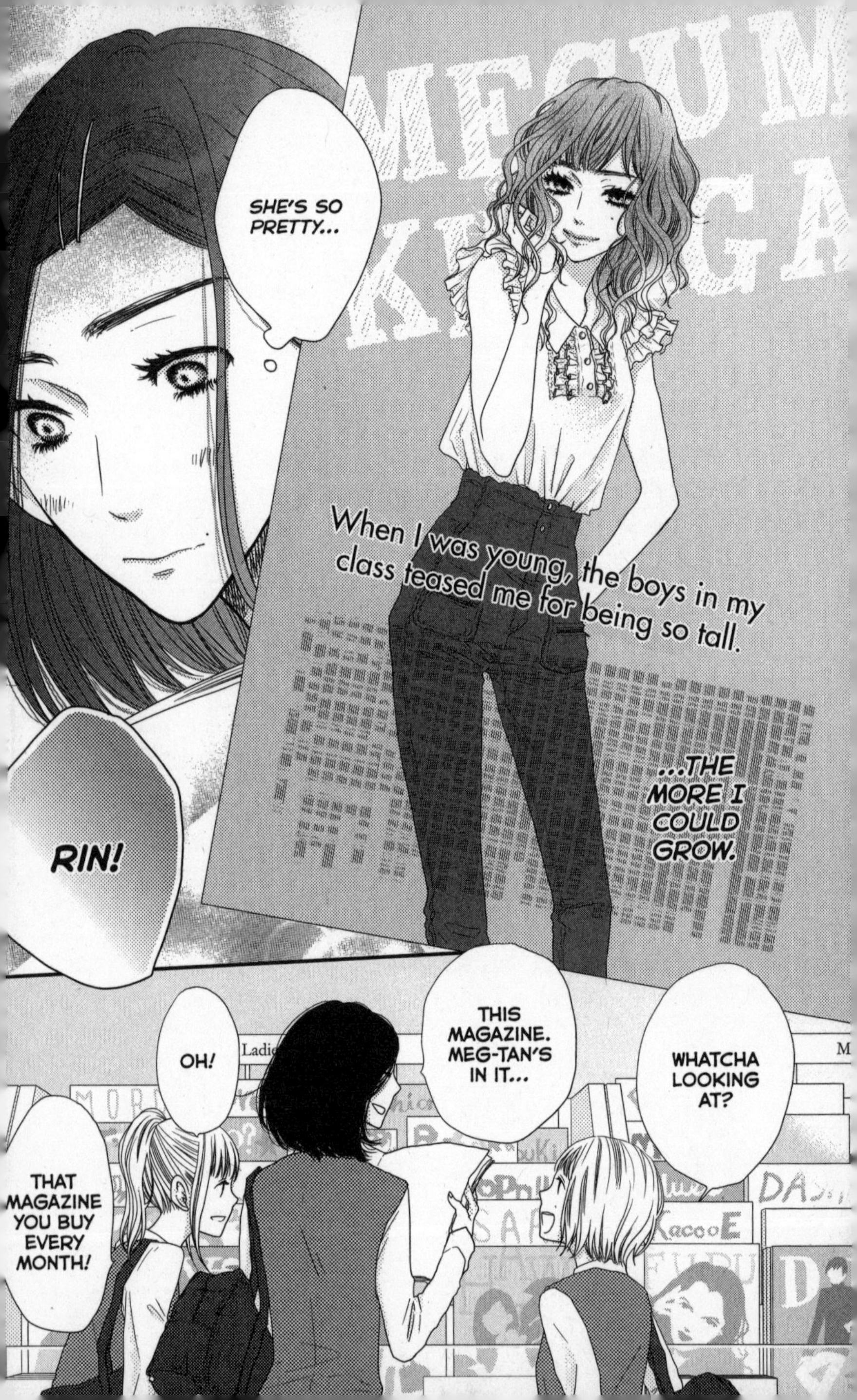
When I was young, the boys in my class teased me for being so tall.
...THE MORE I COULD GROW.
SHE'S SO PRETTY...
RIN!
WHATCHA LOOKING AT?
THIS MAGAZINE. MEG-TAN'S IN IT...
OH!
THAT MAGAZINE YOU BUY EVERY MONTH!

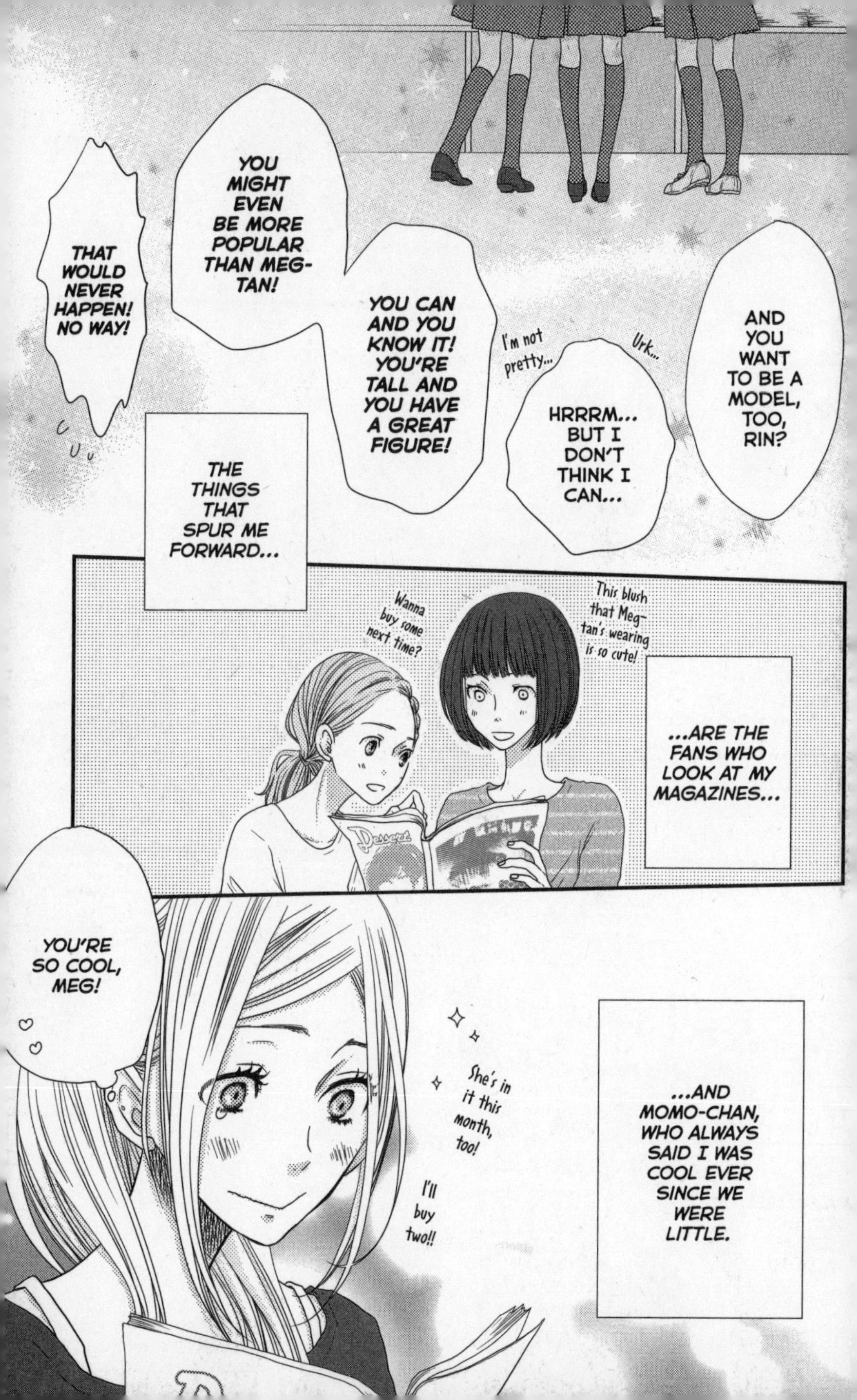
AND YOU WANT TO BE A MODEL, TOO, RIN?
Urk...
HRRRM... BUT I DON'T THINK I CAN...
I'm not pretty...
YOU CAN AND YOU KNOW IT! YOU'RE TALL AND YOU HAVE A GREAT FIGURE!
YOU MIGHT EVEN BE MORE POPULAR THAN MEG-TAN!
THAT WOULD NEVER HAPPEN! NO WAY!
THE THINGS THAT SPUR ME FORWARD...
...ARE THE FANS WHO LOOK AT MY MAGAZINES...
This blush that Meg-tan's wearing is so cute!
Wanna buy some next time?
...AND MOMO-CHAN, WHO ALWAYS SAID I WAS COOL EVER SINCE WE WERE LITTLE.
I'll buy two!!
She's in it this month, too!
YOU'RE SO COOL, MEG!

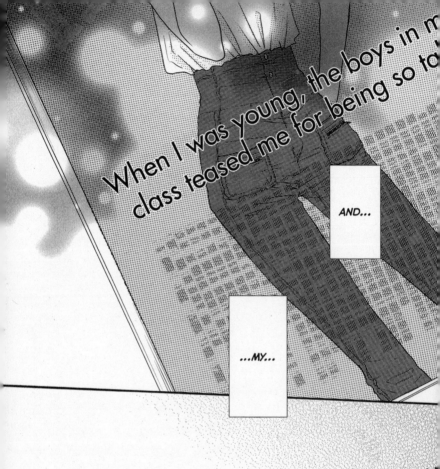

When I was young, the boys in m̶[class teased me for being so t̶a̶[

AND...

...MY...

...more confidence. But anyway, they said so many
̶me, I just hated it. Sometimes I swore to myself, "I'll s̶[

a competitive streak. I hate to lose (ha ha).

̶s surprising! I always imagined you as such an a̶[
girl, and I'm sure all your fans felt the same way̶[

Extra Chapter / end

Say "I love you".

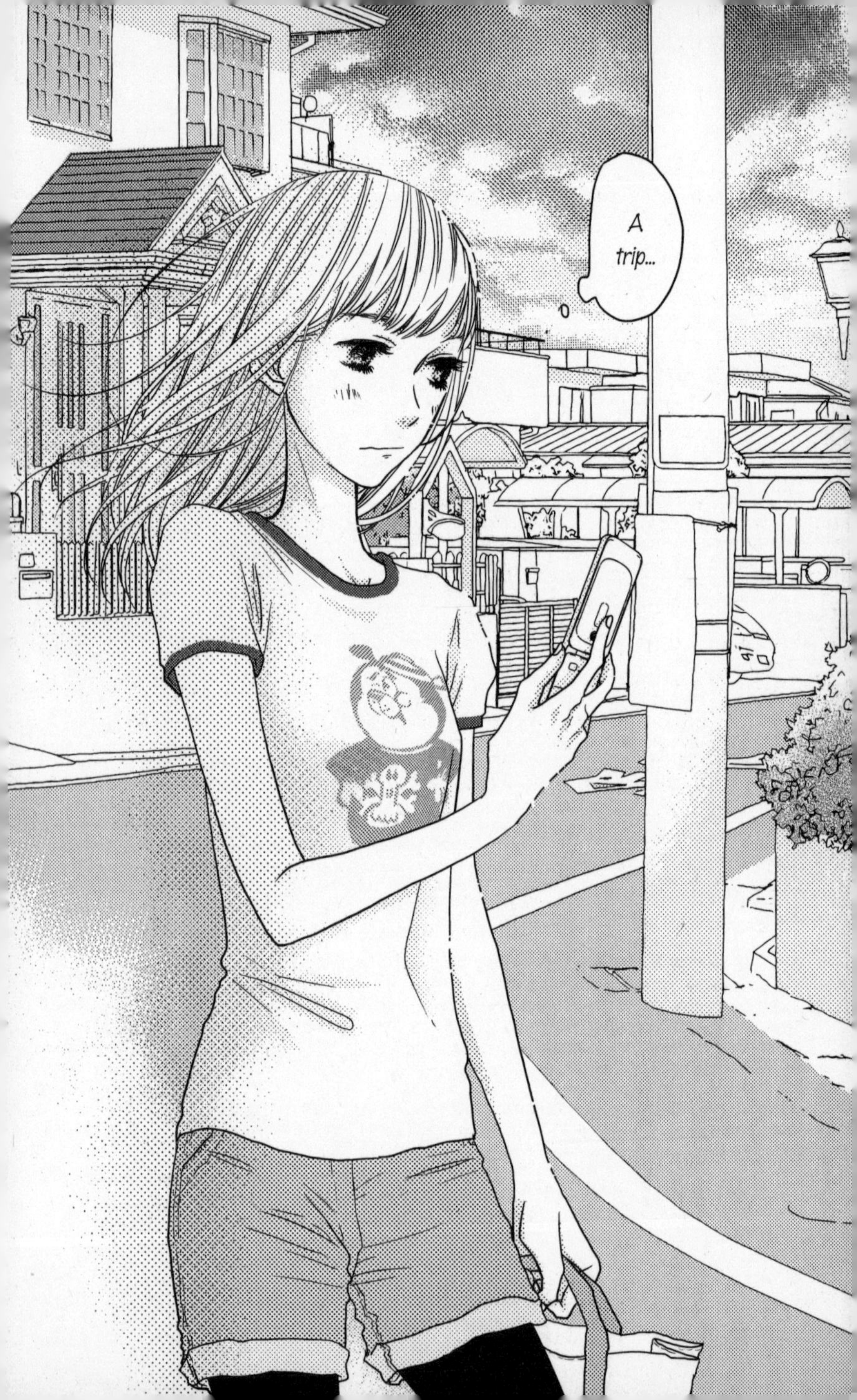
A trip...

Hello. This is volume 13.

I can't believe it went on sale on the same day as the magazine that ran Chapter 52! That's kind of amazing. And you can see the continuation right away in the October issue that goes on sale in August! Times sure have changed. When I was reading manga, it wasn't uncommon to wait four months before the bound volume came out.

Now for this volume. We're continuing the career path thing from the previous volume.

Sorry to be so pushy about it. But I think this kind of thing is really important. Mei aside, Yamato and Megumi are going into special career genres, so every day they run into a lot of things they don't know.
...I guess I wrote that in the last volume (ha ha). I'm sorry...

In this volume, Megumi enjoys the spotlight. Actually, I went to see someone from a modeling agency a long time ago, and as we talked, I just got so fascinated! The more we talked, the more scenes that I wanted draw came to mind, so I was really looking forward to this.

Megumi is mean and a people-pleaser, and kind of a jerk on the inside. She's at the height of unpopularity among my readers (ha ha), but I have fun drawing her, and I like this Megumi girl. Girls who know what they want tend to stand out in a crowd. It's a lot of fun to draw those conspicuous characters.

Her story takes place in France, but I really don't know any French, so I'd get my editor to help me translate, and ask for reference materials about France. There was so much I didn't know, so I was nervous and irritable, but everyone around me was so helpful...Thank you so much!

There are a lot of things I want to draw about Megumi.
She's hurt a lot of people, and now she needs to be hurt (ha ha).
...I guess that makes me the meanie. And Mei and Yamato are going to lose certain circumstances as they grow up. I think I'll be drawing that much later, so...I do hope you'll be patient.

Anyway, now that volume 13 is on sale, that means that the movie has been released, right? I wonder if all you people reading volume 13 will go see it... My heart is pounding. I got to see the movie three times before it was released, and every time, I felt like, "It's so good..." Just watching it once, I did everything I could do to follow the scene changes, and had trouble focusing on every little thing they said, but I could tell through the screen that they really valued the words as they made it.

So I really want you to see it two or three or as many times as you can! You should discover some minor gestures and backgrounds, and good settings! And I would love to hear what you thought about the movie...

Well then, I'll see you in volume 14!

TRANSLATION NOTES

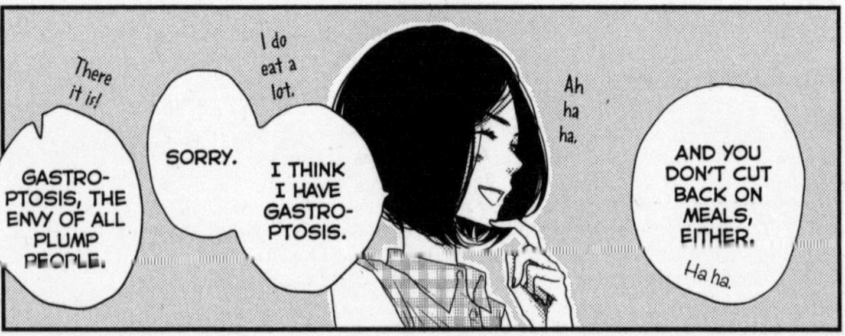
AND YOU DON'T CUT BACK ON MEALS, EITHER.
Ha ha.
Ah ha ha.
I do eat a lot.
I THINK I HAVE GASTROPTOSIS.
SORRY.
There it is!
GASTROPTOSIS, THE ENVY OF ALL PLUMP PEOPLE.

Gastroptosis, page 7

Gastroptosis is a disorder in which the stomach is situated lower than it's supposed to be. It makes it difficult to gain weight by eating, but comes with other adverse health effects.

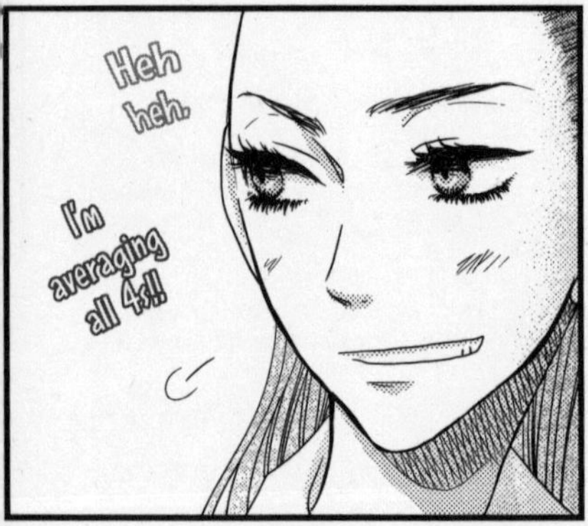
Heh heh.
I'm averaging all 4s!!

Averaging all 4s, page 59

Technically, Aiko said she has a 4.0 grade average, but that's not quite as impressive in Japan as it is in the United States. As mentioned long ago in volume two, Japan grades with numbers instead of letters. A 5 is the equivalent of an A, so if someone had been getting all As, their GPA would be 5.0. Aiko has been averaging all Bs.

Daifuku, page 87
Daifuku is a Japanese treat made of *mochi* (sticky rice cake) and a sweet filling, usually red bean paste.

Oriental Radio, page 94
Oriental Radio is the name of a Japanese comedy duo, consisting of Atsuhiko Nakata and Shingo Fujimori. One of their famous gags involves Fujimori-san hitting on girls by calling them cute, using the same phrase that this man uses here, *"Kimi, kawaii ne."* In the gag, Fujimori-san intentionally mispronounces *kawaii* as *kawa-wii.* It's possible that Megumi is commenting on his phrasing as well as his accent.

+81, page 133
+81 is the country calling code for Japan. Whether Angelo knows that or not, the number would show up on his caller ID, telling him that this is no ordinary phone number.

Gyaru, page 7

Although *gyaru* is simply a slang term that comes from the English word "gal," it refers to a fashion subculture that has fluctuated in popularity among young Japanese women from the 1970s – present. *Gyaru* style usually involves heavy makeup, dyed hair, and flashy, provocative clothes. Clothing brands specializing in *gyaru* styles can easily be found in trendy shopping areas, like Tokyo's famous 109 department store in Shibuya. As Murase-san says, there are plenty of magazines aimed at gyaru girls – notable examples include PopTeen, Egg, and more.

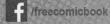 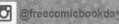

A Kodansha Comics Trade Paperback Original
Say I Love You. volume 13 copyright © 2014 Kanae Hazuki
English translation copyright © 2016 Kanae Hazuki

Published in the United States by Kodansha Comics, an imprint of Kodansha USA Publishing, LLC, New York.

Publication rights for this English edition arranged through Kodansha Ltd, Tokyo.

First published in Japan in 2014 by Kodansha Ltd., Tokyo as *Sukitte iinayo.* volume 13.

ISBN 978-1-63236-214-8

Printed in the United States of America.

www.kodanshacomics.com

9 8 7 6 5 4 3 2 1
Translation: Alethea and Athena Nibley
Lettering: Jennifer Skarupa
Editing: Ajani Oloye
Kodansha Comics Edition Cover Design: Phil Balsman